The Essentials of Teaching Children to Read

The Teacher Makes the Difference

Second Edition

D. RAY REUTZEL
Utah State University

ROBERT B. COOTER, JR.
Bellarmine University

Allyn & Bacon
is an imprint of

Boston   New York   San Francisco
Mexico City   Montreal   Toronto   London   Madrid   Munich   Paris
Hong Kong   Singapore   Tokyo   Cape Town   Sydney

Vice President and Executive Publisher: Jeffery W. Johnston
Senior Editor: Linda Ashe Bishop
Senior Development Editor: Hope Madden
Senior Managing Editor: Pamela D. Bennett
Senior Project Manager: Mary M. Irvin
Editorial Assistant: Demetrius Hall
Senior Art Director: Diane C. Lorenzo
Cover Image and Design: Kellyn E. Donnelly
Operations Specialist: Matt Ottenweller
Director of Marketing: Quinn Perkson
Marketing Manager: Krista Clark
Marketing Coordinator: Brian Mounts

For related titles and support materials, visit our online catalog at www.pearsonhighered.com

Reutzel, D. Ray (Douglas Ray), 1953-
   The essentials of Teaching children to read : the teacher makes the difference / D. Ray
Reutzel, Robert B. Cooter.—2nd ed.
         p. cm.
   Abridged version of: Teaching children to read. 5th ed. c2008.
   Includes bibliographical references and indexes.
   ISBN-13: 978-0-13-500559-0
   ISBN-10: 0-13-500559-0
  1.   Reading (Elementary) 2.   Reading (Elementary)—Language experience approach.
3.   Language arts (Elementary) I. Cooter, Robert B.   II.   Reutzel, D. Ray (Douglas Ray), 1953-
Teaching children to read. III. Title.
   LB1573.R48 2009
   372.4–dc22

                                                                          2007052129

Printed in the United States of America

10 9 8 7 6 5 4   12 11 10

Allyn & Bacon
is an imprint of

For my wife, Pam, my children, and my grandchildren who are my life's inspiration.

—DRR

For Kathy

—RBC

PREFACE

Why is preparation so critical for literacy teachers? Because research tells us it's the teacher who makes the difference in effective reading instruction. As a capable literacy teacher, you will need to think about your teaching decisions and understand and meet the literacy needs of every student in your class. That is a tall order, but this text will outline the essentials you need to succeed.

The Essentials of Teaching Children to Read: The Teacher Makes the Difference, Second Edition, emphasizes the teacher's role in literacy instruction. We examine five pillars of effective instruction, which provide a structure for examining the critical elements that well-prepared literacy teachers are able to implement in classrooms. By organizing every chapter around these pillars of effective instruction, the concept of teacher as lynchpin in literacy learning is reinforced. Using these pillars to ground your teaching, you will be able to recognize your role in developing your students' literacy education.

Text Organization

We believe that a foundation in the scientific research that informs teacher decision making is pivotal. This understanding of the needs of learners leads naturally to the principal literacy topics of phonics, fluency, vocabulary, and comprehension.

With this foundation in place, we build a chapter-by-chapter focus on assessment, capped with a full, dedicated chapter on the topic. This assessment chapter includes information on meeting guidelines of No Child Left Behind, a federal mandate for improving student and school literacy progress.

We then turn our attention to the reality of today's reading classrooms and the programs and standards teachers are asked to examine and follow.

Five Pillars of Effective Instruction

Teacher Knowledge

Chapters examine how teacher knowledge leads to wise teaching decisions. Purple headings, figures, tables, and features mark the chapter sections that cover the important elements of teacher knowledge. This material shares the foundational understandings and research that you need to know to build your background knowledge and assure you are well prepared as an informed literacy decision maker.

Assessment

The role of assessment as an ongoing tool that informs instruction is carefully considered in every chapter. Because teachers must be able to gauge their students' grasp of literacy skills to make informed instructional decisions, orange sections in each chapter are designed to help you create an instructional roadmap pinpointing where children are in their literacy development. These assessment sections also guide you in the use of evaluation tools that will steer you to instruction or intervention, helping you meet specific instructional goals for each child.

Effective Practice

The steps of effective practice are uncovered and illustrated chapter after chapter, topic after topic. Research guides the material provided in these red Effective Practice sections, which lay out practical methods for teaching essential literacy skills and strategies. Great teachers have a large assortment of tools in their educational toolboxes, allowing every child to reach their literacy potential. The applications in these sections provide procedural strategies you can take directly into your classroom.

Differentiated Instruction

Each chapter provides guidance toward differentiating instruction to meet all students' needs. Children come to school with diverse learning needs. Your goal must be to help all the students in your classroom succeed, including students who struggle because English is not their first language or because they have a learning disability or other special need. Green sections in every chapter provide guidance and specific recommendations to focus on the individual needs of striving students. You'll find valuable ideas for adapting instruction to help *all* your students succeed in literacy.

Getting to Know English Learners   In keeping with our differentiated instruction focus, all chapters are peppered with special features that make explicit connections to the needs of English learners. These provide up-to-date information and research-based applications to help you meet the needs of these students.

Family/Home Connections

The value of connections made between the classroom and home is clarified in blue sections in each chapter, leading to important recommendations for creating and nurturing these important relationships. These sections help teachers make powerful learning links between the classroom and the home environment. The goal is to help you communicate with parents and other caregivers, involving them in their children's ongoing literacy success.

What you'll find between the covers of this text is the instructional information essential to you as you journey toward becoming the kind of literacy teacher that makes a difference in all your learners' lives. Good luck!

Acknowledgments

We would like to thank the reviewers of our manuscript for their careful consideration and insights: Ward Cockrum, Northern Arizona University; Anne Gregory, Boise State University; Mandy Grotting, Sun Valley Elementary School; Leslie Hopping, The Columbus Academy; Margot Kinburg, National University; Rita London, New Mexico State University-Carlsbad; Elsie Lunceford, Indian River Community College; Molly Sperling, Devonshire Elementary; Susan Weber, Grandview Schools; and Karen Young, Manatee Community College.

BRIEF CONTENTS

CONTENTS

CHAPTER 5   Teaching Reading Comprehension   152

CHAPTER 6   Assessment   200

Note: Every effort has been made to provide accurate and current Internet information in this book. However, the Internet and information posted on it are constantly changing, so it is inevitable that some of the Internet addresses listed in this textbook will change.

1

Effective Reading Instruction

The Teacher Makes the Difference

Chapter Questions

1. Why is learning to read considered so important for young children?

2. What is reading?

3. What are the seven characteristics of highly effective reading teachers?

4. What do effective teachers know and do to promote success in reading for all students?

The First Day

Selena is a college student preparing to become an elementary school teacher. For her, this is not just another class, but the real beginning of her teaching career. Without doubt, teaching reading will be the centerpiece of her classroom. Selena recalls fondly her own first-grade teacher, Mrs. Roberts, who introduced her to the world of books and reading. Selena hopes she will be a "Mrs. Roberts" to the children she will teach over the course of her career.

Though there are several professors who teach the introductory reading course, Selena has chosen Dr. Favio's class. Professor Favio is known for her many years of successful teaching in public schools and her rigorous, hands-on instructional methods that get her students ready for their first year of teaching. The professor begins by asking students to read a scenario printed on the cover of the course syllabus.

On one occasion, Frank Smith (1985), a well-known literacy expert who had never taught a child to read in a classroom, was confronted with a taunting question by a group of exasperated teachers: "So, what would you do, Dr. Smith, if you had to teach a room full of 30 five-year-olds to read?" Dr. Smith's response was quick and decisive. He first indicated that children learn to read from people—and the most important of these people are teachers. As teachers, therefore, you need to comprehend the general processes of how children develop and learn. And teachers need to understand the specific processes whereby children learn to read.

After everyone has finished reading the quote, Dr. Favio continues the class with a question clearly intended to provoke discussion: "How did *you* learn to read? What do you remember about learning to read? Who helped you? Turn to your neighbor, introduce yourself, and share your thoughts in response to this question." Immediately the room fills with the buzz of students sharing their ideas about how they learned to read. Selena shares her memories with her "elbow partner," Terrence. She tells him how she was first introduced to books by her mom and grandma. "Did they ever read *Clifford, the Big, Red Dog* to you?" asks Terrence. "He was my favorite!"

After a few minutes of discussion, Dr. Favio asks the class to share some of their ideas and records them on a white board at the front of the classroom.

- *Little kids learn to read from someone who reads to them.*
- *I learned to read from my older sister.*
- *I remember writing letters and asking my mother what they spelled.*
- *I had a favorite book I memorized because my grandmother read it to me over and over again.*
- *I remember my teacher reading a great big book to us in kindergarten called* Mrs. Wishy Washy. *I loved that book!*
- *I watched* Sesame Street, Barney, *and* Reading Rainbow. *I learned the letters and some words from watching TV.*

Next, Dr. Favio asks her students to define what it really means to *read.* They are to take one minute of think time, and then share their ideas with their elbow partner. This question makes Selena remember how she struggled in learning phonics. Terrence remarks, "Well, I agree that reading has to include phonics, but I don't see how you can call it "reading" if you don't understand what you are reading. I mean, I can call out all of the words in my geology book, but *understanding* what they mean is another thing. For me, that takes some work!"

Dr. Favio invites comments from the class and records these statements about the nature of reading.

- *I think reading is when you sound out letters to make words.*
- *Reading involves understanding what's on the page.* (This was Terrence's contribution.)
- *I learned to read from little books that used the same pattern over and over again.*
- *Learning phonics is the first part of reading and comprehension is the last.*
- *Reading is about learning information that makes you smarter.*
- *Reading is the ability to put together what you know with what the author wants you to know.*

Dr. Favio stops the discussion at this point. She comments in sincere tones, "While these are critical issues for all teachers to reflect upon, when we look at scientific research there can be no doubt that the teacher's skill and the teacher's knowledge make the greatest difference in whether or not a young child learns to read. And because reading is, in a very real way, the gateway to social justice, your role as a reading teacher has the potential of changing lives and, therefore, our society."

That, thinks Selena, *is why I have chosen to become a teacher.*

Why Is Learning to Read So Important?

The ability to read is a key factor in living a healthy, happy, and productive life. In fact, the ability to read has recently been declared the "new civil right" on the Web site of the National Right to Read Foundation (2001). Without the ability to read, a child cannot fully access his or her democratic rights. Nonreaders and poor readers cannot fully consider political positions and issues; they cannot take complete advantage of available societal or governmental institutions for themselves or their children or thoroughly access their rights and responsibilities as citizens. Stated differently, we believe that the ability to read is—for all America's citizens—the essential hinge upon which the centrally important gate of social justice swings.

Conversely, the *inability to read* has been listed recently as a national health risk. The National Institutes of Health (NIH), an agency of the federal government, has recently registered *reading disability* or *the inability to read* on the nation's list of "life-threatening diseases" because of the devastating and far-reaching effects that reading failure has upon the quality of our citizens' lives. To clearly understand the full impact that reading failure has upon the life of an individual, we offer the following quote from *The 90% Reading Goal,* by Fielding, Kerr, and Rosier (1998):

> The most expensive burden we place on society is those students we have failed to teach to read well. The silent army of low readers who move through our schools, siphoning off the lion's share of administrative resources, emerge into society as adults lacking the single prerequisite for managing their lives and acquiring additional training. They are chronically unemployed, underemployed, or unemployable. They form the single largest identifiable group of those whom we incarcerate, and to whom we provide assistance, housing, medical care, and other social services. They perpetuate and enlarge the problem by creating another generation of poor readers. (pp. 6–7)

Ernest Boyer (1995), former president of the Carnegie Foundation for the Advancement of Teaching, once asserted that the success of every elementary school is judged by its students' achievement in reading and writing. He continued by emphasizing that ". . . learning to read is without question the top priority in elementary education" (p. 69).

What Is Reading?

A substantial task in becoming a teacher is learning what particular terms mean and how to use these terms with other professionals in the field. The term *reading* has been used for many years in a narrow sense to refer to a set of print-based decoding and thinking skills necessary to understand text (Harris & Hodges, 1981). Snow, Burns, and Griffin contend that "Reading is a complex developmental challenge that we know to be intertwined with many other developmental accomplishments: attention, memory, language, and motivation, for example. Reading is not only a cognitive psycholinguistic activity but also a social activity" (1998, p. 15).

Nowadays our understanding of the act of reading has been broadened to include the visual and thinking skills necessary to acquire information from digital video, handheld data assistants, computers, or other technological learning environments (Hobbs, 2005; Messaris, 2005). Add to this broadened definition of reading the idea that the visual and thinking skills needed for acquiring information today are situated in and shaped by increasingly diverse social or cultural settings found in schools, homes, communities, or ethnic groups (Tracey & Morrow, 2006). As a result, the term **reading** is currently interpreted far more broadly and encompasses the learning of a complex set of skills and knowledge that allows individuals to understand visual and print-based information. The goal of reading instruction, then, is to empower *readers* to learn, grow, and participate in a vibrant and quickly changing information-based world.

As children begin the process of learning to read, they need to acquire a set of skills and strategies that will help them reach the ultimate goal associated with learning to read: comprehending what they read whether in traditional print forms or more technology-based formats. On the way to the goal of reading comprehension—that is, understanding the author's message—children must acquire a set of early reading skills or tools that include the following:

- Hearing individual sounds in spoken words (known as *phonemic awareness*)
- Recognizing and identifying letters
- Understanding concepts about how printed language looks and works
- Increasing oral language (speaking) vocabularies
- Understanding that sounds in spoken language "map" onto letters in written language
- Decoding words with accuracy, speed, and expression

Shanahan (2006) and others (e.g., Durkin, 1966) indicate that the desire and ability to learn to read often grow out of a child's initial curiosity about how to write letters and words. Consequently, writing very often represents not only the beginning point in many a young child's journey to learn to read but the finish line as well. At first, young children become aware of letters and words in the world around them. Eventually they may ask how to write their name or spell some other personally significant word or concept (e.g., their pet's name or the name of a relative). When children are able to write letters and words, a "cognitive footprint" or *memory trace* left in the brain is deep and long-lasting—much longer-lasting than that engendered by mere letter or word recognition alone. Similarly, when children can string words together to construct meaning such as that found in a story, they have "comprehended" text at a deeper and longer-lasting level. In a very real sense, children's understanding of what they read is deepened and cemented when they can write about it.

As children learn to write, they must learn a similar set of enabling skills to send them on their way to the ultimate goal of writing: *composition*. To acquire proficiency in writing, younger children need to acquire such skills as:

- handwriting (upper- and lowercase letters).
- understanding writing conventions such as punctuation, headings, paragraph indents, and the like.
- being able to "encode" thoughts into print (i.e., spelling words).

As you can readily see, the components of reading instruction are complementary and reflect a strong and supportive relationship between reading and writing processes (Tierney & Shanahan, 1991). Stated differently, it would be most difficult and terribly ineffective to separate reading from writing in an effective reading instruction program.

Teachers Make the Difference

Question: What is the primary ingredient in the recipe for every child's reading success? Answer: A classroom teacher with the expertise to support the teaching of reading to children having a variety of abilities and needs (Braunger & Lewis, 2006; National Education Association [NEA] Task Force on Reading, 2000; National Research Council, 2001; Snow, Griffin, & Burns, 2005; Strickland, Snow, Griffin, Burns, & McNamara, 2002).

In 1985, the National Academy and Institute of Education issued *Becoming a Nation of Readers: The Report of the Commission on Reading*. In this famous report, commission members concluded that teacher knowledge, skill, and competence is absolutely essential in helping all learners become strong readers. They added:

> An *indisputable* [italics added] conclusion of research is that the quality of teaching makes a considerable difference in children's learning. Studies indicate that about 15 percent of the variation among children in reading achievement at the end of the school year is attributable to factors that related to the skill and effectiveness of the teacher. In contrast, the largest study ever done comparing approaches to beginning reading found that about 3 percent of the variation in reading achievement at the end of the first grade was attributable to the overall approach of the program. Thus, the prudent assumption for educational policy is that, while there may be some 'materials-proof' teachers, there are no 'teacher-proof' materials. (Anderson, Hiebert, Scott, & Wilkinson, 1985, p. 85)

Competent teachers make the difference in effective reading instruction, a fact that has been verified time and again through research. For instance, The National Commission on Teaching and America's Future, or NCTAF, in 1996 declared that by the end of the year 2006, the nation must "provide all students in the country with what should be their educational birthright: access to competent, caring, and qualified teachers" (p. 5), a goal that, sadly, has not yet been achieved (NCTAF, 2006). Likewise, the National Education Association's Task Force on Reading 2000 noted, "The teacher, not the method, makes the real difference in reading success" (p. 7).

From experience, we know parental attitudes confirm that "It all comes down to the teacher—since they [parents] are notorious for competing to get their children into classes taught by the current faculty stars of the school! And why shouldn't they? Nothing in this world can replace the power of a great classroom teacher . . ." (Strickland, Snow, Griffin, Burns, & McNamara, 2002, p. 4). In a national survey by Haselkorn and Harris (2001), 89 percent of Americans responded that it is very important to have a well-qualified teacher in every classroom. These same researchers found that 80 percent of parents agreed strongly that fully qualified teachers should be provided to all children, even if that meant spending more money. Seventy-seven percent said it is a high national priority to develop the professional skills and knowledge of teachers throughout their careers. The National Commission on Teaching and America's Future (1996) reported that, "Without telling parents they are doing so, many districts hire unqualified people as 'teachers' and assign them full responsibility for children. More than 12 percent of all newly hired 'teachers' enter without any training at all, and another 14 percent enter without having fully met state standards" (p. 14). Though these data may have improved somewhat since 1996, it is clear that the problem has not been adequately addressed, especially in large, urban districts having high numbers of disadvantaged children. The poorest children and the most powerless families often receive the least our educational system has to offer (NCTAF, 2006)—what Jonathan Kozol (1991) labels "savage inequalities."

Teacher Development Is a Worthwhile Investment. In a national study of 1,000 school districts, Ferguson (1991) found that every additional dollar spent on more highly qualified teachers netted greater improvement in student achievement than did any other use of school resources. We also know that teachers' general instructional ability and knowledge are strongly related to student achievement (Greenwald, Hedges, & Laine, 1996). And an increasing number of studies now show a strong link between what teachers know about the teaching of reading and their students' achievement in reading (Darling-Hammond, Wise, & Klein, 1999; Snow, Griffin, & Burns, 2005). In fact, research also suggests that teachers influence student academic growth more than any other single factor, including families, neighborhoods, and the schools students attend (Sanders & Rivers, 1996). Successful schools that produce high student reading and writing achievement test scores, regardless of socioeconomic status or the nature of reading and writing instruction, have teachers who are knowledgeable and articulate about their work (Mosenthal, Lipson, Torncello, Russ, & Mekkelsen, 2004; McCardle & Chhabra, 2004).

The Seven Characteristics of Highly Effective Reading Teachers

Emerging from a synthesis of research on effective reading instruction and the practices of exemplary reading teachers in elementary schools, we have determined that there are seven important characteristics that guide us in the central message of this book: The teacher's knowledge about effective reading instruction makes the single greatest difference in whether or not every child will have an equal and effective opportunity to learn to read successfully in elementary school!

Each characteristic of exemplary reading instruction is stated in terms of what highly effective reading teachers must know and be able to do to provide an effective reading instructional program in early childhood and elementary school classrooms. Highly effective reading teachers:

- understand how children learn oral language and how children learn to read.
- are excellent classroom managers.
- begin reading instruction by first assessing what students already know and can do.
- know how to adapt instruction to meet the needs of diverse learners.
- teach the essential components of reading using evidence-based instructional practices.
- model and encourage reading and writing applications throughout the day.
- partner with other teachers, parents, and community members to ensure children's learning.

We outline each characteristic here, but they will be discussed in much greater detail in the remaining chapters of this book.

Characteristic 1: Highly Effective Reading Teachers Understand How Children Learn Oral Language and How Children Learn to Read

The development of oral language is directly linked to success in reading and writing abilities. Children who come to school with thousands of "words in their head"—

Getting to Know English Learners
Literacy exposure and development in first language is generally agreed upon to be a good predictor of an EL student's ability to become a good literacy learner in English.

words they can hear, understand, and use in their daily lives—are already on the path to learning success (Allington & Cunningham, 1996). Similarly, children from what could be termed "language-deprived backgrounds" must receive immediate attention if they are to have any real chance at reading success (National Research Council, 1998; Johnson, 2001; Reutzel & Cooter, 2005). Thus, we have concluded that highly effective reading teachers know and understand the value of early language development.

Language is mainly a verbal (speech sounds) and visual symbol (printed letters/ words) system used in human society that is capable of representing the full range of our knowledge, experiences, and emotions. All humans use language as a tool for having needs met, for thinking and solving problems, and for sharing ideas and feelings (Halliday, 1975). Language is both expressive and receptive. *Expressive language* requires the sender of a message to *encode* or to put his or her thoughts into symbolic systems (verbal and visual) of the language. *Receptive language* requires the receiver of a message to *decode* or unlock the code of the language symbol systems used by the sender in order to construct meaning. Both expressive and receptive forms of language typically take the forms of spoken sounds or written symbols, but may also be represented visually through gestures, art, pictures, video, or dramatization.

The English language is an *alphabetic language*. An alphabetic language is one in which the sounds of spoken or oral language and the symbols or print found in written language relate to one another in more or less predictable ways. For example, the sound /buh/ *maps* onto or is represented by the letter *b*. In some languages the symbols used do not represent sounds in the language at all, but instead represent unified concepts or events such as words or phrases. For example, English uses an alphabetic or orthographic system where symbols represent sounds; Chinese, on the other hand, uses a logographic system that represents entire concepts (words) or events (phrases) with pictures.

The Structure of Language

The structure of language is typically divided into seven interrelated components: (1) phonology, (2) orthography, (3) morphology, (4) syntax, (5) semantics, (6) etymology, and (7) pragmatics.

1. **Phonology** refers to the study of the sound structures of oral language and includes both understanding speech and producing speech.
2. **Orthography** refers to patterns linking letters or **graphemes** to sounds or phonemes in spoken language to produce conventional word spellings (Snow, Griffin, & Burns, 2005).
3. **Morphology** refers to the study of word structure (Carlisle, 2004; Piper, 1998).
4. **Syntax** refers to the rule system of how words are combined into larger language structures, especially sentences. Many persons use the term **grammar** as nearly synonymous with *syntax*.
5. The **semantic** component of language involves connecting one's background experiences, knowledge, interests, attitudes, and perspectives with spoken or written language to comprehend the meaning of that language (Anderson & Pearson, 1984; Kintsch & Kintsch, 2005; Rumelhart, 1980).
6. **Etymology** (Snow, Griffin, & Burns, 2005) is the study of how word meanings and language meanings change over time in popular culture. For example, the meaning of the word *bad* has been changed from "undesirable" or "awful" to "desirable" or "high-quality."
7. **Pragmatics** is the study of how language is used by people in societies to satisfy their need to communicate. Research over the past decade has shown that a teacher's knowledge

Getting to Know English Learners
Children who are learning to become literate in English face a dual task. Besides the characteristics of written language, they have to learn an unfamiliar language that in part refers to an unfamiliar cultural background. In fact, the written system from which these students' home language, culture, and identity are embedded may not even be one that uses alphabetic script as represented by the Greek alphabet. Chinese students, for example, may read symbols that represent whole phrases; Arabic students may read from bottom to top and from right to left.

of language structure and language components relates to and moderately predicts students' early reading achievement (Cunningham, Perry, Stanovich, & Stanovich, 2004; Moats, 1994).

Teachers need to understand how children acquire their ability to speak. There are essentially four major views of how children come by their oral language ability: (1) behaviorist, (2) innatist, (3) constructivist, and (4) social interactionist. **Behaviorists** believe that oral language is learned through *conditioning* and *shaping*—processes that involve a stimulus and a reward or a punishment. **Innatists** believe that language learning is natural or "inborn" for human beings. **Constructivists** believe that language development is built over time and linked to overall thinking ability or cognitive development. **Social interactionists** assume that oral language development is greatly influenced by physical, social, and, of course, linguistic factors found in the child's immediate environment. Whether teachers work with slow learners, gifted students, English Learners (EL), or typically developing children living in the suburbs, they find that oral language among young children develops along a fairly predictable continuum. However, we also know that language development can be slowed through such external influences as poverty.

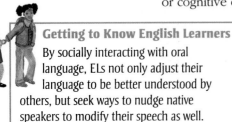

Getting to Know English Learners

By socially interacting with oral language, ELs not only adjust their language to be better understood by others, but seek ways to nudge native speakers to modify their speech as well.

Research tells us that reading teachers who are aware of the oral language developmental stages and average rates of oral language development are more likely to be effective in raising children's oral language development to new and higher levels (Braunger & Lewis, 2006; Burns, Griffin, & Snow, 1999; Snow, Burns, & Griffin, 1998; Snow, Griffin, & Burns, 2005; Strickland, Snow, Griffin, Burns, & McNamara, 2002). Also, highly effective reading teachers understand that rates of oral language development vary radically among children (Smith, 2001) and are able to adjust their instructional pacing and expectations accordingly (Braunger & Lewis, 2006; Burns, Griffin, & Snow, 1999; Snow, Burns, & Griffin, 1998; Snow, Griffin, & Burns, 2005; Strickland, Snow, Griffin, Burns, & McNamara, 2002). Finally, highly effective reading teachers understand the varying explanations of the reading process and are better able to adapt their reading instruction to meet the diverse learning needs of all children (Tracey & Morrow, 2006).

Characteristic 2: Highly Effective Reading Teachers Are Excellent Classroom Managers

The term *classroom management* refers to the ability of a teacher to organize, direct, and supervise the classroom environment so that effective student learning is made possible (Snow, Griffin, & Burns, 2005). Excellent classroom management (Morrow, Reutzel, & Casey, 2006; Reutzel & Morrow, in press) requires teachers to know and use a complex set of skills and strategies to accomplish tasks such as the following:

- Allocate classroom space for multiple uses
- Supply and arrange classroom materials
- Clearly communicate expectations and rules within a positive classroom climate
- Employ effective instructional practices
- Effectively train students in classroom routines and procedures
- Establish a predictable and familiar daily classroom schedule

A supportive and well-thought-out classroom environment is integral to achieving the goals of an effective reading program. When planning for an effective classroom environment, teachers must consider the literacy materials available in the classroom. They may need to think about the quantity of genres (e.g., nonfiction, mysteries, poetry), reading levels, and content of materials provided to children. They see classroom walls as blank palettes for instructional displays and student work. The maintenance of a classroom library, the grouping and accessibility of reading and writing tools, written invitations and encouragements, and directions on how to participate in upcoming literacy events are just a few of the many considerations teachers must deal with to be excellent classroom managers (Hoffman, Sailors, Duffy, & Beretvas, 2004; Wolfersberger, Reutzel, Sudweeks, & Fawson, 2004).

Characteristic 3: Highly Effective Reading Teachers Begin Reading Instruction by First Assessing to Find Out What Students Already Know and Can Do

Reading assessment refers to the observations, record keeping, and ongoing performance tests that a teacher uses to gather information about each student's reading progress (Flippo, 2003). Classroom assessment should be broadly interpreted to allow examination of students' literacy *processes* as well as the *products* they create. The goal of literacy assessment should be to provide sufficient information for teachers to make decisions about "next steps" for students in their literacy learning, and for the selection of effective, evidence-based teaching strategies.

> **Getting to Know English Learners**
> The use of alternative assessment techniques like literacy portfolios maximizes the EL's chance for success, as literacy growth can be documented in powerful and positive ways.

Excellent reading assessment and careful analyses of data (McKenna & Stahl, 2003; Reutzel & Cooter, 2007) are necessary for effective reading instruction and require that teachers know how to use a variety of assessment skills and strategies such as the following:

- Determining what children *can do,* not just what they *cannot do*
- Understanding the multiple purposes for which assessment strategies may be used (i.e., screening, diagnosis, progress monitoring, and outcome assessments)
- Using assessment data to inform the selection of reading instructional strategies
- Gaining insight into the processes students use when reading and writing, not just the final products of their reading and writing
- Documenting children's reading growth and development over time in relation to established benchmarks or standards
- Examining the entire context (the school, the home, and the classroom) of a child's opportunities to learn to read
- Developing a year-long assessment plan for multiple assessment strategies
- Integrating reading assessment data gathering into ongoing reading instruction and practice
- Using computers and electronic technology to collect, store, organize, and analyze assessment data

Teachers must have a well-thought-out assessment plan to achieve the goals of an effective reading program. When planning for reading assessment, teachers may need to consider the purposes for the test(s), testing conditions, and time needed to collect and, most especially, to analyze the data to shape, adapt, and inform later teaching. Great reading teachers think about how to infuse their data gathering into instruction so as to minimize the amount of time taken from teaching. Masterful teachers plan how to use informal data-gathering strategies during whole-group, small-group, and individual instruction. Sometimes, if the school district provides them, teachers are able to use computer software and electronic technological tools like personal data assistants (PDAs) to collect data (Wepner, Valmont, & Thurlow, 2000).

Characteristic 4: Highly Effective Reading Teachers Know How to Adapt Instruction to Meet the Needs of Learners with Special Needs

Meeting every student's needs in learning to read in today's increasingly diverse classroom environments can be complex and challenging. Children's ability to flourish from reading instruction can be influenced by any number of factors, including physical, emotional, behavioral, and intellectual disabilities; differences between the language of instruction and students' primary language, as with English Learners (EL); access to print materials in the home; parenting styles; previous schooling experiences; cultural differences; economic strata; and more. Unfortunately, there is an increasing tendency in some schools to engage in a "one-size-fits-all" reading curriculum that will not address the learning needs of all children (Raphael et al., 2003; Tyner, 2004). However, the only way to provide solid instruction that meets the needs of learners having special needs in today's classrooms is to pursue what is called "differentiating instruction" (Gregory & Chapman, 2002; Tomlinson, 1999). Excellent teachers provide instruction that is responsive to the *specific* needs of every child based on ongoing assessment findings. How one goes about differentiating reading instruction to meet each child's needs is of critical importance for all teachers (Gregory & Chapman, 2002; Tomlinson, 1999).

Today's teachers will need to know how to:

- use a variety of assessment tools for multiple purposes, and then translate their student data into effective teaching plans.
- implement teaching interventions using multiple instructional strategies because one size does NOT fit all.
- make use of multiple organizational and classroom management techniques.

A workable model for many teachers is to begin with a simple, limited, and manageable small-group differentiated instructional system. Small-group differentiated instruction requires that teachers group children by similar abilities and needs for instruction in groups numbering four to eight. Over time and with experience, these same teachers can gradually expand their practice using a range of instructional strategies to include:

- daily, intensive, small-group, teacher-guided reading instruction in appropriately challenging text levels.
- the use of student-selected books and other readings at appropriate reading levels.
- sensibly selected classroom spaces accompanied by clear rules, directions, schedules, and familiar routines.

Of course, there are many other ways effective reading teachers adapt instruction for children with special needs. In this book we show you (1) how to use research-based strategies to help students work collaboratively and develop language skills; (2) how to weave in successful experiences in reading history, science, mathematics, health, and other nonfiction texts; and (3) how to encourage children to become more independent literacy learners (Gregory & Chapman, 2002; Raphael et al., 2003; Tomlinson, 2001; Tyner, 2004).

Hope Madden/Merrill

Characteristic 5: Highly Effective Reading Teachers Teach the Essential Components of Reading Using Evidence-Based Instructional Practices

In the past decade or so, a series of reports has been commissioned dealing with the **essential components of reading** that young children need to learn and be taught to become successful readers. One of the early reports was sponsored by the National Academy of Sciences and the National Research Council. Prominent reading and education experts were convened to review existing research studies to determine which skills must be taught to young children when they are learning to read to prevent them from falling into early reading difficulties or eventual reading failure. This panel issued a report titled *Preventing Reading Difficulties in Young Children* (Snow, Burns, & Griffin, 1998). A companion document, published in 1999 and intended to make the findings of the earlier report more accessible to parents and teachers, was titled *Starting Out Right: A Guide to Promoting Children's Reading Success* (Burns, Griffin, & Snow, 1999). In these two reports, the National Research Council spelled out several essential reading instruction components that simply must be taught to prevent early reading failure.

Two years later, in direct response to a U.S. congressional mandate to examine the status of "scientific" research on teaching young children to read, the report of the National Reading Panel on Teaching Children to Read (2000) was jointly published by the National Institute of Child Health and Human Development, the National Institutes of Health, and the U.S. Department of Education. Like the previously published reading research report, a companion document, titled *Put Reading First: The Research Building Blocks for Teaching Children to Read* (Armbruster, Lehr, & Osborn,

2001), was distributed with the intent to widely disseminate the findings of the National Reading Panel (2000) report to parents and educators. (Note: You can receive a free copy of these reports on the Web from *www.nationalreadingpanel.org.*)

What we now know is that highly effective reading programs focus on (1) curriculum essentials, (2) providing students access to print materials, and (3) effective instruction. Curriculum essentials of evidence-based reading instruction include teaching the following (Burns, Snow, & Griffin, 1999; National Reading Panel, 2000):

- oral language development
- concepts of printed language
- letter name knowledge and production
- sight word recognition
- phonemic awareness
- phonics
- fluency
- vocabulary
- comprehension
- writing/spelling

An equally important component of evidence-based reading instruction is providing children access to various kinds of print materials (e.g., books, poetry, graphic novels, etc.) and print-making supplies (Neuman, 1999; Neuman & Celano, 2001, 2006). Print and print-making supplies or materials include but are not limited to:

- a variety of interesting and appropriately challenging reading and writing materials to include both good literature and information books.
- supportive and assistive technologies for learning to read and write.
- sociodramatic, literacy-enriched play in kindergarten.
- adequate time for reading and writing instruction.
- adequate time for reading and writing practice.
- extra time and expert help for those who struggle.
- outreach to and involvement of parents in interacting with their children around reading and writing.

The third essential component of an evidence-based reading instructional program is, not surprisingly, quality instruction. As noted earlier in this chapter, the quality of instruction provided by the teacher is the single most significant determiner of a child's reading achievement once he or she enters school (Sanders & Rivers, 1996). Evidence-based, high-quality reading instruction includes:

- reading and writing *to, with,* and *by* children.
- making use of captioned television to aid in reading practice at home.
- encouraging the viewing of educational television programming and use of the Internet to increase world knowledge.
- modeling comprehension strategies and encouraging children and teachers to talk about texts to improve comprehension.
- connecting literature study to content learning in other curriculum areas (i.e., science, math, and history).
- creating print-rich, well-organized, and highly interactive classroom environments.
- providing systematic, explicit, and sustained skill and strategy instruction in each of the essential curriculum components of reading instruction.

Characteristic 6: Highly Effective Reading Teachers Model Reading and Writing Applications Throughout the Day

In 1975, New Zealand's renowned reading educator Marie Clay wrote a book titled *What Did I Write?* Children often ask this question while holding up their scribbles and drawings, catching adults off-guard as they begin to explore the world of print. The powerful connection between writing and reading has long been recognized by teachers and researchers alike (Farnan & Dahl, 2003). In 1966, Dolores Durkin wrote the following in her now classic *Children Who Read Early* about how young children become readers:

> In fact, for some early readers, the ability to read seemed almost like a by-product of the ability to print and to spell. For these "pencil and paper kids," the learning sequence moved from (a) scribbling and drawing, to (b) copying objects and letters of the alphabet, to (c) questions about spelling [writing], to (d) ability to read. (p. 137)

Similarly, Clay discovered that

> In the early child's contact with written language, writing behaviours seem to play the role of organizers of reading behaviors . . . which appear to help the child come to grips with learning to attend to the significant details of written language. (1975, p. 3)

Here's what we now know about reading/writing connections: As children read, they learn about how authors structure their writing. They learn about indenting, word spellings, headings, subheadings, and more. They also learn about how authors select words to convey an idea or feeling as well as gain greater insight into how authors organize and present their thoughts in print. No evidence-based reading instructional program is complete without daily, planned opportunities for children to engage in "reading like a writer" and "writing like a reader."

Characteristic 7: Highly Effective Reading Teachers Partner with Other Teachers, Parents, and Community Members to Ensure Children's Learning

Reading teachers in the twenty-first century no longer have the luxury of viewing home involvement as merely a good or even an important idea. There is now substantial agreement among literacy researchers and master teachers that parents can make powerful contributions to their children's success in early literacy learning (Dickinson & Tabors, 2001; Paratore, 2003). Therefore, the teacher's reaching out to parents and homes is vital to young children's progress in learning to read successfully.

For example, in a large-scale, federally funded study of 14 schools in Virginia, Minnesota, Colorado, and California, teachers, administrators, and parents were interviewed, surveyed, and observed to determine the characteristics of effective schools and classroom teachers who were *Beating the Odds in Teaching All Children to Read* (Taylor, Pearson, Clark, & Walpole, 1999). One of the six key school-level factors in this study that was clearly associated with the most effective schools in teaching at-risk children to read successfully was outreach to homes and parents. According to the researchers, "The four effective schools made a more concerted effort to reach out to parents than the other schools. Efforts included conducting focus groups, written or phone surveys, and having an active site council on which parents served" (p. 2).

The findings of the Virginia study were echoed in other research in a major urban school district having high-poverty conditions. In *Perspectives on Rescuing*

Urban Literacy Education, R. Cooter (2004) described results of a privately funded "failure analysis" to learn what teachers must know and be able to do to reverse a 76 percent reading failure rate for this school district's third graders. Five "pillars" or instructional supports, the report concluded, were necessary to ensuring reading success—one of which was family and community involvement. "Most parents help their children at home [with reading] if they know what to do; thus, teachers must be supported in their efforts to educate families in ways they can help their children succeed in the home" (p. 22).

There are many examples of excellent family literacy programs that may serve as models for teachers as they make plans to reach out to families. Perhaps one of the best-known family literacy programs nationally is the **Even Start** program, which has involved over 80,000 children and adults (St. Pierre, Gamse, Alamprese, Rimdziux, & Tao, 1998). **Project FLAME** (Family Literacy Aprendiendo, Mejorando, Educando), a program designed for English Learner (EL) parents and children, is yet another example of a nationally recognized family literacy program (Rodriquez-Brown, Fen Li, & Albom, 1999; Rodriquez-Brown & Meehan, 1998; Shanahan, Mulhern, & Rodriquez-Brown, 1995). Parents involved with the **Intergenerational Literacy Project** (ILP) (Paratore, 2003) as well as those trained in **Project EASE** (Jordan, Snow, & Porche, 2000) significantly influenced their children's early literacy development prior to school and substantially impacted their children's early reading progress once in school.

Getting to Know English Learners
Projects include taking parents and their children to the local library to meet the librarian, tour the children's book section, and get library cards so that parents can aid in their EL children's literacy growth in English.

Effective teachers of reading focus on building strong, sturdy, and easily traversed bridges between the classroom and the homes of the children they serve in order to help every child have a successful experience in learning to read and write.

The Five Pillars of Effective Reading Instruction

In each chapter of this book, we include five sections we think of as the **pillars of effective reading instruction,** derived from the seven characteristics of highly effective reading teachers we have just discussed. We call these "pillars" because these five elements (see Figure 1.1) are like the pillars found in many great buildings that support the integrity of the entire structure.

In the context of our discussion of effective reading instruction, the five pillars provide an integral supporting structure. The five pillars will help you organize your understanding of effective reading instruction like other master teachers of reading. What follows is a brief description of each of the five pillars of effective reading instruction that guide the organization of succeeding chapters in this book.

- *Teacher Knowledge.* Educational research over recent decades has verified the basic skills and strategies of reading and the approximate order in which they should be taught. Effective teachers know this sequence of skills and approach their teaching with this important knowledge.
- *Classroom Assessment.* Teachers must know which reading skills each child has already developed and which he or she has not. Master teachers are able to quickly assess each student's knowledge, create instructional roadmaps of what children know, and then teach students according to their specific needs. Assessment happens in these classrooms *before, during,* and *after*

Figure 1.1   The Five Pillars of Effective Reading Instruction

instruction has taken place. Assessment is essential for making sure every student receives appropriate instruction, and then verifying that learning has taken place.

- *Effective Practice.* There is a veritable mountain of research evidence on the preferred ways of teaching each of the important reading skills and strategies. Great teachers have a plethora of tools in their educational toolbox to ensure that every child is helped to reach his or her full potential.

- *Differentiating Instruction for Diverse Student Needs.* Children come to school with diverse learning needs. For example, in many school districts English is not the first language for a large percentage of students; these students speak

Getting to Know English Learners

The home-school connection—where adults interact with children in a print-rich environment—is crucial for ELs' literacy learning as well. Too often, though, the culture of the EL's home is unlike the culture of the school and ELs' literacy learning can suffer.

Spanish, Chinese, Korean, Arabic, Hmong, and so on. Teachers need to know a variety of ways to help these students learn to read and write in English. In addition, it has been estimated that up to 20 percent of students come to school with various learning differences, such as attention deficit disorder (ADD), dyslexia, cognitive challenges (i.e., "slow learners"), language deficiencies, and behavioral disorders (BD). Our goal must be to help *all* students succeed. Effective reading teachers must have the necessary tools for adjusting instruction to children with diverse learning needs if all are to reach their potential.

- *Family/Community Connections.* It has been said that 80 percent of what students learn occurs outside of school. We know from research, for instance, that children who have been read to a great deal before entering kindergarten have a much stronger language base and are far more likely to succeed in reading (Snow, Burns, & Griffin, 1998). Parents and many involved others in the child's extended family and community are often interested in helping children develop as readers—*if they know what to do.* Thus, teachers can add great power to a child's literacy learning program by educating the adults in their lives in proven reading development strategies that make sense in our busy world.

Summary: Reading Teachers Make the Difference!

So then, we return full circle to our earlier question: *What is the primary ingredient in the recipe for every child's reading success?* We hope that by now you understand the significant role you play in the reading success of each and every child you teach or will teach. You are the hero in every child's literacy learning drama! Research absolutely confirms that your knowledge and skill in the teaching of reading is incredibly important, and we conclude our opening chapter with a little more proof (Braunger & Lewis, 2006; Clark & Peterson, 1986; National Education Association [NEA] Task Force on Reading, 2000; National Research Council, 2001; Snow, Griffin, & Burns, 2005; Strickland, Snow, Griffin, Burns, & McNamara, 2002).

In an interesting reversal of research perspective, students in grades K–12 were asked about the characteristics of their most influential reading teachers. The studies were conducted to discover student perceptions of what teachers do in exemplary reading instruction that helps them succeed (Ruddell & Ruddell, 1995; Ruddell & Harris, 1989; Ruddell & Kern, 1986). The results of the studies indicated that exemplary reading teachers (a) use highly motivating and effective teaching strategies; (b) build strong affective relationships with their students (this relates to interest, attitude, and motivation); (c) create a feeling of excitement about what they are teaching; (d) adjust instruction to meet the individual needs of their students; (e) create rich classroom environments to support their teaching; and (f) have strong organization and management skills.

Taylor and colleagues (1999) studied the literacy practices of exemplary teachers in high-poverty schools that "beat the odds" in teaching children to read. Students in this study were considered at-risk because they came from low-income families, but had average or above-average scores on reading achievement tests. Two teachers each from grades K–3 in 14 schools from across the United States participated in the study. Each teacher was observed five times from December to April for an hour of reading instruction. Teachers also completed a written survey, kept a weekly log of reading and writing activities in their classrooms, and were interviewed at the end of the school year. These masterful teachers focused their reading instruction on small-group instruction, provided time for students to read independently, monitored students' on-task behaviors, and provided strong links to homes with consistent communication. These tremendous teachers also included in their reading instruction a focus on explicit phonics instruction and the application of phonics while reading and writing connected text. They asked high-level comprehension questions, and were more likely to ask students to record their responses to reading in writing.

Metsala and Wharton-McDonald (1997) carefully collected survey and interview data about the most important reading instructional practices among 89 K–3 regular education and 10 special education teachers identified by their school principals as "outstanding." These first-rate reading teachers were described by their peers and supervisors as "masterful" classroom managers who handled time, materials, and student behavior with finesse. These superior reading teachers held high expectations for their students and had a real sense of purpose, direction, and objective. At the top of the list of common practices was a print-rich classroom environment. They also provided daily doses of skill and strategy instruction, access to varied types of text, and adapted their classroom reading instruction to the ability levels or needs of their students. These extraordinary teachers worked to motivate their students to engage in reading and writing regularly and consistently monitored student progress.

In yet another study of primary-level exemplary reading teachers, Morrow, Tracey, Woo, and Pressley (1999) found that these teachers, as we saw in earlier studies, created print-rich classroom environments. See a pattern forming? In these print-rich classrooms, teachers orchestrated a variety of learning activities involving the whole class, small groups, and independent seatwork. Instruction was often individualized and occurred on a one-to-one basis. Learning was sometimes teacher-directed, sometimes self-directed through the use of learning centers. Classrooms were rich with student conversation and interaction. Teachers planned and implemented regular times for writing, word analysis instruction, and comprehension strategy instruction. They also made consistent efforts to connect reading and writing instruction to the content taught at other times of the day in core subjects like science, math, and social studies. Many of these same effective practices were reported and confirmed by Cantrell (1999a, 1999b) two years later in her study of the effects of reading instruction on primary students' reading and writing achievement.

In summary, a synthesis of several case studies of exemplary reading teachers in the early childhood and elementary grades found that effective reading teachers share several important characteristics (Allington & Johnston, 2002; Block, 2001; Cantrell, 1999a, 1999b; Morrow, et al., 1999; Morrow & Casey, 2003; Pressley et al., 1996; Pressley, Allington, Taylor et al., 1999; Taylor et al., 2002; Wharton-McDonald et al., 1997; Pressley, Allington, Wharton-McDonald, Collins-Block, & Morrow, 2001). Masterful reading teachers:

- provide clear explanations and model how to perform specific reading and writing skills, strategies, and behaviors.
- engage students in constructive conversations with teachers and with other students.
- create a supportive, encouraging, and nurturing classroom climate.
- weave reading and writing throughout the curriculum and throughout the day.

- integrate content area topics into literacy instruction.
- create print-rich classroom environments with a variety of literacy materials that support instruction readily accessible.
- meet individual needs in whole-class, small-group, and independent settings.
- implement excellent organization and management decisions.
- develop strong connections with their students' families, homes, and communities.

A common myth about teachers goes something like this: "Those who can, do. Those who can't, teach." Another equally distasteful myth alleges that "Teachers are born, not made." Neither could be farther from the truth. Teachers today must understand a great deal about how children develop and learn generally, about how they develop and learn to read specifically, and about how to assess and teach children in a classroom filled with diversity that did not seem to exist in the past. Today's teachers are expected to know more and do more than teachers at any other time in our history. Teachers must know how to teach by mastering and implementing a body of knowledge related to language development, children's literature, curriculum standards, classroom management, and learning. They must be able to assess students' strengths and needs, plan effective instruction that focuses on the essential components of reading, and ensure that every child makes adequate yearly progress so that no child is left behind. In the end, the expert teaching of reading requires some of the best minds and talent to be found in our nation. Like Louisa Moats (1999), we too, believe that teaching reading is rocket science!

Classroom Applications

1. Read *Using Research and Reason in Education: How Teachers Can Use Scientifically Based Research to Make Curricular and Instructional Decisions.* Working with other members of a small group, list 10 reasons why teachers should rely on the results of scientific research to inform their instructional and curricular choices. Share your group's list with the rest of the class. Collapse all of the small-group charts into a single class chart.
2. Read "Beginning Reading Instruction: The Rest of the Story from Research" at *http://www.nea.org/reading/images/beginningreading.pdf.* Compile a list of practices in reading instruction that research supports in addition to those found in the Report of the National Reading Panel: Teaching Children to Read (2000).
3. Organize into small research groups. Select a grade level from kindergarten to third grade. Read *Starting Out Right: A Guide to Promoting Children's Reading Success.* Prepare a class presentation on student accomplishments in reading and writing at the grade level you selected.
4. Read "Beating the Odds in Teaching All Children to Read" (Ciera Report No. 2–006), available on the Web at *www.ciera.org.* In small groups, prepare a brochure or pamphlet that explains to parents, teachers, and school administrators the characteristics of schools and teachers who succeed in teaching all children to read. Share your pamphlet with your class or with parents at your first open house.

Recommended Readings

Armbruster, B. B., Lehr, F., & Osborn, J. (2001). *Put reading first: The research building blocks for teaching children to read.* Washington, DC: U.S. Department of Education. Available at *http://www.nifl.gov/partnershipforreading/publications/reading_first1.html*

Burns, M. S., Griffin, P., & Snow, C. E. (1999). *Starting out right: A guide to promoting children's reading success.* Washington, DC: National Academy Press.

National Institute of Child Health and Human Development. (2000). *Report of the National Reading Panel: Teaching children to read.* Washington, DC: Available at *www.nationalreadingpanel.org/Publications/researchread.htm*

Pressley, M. (2002). Beginning reading instruction: The rest of the story from research. Washington, DC: National Education Association. Available at *http://www.nea.org/reading/images/beginningreading.pdf*

Pressley, M. (2003). A few things reading educators should know about instructional experiments. *The Reading Teacher, 57*(1), 64–71.

Shannahan, T. (2003). Research-based reading instruction: Myths about the National Reading Panel Report. *The Reading Teacher, 56*(7), 646–654.

Slavin, R. E. (2003, February). A reader's guide to scientifically-based research. *Educational Leadership,* pp. 12–16.

Snow, C. E., Burns, M. S., & Griffin, P. (1998). *Preventing reading failure in young children.* Washington, DC: National Academy Press.

Snow, C. E., Griffin, P., & Burns, M. S. (2005). *Knowledge to support the teaching of reading: Preparing teachers for a changing world.* San Francisco, CA: Jossey-Bass.

Stanovich, P. J., & Stanovich, K. E. (2003). *Using research and reason in education: How teachers can use scientifically based research to make curricular and instructional decisions.* Washington, DC: National Institute for Literacy. Available at *www.nifl.gov/partnershipforreading/publications/pdf/Stanovich_Color.pdf*

U.S. Department of Education. (2001). *No Child Left Behind.* Washington, DC: U.S. Department of Education. Available at *http://www.ed.gov/index.jhtml*

U.S. Department of Education. (2003). Identifying and implementing educational practices supported by rigorous evidence: A user-friendly guide. Washington, DC: Coalition for Evidence-Based Policy. Available at *http://www.ed.gov/rschstat/research/pubs/rigorousevid/guide.html*

chapter

2

Phonics and Word Identification

Chapter Questions

1. How do children learn to decode words?
2. How do effective teachers assess students' letter and word identification abilities?
3. What does research show are the best ways of teaching phonics?
4. Who has difficulty learning phonics and what can be done to assist them?
5. What strategies can parents use to help their child learn phonics skills?

Mr. Bill and Emily

Mr. Bill, as his students like to call him, is a second-grade teacher beginning his third year of teaching at Doolittle Elementary in downtown Chicago. As is his practice, Mr. Bill conducts a number of short assessments in the first two weeks of school to get a better handle on where his students are in their reading development and to help in planning small-group instruction. While his students are engaged in independent work, Mr. Bill invites Emily, apparently one of his more precocious readers, to join him in the reading center. He had asked her to pick a favorite book or two and show him her "very best reading."

"Emily," asks Mr. Bill, "what book did you choose to share with me today?"

Emily proudly holds up a copy of *The Summer of the Swans* by Betsy Byars and says, "I'm ready to show you my very best reading, Mr. Bill."

"Go for it!" responds Mr. Bill. "Let's do it! Pick out a page and show me your very best reading." He then turns on the tape recorder.

Emily opens her book to page 46, where she had placed her bookmark, and begins reading. At one point, Emily reads tentatively: "'Already he had started shhh—aaakkk—ing, *shaking* his head again, all the while waaa—chh—ing the swans gliding across the dark water.'" Emily looks up for a reaction from her teacher.

Mr. Bill says, "I like how you stretched out those words you didn't know like a rubber band so you could *hear* the sounds and blend them. Well done! Let's continue."

Emily reads, "'Sss—kwint—ing, *squinting!*'" then quickly looks up with a mix of anticipation and dread in her eyes.

"Right again! You're quite a reader, Miss Emily!" says Mr. Bill. Emily beams at Mr. Bill's words of praise.

When Emily's recitation is finished, she looks up, obviously hoping for some sign of approval from the room's best reader. Mr. Bill says, "Emily, I've already noticed this year how much you enjoy poetry." When Emily nods, Mr. Bill says, "Me, too! I love poetry that rhymes and also tells a story. One of my favorite poems is by a man named Pek Gunn. He was from Tennessee and liked to tell stories from his childhood."

Mr. Bill continues. "Pek Gunn wrote a poem called 'June Bug on a String'* that talks about how children a hundred years ago used to catch June bugs. They're bugs kind of like bumblebees, except they don't sting. Kids would tie a thread around a June bug and then let it fly around while they held the string and watched."

"That sounds mean," responds Emily.

"I see your point. But they didn't hurt the bug—they just watched it fly slowly around."

"I guess that's okay," says Emily. "As long as they let the June bug go after they played awhile."

"They did. The point of the poem is that whoever holds the string in life is in control. So, the child in the poem holding the string was in control!"

"Mr. Bill, I see what you mean. But what are you trying to tell me?" Emily queries.

"Only this. When I see how well you are coming along with your reading, I see a girl who is getting control over reading like a grown-up! This year we are

David Mager/Pearson Learning Photo Studio

* The poem "Junebug on a String" was written by the late poet laureate of Tennessee, Richard "Pek" Gunn. His two self-published books of poetry, *Keep On Laughin'; It's Good for What Ails You: Nostalgic in Verse and Short Story,* and *Tumblin' Creek Tales and Other Poems* are out of print, but can be found for purchase from online bookstores.

going to learn new ways to make sure that, whenever you come to a new word in a book, you'll be able to pronounce that new word as fast as lightning. That way, *you* will be the one holding the string. You'll be in control of reading all the time!"

How Do Children Learn to "Decode" Words?

What do you think of when you hear the word *phonics?* Does it call to mind the old phrase "sounding out words"? If so, you're not alone. But the truth is, there is much more to learning to unlock the code of written language than you may think. An understanding of the development of phonics and other decoding skills is essential for effective assessment and teaching. In this chapter we take a close, evidence-based look at what children must know and be able to do to effectively "decode" words using phonics and related word identification skills, and the teacher's role in fostering the learning process.

What Is *Phonics?*

Phonics refers to how alphabet spellings relate to speech sounds in systematic and predictable ways (letter-sound relationships or **graphophonemic knowledge**), and how this knowledge can be used to identify words in print (National Research Council, 1998; Rasinski & Padak, 1996). Before we go further in this conversation about phonics, let's clarify the difference between two important skills: word identification and word recognition.

Word identification has to do with the skills students learn that help them to figure out the pronunciation of a word in print. This is what the old phrase, *sound out* means. When a reader sees a new word in print (for example, *preamble*), he or she must be able to blend the speech sounds together that are represented by the letters *pre/am/ble* to pronounce the word correctly. The act of correctly pronouncing the word in print is what we mean by *word identification.* Word identification skills are sometimes referred to as *word attack skills* because the purpose is to break the code of written words and translate the letters, affixes, syllables, and so forth back to a spoken word.

Word recognition, on the other hand, has to do with connecting a printed word's pronunciation with its meaning. It is possible for a student to use word identification skills to pronounce a word in print, yet not be able to connect the pronunciation of the word to its meaning, thereby failing at word recognition. For instance, a child may well be able to use word identification skills to pronounce the word *mordant,* yet have no idea what the word means. By the way, do *you* know the meaning of the word *mordant?* If not, then you now know the difference between word identification (the ability to pronounce a word in print— *mordant* is pronounced /*more•dent*/), and word recognition (the ability to understand the word's meaning). Thus, when we think of phonics, structural analysis, application of onset and rime, and so forth, we are talking about word identification.

Learning the Alphabetic Principle

Getting to Know English Learners

While the spelling of most words in American English remains the same, some ELs have learned English in countries that use British English spelling (like Canada and India), so words like "color" are spelled "colour," "recognize" is "recognise," and "judgment" is "judgement."

Research informs us that, from birth, children begin learning oral language (which never stops, of course) then learn, either on their own or with help, that spoken words have individual speech sounds called *phonemes*. By developing an awareness of phonemes in words, they have learned to hear the parts of spoken words. We call this ability to pull apart spoken words and attend to the individual phonemes as **segmentation.** Next in children's literacy learning journey comes an awareness of the alphabetic principle.

The **alphabetic principle** is the concept that letters or letter combinations represent speech sounds in whole, spoken words. Understanding of the alphabetic principle is the first step toward learning to decode words using phonics. It is a critical conceptual connection between spoken language and written language that young children must acquire to profit from phonics instruction. Primary-grade teachers create instructional strategies that help children learn the following:

- Speech is made up of individual speech sounds (phonemes) that are represented by specific letters (graphemes) and letter combinations (e.g., the speech sound /r/ is always written using the letter *r*).
- The 26 letters of the English alphabet represent certain sounds.
- The spelling of most words remains the same across the various books and texts students will encounter (i.e., the words *open* and *weather* are always spelled the same in print).

In summary, when phonemic awareness is combined with letter–name knowledge, students attain a new conceptual understanding—the alphabetic principle (Byrne & Fielding-Barnsley, 1989). This understanding is necessary for students to progress in their reading development, particularly in learning phonics. As students become aware of the alphabetic principle, teachers can expect to effectively provide them phonics instruction.

Phonics and Related Word Attack Skills

Surveys conducted by the International Reading Association (IRA) found that "phonics" is one of the most talked-about subjects in the field of reading education. Before we plunge into an "executive briefing" for teachers of phonics and related decoding and word recognition skills, we invite you to take a short pretest to find out what you already know—or what you need to know—about phonics. Complete the *Phonics Quick Test* (Figure 2.1) before reading further. The results may surprise you!

Important Phonics Patterns

Most states and local school districts have either developed or purchased a reading program with a *scope and sequence* of reading skills to help teachers know which reading skills should be taught at each grade level. The primary value of a scope and sequence of skills is that it helps teachers approach decoding instruction systematically. A secondary value is that it helps coordinate instruction across the state, which

Figure 2.1 The Phonics Quick Test

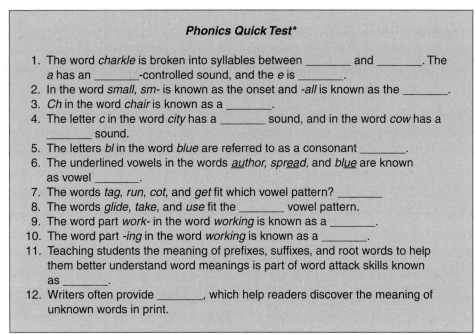

*Answers to the *Phonics Quick Test* are found at the end of this chapter, on p. 60.

is especially useful in maintaining continuity in learning for highly mobile students. Texas, California, Mississippi, Kansas, and Oklahoma are just a few states that have developed their own scope and sequence of reading skills. Following are a few phonics skills that seem to be included in virtually all commercial or locally developed scope and sequence charts of reading skills.

Beginning Consonant Sounds in Words. Arguably the single most efficient phonics generalization to teach has to do with identifying beginning consonant sounds in words. This is the best starting point for phonics instruction because consonants more regularly represent consistent phonemes than do vowels. It is easy to see this consistency of grapheme-phoneme relationship of consonants with the sounds they represent in Tables 2.1 and 2.2 that follow. In other words, consonant sounds tend to be more constant or reliable compared to vowel sounds. However, not all consonants are created equal—some are much more stable than others! The most consistent or stable consonants and their sounds are listed in Table 2.1.

Just to prove the point that not all consonants are created equal (i.e., some consonants are not as consistent as others), we share in Table 2.2 some of the not-very-consistent consonants that should not be taught until after students make some significant gains in phonics knowledge.

The C Rule. The letter *c* is an irregular consonant because it represents more than one phoneme. Rather, it can be used to represent two other phonemes that are already represented by the letters *k* and *s*. In general, when the letter *c* is followed by the letters *a, o,* or *u,* it will represent the sound we associate with the letter *k,* also known as the *hard c* sound. Some examples are the words *cake, cosmic,* and *cute.*

Table 2.1 Most Consistent Consonants

Sound	Spelling and Percentage of Use in English	Example(s)
/b/	b (97%)	ball
/d/	d (98%)	doll
/h/	h (98%)	hall
/l/	l (91%)	lost
/m/	m (94%)	Molly
/n/	n (97%)	not
/p/	p (96%)	put
/r/	r (97%)	road
/t/	t (97%)	tell
/v/	v (99.5%)	vault

Table 2.2 Some Not-Very-Consistent Consonants

Sound	Spellings and Percentage of Use in English	Example(s)
/f/	f (78%), ff, ph, lf	fun, staff, phone, wolf
/g/	g (88%), gg, gh	good, egg, ghost
/j/	g (66%), j (22%), dg	giraffe, jelly, judge
/k/	c (73%), cc, k (13%), ck, lk, q	can, stucco, rock, Chuck, chalk, bisque
/s/	s (73%), c (17%), ss	some, cent, stress
/y/	i (55%), y (44%)	onion, yell
/z/	z (23%), zz, s (64%)	zip, jazz, easy

On the other hand, the letter *c* can sometimes represent the sound associated with the letter *s*. This is referred to as the *soft c* sound. The *soft c* sound is usually produced when *c* is followed by *e, i,* or *y*. Examples of the *soft c* sound are found in the words *celebrate, circus,* and *cycle*.

The G Rule. *G* is the key symbol for the phoneme we hear in the word *get* (Hull, 1989, p. 35). The consonant *g* is also irregular, having both a soft and a hard sound. The rules are the same as for the letter *c*: When *g* is followed by the letters *e, i,* or *y,* it represents a soft *g* or /j/ sound, as with the words *gently, giraffe,* and *gym*. If *g* is followed by the letters *a, o,* or *u,* then it usually represents the hard or regular sound, as with the words *garden, go,* and *sugar*.

The CVC Pattern. When a vowel comes between two consonants, it usually represents what is referred to as a *short* vowel sound. Examples of words following the CVC pattern include *sat, ran, let, pen, win, fit, hot, mop, sun,* and *cut*.

Vowel Digraphs (CVVC). When two vowels come together in a word, the first vowel usually carries what is referred to as a *long* sound and the second vowel is silent. This occurs especially often with the *oa, ee,* and *ay* combinations. Some examples are *toad, fleet,* and *day.* A common slogan used by teachers to help children remember this generalization is "When two vowels go walking, the first one does the talking."

The VCE (Final Silent E) Pattern. When two vowels appear in a word and one is an *e* at the end of the word, the first vowel is generally long and the final *e* is silent. Examples include *cape, rope,* and *kite.*

The CV Pattern. When a consonant is followed by a vowel, the vowel usually produces a long sound. This is especially easy to see in two-letter words such as *be, go,* and *so.*

R–Controlled Vowels. Vowels that appear before the letter *r* are usually neither long nor short but tend to be overpowered or "swallowed up" by the /r/ sound. Examples include *person, player, neighborhood,* and *herself.*

Other Important Phonics Terms and Skills to Be Taught

Even though the phonics generalizations just noted are some of the most useful, most commercially published reading programs focus attention on many others. Following are several more terms, definitions, and examples of other phonics skills related to consonants and vowels not already discussed in this chapter.

Consonant Digraphs. Two consonants that produce only one speech sound *(th, sh, ng)* are called **consonant digraphs.** Examples of words containing consonant digraphs follow.

> *ch—children, change, merchant, search, which, branch*
>
> *th—thank, author, both, that, mother, smooth*
>
> *ng—sling, gang, long, fang, hung, wrong*

Consonant Blends or Clusters. Two or more consonants coming together in which the speech sounds of all the consonants may be heard *(bl, fr, sk, spl)* are referred to as **consonant blends** or *clusters.* Examples of words containing consonant blends follow:

> *bl—black, block, blast, blur, oblige, nimbly*
>
> *fr—frost, fruit, afraid, befriend, leapfrog, refresh*
>
> *sk—sky, skunk, outskirts, desk, task*
>
> *spl—splash, splat, split, splotch*

Vowel Digraphs. Two vowels together in a word that produce only one speech sound *(ee, oo, ie, ai)* are called **vowel digraphs.** The usual rule is "When two vowels go walking, the first one does the talking," but this is not always so. Examples of words containing vowel digraphs follow:

> *ee—eel, sleep, week, three, spree*
>
> *ea—head, each, threat, heaven*
>
> *oa—houseboat, oak, coat, loaf, toad*

Schwa. Some vowel letters produce the /*uh*/ sound (*a* in *America*). The schwa is represented by the backward upside-down *e* symbol: ə. Examples of words containing the schwa sound follow:

> *a—about, ago, several, canvass, china, comma*
> *e—effect, erroneous, happen, children, label, agent*
> *o—other, mother, atom, riot, second, objection*

Diphthongs. Two vowels together in a word that produce a single, glided sound (*oi* in *oil, oy* in *boy*) are known as **diphthongs.** Here are some examples:

> *ow—down, flower, crowd, towel, how, bow, avow*
> *oi—oil, voice, exploit, soil, void, typhoid*
> *ou—out, hour, doubt, our, around, count*

Onset and Rime

Because many phonics generalizations are not as consistent in English as we would like, teachers buttress their instruction with other word attack strategies. Adams (1990b) states that linguistic researchers have found an instructionally useful alternative form of word identification involving onsets and rimes. An **onset** is that part of the syllable that comes before the vowel; the **rime** is the rest (Adams, 1990b, p. 55). Although all syllables must have a rime, not all have an onset. The following are a few examples of onsets and rimes in words.

Word	Onset	Rime
a	—	*a*
in	—	*in*
aft	—	*aft*
sat	*s-*	*-at*
trim	*tr-*	*-im*
spring	*spr-*	*-ing*

One may wonder about usefulness of onset and rime in the classroom, at least as far as word identification instruction is concerned. First, some evidence indicates that children are better able to identify the spelling of whole rimes than of individual vowel sounds (Adams, 1990b; Barton, Miller, & Macken, 1980; Blevins, 1997; Mustafa, 1997; Treiman, 1985). Second, children as young as 5 and 6 years of age can transfer what they know about the pronunciation of one word to another that has the same rime, such as *call* and *ball* (Adams, 1990b). Third, although many traditional phonics generalizations with vowels are very unstable, even irregular phonics patterns seem to remain stable within rimes! For example, the *ea* vowel digraph is quite consistent within rimes, with the exceptions of *-ear* in *hear* compared to *bear*, and *-ead* in *bead* compared to *head* (Adams, 1990b). Finally, there appears to be some utility in the learning of rimes for children. Nearly 500 primary-level words can be derived through the following set of only 37 rimes (Adams, 1990b; Blachman, 1984):

-ack	*-at*	*-ide*	*-ock*	*-ain*	*-ate*
-ight	*-oke*	*-ake*	*-aw*	*-ill*	*-op*
-ale	*-ay*	*-in*	*-or*	*-all*	*-eat*
-ine	*-ore*	*-ame*	*-ell*	*-ing*	*-uck*
-an	*-est*	*-ink*	*-ug*	*-ank*	*-ice*
-ip	*-ump*	*-ap*	*-ick*	*-ir*	*-unk*
-ash					

The application of onset and rime to reading and word identification instruction seems almost obvious. Many students will find it easier to identify new words in print by locating familiar rimes. Spelling efficiency may also increase as rimes are matched with onsets to construct "invented" spellings. (We prefer to call them "temporary" spellings so that children and parents understand that we intend to develop correct spellings.)

One teacher remarked that the easiest way to teach rimes is through *rhymes!* She was exactly right. Children learn many otherwise laborious tasks through rhymes, songs, chants, and raps. Any of these that use rhyming words can be very useful to teachers. For example, a teacher may wish to use an excerpt like the one shown below from the book *Taxi Dog* by Debra and Sal Barracca to emphasize the *-ide* and *-ill* rimes. The rimes are noted in bold type for easy identification by the reader.

> It's just like a dream,
> Me and Jim—we're a team!
> I'm always there at his s**ide.**
> We never stand st**ill,**
> Every day's a new thr**ill**—
> Come join us next time for a r**ide!** (1990, p. 30)

Structural Analysis: An Important Decoding Tool

Another strategy readers use to decode unfamiliar words in print is called **structural analysis.** Rather than attacking words on the letter-phoneme level or on the onset and rime level, this kind of word identification uses a reader's knowledge of meaning "chunks" in words. Here's how it works. A reader encounters a word, usually a multi-syllabic word, that is unknown to him in print (that is, the word is known to him when he hears it; just not familiar in print)—let's say the word is *unbelievable*. Let's say our reader in this example has heard the word part or root word *believe* dozens of times in conversations and has seen it in print (e.g., in sentences like "Yes, I believe you" or "I believe that all children should have a nice birthday party") and immediately recognizes it. The prefix *un-* is likewise very familiar to the reader from other words he has learned to read, such as *untie, unreal,* and *unhook.* He is able to infer from his prior knowledge of words that *un-* means something like "not" or "to reverse." Finally, the reader's mind focuses briefly on the suffix (and word) *-able* and its meaning, also deduced from his prior knowledge of words like *workable.* In our example, then, the reader has found a new way of decoding words at something larger than the sound–symbol level. He progressed from the root word *(believe),* to the prefix *(un-),* to the suffix *(-able).* Furthermore, it was the meaning of these word parts that led to successful decoding. Structural analysis of words takes decoding to a new and higher level. This is a particularly important strategy for children in second and third grade, during which multisyllabic words become more common and must be decoded in chunks!

How Structural Analysis Works. Words are made up of basic meaning units known as **morphemes**. Morphemes may be divided into two classes—bound and free. Bound morphemes must be attached to a root word (sometimes called a base word) to have meaning. Prefixes and suffixes are bound morphemes (e.g., *pre-, un-, dis-, en-, inter-, extra-, -ed, -ies, -er, -ing*). Free morphemes (base words or root words) are meaning units that can stand alone and have meaning. The word *replay* has both a bound and free morpheme: *re-,* the bound morpheme (prefix) meaning "again," and *play,* the free morpheme that has meaning on its own. Sometimes two free morphemes combine to form a new compound word, such as *doghouse, outdoors, playground,* and *tonight.*

Teachers can help children begin to practice structural analysis of words in the same ways as they do onset and rime. The idea to get across to students is that whenever a good reader comes to a word she cannot identify through context and phonics alone, she sometimes looks within the word for a recognizable base (root) word and its accompanying prefix, suffix, or endings (Durkin, 1989; Lass & Davis, 1985). In other words, we tell our students to "look for something you know within the word."

Figure 2.2 shows selected examples of affixes adapted from *The Reading Teacher's Book of Lists* (Fry, Kress, & Fountoukidis, 2000).

> **Getting to Know English Learners**
>
> ELs may apply their knowledge of cognates when they come across unfamiliar vocabulary words. Romance languages like Spanish, Italian, French, and Germanic-based English have a large number of cognates. (Latin heavily influenced English and the romance languages' linguistic roots are distinctly Latin). Examples of Spanish/English cognates are: curioso/curious, decidir/to decide, naturalmente/naturally, and novelas/novels.

Figure 2.2 Examples of Affixes

Prefixes

Prefix	Meaning	Example	Prefix	Meaning	Example
intro-	inside	*introduce*	*ad-*	to, toward	*adhere*
pro-	forward	*project*	*para-*	beside, by	*paraphrase*
post-	after	*postdate*	*pre-*	before	*predate*
sub-	under	*submarine*	*per-*	throughout	*pervade*
ultra-	beyond	*ultramodern*	*ab-*	from	*abnormal*
dis-	opposite	*disagree*	*trans-*	across	*transatlantic*

Suffixes

Suffix	Meaning	Example	Suffix	Meaning	Example
-ant	one who	*servant*	*-ee*	object of action	*payee*
-ist	one who practices	*pianist*	*-ary*	place for	*library*
-ence	state/quality of	*violence*	*-ity*	state/quality of	*necessity*
-ism	state/quality of	*baptism*	*-ette*	small	*dinette*
-s, -es	plural	*cars*	*-ard*	one who	*coward*
-kin	small	*napkin*	*-ing*	material	*roofing*

Putting It All Together: A Sequence for Phonics and Word Identification Skill Instruction

Evidence-based reading research allows us to suggest a general sequence of early literacy skills that directly relate to word identification. This sequence is shown in Figure 2.3. Children who become proficient in these word identification skills by the end of grade 3 and who practice them regularly in reading for pleasure will attain a high degree of fluency. Note that these benchmark skills are appropriate for children learning to read in English or Spanish. We also include benchmark skills for the closely related areas of spelling and writing.

Figure 2.3   End-of-year benchmark skills: K–3

Kindergarten End-of-Year Benchmarks for English and Spanish

DECODING AND WORD RECOGNITION

✓ Recognizes and names all uppercase and lowercase letters

✓ Knows that the sequence of written letters and the sequence of spoken sounds in a word are the same

✓ (Spanish only) Applies letter sound knowledge of consonant-vowel patterns to produce syllables

SPELLING AND WRITING

✓ Writes independently most uppercase and lowercase letters

✓ Uses phonemic awareness and letter knowledge to spell independently (invented/temporary spelling)

ORAL READING

✓ Recognizes some words by sight, including a few common words

First Grade End-of-Year Benchmarks for English and Spanish

DECODING AND WORD RECOGNITION

✓ Decodes phonetically regular one-syllable words and nonsense words accurately

✓ (Spanish only) Decodes two-syllable words, using knowledge of sounds, letters, and syllables including consonants, vowels, blends, and stress

SPELLING AND WRITING

✓ Spells three- and four-letter short vowel words correctly (English only)

✓ Uses phonics to spell independently

✓ Uses basic punctuation and capitalization

✓ Uses graphic organizers to plan writing with guidance

✓ Produces a variety of types of compositions like stories, descriptions, journal entries, and so on.

(continued)

Figure 2.3 (Continued)

✓ (Spanish only) Recognizes words that use specific spelling patterns such as *r/rr, y/ll, s/c/z, q/c/k, g/j, j/x, b/v, ch, h, i/y, gue,* and *gui*

✓ (Spanish only) Spells words with two syllables using dieresis marks, accents, *r/rr, y/ll, s/c/z, q/c/k, g/j, j/x, b/v, ch, h,* and *i/y* accurately

✓ (Spanish only) Uses verb tenses appropriately and consistently

ORAL READING

✓ Reads aloud with fluency any text that is appropriate for the first half of grade 1

✓ Comprehends any text that is appropriate for the first half of grade 1

✓ Uses phonic knowledge to sound out unknown words when reading text

✓ Recognizes common, irregularly spelled words by sight

Second-Grade End-of-Year Benchmarks for English and Spanish

DECODING AND WORD RECOGNITION

✓ Decodes phonetically regular two-syllable words and nonsense words

✓ (Spanish only) Decodes words with three or more syllables using knowledge of sounds, letters, and syllables including consonants, vowels, blends, and stress

✓ (Spanish only) Uses structural cues to recognize words such as compounds, base words, and inflections such as *-mente, -ito,* and *-ando*

SPELLING AND WRITING

✓ Spells previously studied words and spelling patterns correctly in own writing

✓ Represents the complete sound of a word when spelling independently

✓ Begins to use formal language patterns in place of oral language patterns in own writing

✓ Uses revision and editing processes to clarify and refine own writing with assistance

✓ Writes informative, well-structured reports with organizational help

✓ Attends to spelling, mechanics, and presentation for final products

✓ Produces a variety of types of compositions like stories, reports, correspondence, and so on

✓ Uses information from nonfiction text in independent writing

✓ (Spanish only) Spells words with three or more syllables using silent letters, dieresis marks, accents, verbs, *r/rr, y/ll, s/c/z, q/c/k, g/j, j/x, b/v, ch, h,* and *i/y* accurately

ORAL READING

✓ Reads aloud with fluency any text that is appropriate for the first half of grade 2

✓ Comprehends any text that is appropriate for the first half of grade 2

Figure 2.3 (Continued)

✓ Uses phonic knowledge to sound out words, including multisyllable words, when reading text

✓ Reads irregularly spelled words, diphthongs, special vowel spellings, and common word endings accurately

Third-Grade End-of-Year Benchmarks for English and Spanish

DECODING AND WORD RECOGNITION

✓ Uses phonic knowledge and structural analysis to decode words

SPELLING AND WRITING

✓ Spells previously studied words and spelling patterns correctly in own writing

✓ Uses the dictionary to check and correct spelling

✓ Uses a variety of formal sentence structures in own writing

✓ Incorporates literary words and language patterns in own writing (elaborate descriptions, figurative language)

✓ Uses all aspects of the writing process in compositions and reports with assistance

✓ Combines information from multiple sources in written reports

✓ Suggests and implements editing and revision to clarify and refine own writing with assistance

✓ Reviews written work for spelling, mechanics, and presentation independently

✓ Produces a variety of written work (response to literature, reports, semantic maps)

✓ Uses graphic organizational tools with a variety of texts

✓ (Spanish only) Writes proficiently using orthographic patterns and rules such as *qu*, use of *n* before *v*, *m* before *b*, *m* before *p*, and changing *z* to *c* when adding *-es*

✓ (Spanish only) Spells words with three or more syllables using silent letters, dieresis marks, accents, verbs, *r/rr*, *y/ll*, *s/c/z*, *q/c/k*, *g/j*, *j/x*, *b/v*, *ch*, *h*, and *i/y* accurately

ORAL READING

✓ Reads aloud with fluency any text that is appropriate for the first half of grade 3

✓ Comprehends any text that is appropriate for the first half of grade 3

How Do Effective Teachers Assess Letter and Word Identification?

We have seen in this chapter that word identification skills proceed from grasp of the alphabetic principle to early phonics skills, then to structural analysis and onset and rime. In this section we present essential assessment strategies used by effective teachers in determining student needs.

Letter Naming Test (LNT)

A critical first step for children moving from phonemic awareness to alphabetic principle and phonics is letter naming. *Rapid* letter-naming ability is the goal. Based on the work of Marie Clay (1993), this task determines whether readers can identify letters of the alphabet in uppercase and lowercase forms. Walsh, Price, and Gillingham (1988) found that letter naming was strongly related to early reading achievement in kindergarten children. Cooter, Flynt, and Cooter (2007) include in their new *Comprehensive Reading Inventory* several letter-naming subtests for this purpose. We present one of these subtests here for your use in the classroom.

Administration of the Letter-Naming Test. Ask the student to be seated next to you and explain that you would like to find out which letters of the alphabet she can name as you point to them on the chart found in the alphabet letter display in Figure 2.4. Begin by pointing to the top of the form and ask the student to identify each letter work line by line and left to right to the bottom of the display, keeping letters below your line of focus covered. Using a photocopy of the alphabet letter display, mark the letters the student correctly identifies. Also make note of those letters the students cannot identify and whether the case of the letter appears to be an issue. Ask the child to point to the letter you named in the display. Record this information. Most children, even readers with special learning needs, will be able to identify at least 50 percent of the letters requested (Reutzel & Cooter, 2007).

Determining the Student's Developmental Level. Cooter, Flynt, and Cooter (2007) explain that the developmental levels derived from their assessment tool are indications of students' skill in performing a particular task. **Proficient** means that the student has attained relative mastery of the skill being assessed and does not require further instruction. **Developing** means that the student has demonstrated a degree of skill in the task being assessed, but has not yet achieved mastery. **Emergent** essentially means that the student has little or no skill in the task assessed and requires instruction.

In relation to the Letter-Naming Test (LNT), we are interested in (1) whether the student can name all 26 letters of the alphabet, and (2) how quickly he or she can identify each letter (rapid letter naming). Perfect letter identification is the goal. While research-based criteria for speed of letter identification is unavailable at this time, we believe teachers should consider how long students take to identify each letter. A pause of more than, say, 5 seconds is viewed as problematic and indicates that more practice is in order for the student.

Developmental Level	Items Correct
Proficient	26
Developing	20–25
Emergent	0–19

Word Attack Survey

Sometimes teachers choose to conduct a quick, informal assessment of students' phonics and word attack skills. Reutzel and Cooter (2007) have developed an instrument to assess these skills titled the *Reutzel/Cooter Word Attack Survey* (WAS). This tool has been tested extensively in classroom trials since 1999. Like many

Figure 2.4 Alphabet Letter Display (Mixed-Case Letters)

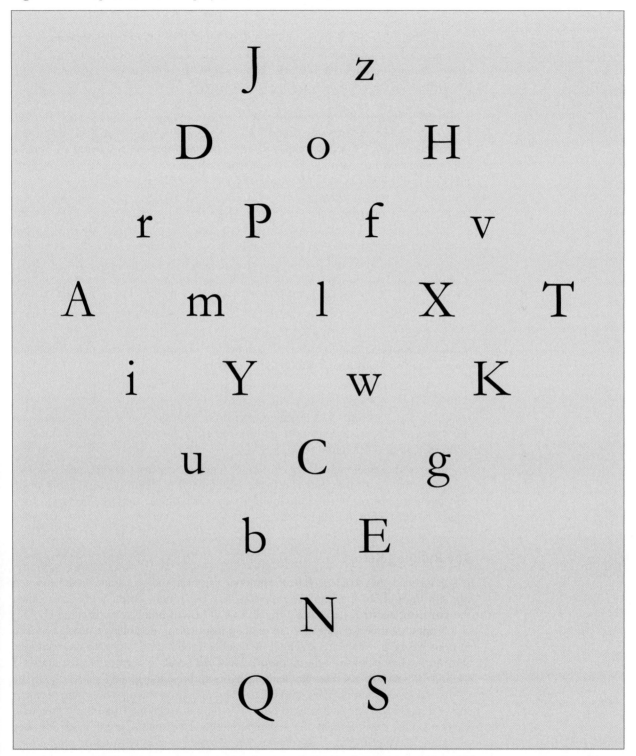

Source: Cooter, R. B., Flynt, E. S., & Cooter, K. S. (2007). *Comprehensive Reading Inventory*. Upper Saddle River, NJ: Pearson/Merrill/Prentice Hall. Used with permission of the authors.

commercially available word attack tests, the WAS uses "nonsense" words that fit common spelling patterns. The primary focus of the WAS is on vowel and consonant generalizations.

To administer the WAS you will need to reproduce the word cards provided at the end of this chapter for students to read. Also, make copies of the Word Attack Survey Form (see Figure 2.5) for use in noting student responses.

Directions for administering the WAS follow:

1. Seat the student across from you at a small table.

2. Show him the premade flash cards (see Figure 2.6). Say: "I would like for you to read aloud some words on these flash cards. These are not real words. They are make-believe words, so they may sound kind of funny to you. Just try to say them the way you think they should be pronounced. For example, this first word *(sim)* is pronounced "sim." (Pronounce the word for the student.) "Now I'd like for you to pronounce the next word for me." (Show the word *cip*.) Praise the child for saying the word correctly (or explain the directions again, if necessary). After asking the student to pronounce the third example word *(sar)*, proceed to the next step.

3. Say: "Now I would like for you to say each word as I show it to you. These are also make-believe words, so they will not sound like any word you know. Just say them the way you think they should be pronounced." Work your way through the words and note any mispronunciations on the Word Attack Survey Form (Figure 2.5).

4. Once the student has read through the word cards, praise him for his hard work and allow him to go on to other activities. Compute the total number of miscues using the Word Attack Survey Form (Figure 2.5).

5. Determine areas of phonic knowledge the student may be having difficulty with based on repeated miscues. We recommend that your instructional decisions be based on a pattern of errors repeated over time. Thus, you will need to administer this assessment to a student more than once before deciding which areas must be addressed in phonics mini-lessons.

One of the challenges busy classroom teachers confront is organizing assessment information so that they can make enlightened teaching decisions and group effectively for instruction. To help in this process, we offer a Student Phonics Knowledge Checklist, shown in Figure 2.7.

The Running Record

It is important that teachers follow students' phonics and word attack skills development throughout the year. The most widely used method for doing so is called the **running record.** Let's take a quick look at how running records came about.

From the earliest days of formal reading instruction, the ability to decode words in print has been viewed as essential (Reutzel & Cooter, 2005). In 1915, for example, William S. Gray published the *Standardized Oral Reading Paragraphs* for grades 1 through 8, which focused on oral reading errors and reading speed exclusively. In the 1930s and 1940s, Durrell (1940) and Betts (1946) discussed at length the value of studying oral reading errors as a way to inform reading instruction. These and other writings began the development of assessment methods for analyzing oral reading errors.

Marie Clay (1972), in her manual *The Early Detection of Reading Difficulties,* sought to formalize methodology for teachers conducting decoding assessments. Clay's running records for analyzing oral reading errors proved to be functional for

Figure 2.5 The Reutzel/Cooter Word Attack Survey Form

Student Name _____ Date _____

Part 1: Vowel Generalizations

Sample Item	sim	cip	sar

A. CVC/Beginning Consonant Sounds

1. tat _____
2. nan _____
3. rin _____
4. mup _____
5. det _____
6. sim _____
7. loj _____
8. cal _____
9. pif _____
10. fek _____

B. Vowel Digraphs

11. geem _____
12. hoad
13. kait _____
14. weam _____

C. VCE Pattern

15. jape _____
16. zote _____

17. gipe _____
18. tope _____

D. CV Pattern

19. bo _____
20. ka _____
21. fi _____
22. tu _____

E. R-Controlled Vowels

23. sar _____
24. wir _____
25. der _____
26. nur _____

F. Schwa Sound

27. ahurla _____
28. thup _____
29. cremon _____
30. laken _____

Part 2: Consonant Generalizations

G. Hard and Soft *C*

31. cale _____
32. cose _____
33. cimmy _____
34. cyler _____

H. Hard and Soft *G*

35. gare _____
36. gob _____
37. gime _____
38. genry _____

I. Consonant Digraphs

39. ohur _____
40. thim _____
41. shar _____
42. whilly _____
43. thar _____

J. Double Consonants

44. nally _____
45. jpple _____
46. attawap _____
47. urrit _____

K. Ph (f sound)

48. phur _____
49. phattle _____
50. phenoblab _____

L. Single Consonants*
M. Syllabication Rule**

51. lappo _____
52. pabute _____
53. larpin _____
54. witnit _____

*See section A
**Besides Items 51–54, there are many other syllabication examples throughout the *R/CWAS*.

Comments:

Reutzel, D. Ray; Cooter, Robert B. *Strategies for Reading Assessment and Instruction: Helping Every Child Succeed*, 3rd Edition, © 2007. Reprinted by permission of Pearson Education, Inc.

Figure 2.6   Word Cards for the Reutzel/Cooter Word Attack Survey

Figure 2.6   (Continued)

mup
cremon
laken
cale

cose
cimmy
cyler
gare
gob

gime
genry
chur
thim

shar
whilly
thar
nally
ipple

attawap
urrit
phur
phattle

phenoblab
lappo
pabute
larpin
witnit

Figure 2.7   Student Phonics Knowledge Checklist

Student Phonics Knowledge Checklist

Student Name _____

Skill(s)	**Date Observed**
Level 1: Phonemic Awareness	
1. Rhyming	_____
2. Alliteration	_____
3. Oddity tasks	_____
4. Oral blending syllables, onset/rime, phoneme by phoneme	_____
5. Oral segmentation syllables, onset/rime, phoneme by phoneme	_____
6. Phonemic manipulation substitution *(i, f, v);* deletion *(s, i, f)*	_____
Level 2: Alphabetic Principle	
7. Making the connection between sounds and symbols	_____
Level 3: Explicit Phonics Instruction	
8. Specific letter sounds/Specific letter names	_____
a. Onset/consonants and rimes	_____
b. Continuous consonants	_____
c. Short vowel sounds	_____
d. Continue teaching both vowels and consonants	_____
e. Consonant digraphs *wh, ch, th, sh*, etc.	_____
f. Vowel dipthongs *oi, oy, ou*	_____
g. Vowel digraphs *ee, ea, ai, ay*, etc.	_____
9. Word play with onset and rime blending	_____
10. L → R blending of letter-sounds in words	_____
11. Segmentation of sounds in words and writing segmented sounds	_____

Source: From Phonemic Awareness for Early Reading Success, by W. Blevins, 1997. Reprinted by permission of Scholastic, Inc.

many classroom teachers. A New Zealand educator and former president of the International Reading Association, Clay described the running record as an informal assessment procedure with high reliability (.90 on error reliabilities) that informs teachers regarding students' decoding development.

The procedure for maintaining a running record is not difficult, but does require practice.

In essence, the teacher notes everything the student says while reading a selected passage, including all words read correctly as well as all miscues (Wiener & Cohen, 1997). Clay recommends that three running records be obtained for each child on various levels of difficulty for initial reading assessment. Her criteria for oral reading evaluation are based on words correctly read aloud:

Independent Level (easy to read)	95–100% correct
Instructional Level (ideal for teaching)	90–94% correct
Frustration Level (too difficult)	80–89% correct

Running records using Clay's method are taken using books on different reading levels; student errors (miscues) can be recorded on a sheet of paper. In recent research

(Fawson, Ludlow, Reutzel, Sudweeks, & Smith, in press), it was found that reliable scores are obtained when teachers take three running records within the same reading level of text and average the three scores.

Guidelines for generating running records follow:

1. Gather passages from a number of reading materials representing a variety of reading levels. Each reading level should be represented by three passages; passages should be 100 to 200 words in length (for early readers, texts may fall below 100 words).

2. Have the student read the passage one or two times orally before you begin the running record.

3. Sit alongside the student while she reads so that both of you can see the page of text. Record a check mark on a sheet of blank paper for each word the student says correctly. Miscues (errors) should be recorded using the notations indicated in Figure 2.8. Figure 2.9 shows an example of a running record based on a passage from the *Flynt-Cooter Reading Inventory for the Classroom* (Flynt & Cooter, 2004).

Understanding Miscues: MSV Analysis. Clay (1985) developed a way of interpreting miscues for use in her widely acclaimed Reading Recovery program, commonly referred to as **MSV analysis.** This interpretive strategy enables you to determine whether the student uses three primary **cueing strategies** when she encounters a new word and a miscue occurs: meaning cues (M), syntax cues (S), and visual cues (V). Here is a summary of Clay's work compiled by Flynt and Cooter (2004).

> **Getting to Know English Learners**
> Word order and syntax may vary by language and may therefore cause confusion among ELs. A modern example of a language with a different word order is German; Latin is an antiquated example.

M = Semantic (Meaning—Does it make sense?). In reviewing each miscue, consider whether the student is using meaning cues in her attempt to identify the word. Context clues, picture cues, and information from the text are examples of meaning cues used by the reader.

S = Structure (or Syntax—Does it sound right?). A rule system, or *grammar,* governs all languages. The English language is essentially based on a "subject-verb" grammar system. *Syntax* is the application of this subject-verb grammar system in creating sentences. The goal of studying syntax cues as part of your miscue analysis is to determine the extent to which the student unconsciously uses rules of grammar in attempting to identify unknown words in print. For example, if a word in a passage causing a miscue for the reader is a verb, ask yourself whether the student's miscue was also a verb. Consistent use of the appropriate part of speech in miscues (i.e., a noun for a noun, a verb for a verb, articles for articles, etc.) is an indication that the student has internalized the rule system of English grammar and is applying that knowledge in attacking unknown words.

V = Visual (Graphophonic—Does it look right?). Sometimes a miscue looks a good bit like the correct word appearing in the text. The miscue may begin with the same letter or letters, for example, *top* for *toy,* or *sit* for *seat.* Another possibility is that the letters of the miscue may look very similar to the word appearing in text (e.g., *introduction* for *introspection*). Use of visual cues is essentially the student's ability (or inability) to apply phonics skills. The extent to which students use visual cues is an important factor to consider when trying to better understand the decoding skills employed by developing readers.

Figure 2.8 Notating Miscues in a Running Record

Reading Behavior	Notation	Explanation
Accurate Reading	✓ ✓ ✓ ✓ ✓	*Notation:* A check is noted for each word pronounced correctly.
Self-Correction	✓ ✓ ✓ ✓ attempt | SC ──────────── word in text |	The child corrects an error himself. This is not counted as a miscue. *Notation:* "SC" is the notation used for self-corrections.
Omission	───── ──────────── Word in text	A word or words are left out during the reading. *Notation:* A dash mark is written over a line above the word(s) from the text that has been omitted.
Insertion	Word inserted ──────────── ───────	The child adds a word that is not in the text. *Notation:* The word inserted by the reader is placed above a line and a dash placed below it.
Student Appeal and Assistance	─────── | A ──────────── Word from text |	The child is "stuck" on a word he cannot call and asks (verbal or nonverbal) the teacher for help. *Notation:* "A" is written above a line for "assisted" and the problem word from the text is written below the line.
Repetition	↓┌──┐ ✓ ✓ ✓ R ✓ ✓ ✓	Sometimes children will repeat words or phrases. These repetitions are not scored as an error, but *are* recorded. *Notation:* Write an "R" after the word repeated and draw a line back to the point where the reader returned.
Substitution	Substituted word ──────────── Word from text	The child says a word that is different from the word in the text. *Notation:* The student's substitution word is written above a line under which the correct word from text is written.
Teacher Assistance	─────── | ──────────── Word from text | T	The student pauses on a word for five seconds or more, so the teacher tells him/her the word. *Notation:* The letter "T" is written to the right of a line that follows the word from text. A blank is placed above a cross-line to indicate that the student didn't know the word.

Figure 2.9 Running Record Example

Student _____ Paco _____ (Grade 2) _____	
Title: **The Pig and the Snake**	
One day Mr. Pig was walking to	✓ ✓ ✓ ✓ ✓ ✓ ✓
town. He saw a big hole in the	✓ ✓ sam| sc / saw | ✓ ✓ ✓ ✓ ✓
road. A big snake was in the	✓ ✓ — / big ✓ ✓ ✓ ✓ ✓
hole. "Help me," said the snake,	✓ ✓ ✓ ouT / — ✓ ✓ ✓
"and I will be your friend." "No, no,"	✓ ✓ ✓ ✓✓ — |A / friend | ✓ ✓
said Mr. Pig. "If I help you get	✓ ✓ ✓ ✓ ✓ ✓ ✓ ✓
out you will bite me. You're	✓ ✓ ✓ R ✓ ✓
a snake!" The snake cried and	✓ ✓ ✓ ✓ ✓ ✓
cried. So Mr. Pig pulled the	✓ ✓ ✓ ✓ popped / pulled
snake out of the hole.	✓ ✓ ✓ ✓ ✓
Then the snake said, "Now I am	✓ ✓ ✓ ✓ ✓ ✓ ✓
going to bite you, Mr. Pig."	✓ ✓ ✓ ✓ ✓ ✓
"How can you bite me after	✓ ✓ ✓ ✓ ✓ — / after | T
I helped you out of the hole?"	✓ ✓ ✓ ✓ ✓ ✓ ✓
said Mr. Pig. The snake said, //	✓ ✓ ✓ ✓ ✓ ✓
"You knew I was a snake	✓ ✓ ✓ ✓ ✓ ✓
when you pulled me out!"	✓ ✓ ✓ ✓ ✓

Source: Flynt, E. S., & Cooter, R. B. (2004). *The Flynt/Cooter Reading Inventory for the Classroom* (5th ed.), Upper Saddle River, NJ: Merrill/Prentice Hall. Used with permission of the authors.

Applying MSV thinking is fairly simple once you get the hang of it. In Figure 2.10 we return to the miscues noted in Figure 2.9 and conduct an MSV analysis on each. Do you see why each interpretation was made?

An Alternative Running Records System. Flynt and Cooter (2004) developed a method of generating running records that makes the process both efficient and useful to classroom teachers. This system involves what they call a "miscue grid" and can be extremely effective when used with reading passages that are matched to student interests.

Figure 2.11 shows how miscues can be noted on the left side of the grid over the text, then tallied in the appropriate columns to the right according to miscue type. This process expedites administration and enables teachers to identify error patterns for each oral reading. The "grid method" can easily be adapted by teachers for use with excerpts from any piece of literature.

Teachers should select passages representing a range of reading levels (or have students select the passage(s) to be read) one day prior to assessment so that the first 100 words can be transcribed onto the left-hand side of a blank grid patterned after the one shown in Figure 2.11. Tape record the student's oral reading so that it can be reviewed later for accuracy of transcription. Miscues should be noted in the left-hand column over the text facsimile using the symbols described earlier. After all miscues are noted, examine each and make a final determination about its type (mispronunciation, substitution, insertion, etc.). Then make a mark in the appropriate grid box on the right side of the form. Only one mark is made for each miscue. Once this process is completed, each column is tallied.

In Figure 2.11 you will note that the reader had two mispronunciations, four substitutions, and so on. When the student has read several passages for the teacher over a period of weeks and months, it becomes easy to identify "error patterns"— types of miscues that happen regularly—and to plan appropriate instruction for small groups or individuals.

If you decide to use the grid system, be sure to conduct an MSV analysis on each miscue to better understand which cueing systems the reader is using.

A Running Record Self-Assessment. It is critical that all assessments be carried out with precision. When we are learning how to do a running record, which takes six or so practice sessions, it is helpful to have a way of judging for ourselves how we are doing and make corrections as needed. If a literacy coach is available to help us with modeling and feedback, so much the better; but that is not always an available resource. R. Cooter and colleagues (Cooter, Mathews, Thompson, & Cooter, 2004) developed a self-assessment tool to help teachers with "fidelity of implementation" in administering running records. Their running record self-assessment is offered in Table 2.3 for your use in the classroom.

Commercial Diagnostic Reading Tests. Teachers sometimes believe it necessary to assess an individual student's reading ability using norm-referenced measures. This often happens when new students move into a school district without their permanent records, or when struggling readers are being considered for extra assistance programs such as Title 1 or special education services provided in inclusive classrooms. Here we describe for you one such measure, a diagnostic tool called the *Woodcock Reading Mastery Tests–Revised* (Woodcock et al., 1987, 1997).

Figure 2.10 Running Record with MSV Analysis

Student _____ Paco _____ (Grade 2)

Title: **The Pig and the Snake**		E MSV	SC MSV
One day Mr. Pig was walking to	✓ ✓ ✓ ✓ ✓ ✓ ✓		
town. He saw a big hole in the	✓ ✓ sam|sc / saw| ✓ ✓ ✓ ✓ ✓		Ⓜ Ⓢ Ⓥ
road. A big snake was in the	✓ ✓ ＝/big ✓ ✓ ✓ ✓ ✓	M S V	
hole. "Help me," said the snake,	✓ ✓ ✓ ouT/＝ ✓ ✓ ✓	Ⓜ Ⓢ V	
"and I will be your friend." "No, no,"	✓ ✓ ✓ ✓✓ —|A / friend| ✓ ✓	M S V	
said Mr. Pig. "If I help you get	✓ ✓ ✓ ✓ ✓ ✓ ✓ ✓		
out you will bite me. You're	✓ ✓ ✓ R ✓ ✓		Ⓜ Ⓢ Ⓥ
a snake!" The snake cried and	✓ ✓ ✓ ✓ ✓ ✓		
cried. So Mr. Pig pulled the	✓ ✓ ✓ ✓ popped/pulled	Ⓜ Ⓢ Ⓥ	
snake out of the hole.	✓ ✓ ✓ ✓ ✓		
Then the snake said, "Now I am	✓ ✓ ✓ ✓ ✓ ✓ ✓		
going to bite you, Mr. Pig."	✓ ✓ ✓ ✓ ✓ ✓		
"How can you bite me after	✓ ✓ ✓ ✓ ✓ —/after|T	M S V	
I helped you out of the hole?"	✓ ✓ ✓ ✓ ✓ ✓ ✓		
said Mr. Pig. The snake said, //	✓ ✓ ✓ ✓ ✓ ✓		
"You knew I was a snake	✓ ✓ ✓ ✓ ✓ ✓		
when you pulled me out!"	✓ ✓ ✓ ✓ ✓		

Source: Flynt, E. S., & Cooter, R. B. (2004). *The Flynt/Cooter Reading Inventory for the Classroom* (5th ed.). Upper Saddle River, NJ: Merrill/Prentice Hall. Used with permission of the authors.

Figure 2.11 Sample of a Miscue Grid

	ERROR TYPES							ERROR ANALYSIS		
	Mis-pronun.	Sub-stitute	Inser-tions	Tchr. Assist	Omis-sions	Error Totals	Self-Correct.	Meaning (M)	Syntax (S)	Visual (V)
Hot Shoes										
The guys at the I. B. Belcher										
Elementary School ~~loved~~ *lived* all the new sport		1								
shoes. Some ~~were~~ *wear* the "Sky High"		1				1		1	1	
~~model~~ *mobil* by Leader. Others who		1				1				
couldn't afford Sky Highs would settle					2	2		1 / 1	1 / 1	
for a lesser shoe. Some liked the "Street							1			
Smarts" by Master, or the										
"Uptown-Downtown" by Beebop.										
The Belcher boys got to the point										
with their shoes that they could										
~~identify~~ *in-dub-fee* their friends just by	1					1				
looking at their feet. But the boy who										
was the ~~envy~~ *enemy* of the entire fifth		1				1		1	1	
grade was Jamie Lee. He had a										
pair of "High Five Pump'em Ups" *sc*							1			
by ~~Superior~~ *sooner*. The only thing Belcher //	1				1	2		1	1	
boys loved as much as their										
shoes was basketball.										
TOTALS	2	4			3	9	2	5	5	

Summary of Reading Behaviors (Strengths and Needs)

Source: Cooter, R. B., Flynt, E. S. & Cooter, K. S. (2007). *Comprehensive reading inventory.* Upper Saddle River, NJ: Pearson/Merrill/Prentice Hall. Used with permission of the authors.

Table 2.3 Self-Assessment/Goal Continuum: Running Records

Directions: Using a red marker, draw a vertical line after the description on each row that best describes your current implementation of each aspect of running record. Using a yellow marker, indicate your end-of-the-year goal for each aspect.

Conventions: marking system	I have never received training on a universal marking system.	I created my own marking system.	I use markings that can be interpreted by my grade level.	I use markings that can be interpreted by my school. Some markings can be universally read.	I use markings that can be interpreted by district teachers. Most markings can be universally read.	I use markings that can be interpreted universally by teachers.
Scoring • Accuracy rate • Error rate • Self-correction	I do not score running records.	I score for accuracy rate.	I use the conversion chart to score for accuracy rate to group my students.	I use the conversion chart to score for accuracy rate and error rate to group my students.	I use the conversion chart to calculate accuracy rate, error rate, and self-correction rate for grouping.	I use the conversion chart to calculate accuracy, error rate, and self-correction rates daily to inform my instruction.
Analysis: cueing systems (MSV) • Meaning • Structure • Visual	I do not analyze my running records.	I sometimes analyze errors on running records.	I analyze all errors on each running record.	I analyze all errors and self-corrections on each running record.	I analyze all errors and self-corrections for meaning, structure, and visual on each running record to guide and inform instruction.	I analyze all errors and self-corrections for meaning, structure, and visual on each running record. In addition, I look for patterns over time to further guide instruction.
Frequency	I do not use running records.	I use running records two times a year, at the beginning and end of school.	I do running records occasionally throughout the year.	I do one running record on my struggling students once per six weeks.	I do one running record on all my students once per six weeks.	I perform running records daily so that each student is assessed every six weeks. My struggling students are done twice every six weeks.

From "Searching for Lessons of Mass Instruction," by Cooter, R., Matthews, B., Thompson, S., and Cooter, K. *Reading Teacher, 58*(4), December, 2004. Copyright 2004 by International Reading Association. Reproduced with permission of International Reading Association in the format Textbook via Copyright Clearance Center.

The WRMT–R/NU is a battery of six individually administered subtests intended to measure reading abilities from kindergarten through adult levels. Subtests cover visual-auditory learning, letter identification, word identification, word attack, word comprehension, and passage comprehension. The test's design aligns with a skills perspective of reading. The assessment is divided into two sections according to age and ability levels: readiness and reading achievement. The WRMT–R/NU reports norm-referenced data for both of its forms and offers insights into remediation. Results may be calculated either manually or by using the convenient scoring program developed for personal computers (PCs). The WRMT–R/NU is frequently used by teachers in special education and Title I reading programs.

Commercial Reading Assessment Tools

There are a number of commercial products on the market to help teachers gather information about students' reading skills. While such products may be helpful, they can also be expensive. In this section we present products that have been useful in our classroom practices and that meet with our general approval. We begin with the most valid instruments of all: informal reading inventories or IRIs.

Informal Reading Inventories. An **informal reading inventory** (IRI) is normally individually administered (though some can be given to groups of children), and is usually comprised of graded word lists and story passages. Emmett A. Betts is generally considered to be the developer of the first IRI; however, several other individuals contributed to its development in concept as far back as the early 1900s (Johns & Lunn, 1983).

The Teacher's Guide to Reading Tests (Cooter, 1990) lists several advantages and unique features of IRIs that help explain why teachers continue to find them useful. One benefit is that IRIs provide for authentic assessment of the reading act: that is, an IRI closely resembles real reading. Students are better able to "put it all together" by reading whole stories or passages. Another advantage of IRIs is that they usually provide a systematic procedure for studying student miscues or reading errors.

IRIs are rather unusual when compared to other commercial forms of reading assessment. First, because they are informal, no norms, reliability data, or validity information are usually available. This is often seen as a disadvantage by some public school educators, especially when assessing students enrolled in federally funded remedial programs where reliability data are often required. Second, IRIs are unusual (in a positive way) because they provide a great deal of information that is helpful to teachers in making curricular decisions, especially teachers who place students into needs-based or guided reading groups (Fountas & Pinnell, 1996). IRIs provide an approximation of each child's ability in graded or "leveled" reading materials, such as basal readers and books used for guided reading.

IRIs tend to be somewhat different from each other. Beyond the usual graded word lists and reading passages, IRIs vary a great deal in the subtests offered (e.g., silent reading passages, phonics, interest inventories, concepts about print, phonemic awareness, auditory discrimination) and in the scoring criteria used to interpret reading miscues. Some argue (we include ourselves among them) that the best IRIs are those constructed by classroom teachers themselves using their own reading materials. Several examples of IRIs now used in many school systems follow.

The Comprehensive Reading Inventory (CRI) (Cooter, Flynt, & Cooter, 2007). The CRI is a research-based version of the traditional IRI. The authors incorporate phonemic awareness, letter naming, word identification, comprehension processes, reading fluency, and miscue analysis into an authentic reading assessment. Unlike most other commercial IRIs, the new CRI offers validity and reliability data based on scientific research. The CRI includes appropriate length passages, both expository and narrative, and an efficient miscue grid system for quick analyses of running records. The CRI also includes a spanish version for bilingual teachers use with EL students.

Developmental Reading Assessment (DRA) (Beaver, 2001). This is an informal reading inventory offering graded reading passages, rubrics for evaluating students' oral reading, and a storage box for student portfolios.

The English–Español Reading Inventory (Flynt & Cooter, 1999). This easy-to-use tool offers complete informal reading inventories for prekindergarten through grade 12 students in both Spanish and English. The Spanish passages were carefully developed and field-tested with the aid of native Spanish-speaking teacher-researchers from the United States, Mexico, and Central and South America to avoid problems with dialect differences and to maximize their usefulness in U.S. classrooms.

Qualitative Reading Inventory–3 (Leslie & Caldwell, 2000). This IRI includes both narrative and expository passages, has pictures for each level passage, and methods for assessing prior knowledge. This IRI also includes a text link to the Internet.

Dynamic Indicators of Basic Early Literacy Skills (DIBELS). The *Dynamic Indicators of Basic Early Literacy Skills,* or DIBELS, is a set of standardized, individually administered measures of early literacy development. DIBELS was specifically designed to assess three of the "five big ideas" of early literacy development: phonological awareness, alphabetic principle, and oral reading fluency (measured as a corrected reading rate) with connected text. Because of its prominence in schools today, we discuss DIBELS in detail in Chapter 6.

What Does Research Show Are the Best Ways of Teaching Phonics?

Phonics: What Do We Know from Research and Practice?

Research confirms that systematic and explicit phonics instruction is more effective than nonsystematic instruction or programs that ignore phonics (National Reading Panel, 2000). When delivered as part of a comprehensive reading program—one that includes expansive vocabulary instruction, reading practice in great books, and writing development—by a skillful teacher, phonics instruction can help children become enthusiastic lifelong readers.

Approaches to Phonics Instruction

Several approaches to phonics instruction have found support in the research (National Reading Panel, 2000). These approaches are sometimes modified or combined in reading programs.

Synthetic Phonics Instruction. Traditional phonics instruction in which students learn how to change letters or letter combinations into speech sounds, then blend them together to form known words ("sounding out").

Embedded Phonics Instruction.   The embedding of phonics instruction in text reading, which results in a more implicit approach that relies to some extent on incidental learning (National Reading Panel, 2000, p. 8).

Analogy-Based Phonics Instruction.   A variation of onset and rime instruction that encourages students to use their knowledge of word families to identify new words that have that same word part. For example, students learn to pronounce *light* by using their prior knowledge of the *-ight* rime from three words they already know: *right, might,* and *night.*

Analytic Phonics Instruction.   A variation of the previous two approaches; students study previously learned whole words to discover letter–sound relationships. For example, *Stan, steam,* and *story* all include the *st* word element (*st* is a consonant blend).

Phonics-Through-Spelling Instruction.   Students segment spoken words into phonemes and write letters that represent those sounds to create the word in print. For example, *rat* can be sounded out and written phonetically. This approach is often used as part of a process writing program.

Favorite Strategies for Teaching Phonics

Letter–Sound Cards.   Letter–sound cards are intended as prompts to help students remember individual and combination (i.e., digraphs and blends) letter sounds that have been introduced during mini-lessons or other teachable moments. You will need to have a word bank for each child (children's shoe boxes, recipe boxes, or other small containers in which index cards can be filed), alphabetic divider cards to separate words in the word bank, index cards, and colored markers.

The idea is to provide students with their own word cards on which you (or they) have written a key letter sound or sounds on one side and a word that uses that sound on the other. Whenever possible, it is best to use nouns or other words that can be depicted with a picture, so that, for emergent readers, a drawing can be added to the side having the word (as needed). Two examples are shown in Figure 2.12.

Phonics Fish (or Foniks Phish?) Card Game.   Remember the children's card game Fish (sometimes called Go Fish)? This review activity helps students use their growing awareness of phonics sounds and letter patterns to construct word families (i.e., groups of words having the same phonetic pattern). It can be played in small groups, at a learning center with two to four children, or during reading groups with the teacher.

You will need a deck of word cards. The words can be selected from the students' word banks or chosen by the teacher or parent/teaching assistant from among those familiar to all students. The word cards should contain ample examples of at least three or four phonetic patterns that you wish to review (e.g., beginning consonant sounds, *r*-controlled vowels, clusters, digraphs, rime families, etc.).

Before beginning the game, explain which word families or sound patterns are to be used. Next, explain the rules of the game.

1. Each child will be dealt five cards.
2. The remaining cards (deck of about 50) are placed facedown in the middle of the group.
3. Taking turns in a round-robin fashion, each child can ask any other if he or she is holding a word having a particular sound or pattern. For example, if one of the patterns included is the */sh/* sound, then the first student may say something

Figure 2.12   Letter–Sound Card Examples

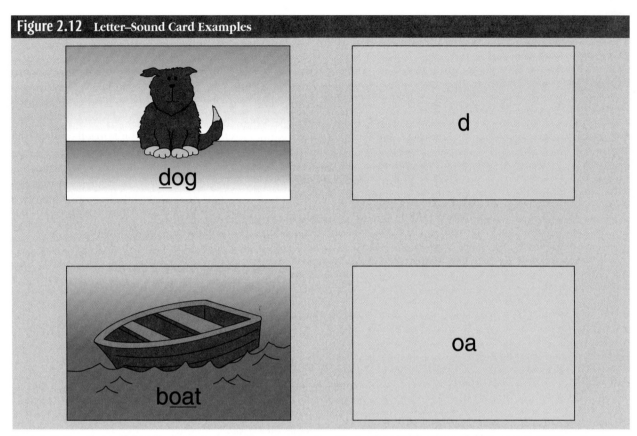

Reutzel, D. Ray; Cooter, Robert B., *Strategies for Reading Assessment and Instruction: Helping Every Child Succeed,* 3rd Edition, © 2007, Reprinted by permission of Pearson Education, Inc.

like, "Juanita, do you have any words with the */sh/* sound?" If the student being asked does not have any word cards with that pattern, he or she says, "Go Fish!" The student asking the question then draws a card from the deck.

4. Cards having matching patterns (two or more) are placed faceup in front of the student asking the question.
5. The first student to get rid of all his or her cards wins the game.

Stomping, Clapping, Tapping, and Snapping Sound. Helping children hear syllables in words enables them to segment sounds. This knowledge can be used in myriad ways to improve writing/spelling, increase awareness of letter combinations used to produce speech sounds, and apply knowledge of onsets and rimes. All these skills and more enable students to sound out words in print more effectively. Many teachers have found success in helping children hear syllables by clapping them out when reading nursery rhymes: "Mar-y had a lit-tle lamb, lit-tle lamb, lit-tle lamb. . . ."

We prefer to use rhyming poetry, songs, chants, or raps for these syllabication activities. Use an enlarged version produced for an overhead projector, a big book version, or simply rewrite the text on large chart paper using a watercolor marker. First, model-read the enlarged text aloud in a normal cadence for students. Reread the selection, again at a normal cadence, inviting students to join in as they wish. Next, explain that you will reread the selection, but this time you will clap (or snap, stomp, etc.) the syllables in the words. (Note: If you have not already explained the concept of syllables, you will need to do so at this point.) Finally, invite students to clap (or make whatever gesture or sound you have chosen) as you reread the passage.

Tongue Twisters. Many students enjoy word play. Tongue twisters can be a wonderful way of reviewing consonants (Cunningham, 1995) in a way that is fun for students. We have found that tongue-twister activities can combine reading and creative writing processes to help children deepen their understanding of phonic elements.

There are many traditional tongue twisters in published children's literature that may be used. However, we find that children enjoy creating their own tongue twisters. All you need to do is decide which sounds/letter pattern families are to be used.

Cunningham (1995) suggests that you begin by simply reciting some tongue twisters aloud and inviting students to join in. We recommend that you produce two or three examples on chart paper and post them on the wall as you introduce the concept of tongue twisters. For example, you might use the following.

> Silly Sally sat in strawberries.
>
> Peter Piper picked a peck of pickled peppers.
> If Peter Piper picked a peck of pickled peppers,
> Then how many peppers did Peter Piper pick?
>
> Peter Piper panhandles pepperoni pizza,
> With his pint-sized pick-up he packs a peck of pepperoni pizzas,
> For Patti, his portly patron.
>
> Simple Simon met a pieman going to the fair,
> Said Simple Simon to the pieman,
> "Let me taste your wares!"
> Said the pieman to Simple Simon,
> "Show me first your penny!"
> Said Simple Simon to the pieman,
> "I'm afraid I haven't any."

Children especially love it when teachers create tongue twisters using names of children in the class, such as the following example:

> Pretty Pam picked pink peonies for Patty's party.

Challenge students to create their own tongue twisters to "stump the class." It may be fun to award students coupons that can be used to purchase take-home books for coming up with clever tongue twisters.

Creating Nonsense Words

Many popular poets, such as Shel Silverstein and Jack Prelutsky, have tapped into children's fascination with word play in their very creative poetry. For instance, when Silverstein speaks of "gloppy glumps of cold oatmeal," we all understand what he means, even though *gloppy* and *glumps* are nonsense words. Having students create nonsense words and then apply them to popular poetry is a motivating way to help them practice phonic patterns.

First decide which phonic sound/letter pattern families you wish to emphasize. For instance, it may be appropriate to review the letter/sound families represented by *-ack, -ide, -ing,* and *-ore.* You will also need books of poetry or songs with rhyming phrases, chart paper or overhead transparencies, and markers.

As with all activities, begin by modeling what you expect students to do. On a large sheet of chart paper or at the overhead projector, write the word family parts that you wish to emphasize (for this example, we used *-ack, -ide, -ing,* and *-ore*). Illustrate how you can convert the word parts into nonsense words by adding a consonant, consonant blend, or consonant digraph before each one, such as shown here.

-ack	**-ide**	**-ing**	**-ore**
gack	spide	gacking	zore
clack	mide	zwing	glore
chack	plide	kaching	jore

In the next phase of the demonstration, select a poem or song that rhymes and review it with students (use enlarged text for all of your modeling). Next, show students a revised copy of the song or poem in which you have substituted nonsense words. Here is one example we have used with the song "I Know an Old Lady Who Swallowed a Fly." We show only the first verse here, but you could use the entire song, substituting a nonsense word in each stanza.

> I know an old lady who swallowed a fly,
> I don't know why,
> she swallowed the fly,
> I guess she'll die.

A nonsense-word version follows:

> I know an old lady who swallowed a **zwing,**
> I don't know why,
> she swallowed the **zwing,**
> I guess she'll die.

Online Phonics and Word Attack Activities

Many wonderful phonics activities are available on the Internet. The following Web sites offer useful, creative, and pedagogically sound activities.

First School Years—*www.firstschoolyears.com*
Reading Rockets—*www.readingrockets.org/*
BBCEducation—*www.bbc.co.uk/schools/wordsandpictures/*
EdHelper.com—*www.edhelper.com/phonics/Phonics.htm*
Phonics Link—*www.sdcoe.k12.ca.us/SCORE/Phonics_Link/phonics.html*

Who Has Difficulty in Learning Phonics and What Can Be Done to Assist Them?

There are many reasons why children may have difficulty learning phonics and other word identification skills. As we have seen in the past two chapters, if students have not developed phonemic awareness knowledge of letter names and an understanding of concepts of print, learning phonics will be difficult if not impossible. Research also suggests that most students who have reading difficulties may have deficits in oral language, language comprehension, and background knowledge (Snow, Burns, & Griffin, 1998; Stanovich & West, 1989). We have seen that this is often the case with many children living at the poverty level. Other factors affecting the learning of phonics include challenges faced by English learners (ELs), issues of focusing attention on learning activities (as with children having attention deficit disorder [ADD]), dyslexia, language impairments affecting sound perception, and children who are less cognitively able ("slow learners"). In this section we offer strategies for meeting the needs of many of these learners.

Interactive Strategies

Vellutino and Scanlon (2002) developed and field-tested a sequence of instructions for struggling readers called **interactive strategies.** These strategies for providing differentiated instruction appear to be adapted in part from the Reading Recovery model originally developed by Marie Clay (1993b). Aimed at improving decoding skills, interactive strategies are comprised of five "lessons" in the intervention format. Walpole and McKenna (2004) recommend this sequence as one that provides "strategic integration" of new decoding skills. Here are the five steps in the integrative strategies model.

1. *Five minutes of rereading familiar texts.* Repeated readings of familiar texts is an effective way to improve word identification skills and automaticity in decoding (National Reading Panel, 2000). Daily rereading of familiar or decodable texts can be a powerful reinforcement in phonics acquisition.

2. *Five minutes of phonics skills instruction.* This focused and intensive instruction is based on individual student needs in learning phonics and related skills. In the research by Vellutino and Scanlon (2002), students received short, focused "bursts" of instruction and practice in such areas as phonemic awareness, alphabet recognition, phonics, studying word families (onset and rime), and producing spelling patterns.

Laura Bolesta/Merrill

3. *Ten minutes of reading and applying decoding skills to new text.* Children read a new text each day on their **instructional reading level** (90–95 percent correct word identification). Before reading, the teacher introduces the book in an enticing way (sometimes referred to as a "book talk"). As the child reads the text aloud, the teacher may intervene to offer prompts when the child encounters an unknown word.

4. *Five minutes of word work using high-frequency words in isolation.* We have long been proponents of students having **word banks** or

vocabulary notebooks in which they keep the most frequently occurring words in print (e.g., *was, the, run, are, and, there, this,* etc.), or **high-frequency words,** as well as other content-related words the teacher has selected from science, social studies, and mathematics curricula. We discuss high-frequency words in Chapter 3, in the context of fluency. In the interactive strategies model, teachers have students spend five minutes each day identifying high-frequency words and others selected by the teacher. These practice sessions can be conducted easily with students working in pairs.

5. *Five minutes of writing.* In the final step of the interactive strategies model, teachers begin (as they always should for any practice activity) with building background or activating students' prior experiences that are related to the task students are being asked to do. The writing activity may involve dictation by the teacher or student, spelling practice with the target words, or sentence writing according to criteria established by the teacher.

Students with Dyslexia

Dyslexia is defined by the International Dyslexia Association (n.d.) as a

specific learning disability that is neurological in origin. It is characterized by difficulties with accurate and/or fluent word recognition and by poor spelling and decoding abilities. These difficulties typically result from a deficit in the phonological component of language that is often unexpected in relation to other cognitive abilities and the provision of effective classroom instruction. Secondary consequences may include problems in reading comprehension and reduced reading experience that can impede growth of vocabulary and background knowledge. . . . Many people who are dyslexic are of average to above average intelligence.

Recommended instruction for students with dyslexia typically involves individualized, intensive, **multisensory** (i.e., visual, tactile, auditory, kinesthetic) methods and writing and spelling components. Remedial teaching of phonics for dyslexic students may include direct instruction in phonics and structural analysis.

It is recommended that instruction for students with dyslexia be individualized to meet their specific learning needs. Materials used should be matched to each student's individual ability level. Following are key recommendations of the International Dyslexia Association (IDA):

- *Linguistic.* Instruction should be aimed at insuring fluency with the patterns of language in words and sentences.
- *Meaning-based.* All instruction should lead to an emphasis on comprehension and composition.
- *Multisensory.* The simultaneous use of two or more sensory pathways (auditory, visual, kinesthetic, tactile) during presentation and practice are often effective.
- *Phonemic awareness.* It can be beneficial to offer instruction that reteaches students to detect, segment, blend, and manipulate sounds in spoken language.
- *Explicit direct instruction.* Phonics instruction should be systematic (structured), sequential, and cumulative, and presented in a logical sequential plan that fits the nature of language (alphabetic principle), with no assumption of prior skills or language knowledge.

English Learners

Recently, the *Report of the National Literacy Panel on Language-Minority Children and Youth* (August & Shanahan, 2006) was released, shedding new light on the reading instruction needs of English learners (EL). First, it was found that evidence-based reading research confirms that focusing instruction on key reading components—phonemic awareness, decoding, oral reading fluency, reading comprehension, vocabulary, and writing—has clear benefits. The researchers went on to say that differences due to children's second-language proficiency make it important to adjust instruction to meet the needs of second-language learners.

A second finding was that language-minority students who become literate in their first language are likely to have an advantage in the acquisition of English literacy. This finding was supported by studies demonstrating that language-minority students taught in both their native language and English performed, on average, better on English reading measures than language-minority students instructed only in English. Unfortunately, it is often difficult for large school districts to find enough well-qualified bilingual teachers to serve these children.

This important study makes it clear that phonics instruction is critical to English learners and must be delivered by a knowledgeable teacher.

English Learners (Spanish). Native Spanish speakers are the most rapidly growing population of English learners (EL) in many states. Some basic similarities and differences between English and Spanish languages may cause some problems in the learning of phonics. Table 2.4 shows a few points for you to consider in planning phonics instruction with EL students, adapted from Honig, Diamond, and Gutlohn (2000).

More similarities and exceptions are noted earlier in this chapter. Happily, most phonics generalizations in English and Spanish are the same. If anything, Spanish is far more consistent than English!

Table 2.4 Planning Phonics Instruction

Sound	Explanation	Examples
/s/	This sound is spelled with *s* in English and Spanish.	English: *seed, secret* Spanish: *semilla, secreto*
/m/	This sound is spelled with *m* in English and Spanish.	English: *map, many* Spanish: *mapa, mucho*
Spanish *e*	The letter *e* in Spanish has the long -*a* sound, as in *eight*.	
/ch/	In Spanish, the digraph *ch* also make the /ch/ sound. However, *ch* only appears in the beginning or medial positions in Spanish.	English: *church, each* Spanish: *chico, ocho*
/sh/	The *sh* digraph does not exist in Spanish. Sorting new words with *sh* and *ch* will be helpful. Be sure to also focus on the meaning of each word.	

What Strategies Can Parents Use to Help Their Child Learn Phonics Skills?

Activities for Parents to Increase Children's Print and Phonological Awareness

The Public Library Association (*www.pla.org*) and the Association for Library Service to Children conduct a joint project known as Every Child Ready to Read @ Your Library. In this section we paraphrase some of this project's excellent ideas. We have worded them in language you might use with parents. The activities listed below are arranged, like our benchmark skills, from easiest to most difficult. It is wisely recommended that parents be sure that their children can perform tasks at the simpler level before moving on to a higher level.

Words from Pictures. Have your child glue pictures cut from magazines donated for this purpose onto paper. Have him or her tell a "story" about the picture *as you write* what he or she says. You can teach new words at this time, but be sure to draw the child's attention to the printed word. After the story is written, go back and take turns "reading" the story to each other. Collect these pictures and stories and make them into a book that can be looked at again and again.

Nursery Rhymes. A somewhat lost tradition in the United States is reading nursery rhymes to children, though hearing rhymes helps children later learn rimes (and onsets). Read nursery rhymes to your child. After he or she can say the rhyme and is very familiar with it, practice counting the words in one sentence at a time. Focus on hearing like sounds in words and how the sounds look in print.

Rhyming Picture Cards. Create picture cards with words beneath and practice categorizing the rhyming words. If your child has trouble matching rhyming words, provide help by drawing attention to the fact that words that rhyme have the same sound at the end. For example, *cat* and *rat* rhyme because they both have the *at* sound at the end; *clock* and *block* rhyme because they both have the *ock* sound at the end (emphasize the ending that makes the words rhyme when saying them). Adding some examples that do not rhyme may help your child understand (e.g., *clock* and *ball* do not rhyme because they have different ending sounds).

Silly Words. Make up "silly" words by changing the first letter in a known word. Play a game of seeing how many silly words you and your child can create and then have your child tell you whether or not the silly word is a real word. To play this game at the easiest level, you should make up several words by changing the first sound (e.g., *cook—sook, book, wook, took*) and then asking your child whether or not each is a real word. At a more advanced level, you can model and ask your child to change the first sound in a word from one word to another. For example, say: "My word is *be* and the new sound is /*m*/." (Say the sound, not the word.) "What is the new word?" (*Me.*) There are many familiar words in which the first sound can be changed to make a new word (*light–night, boat–goat, pail–sail, cat–rat, ball–wall*).

Many states have established their own collaborative Web sites featuring valuable information about family involvement in early reading development. You can find many more activities like these online at *www.ala.org/ala/pla/plaissues/earlylit/workshopsparent/workshopsparents.htm.*

Summary

Reading research has confirmed the importance of teaching children alphabetic principle, phonics, and other word attack skills explicitly. In this chapter, we have offered an evidence-based sequence for teaching phonemic awareness skills, moving from a simple understanding that, as competence in phonemic awareness is reached, students are helped to gain an understanding that the sounds in spoken words can be symbolically represented by letters (alphabetic principle). This level of understanding brings students to the point of development where they are ready to acquire basic phonics skills.

After basic phonics skills have been learned, readers are ready to learn an even higher level of word identification called *structural analysis*. Here the reader uses prior knowledge of word parts and their meaning to both pronounce and understand unfamiliar words in print. This chapter presents a practical sequence of instruction leading to fluent word identification. In later chapters we present evidence-based strategies teachers can use to teach each of these important reading skills.

Classroom Applications

1. Conduct a library and Internet search for books that could be used to help you introduce the alphabetic principle to emergent readers. Prepare an annotated bibliography of your sources to share with your colleagues in class.

---

*Phonics Quick Test**

1. The word *charkle* is broken into syllables between __r__ and __k__. The *a* has an __r__-controlled sound, and the *e* is __silent__.
2. In the word *small*, *sm-* is known as the onset and *-all* is known as the __rime__.
3. *Ch* in the word *chair* is known as a __consonant digraph__.
4. The letter *c* in the word *city* has a __soft__ sound, and in the word *cow* has a __hard__ sound.
5. The letters *bl* in the word *blue* are referred to as a consonant __blend__.
6. The underlined vowels in the words *au̱thor, sprea̱d,* and *blu̱e* are known as vowel __digraphs__.
7. The words *tag, run, cot,* and *get* fit which vowel pattern? __CVC__
8. The words *glide, take,* and *use* fit the __VCE__ vowel pattern.
9. The word part *work-* in the word *working* is known as a __root or base word, or free morpheme__.
10. The word part *-ing* in the word *working* is known as a __suffix or bound morpheme__.
11. Teaching students the meaning of prefixes, suffixes, and root words to help them better understand word meanings is part of word attack skills known as __structural analysis__.
12. Writers often provide __context clues__, which help readers discover the meaning of unknown words in print.

2. Locate the Web page for your state's education department. Print out the scope and sequence of recommended skills in the areas of alphabetic principle and phonics. Compare this list to the curriculum guide or map from the school district in which you plan to carry out your internship (student teaching). Prepare a "Comprehensive Decoding Checklist" to use in profiling each child's decoding abilities. This will be useful to you later, when we discuss reading assessment in this text. More important, you will have created a valuable tool for informing your teaching.

3. Develop your own *Words to Go!* activity for parent involvement. Use new examples. Find a resource for making all materials for the activity available in both English and Spanish.

4. Through your college or university teacher-preparation program, find a teacher who will allow you to perform running records on two of his or her students. Analyze your findings using MSV analysis. Be sure to do three running records on each level of difficulty with each child as recommended by research cited in this chapter.

5. With a classmate, assemble a PowerPoint presentation summarizing important concepts from this chapter that could be shared with parents. Share your presentation with two or three adults; solicit their feedback.

Recommended Readings

American Federation of Teachers. (1999). *Teaching reading is rocket science: What expert teachers of reading should know and be able to do.* Washington, DC: American Federation of Teachers.

Burns, M. S., Griffin, P., & Snow, C. E. (1999). *Starting out right: A guide to promoting children's reading success.* Washington, DC: National Academy Press.

Cooter, R. B., Matthews, B., Thompson, S., & Cooter, K. S. (2004). Searching for lessons of mass instruction? Try reading strategy continuums. *The Reading Teacher, 58*(4), 388–393.

Cunningham, P. M. (2004). *Phonics they use: Words for reading and writing* (4th ed.). Boston: Pearson/Allyn & Bacon.

Fry, E. B., Kress, J. E., & Fountoukidis, D. L. (2000). *The reading teacher's book of lists* (4th ed.). New York: Jossey-Bass.

Leu, D. J., Kinzer, C. K., Wilson, R. M., & Hall, M. A. (2006). *Phonics, phonemic awareness, and word analysis for teachers: An interactive tutorial* (8th ed.). Upper Saddle River, NJ: Pearson/Merrill/Prentice Hall.

National Institute for Literacy. (2003). *Put reading first: The research building blocks for teaching children to read.* Washington, DC: National Institute for Literacy at Ed Pubs. Free download available at *www.nifl.gov/partnershipforreading.*

Reutzel, D. R., & Cooter, R. B. (2007). *Strategies for reading assessment and instruction: Helping every child succeed* (3rd ed.). Upper Saddle River, NJ: Pearson/Merrill/Prentice Hall.

3

Developing Children's Reading Fluency

Chapter Questions

1. According to evidence-based research, what is fluent reading?

2. What is the nature of the relationship between fluency and reading comprehension?

3. How do young children develop fluency in reading?

4. How is reading fluency assessed?

5. What are evidence-based instructional practices or strategies for developing reading fluency?

"One Minute of Reading"

Michelle, a second-grade student, settles in next to Mrs. Chang, who is waiting to take a one-minute reading sample. Mrs. Chang hands her the second-grade passage and sets a one-minute timer. "Michelle, I am glad to spend some time today listening to you read. Are you ready?" queries Mrs. Chang.

"Yes, I think so," answers Michelle.

"I want you to read the passage aloud as quickly as you can without making mistakes. Do you understand?"

"Yes, Mrs. Chang, I understand," replies Michelle.

"Okay, then. When I say 'Start,' you may begin reading."

Michelle nods and clears her throat.

"Start!" says Mrs. Chang.

Michelle begins reading. "My Friend. I have a new friend at school. She can't walk so she uses a wheelchair to get around. She comes to school in a special van. . . ."

When Michelle finishes the reading, Mrs. Chang praises her: "Michelle, you are reading very fluently. You made only two errors, read quickly enough for a second grader, had expression in your voice, and read more than one word at a time!"

Michelle beams with pride. "Thanks," she says quietly.

"Can you tell me what you remember from the pages you read?"

"I think so," responds Michelle.

When Michelle finishes retelling what she can remember, Mrs. Chang praises her again. "Would you like to add anything to what you remember from your reading?" she questions.

"Uh-huh."

Mrs. Chang listens while Michelle adds one more detail she has remembered to her oral retelling.

"Michelle, I'm going to ask you a few questions about what you have just read. I would like for you to answer the questions as best you can."

"Okay," responds Michelle.

Mrs. Chang probes Michelle's comprehension of the passage with a few well-chosen questions to see if she remembers more than she has retold.

That afternoon, Mrs. Chang looks at the record she made of Michelle's earlier oral reading. She read the text with 95 percent accuracy, so Mrs. Chang knows that decoding this text wasn't a problem for Michelle. She had timed Michelle's reading and calculated her reading rate in words read correctly per minute. She now compares Michelle's words read correctly per minute (wcpm) to a chart showing expected oral reading rate ranges by grade level. Michelle scores near the 75th percentile for her grade level. Next, Mrs. Chang reviews the oral reading expression rating scale she had filled out right after listening to Michelle read. Michelle averaged three out of four points on expression, pacing, smoothness, and phrasing using this rating scale as a measure. Finally, Mrs. Chang carefully reviews what she wrote down while listening to Michelle's oral retelling of the pages she had read aloud. Michelle remembered the major ideas and more than half of the details in the passage, evidencing her comprehension of the text.

All things considered, Michelle has performed well! There is no doubt in Mrs. Chang's mind that Michelle is progressing well toward the goal of becoming a fluent reader!

For many years, fluency has been acknowledged as an important goal in becoming a proficient and strategic reader (Allington, 1983a, 1984, 2001; Klenk & Kibby, 2000; Opitz & Rasinski, 1998; Rasinski, 2000; Rasinkski & Padak, 1996; The Report of the National Reading Panel, 2000). As a result of the publication of the *Report of the National Reading Panel* in 2000, there has been a marked increase in attention given to teaching, practicing, and assessing reading fluency in the elementary school grades. To help children become fluent readers, teachers need to know the answer to four important questions. First, what is fluency? Second, how do children develop fluency in reading? Third, how is reading fluency assessed to determine which elements of fluent reading require instruction and practice? And finally, what are evidence-based strategies for fluency instruction and practice that will assist all children to develop fluent reading behaviors? This chapter develops teacher knowledge in the area of reading fluency, describes valid and reliable fluency assessment instruments and procedures, and explains evidence-based reading fluency instructional strategies.

What Is Reading Fluency?

Fluency is defined as (1) accuracy and ease of decoding (automaticity); (2) age- or grade-level-appropriate reading speed or rate; (3) appropriate use of volume, pitch, juncture, and stress (prosodic features) in one's voice; and (4) appropriate text phrasing or "chunking." There seems to be a high degree of agreement among researchers as to the skills one must develop to become a fluent reader (Allington, 2001; Juel, 1991; National Reading Panel, 2000; Richards, 2000; Samuels & Farstrup, 2006). These skills include the following:

- **Automaticity**—Translating letters to sounds to words effortlessly and accurately
- **Expression**—Using proper intonation (i.e., prosodic features such as pitch, juncture, and stress) in one's voice

Figure 3.1 A Model of Fluent Reading

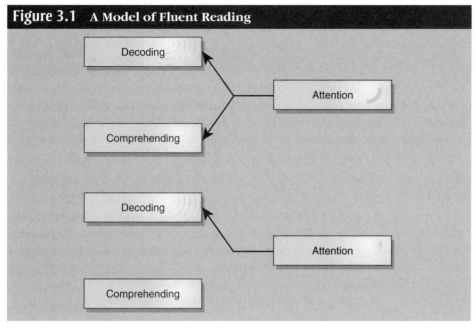

Adapted from Chall, 1967.

- **Rate**—Attaining appropriate reading speed according to the reader's purpose or the type of passage
- **Phrasing**—Reading orally large chunks of text such as phrases or sentences smoothly without hesitating, stopping to decode, or rereading

In summary, fluent readers can decode the words in text accurately and effortlessly, and read with correct volume, phrasing, appropriate intonation, and at a reasonably rapid rate so that their reading has become "automatic." When fluent readers read aloud effortlessly with speed, accuracy, and proper expression, their mind is free to focus on comprehension of text. The top half of Figure 3.1 presents a model reflecting the automaticity of fluent readers.

On the other hand, less fluent readers struggle through text in a labored, word-by-word manner. They focus most of their attention on decoding or figuring out how to pronounce the words, so reading comprehension suffers. The bottom half of Figure 3.1 shows how comprehension can be virtually ignored when readers devote most of their mental energies to decoding. Thus, reading fluency is important because it provides a much-needed bridge between word recognition and reading comprehension (National Reading Panel, 2000; Rasinski, 1989; Reutzel & Hollingsworth, 1993; Samuels & Farstrup, 2006).

How Do Children Develop Reading Fluency?

The answer to this question has been the focus of many years of research and theory development (Jenkins, Fuchs, Van den Broek, Espin, & Deno, 2003; Kame'enui & Simons, 2001; National Reading Panel, 2000; Stahl, 2004; Wolf & Katzir-Cohen, 2001).

Perhaps the most prominent theory devised to explain how readers become fluent is the the LaBerge and Samuels (1974) theory of automatic information processing, or *automaticity theory*. This popular and well-researched explanation of how reading fluency develops hypothesizes that the human mind functions much like a computer, and that visual input (letters and words) is sequentially entered into the mind of the reader. Almost without exception, humans have the ability to perform more than one task at a time (computer specialists sometimes call this "multitasking"). Because each computer—and, by extension, the human mind—has a limited capacity for multitasking, attention must be shifted from one job to another. If one job requires a large portion of the available computer's attention capacity, then capacity for another job is limited. The term *automaticity* implies that human minds of readers, like computers, have a limited amount of ability to shift attention between the processes of decoding (sounding out words) and comprehending (thinking about the meaning of the author's message in the text). If readers are too bogged down in decoding the text, they will not be able to focus on the job of comprehending the author's message. Particularly in the earliest stages of reading development, the relationship between fluency and comprehension is relatively high (Paris, Carpenter, Paris, & Hamilton, 2005).

> **Getting to Know English Learners**
> a. Human beings have an innate ability to acquire language, almost without exception, when appropriate sociocultural factors, such as socialization, are in place.
> b. Automaticity also occurs when a speaker of a language acquires his or her language fluently, and can therefore "automatically" draw upon this knowledge in most situations.

An example of automaticity in action can be seen in the skill of riding a bike. Novice bike riders focus so intently on balancing, turning the handlebars, and pedaling that they sometimes fail to attend to other important tasks like direction and potential dangers. Similarly, a reader who is a poor decoder focuses so much of his attention on phonics and other sounding out strategies that he has little brainpower left for comprehending. When this happens the reading act, like an overloaded computer or a novice bike rider, "crashes." In contrast, children who are accomplished bike riders can ride without hands, carry on a conversation with a friend, dodge a pothole in the road, and chew gum at the same time. Like the accomplished bike rider, fluent readers can rapidly shift attention and focus on the author's message because decoding no longer demands the lion's share of their attention capacity. LaBerge and Samuels's theory of automaticity predicts that if reading can occur automatically without too much focus or effort devoted to the decoding process, then reading comprehension, while not guaranteed, is at least made possible (Samuels, 2006).

Chall's Stages of Reading Fluency

Jeanne Chall (1983) proposed six stages of becoming a fluent, accomplished reader, as shown in Figure 3.2. In the first stage, or Stage 0, children have not yet begun to pay much attention to the letters and words on the page. Rather, they ask for books to be read aloud repeatedly so that they can internalize both the language and structure of the stories. They also rely rather heavily on pictures for making their way through a text. During this prereading or nonreading stage, children often need someone to read to or with them in order to successfully navigate their way through text.

> **Getting to Know English Learners**
> Remember, print direction may differ for certain ELs.

Stage 0. In Stage 0, children engage in a kind of pseudo-reading— the "reading" common among preschoolers who retell a familiar story with the aid of pictures, recognizing an occasional word to help them remember the events and language of the story.

Figure 3.2 Stage Model of Reading Development

Children pass through stages of reading development one at a time in order. Each stage must be completed before the child moves on to the next stage of reading development.

- *Stage 0: Children love to hear books read aloud to them again and again, enjoying the language and repetition. They can pretend read by retelling the story with the aid of the pictures in the book.*
- *Stage 1: Children start to notice letters and sounds and how these connect. When this happens they may recognize that they cannot read the print and refuse to read aloud. They first try to guess words based on meanings. Next they pay so much attention to how words look that they may not care about meaning. Eventually they become concerned with how the words look and what they mean.*
- *Stage 2: Children love to read familiar books again and again to gain fluency and confidence.*
- *Stage 3: Children want to read books to learn new information about the world.*
- *Stage 4: Children learn to read books that present more than a single point of view.*
- *Stage 5: Children learn to selectively sample print to get what they want for their own purposes. They also know what they don't want to read. They become critical readers who use print to think and reason.*

Stage 1. Once children understand that reading requires more than listening to a story read aloud repeatedly and following along with the pictures, they begin to focus their attention on the print on the page. As they do so, they come to understand that reading involves looking at and understanding how to process that print. At this point, children move into Stage 1 of reading development, which involves learning the ways in which letters and sounds connect to form words that may be spoken. Chall (1983) says that Stage 1 reading has been referred to pejoratively as a "guessing and memory game," or as "grunting and groaning," "mumbling and bumbling," or "barking at print," depending on whether the prevailing and currently popular methodology for teaching beginning reading is a sight word or a phonics approach.

As children focus intently on reading the print on the page, they will often say that they can't read and refuse for a time to try to do so. They may even retreat to old habits of guessing the words using pictures. When children begin to attend to the print on the page, they often make errors while reading that are semantically or syntactically acceptable, such as substituting the word *home* for *house.* Later on, as they focus more intently on decoding the actual print on the page, their errors shift to saying words that "look" about the same but do not mean the same, such as *horse* rather than *house.* This shift in errors signals that children are now paying greater attention to how words appear rather than focusing on what they mean. As children's reading development progresses and they can more quickly assign sounds to letters and blend these sounds together to form spoken words, they begin to return to a concern for not only how a word *looks* but also what it *means.* Chall indicates that children need to temporarily unglue from meaning in language to focus their attention on the print in order to later process print well enough (accurately, quickly, effortlessly, and expressively) or fluently to unglue from the print and return again to meaning. Chall also indicates that all children seem to move through the learning-to-read process in the same way. Better readers progress through these stages faster, and poor readers continue to make the first type of reading error—substituting or guessing the word on the basis of meaning and syntax. Chall insists that it is only when the children appear to let go of "meaning" substitutions and work instead on what words look and sound like that they make substantial progress.

Stage 2. In Stage 2, children consolidate what they have learned about reading in Stage 1—the connections between letters and sounds—by reading easy books that are familiar or well-known to gain a sense of fluency. For children of low socio-economic status (SES), Chall notes that discrepancies between good and poor readers reported in Stages 0 and 1 seem to widen at Stage 2. Chall assumes the reasons for this widening of the fluency gap to be that the parents of children in poverty cannot afford to buy books, and that their patterns of recreation and work do not include borrowing books and magazines from a public library. As a result, children of poverty lose access to needed time for reading practice in appropriately challenging texts. They also are deprived of opportunities to develop their oral language and to enjoy emotionally confirming responses that reading books with caregivers can bring.

Getting to Know English Learners
ELs may also lose time with reading books because their parents may not yet be able to read in English.

Stages 3–5. Once children can read fluently or with automaticity, Chall contends, reading development progresses on to Stage 3, during which children read for knowledge or for information, and then to Stage 4, during which children and adolescents read books that require dealing with more than one point of view. This means Stage 4 readers gradually become able to look beyond the literal meaning of text and consider content from more than a single point of view. In other words, they become critical readers, both learning from and questioning the text. In the final stage of development, Stage 5, readers are self-directed and have learned to read many genres of text. They know what not to read as well as what to read: they selectively use printed material in pursuit of areas of knowledge central to their own learning and responsibilities. They know how to skim and scan text to find information they want or need. They understand that various types of printed materials are organized differently, and they know how to make efficient use of search strategies in relation to this knowledge of text organization.

Thus, children develop reading fluency in a whole-to-parts-to-whole manner. They begin by using pictures to memorize texts that are repeatedly read aloud. This process encourages them to pay attention to the meaning of spoken language. Eventually, children understand that the story is not coming from the pictures on the page and begin to pay attention to the print. As they pay greater attention to the print, they continue to try to figure out the meaning of text using picture clues, a few known sight words, and their emerging understandings of letter, sound, and blending processes. They make meaning-related and grammatically acceptable errors as they read. As they progress, they understand that they need to learn letter names to connect these with sounds in spoken language.

The Stages of Reading in Action

In kindergarten and early first grade, children benefit from learning to decode easy words, for example, CVC or consonant-vowel-consonant words such as *fat, sit,* or *run.* Fluency in decoding and writing these simple CVC words in kindergarten leads to increased reading achievement and oral reading fluency at the end of first grade, helping children move successfully through Chall's (1983) Stage 1 reading development (Good, Simmons, & Kame'enui, 2001). In Stage 2, children need to read large amounts of text that are appropriately selected for challenge. This means that texts should support students' abilities to continuously add new words to their reading vocabularies. Most scholars currently agree that children should practice their fluency in texts that are written at the instructional level—90–94 percent known words—with guidance or feedback from peers, teachers, or other caregivers (Stahl, 2004). Hiebert & Fisher (2006) caution teachers to consider how many unfamiliar words are found in texts children read and the balance between sight words and decodable words as they work their way into uncontrolled texts for fluency practice. We have found that Dr. Seuss books typically present young readers with an appropriate balance of sight words to decodable words for beginning reading fluency practice (Hiebert, 2006).

Fluency involves a developmental process that looks different over time. It begins with fluent letter and sight word recognition, then moves to fluent decoding or automaticity, and then to fluent access to vocabulary and comprehension strategies (Pikulski, 2006). Fluency develops differently across text difficulty levels and genres, and teachers must not take for granted that fluent reading at one level of text difficulty or within one type of text genre indicates that fluency is fully developed for other levels of text difficulty or genres (Pikulski, 2006; Reutzel, 2006).

Finally, teachers need to know what to expect from children as they develop reading fluency. The Committee on the Prevention of Reading Difficulties in Young Children included in their report, titled *Preventing Reading Difficulties in Young Children* (Snow, Burns, & Griffin, 1998), desired "benchmarks" for kindergarten through third grade in reading and writing. Figure 3.3 presents fluency benchmark standards from their report.

Figure 3.3 Fluency Benchmark Standards*

Kindergarten: "Reads" familiar texts emergently, i.e., not necessarily verbatim from the print alone.

Grade 1: Reads aloud with accuracy any text that is appropriately designed for the first half of grade 1.

Grade 2: Accurately decodes orthographically regular multisyllable words and nonsense words. Accurately reads many irregularly spelled words and such spelling patterns as diphthongs, special vowel spellings, and common word endings.

Grade 3: Reads aloud with fluency any text that is appropriately designed for grade level.

*Criteria derived for the research by the *Committee on the Prevention of Reading Difficulties in Young Children.* Snow, C. E., Burns, M. S., & Griffin, P. (Eds.). (1998). *Preventing reading difficulties in young children.* Washington, D.C.: National Academy Press.

What Does Research Say About Fluency and Reading?

The history of fluency instruction in reading is characterized by the swinging of the pendulum of fashion (Rasinski, 2006b). Prior to and during the early part of the twentieth century, oral reading ability and performance were highly valued as a cultural asset (Rasinski, 2006; Smith, 2002). But modern research disclosed that reading silently seems to hold an advantage for readers in terms of reading rate and comprehension (Huey, 1908). Moreover, the utility and superiority of silent reading seemed apparent, since most adult readers engage almost exclusively in silent reading as opposed to oral reading (Rasinski, 2003). Allington (1983) indicated that fluency instruction was often neglected in reading programs. Results of this neglect were highlighted in a large-scale study of fluency achievement in U.S. education, in which the National Assessment of Educational Progress found that "44% of fourth grade students tested were disfluent *even with grade-level stories that the student read under supportive testing conditions*" (National Reading Panel, 2000, pp. 3–1; emphasis added). Due to the analyses and findings of the National Reading Panel (2000) about effective fluency practice, the importance of oral reading practice—at least in the earliest stages of fluency development—has been called to our collective attention once again.

The National Reading Panel's (2000) meta-analysis of fluency studies showed that fluency practice is most effective when (1) the reading practice is oral; (2) when it involves repeated readings of a text (more than twice); and (3) when students receive guidance or feedback from teachers, parents, volunteers, and peers (pp. 3–11). The National Reading Panel was unable to locate sufficient evidence showing a significantly positive impact for silent reading practice on students' reading fluency acquisition. Of the 14 studies that met the National Reading Panel's selection criteria dealing with silent reading practice, only three showed any evidence of gains in reading achievement from more time spent in silent reading practice, and the size of the gains were so small as to be "of questionable educational value" (pp. 3–26). The Panel further noted that none of the 14 silent reading studies even attempted to measure the impact of increased amounts of silent reading on children's development of reading fluency. From these findings, we have concluded that younger students will likely benefit far more from oral, repeated reading practice with feedback during the early stages of reading fluency acquisition, instruction, and practice than from silent reading.

More recently, Stahl (2004) reported an investigation of the effects of FORI (fluency-oriented reading instruction) using two variations of practice: monitored, wide silent reading practice compared with oral repeated readings with feedback. He also used a control group to determine whether one form of reading practice was superior to the other in terms of fluency acquisition of second grade readers. Stahl found that repeated oral readings with feedback *and* wide silent readings with monitoring were *both* superior to the control group performance. On the other hand, the two variations—oral readings with feedback and wide silent readings with monitoring—were roughly equivalent to one another, suggesting that "the increased amount of reading and the support given during the reading are what underlie the success of the two approaches" (p. 205). This finding has been replicated in a more recent study of struggling readers by M. Kuhn (2005b).

Hasbrouck and Tindal (2006) provide a study of oral fluency reading rates that span grades 1–8. These reading rate norms adjust reading rate for accuracy using a metric called *words correct per minute (wcpm)*. Their research suggests that children ought to be able to read about 53 wcpm by the end of first grade (Hasbrouck & Tindal, 2006). Rates for other grades and ages will be discussed later in this chapter as they relate to assessing oral reading fluency.

There is precious little research available about how expression and intonation affect fluency or comprehension (Dowhower, 1991; Reutzel, 2006). Most measures of expression in the reading literature make use of informal scales (Rasinski, 2003; Zutell & Rasinski, 1991) that ask teachers to make judgments about the prosodic features of oral reading rather than more exacting prosodic measures similar to those used by speech-language pathologists.

At present, research is unclear about which levels of text to use for fluency practice and instruction. In answer to this continuing concern, Kuhn and Stahl (2000) recommend the use of instructional-level text for fluency instruction and practice in their review of fluency developmental and remedial practices. Fluency, much like reading comprehension, also needs to be developed across text types. An ability to read narrative or poetry texts fluently does not necessarily imply an ability to read information or expository texts with similar facility. These findings suggest that fluency when reading different text genres and difficulty levels is not a perfectible process—at least not in the primary grades.

Even though most research indicates that fluency practice and instruction are an essential component of high-quality reading instruction in the elementary years (Stahl, 2004), too much of a good thing can be a bad thing! In one short-term study, Anderson, Wilkinson, and Mason (1991) reported that too much attention and time spent on developing fluency, especially when the emphasis is largely focused on accuracy and rate, may detract from students' ability to comprehend text. The National Reading Panel (2000) found in its review of fluency instruction that fluency lessons ranging in length from 15 to 30 minutes showed positive effects on students' fluency development.

Finally, research on fluency has generally shown there is a strong relationship between fluency development in the early grades and children's later reading comprehension (Paris, Carpenter, Paris, & Hamilton, 2005). Recent studies show, however, that this relationship between fluency and comprehension is transitory, diminishing over time. Some educators believe that fluency is the key that unlocks the door to comprehension. But this is only partially true. Fluency may *unlock* the door, but it does not *open* the door to reading comprehension. Rather, it is best to think of fluency as necessary but insufficient for children to comprehend what they read. To comprehend, children must be more than fluent. They must learn how to select and use a variety of cognitive strategies to help them understand text (Pressley, 2000; 2006).

How Is Reading Fluency Assessed?

Assessing fluency is the first step in understanding and planning effective fluency instruction. With a wide variety of fluent reading levels within classrooms and across grade levels, it is highly unlikely that a single approach to fluency instruction will address the diverse needs of all children. To begin fluency assessment, we focus on children's ability to read high-frequency sight words.

Assessing Sight Word Fluency

We suggest beginning sight word fluency assessment with the Thorndike-Lorge Magazine Count list of 25 high-frequency words shown in Table 3.1. This tool is typically used with kindergarten children. Neatly print each of the 25 words onto individual cards using white card stock and black block printing or computer-produced print. Shuffle the deck of 25 sight word cards to randomize the order. Next, invite a student to be seated next to you. Explain that you would like to find out which words the child knows by sight. Begin by showing the child the first card in the deck and continue until all 25 randomly presented words from the list are shown to the child.

Progress monitoring of early readers' accurate and fast recognition of these 25 highly frequent words should occur at least monthly in the second half of kindergarten and early half of first grade. By the end of kindergarten or early first grade, children should be able to accurately and quickly recognize all 25 sight words.

Table 3.1   The Thorndike-Lorge Magazine Count

	Word	Frequency of Use	Cumulative % of Use
1	the	263,472	.0515
2	and	138,672	.0817
3	a	117,222	.1072
4	to	115,358	.1323
5	of	112,601	.1568
6	I	89,489	.1763
7	in	75,253	.1926
8	was	58,732	.2055
9	that	55,667	.2176
10	it	52,107	.2290
11	he	49,268	.2397
12	you	42,581	.2490
13	for	39,363	.2576
14	had	34,341	.2651
15	is	33,404	.2723
16	with	32,903	.2795
17	her	31,824	.2884
18	she	31,087	.2932
19	his	30,748	.2999
20	as	30,693	.3066
21	on	30,244	.3132
22	at	26,250	.3189
23	have	24,456	.3242
24	but	23,704	.2392
25	me	23,364	.3345
	Sum = 1,535,783		
	Total Number of Words = 4,591,125		

Reprinted by permission of Teachers College Press from *Teacher's word book of 30,000 words*.

To expand the assessment of early readers' sight words into the first and second grade levels, we suggest using the 107 High-Frequency Word List by Zeno, Ivens, Millard, and Duvvuri (1995), shown in Table 3.2.

Neatly print each of the 107 words onto individual cards using white card stock and black block printing or computer-produced print. Shuffle the deck of 107 sight word cards to randomize the order. Next, invite a student to be seated next to you. Explain that you would like to find out which words the child knows by sight. Begin by showing the child the first card in the deck and continue until 25 randomly presented words from the list of 107 are shown to the child.

Progress monitoring of early readers' accurate and fast recognition of these 107 highly frequent words should occur at least monthly in the second half of first grade and into second grade. By the end of second grade, children should be able to accurately and quickly recognize all 107 sight words.

If children have difficulty recognizing the sight words in the instruments we have presented here, they can be assisted in committing the words to memory through the use of instructional strategies presented later in this chapter.

Assessing Oral Reading Fluency

Assessing oral reading fluency has for many years focused somewhat exclusively on how quickly students could read a given text. This is known as **reading rate** or **reading speed.** More recently, reading teachers have used **words correct per minute** (wcpm) to indicate reading rate. Although wcpm is one indicator of fluent oral reading, it is *only*

Table 3.2 The 107 Most Frequently Used Words in Written English (Zeno et al., 1995)

the	at	we	many	first	know
of	or	what	these	new	little
and	from	about	no	very	such
to	had	up	time	my	even
a	I	said	been	also	much
in	not	out	who	down	our
is	have	if	like	make	must
that	this	some	could	now	
it	but	would	has	way	
was	by	so	him	each	
for	were	people	how	called	
you	one	them	than	did	
he	all	other	two	just	
on	she	more	may	after	
as	when	will	only	water	
are	an	into	most	through	
they	their	your	its	get	
with	there	which	made	because	
be	her	do	over	back	
his	can	then	see	where	

Excerpt from "The 107 most frequently used words in wrtitten English" from Zeno, S. M., Ivens, S. H., Millard, R. T., & Duvvuri, R. (1995). *The educator's word frequency guide.* New York: Touchstone Applied Science Associates, Inc. Used with permission.

one. To adequately assess fluency, teachers should consider at least four different components: (1) accurate decoding of text; (2) reading rate or speed; (3) use of volume, stress, pitch, and juncture (prosodic markers); and (4) mature phrasing or "chunking" of text.

Teachers have in recent years begun to discuss how they might more efficiently and authentically assess the ability to read fluently (Kuhn & Stahl, 2000). Most teachers believe that paper and pencil assessment tools such as standardized reading tests are inadequate or at least incomplete measures of reading fluency. Another significant issue for many teachers today is accessing valid and reliable estimates of reading rates appropriate for children of differing ages and grades.

One of the simplest and most useful means of collecting fluency data is the **one-minute reading sample** (Rasinski, 2003). A one-minute reading sample is typical of that used in the Oral Reading Fluency (ORF) test drawn from the *Dynamic Indicators of Basic Early Literacy Skills* (DIBELS) battery (Good & Kaminski, 2002).

To take a one-minute reading sample, teachers need a grade-level text of between 200 and 300 words, a one-minute cooking timer with an alarm sounding at zero or a stop watch, and a pencil for marking the text. Children are asked to read aloud a grade-level passage for one minute. Words omitted, substituted, or hesitations of more than three seconds are scored as errors. Words self-corrected within three seconds are scored as accurate. After one minute, the student stops reading. The teacher subtracts the total number of errors from the number of words read by the student to obtain a score of words correct per minute (wcpm). This number constitutes the student's reading rate. Using more than one passage to assess fluency rates helps to control for any text-based or genre-type differences or variations. However, if standardized passages are used, such as those from published sources of CBM materials (e.g., *DIBELS, Reading Fluency Monitor, AimsWEB*), a score from a single passage is considered valid (Hintze & Christ, 2004). The final wcpm score can then be compared to the ORF norms (see Table 3.3) for making screening, diagnostic, or progress-monitoring decisions. By using words correct per minute (wcpm), reading rate is corrected for the accuracy of the reading. The new ORF norms align closely with those published in 1992, and also closely match the widely used DIBELS norms for fall, winter, and spring.

If you want to use the DIBELS oral reading fluency test to augment one-minute fluency samples you take during the year, the full directions for using the ORF measurement can be obtained by going to the DIBELS Web site at *http://dibels.uoregon.edu/*, registering as a user, and downloading grade-level passages and administration and scoring procedures.

Assessing Expressive Reading

As we mentioned earlier in this chapter, reading fluency is not just described or defined as accurate reading at an age-appropriate rate. It also includes reading that is appropriately expressive. To augment one-minute reading sample measurement of accuracy and rate, Rasinski (2003) provides a practical measurement of students' oral reading fluency, the *Multidimensional Fluency Scale* (see Figure 3.4). This rating tool provides more extensive and reliable information about four components of fluent reading: (a) volume and expression, (b) phrasing, (c) smoothness, and (d) pace. Rasinski's (2003) recent revision of the original Zutell and Rasinski's (1991)

Table 3.3   Grades 1–8 Oral Reading Fluency Norms*

Grade	Percentile	Fall WCPM	Winter WCPM	Spring WCPM
1	90	XX	81	111
	75	XX	47	82
	50	XX	23	56
	25	XX	12	28
	10	XX	6	15
2	90	106	125	142
	75	79	100	117
	50	51	72	89
	25	25	42	61
	10	11	18	31
3	90	128	146	162
	75	99	120	137
	50	71	92	107
	25	44	62	78
	10	21	36	48
4	90	145	166	180
	75	119	139	152
	50	94	112	123
	25	68	87	98
	10	45	61	72
5	90	166	182	194
	75	139	156	168
	50	110	127	139
	25	85	99	109
	10	61	74	83
6	90	177	195	204
	75	153	167	177
	50	127	140	150
	25	98	111	122
	10	68	82	93
7	90	180	192	202
	75	156	165	177
	50	128	136	150
	25	102	109	123
	10	79	88	98
8	90	185	199	199
	75	161	173	177
	50	133	146	151
	25	106	115	124
	10	77	84	97

*Compiled by Jan Hasbrouck, Ph.D. & Gerald Tindal, Ph.D. (2006). Oral reading fluency norms: A valuable assessment tool for reading teachers. *The Reading Teacher, 59(7)*, 636–645.
Count 5546 3496 5335
WCPM: Words correct per minute
TABLE SUMMARIZED FROM: Behavioral Research & Teaching (2005, January). Oral Reading Fluency: 90 Years of Assessment (BRT Technical Report No. 33), Eugene, OR: Author.
Data available at: *http://brt.uoregon.edu/*TECHNICAL REPORTS
Table available at: *www.jhasbrouck.com/*Q&A: Fluency

Figure 3.4 Multidimensional Fluency Scale

Use the following scale to rate reader fluency on the five dimensions of accuracy, expression and volume, phrasing, smoothness, and pace.

A. Accuracy

1. Word recognition accuracy is poor, generally below 85%. Reader clearly struggles in decoding words. Makes multiple decoding attempts for many words, usually without success.
2. Word recognition accuracy is marginal: 86–90%. Reader struggles with many words. Many unsuccessful attempts at self-correction.
3. Word recognition accuracy is good: 91–95%. Reader self-corrects successfully.
4. Word recognition accuracy is excellent: 96%–100%. Self-corrections are few but successful, as nearly all words are read correctly on initial attempt.

B. Expression and Volume

1. Student reads with little expression or enthusiasm. Reads words as if simply to get them out. Little sense of trying to make text sound like natural language. Tends to read in a quiet voice.
2. Student reads with some expression. Begins to use voice to make text sound like natural language in some areas of the text, but not others. Focus remains largely on saying the words. Still reads in a voice that is quiet.
3. Student's reading sounds like natural language throughout the better part of the passage. Occasionally slips into expressionless reading. Voice volume is generally appropriate throughout the text.
4. Student reads with good expression and enthusiasm throughout the text. Sounds like natural language. Reader is able to vary expression and volume to match his/her interpretation of the passage.

C. Phrasing

1. Monotonic with little sense of phrase boundaries; frequent word-by-word reading.
2. Student uses frequent two- and three-word phrases, giving the impression of choppy reading; improper stress and intonation that fails to mark ends of sentences and clauses.
3. Student reads in mixture of run-ons, with mid-sentence pauses for breath and possibly some choppiness; reasonable stress/intonation.
4. Reading is generally well-phrased, mostly in clause and sentence units, with adequate attention to expression.

D. Smoothness

1. Student reads with frequent extended pauses, hesitations, false starts, sound-outs, repetitions, and/or multiple attempts.
2. Student experiences several "rough spots" in text, where extended pauses, hesitations, etc., are more frequent and disruptive.
3. Reader experiences occasional breaks in smoothness caused by difficulties with specific words and/or structures.
4. Generally smooth reading with some breaks, but word and structure difficulties are resolved quickly, usually through self-correction.

E. Pace (during sections of minimal disruption)

1. Slow and laborious.
2. Moderately slow.
3. Uneven mixture of fast and slow reading.
4. Consistently conversational.

Multidimensional Fluency Scale (MFS) adds assessment of reading volume and expression. Zutell and Rasinski (1991) report a .99 test-retest reliability coefficient for the original MFS.

To use the *Multidimensional Fluency Scale,* teachers take a one-minute reading sample as previously described and fill in the required ratings using a paper copy of the MFS. The MFS can also be used to rate group performances such as plays, readers' theater, and radio readings (Reutzel & Cooter, 2004).

What Are the Characteristics of Effective Fluency Instruction?

In this section we provide seven characteristics of effective fluency instruction and practice drawn from evidence-based research.

1. *Explicit Instruction.* Hoffman (2003) asserts that teachers should "Work to develop the meta-language of fluency with . . . students, which includes concepts of expression, word stress, and phrasing" (p. 6). Young readers need to know that fluency is an important goal of their reading instruction. They need to know what fluency is. They need to know the academic language or terms used by teachers and researchers to describe fluency, so that they, too, can think and talk specifically about fluency as a concept and skill with their peers and their teachers. They also need the language of fluency to be able to examine and regulate their own reading fluency as an independent reader. Students must develop an awareness of the various elements of fluency in order to monitor them, fix them, and improve their fluency. Students must know how to use fluency fix-up strategies and understand the varying purposes of fluency in order to self-regulate and improve it. As classroom teachers, we must not only facilitate reading fluency practice but also cultivate a deeper appreciation among students of the importance of fluency as a personal goal of reading improvement. Equally important, we need to develop students' understanding of what we mean when we say that reading is fluent so that they can go about fixing fluency up when it isn't going along as it should (Rasinski, Blachowizc, & Lems, 2006; Reutzel, 2006; Worthy & Broaddus, 2002).

> **Getting to Know English Learners**
> Modeling oral reading to ELs may be especially helpful if their parents do not yet read English. Assigning a capable reading buddy in the classroom may help alleviate this problem.

2. *Modeling.* Exposure to rich and varied models of fluent oral reading helps *some* children. For other students, modeling of nonfluent oral reading seems to alert attention to the specific characteristics of fluent reading that are sometimes transparent or taken for granted when teachers only model fluent oral reading. In other words, some students need to know what fluency *is* and *is not* to achieve clarity on the concept of fluency and its attendant characteristics (Reutzel, 2006). In this case, parents, teachers, or siblings spend significant amounts of time reading aloud to children while modeling fluent oral reading. Through this process of modeling fluent (and sometimes nonfluent) oral reading, children learn the behaviors of fluent readers as well as the elements of fluent oral reading. Many researchers have documented the significant impact of modeling on the acquisition of fluency in reading (Rasinski, 2003; Rasinski et al., 2006; Reutzel, 2006; Stahl, 2004).

3. *Reading Practice.* Good readers are given more opportunities to read connected text for longer periods of time than are students having reading problems. This dilemma led Allington (1977) to ask, "If they don't read much, how are they ever gonna get good?" The National Reading Panel (2000) has emphasized the need for children to experience regular, daily reading practice.

4. *Access to Appropriately Challenging Reading Materials.* Proficient readers spend more time reading appropriately challenging texts than students having reading problems (Gambrell et al., 1981). Reading appropriately challenging books with instruction and feedback may help proficient readers make the transition from word-by-word reading to fluent reading, whereas poorer readers often spend more time in reading materials that are relatively difficult. Doing so denies those students who are having reading problems access to reading materials that could help them develop fluent reading skills. For the most part, children need to be reading in instructional level texts with instruction, modeling, support, monitoring, and feedback (Bryan, Fawson, & Reutzel, 2003; Kuhn, 2005a; Kuhn & Schwanenflugel, 2006; Kuhn & Stahl, 2000; Rasinski & Hoffman, 2006; Stahl, 2004). Menon and Hiebert (2005) and Hiebert and Fisher (2006) found that texts for supporting early readers' fluency development need to be controlled to contain fewer unfamiliar words than is typical in many beginning reading texts as well as a balance between high-frequency words and decodable words. When children read in such texts, they made weekly gains of over 3.4 words correct per minute! Carefully selected texts, in a very real way, are the scaffolding teachers use to support students' reading fluency practice (Brown, 1999). Teachers need to increase the volume of students' reading in appropriately designed, controlled reading texts in the early stages of fluency development (Hiebert & Fisher, 2006).

5. *Use of Oral and Silent Reading.* The *Report of the National Reading Panel* (2000) indicated there was ample scientific evidence to support reading practice for fluency that included the following elements: (a) oral reading, (b) repeated reading of the same text, and (c) feedback and guidance during and after reading of a text. On the other hand, silent reading of self-chosen books without monitoring or feedback did not have substantial scientific evidence to support its exclusive use for reading practice across elementary grades. Recent experimental research suggests that silent, wide reading (across genre or text types) with monitoring seems to produce equivalent or better fluency gains in second- and third-grade students as compared to oral repeated readings (Kuhn & Schwanenflugel, 2006; Pikulski & Chard, 2005; Reutzel, Fawson, & Smith, 2006 in preparation; Stahl, 2004). There is mounting evidence that the old practice of SSR where the teacher read as a model for children is giving way to a new model of silent reading practice that incorporates book selection instruction, student monitoring and accountability, and reading widely (Bryan, Fawson, & Reutzel, 2003; Kuhn, 2005b; Marzano, 2004; Stahl & McKenna, 2006; Reutzel, Smith, & Fawson, in preparation; Stahl, 2004).

6. *Monitoring and Accountability.* For many years, teachers believed that their sitting and reading a book silently provided modeling sufficient to promote students' desires and abilities to read. This has never been proven to be the case. In recent years, Bryan, Fawson, and Reutzel (2003) have reported that monitoring disengaged readers with quick, stop-in visits to listen to oral reading and discuss a piece of literature during silent reading has a beneficial effect on their engagement during silent reading. Furthermore, having children account for their fluency practice time by reading onto a tape or for a teacher has a positive impact upon fluency engagement and growth (Reutzel, 2006; Reutzel, Smith, & Fawson, in preparation; Stahl, 2004).

7. *Wide and Repeated Reading.* There is considerable evidence that repeated readings of the same text leads to automaticity—fast, accurate, and effortless word recognition (Dowhower, 1991; NRP, 2000). However, once automaticity is achieved, reading widely seems to provide the necessary ingredient to move students' fluency from automaticity to comprehension. Thus, it is important that when a student achieves grade-level automaticity, he or she be encouraged to read widely as well as repeatedly to develop connected text comprehension (Kuhn, 2005a; Kuhn & Schwanenflugel, 2006; Pikulski & Chard, 2005; Reutzel, 2006; Stahl, 2004). From the currently available evidence, this occurs in second or third grade for some children while others may need to continue to read texts repeatedly until they achieve automaticity at grade level into the intermediate years.

An awareness of the seven characteristics of effective fluency instruction and practice can help you, the teacher, create optimal conditions for students to become fluent readers.

Fluency Begins Early

Even though an emphasis on reading fluency is recommended to begin midyear in the first grade, recognizing a few common words by sight is also an important part of early reading development (Burns, Griffin, & Snow, 1999). Young children should be taught to recognize several common, high-frequency words (known as **sight words**) instantaneously and without phonic analysis. Many years ago, Thorndike and Lorge (1944), researchers at Columbia University, reported a study in which they counted the frequency of words found in a 4.5 million-word sample drawn from popularly published U.S. magazines. At the conclusion of this study, these researchers found that a corpus of only 25 words accounted for 1.5 million of the total 4.5 million words in these magazines (see Table 3.1). In fact, three words in this list accounted for nearly 11 percent of frequency of words in the sample; these words were *a, and,* and *the,* with the word *the* accounting for nearly 5 percent of all words in the sample. Years later, Zeno, Ivens, Millard, and Duvvuri (1995) found that a corpus of 107 words accounted for 50 percent of all words typically found in printed materials read by U.S. adults (see Table 3.2).

These studies show that with a relative few words known by sight—somewhere between 25 and 107—young children can fluently recognize approximately 33 to 50 percent of the words they will be likely to encounter in commonplace adult reading materials. Thus it seems reasonable for teachers to focus significant and early attention on helping young children acquire the ability to automatically identify a small corpus of common, high-frequency words by sight in the future service of reading fluency.

What Are Effective Fluency Teaching Strategies?

Careful planning is always crucial for successful teaching. In fluency instruction, as with most other reading skill areas, the teacher must choose a "balanced diet" of reading materials for practice exercises (i.e., stories, nonfiction materials, poetry), and provide explicit, teacher-led instruction, modeling, guided student practice, practice with peers, and independent practice. An effective model for organizing fluency instruction that includes these elements was developed for Title I reading teachers in Kansas

Figure 3.5　The Fluency Formula

The Fluency Formula

A Blueprint for Improving Accuracy, Rate, Expression, and Phrasing

---

Planning for Instruction

A.　Identify instructional standards (objectives).
B.　List necessary supplies and check-off selection of passage.
C.　Introduce passages for modeling and practice (fluency pyramid).
D.　Develop explicit fluency instructional plans.

Step I: Explicit Fluency Instruction and Modeling

A.　Explain the specific fluency instructional objective—targeted fluency skill.
- Explain *what* is to be learned about fluency—accuracy, rate, expression, or phrasing.
- Explain *why* learning this information is important.
- Explain *when* and *where* this information will be useful.

B.　Introduce the passage and concepts.
- Teach high-frequency sight words.
- Introduce vocabulary.
- Introduce the fluency skill to be learned.

C.　Model the targeted fluency skill.

Step II: Guided Oral Reading Practice

A.　Guided oral reading strategies: teacher with students
- Choral reading

B.　Peer-supported practice: *students helping students*
- Partner or "buddy" reading
- Neurological impress method (NIM)

Step III: Independent Practice Reading

- Assisted repeated oral readings
- Scaffolded Silent Reading (ScSR)

Step IV: Performance Reading for Fluency Practice

- Readers' theatre
- Radio reading
- Recitation

Step V: Goal Setting and Monitoring Student Progress

- Fluency assessment rubric
- Tracking fluency progress
- Goal setting

(R. Cooter & K. Cooter, 2002) called **the Fluency Formula** (summarized in Figure 3.5). A sample lesson plan for teaching children about phrasing in fluency is shown in Figure 3.6. In the description that follows, you will see that evidence-based elements of effective fluency instruction have been included.

Implementing the Fluency Instructional Plan

An effective teacher always maps out her lesson plan well before implementing it. Lesson planning always begins with the decision about an appropriate objective. Objectives for fluency instruction, as with anything else in any curriculum, should be drawn from three sources:

1. a careful review of grade-level expectations and state standards,
2. an assessment of each child's needs and abilities relative to the standards, and
3. a collation of all students' needs into a classroom profile to better understand more universal group needs.

Identifying Standards for Fluency Instruction. Standards for fluency have been developed by most states for each grade level, as well as by the U.S. Department of Education. In Chapter 6, "Assessment," we discuss ways of developing both individual and group objectives from assessment data. Fluency standards almost invariably pertain to one of three principal areas: accuracy, rate, or expression. These three areas are described later in the description of Stage 1 of the Fluency Formula.

Selecting Reading Materials: Varying Literary Genre. Once you have selected a fluency objective, reading materials should be selected for (1) reading aloud (modeling), and (2) for instruction (guided oral reading). Your primary goal in the first part of fluency instruction should be to *model* fluent reading behavior. As the teacher, you are—theoretically—the *best* reader in the room and your young charges want to see and hear what fluent reading behavior is like. Because you will have a wide range of reading ability represented in your class, you will want to think about modeling for students in two venues: whole class and small groups based on reading level (i.e., guided reading groups).

For whole-group modeling, remember the "balanced diet" idea mentioned earlier: *model fluent reading using a variety of genres in children's literature.* Here's what we mean: Think of the balanced reading diet at each grade level as you would the famous food pyramid. At the bottom of the **fluency pyramid** we place the ever-popular narrative selections or stories. Some of your oral reading to the class for fluency modeling and practice should come from high quality children's stories and books. At the center of the fluency pyramid are interesting nonfiction books that not only provide a medium for modeling and practicing fluency, but also help children develop an understanding of new concepts and vocabulary. Notice that nonfiction text examples are almost equal in proportion to narrative texts. At the top of the pyramid, less frequent in comparison to the first two types, is some extra spice for children's fluency diet: songs, poetry, chants, and raps. Figure 3.7 shows a fluency pyramid scheme for passage selection in the elementary grades.

Selecting Appropriately Challenging Reading Materials. Passages *only* read aloud by the teacher during modeling can be at reading levels well above the abilities of the listeners. In these cases, the teacher is

> **Getting to Know English Learners**
> It is important to read aloud to ELs, regardless of reading level, so that they can hear the rhythm of the English language as their brains actively process the new language.

Figure 3.6   Sample Lesson Plan: The Fluency Formula

Instructional Standard or Objective: *Children will pay attention to punctuation to help them read expressively.*

Materials

- Book—*In a Tree*, pp. 18–19
- Overhead transparency
- Overhead projector
- Fluency phones
- Three colored overhead markers
- Text types: Narrative ( ) Information Books (x) Poetry ( )

Explain

- **What**

Today, boys and girls, we are going to be learning about how to read expressively. Important parts of reading expressively are pausing, stopping, and raising or lowering our pitch as we read. Pitch is how high or low the sounds are that we make with our voices. *(Demonstrate high and low pitch.)* "Stopping" means we quit reading for a moment, like this. *(Demonstrate.)* "Pausing" means we take a breath and keep reading. Marks on the page called *punctuation marks (Point.)* help us to know when we need to pause, stop, or raise or lower our pitch.

- **Why**

We need to read expressively with pauses or stops so that we can show that we understand what we are reading. Punctuation tells us what we need to know about how to express the words, phrases, and sentences with the right pauses, stops, and pitch.

- **When/Where**

Whenever we read, we should pay attention to the punctuation so that we know where to pause, stop, and raise or lower our pitch.

Teacher Modeling

- **Example**

I am going to begin by reading this page with good expression, paying attention to what the punctuation tells me to do, such as pause, stop, or raise or lower my pitch. Please look at the page on the overhead. Notice that I have colored each punctuation mark with a different color to help you see it more clearly. Follow what I read with your eyes. Listen very carefully to see if I stop, pause, or change my pitch where I should.

- **Non-example**

Now I am going to read this page with poor expression, paying little or no attention to what the punctuation tells me to do. I won't pause, stop, or raise or lower my pitch. Please look at the page on the overhead. Notice that I have colored each punctuation mark with a different color to help you see it more clearly. Follow what I read with your eyes. Listen very carefully to see where I should have changed my reading to stop, pause, or raise or lower my pitch.

Guided Oral Reading Practice: Teacher and Students; Students with Students

Teacher and Students

Now that I have shown you how and how not to read this page, let's practice it together! We will begin reading this page all together. *(Point.)* Watch my pen so that we can all stay together.

Figure 3.6 (Continued)

Next, we will read this again using echo reading. How many of you have ever heard an echo? If I say, "Hello," the echo will say, "Hello." Now I will read and you will echo me. Let's begin.

Students with Students

Turn to your neighbor. One person will read and the other will echo.

Independent Practice

Take your fluency phone (PVC pipe shaped into a phone as shown in photo) and read this again to yourself, listening carefully to see where you are stopping, pausing, or raising or lowering your pitch.

Take your fluency phone and read this again to yourself, listening carefully to see where you are stopping, pausing, or raising or lowering your pitch.

Ray Reutzel

Performance

Today we will perform our fluency readings by standing and reading the passage aloud in unison in pairs. We will number off into pairs. Get with your partners and prepare to read this aloud for the class. I will roll two or three dice to see which pair is picked to read aloud. After reading, we will ask each pair to use the fluency assessment rubric and evaluate their performance.

Assess

- Rubric for assessment
- Set personal goals
- Graph progress

Reflect

- What went well?
- How would you change the lesson?

simply demonstrating how a passage can be read with proper intonation and rate. When selected for children to read themselves, either with the teacher or with another student, passages should conform to the following guidelines.

- *Use selections within the decoding range of the learner—95 percent or better accuracy.* A good rule of thumb to remember is that the range of readers in a classroom

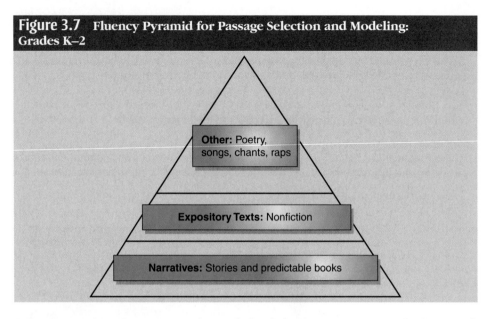

Figure 3.7 Fluency Pyramid for Passage Selection and Modeling: Grades K–2

Other: Poetry, songs, chants, raps

Expository Texts: Nonfiction

Narratives: Stories and predictable books

is usually equal to plus or minus the grade level designation. For example, in second-grade classrooms there can be a range of readers from a pre-primer level to fourth grade. In a fourth-grade classroom there can be struggling readers at emergent or first-grade levels, as well as students reading at an eighth-grade level.

• *Text type and your objective should be a good match.* The objective of your lesson, depending on the needs of your students, should fall within the domain of accuracy, rate, or expression. If your purpose is to practice accuracy of decoding, then you may want to choose what is called **decodable text.** Decodable texts are usually short books that use common spelling patterns, or **orthography.** If, on the other hand, your objective is to help readers adjust their reading speeds according to their purpose or type of text, then you may want to choose a variety of text samples for demonstration and practice sessions, such as stories, mathematics word problems, history readings, and poetry.

• *Limit the number of unfamiliar words.* Words that are new to students should appear in the passage rarely—about 1 in 150 words—for children to have a high probability of learning to read these words (Hiebert, 2006).

• *Target oral reading rates.* Identify these rates using grade level, time of year, and 50th percentile performance as desirable goals (see Table 3.3).

• *Practice with a variety of text genres.* A variety of literary genres should be used in balanced proportions (see the Fluency Pyramid in Figure 3.7).

Developing an Explicit Lesson Plan. Once you have completed the above tasks, begin lesson planning. Using the sample lesson plan in Figure 3.6 as a template, you will be able to map out in some detail the flow of explicit fluency instruction to offer. It is important that new teachers work through this process so that instruction is presented in a seamless and explicit way. Scaffold instruction to help students work through their individual zones of proximal development, and use verbal instructions and explanations to help them make sense of fluency concepts so that nothing important is omitted. Even veteran teachers

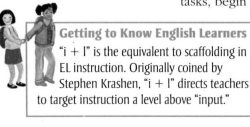

Getting to Know English Learners
"i + 1" is the equivalent to scaffolding in EL instruction. Originally coined by Stephen Krashen, "i + 1" directs teachers to target instruction a level above "input."

who are new to fluency instruction should fully complete the explicit fluency instruction lesson template, since they are very often "first-time" teachers in the reading skill area of fluency. Once you get your "sea legs" with this model, lesson planning can become less detailed in terms of language, but the steps given should always be followed to ensure comprehensive instructional coverage of fluency elements and practice.

Each of the remaining parts of the lesson plan is briefly described in the sections that follow.

Lesson Part I: Passage Introduction and Sight Word Instruction

The Fluency Formula (R. Cooter & K. Cooter, 2002) begins in earnest with your introducing the selection to be read, much as you might for a book talk. Start by showing the book jacket and telling about the author. Explain why you chose this selection. Children should feel excited about hearing the selection.

Teach High-Frequency Sight Words. Words can be fluently recognized in one of two ways (Sadoski & Pavio, 2004). First, words can be recognized as wholes without analysis of the parts—this is called **logographic reading.** Second, words can be recognized through recoding each letter into a sound, holding the sounds in sequence in short-term memory, and then blending the sequenced sounds together. This is referred to as **phonological recoding.** Regardless of the way words are initially recognized, for mature readers, most words have become sight words through repetitious exposure (practice) and attention to visual (logographic) and/or letter-sound (phonological recoding) details.

When young children begin to read, they often try to memorize words as wholes to avoid the difficult task of learning letter–sound relationships and using these relationships to analyze unknown words. This is often characterized as an immature and inefficient way for children to learn to read (Chall, 1983). There is, however, a group of words that occur so frequently in written language that it is better if children are helped to remember these words logographically, or as wholes, without resorting to repetitious letter–sound analysis. These words, called *high-frequency words* or *sight words*, are words that teachers should help children recognize instantaneously.

Snow, Burns, and Griffin (1998) and Burns, Griffin, and Snow (1999) recommend that early reading instruction include the learning of sight words. How can teachers help young children learn a corpus of high-frequency words by sight? One of the most popular and pervasive practices in today's elementary classrooms for teaching sight words is the use of a **word wall.**

A word wall is a large visual display, usually posted on a wall of the classroom, featuring high-frequency words. Many teachers struggle with deciding how many high-frequency words should be displayed. We recommend that kindergarten children fluently recognize a core of up to 25 of the most-frequently occurring sight words as featured in the Thorndike-Lorge high-frequency word list shown in Table 3.1. We further recommend that first- and second-grade students fluently recognize a core of 107 high-frequency words as shown in the Zeno et al. (1995) word list contained in Table 3.2.

Word walls are usually organized in alphabetical order. High-frequency words are typically displayed underneath an alphabet letter category in the order in which they were introduced or taught. Some word walls use colored ink to help children distinguish one sight word from another. Still other word walls make use of word shapes to help children remember high-frequency words. These three practices, while intuitively appealing, often conflict with the goal of helping children learn high-frequency words by sight. Displaying words underneath a particular letter is not the problem; rather, leaving the words in fixed order for long periods of time may cause children to use order cues rather than careful examination of the word to remember it. For example, a child might remember the word *the* because it is the fourth word in the list under the letter T. We strongly recommend that the order of sight words within each alphabetical category be regularly altered so that a word's position does not replace looking at it to identify it.

We also caution teachers against the use of color cues for displaying sight words on the word wall. Young children often learn colors long before they recognize words. Here again, a kindergarten child may remember the word *the* as the "green" word on the word wall, memorizing its color rather than the word itself.

Finally, we recommend that teachers not use word shapes or configuration when displaying sight words. Research has shown that configuration is one of the least reliable and least relied-upon cues for recognizing high-frequency words among those available to children (Harris & Sipay, 1990). Imagine, for a moment, that a kindergarten child is viewing a word wall that displays the words in the same order all year, using different colored ink and the configuration (shape) of words. It is highly probable that such a child might know the word *the* because it is the fourth word under the letter T, it is green, and it has one hump at the beginning of the word. Instead, we recommend that teachers use light or white card stock cut in standard rectangular size, standard black ink, and familiar print styles when making a word wall. Of course, a word wall should be in a location that can be clearly seen by teacher and children from all angles. Print size should also be large enough to meet the same test.

We have also found that the effectiveness of a word wall is not found in *having* it, but rather in *using* it in daily reading and writing instruction and practice. As young children learn to recognize basic sight words, they benefit from three interrelated processes in remembering these words: recognition, searching, and writing. Each of the three should be used in conjunction with the others.

Recognition involves visually distinguishing one sight word from others. This is accomplished by simple, game-like practices using word wall words, such as matching pairs. Make two copies of the 25 sight words (50 total cards) in kindergarten or 107 (214 total cards) in first and second grades. Shuffle the deck of sight word cards. Lay them out on a table top in five rows of five (or ten rows of eleven). The first player turns over two cards and reads each sight word exposed. If the two cards match, the player takes the cards and gets another turn. If they do not match, the player must put them back face down in exactly the same place, and the next player gets a turn. Play continues until all card pairs have been matched. Students can review the words after the game.

Searching for sight words is another process that may be used to aid retention. Look for sight words in easy books or other printed text like magazine or newspaper pages. Use highlighter tape or highlighter pens, or place a clear overhead transparency over the pages of the text selected. Give students one to three sight words to search for and a specific time frame (such as three minutes) to circle or cover with tape as many of those sight words as they can. Using a transparency and an overhead marker does not damage the book or text; the transparency can be cleaned repeatedly and used with other books or texts.

Writing sight words from teacher dictation leaves a more permanent "cognitive footprint" than do recognition or searching tasks. Children can be directed to quickly and accurately write the words dictated in a Beat-the-Clock format. This game requires that children have paper and pencil or, better yet, a gel board or white board and dry erase marker for writing. Set a timer for three minutes. Start by saying, "Go! Write the sight word *the*." Count 10 seconds and say, "Write the sight word *me*." Proceed until three minutes have elapsed. Then ask children to show you their sight word dictation. Make quick notes about each student's performance on the dictation task. Then say, "Let's see if we can beat the clock." This time, only count to nine between each sight word dictated. This slightly faster pace challenges children to write their sight words as dictated more quickly, yet legibly and accurately. Using a simple graph for each child can also be used to help them beat their own best time.

Other questions related to the teaching of sight words relate to the pacing of sight word instruction and sight word review. We recommend teaching a new sight word each day in kindergarten and three sight words per day in first and second grade. Reviews of sight words already taught should occur using the "law of 10-20" recently researched by H. Pashler (2006). Sight word review cycles should take place between 10 and 20 percent of the time to be remembered. Hence six months is 183 days. The law of 10-20 suggests that a complete review of 25 kindergarten sight words should occur between every 18–36 days. Thus sight words, like other memory tasks, are best learned through distributed practice and review rather than from massed practice. Rather than teaching one to two sight words a week, these sight words should be taught quickly over time with spaced reviews. For example, the 25 sight words taught in kindergarten would take 5 weeks at one word per day, with seven review cycles occurring during the year. In first grade, the remaining 82 (of the 107) taught 3 per day would allow for seven review cycles during the school year in grades 1–2.

Some children will struggle to remember specific sight words. If this is the case, we recommend using Cunningham's (1980) "drastic strategy." Although this strategy was intended to be used for teaching hard-to-remember "four-letter" function words, glue words, or structure words that do not have concrete meanings, the strategy is easily adapted for helping young children remember difficult-to-learn, high-frequency sight words.

You will need word cards, envelopes, markers, scissors, and classroom chalk or dry erase boards. Although the "drastic strategy" uses a six-step process, not all steps are always necessary. Carefully observe the progress of children to determine at which step the strategy has produced the desired memory for sight word learning. The six steps follow:

Step 1: Teacher Storytelling
Select a sight word and enlarge it on a card for each child in the class or group. Tell a story in which the displayed word—*the*—is used. Before you begin your story, tell students that they are to hold up their cards each time they hear the targeted word in your story. As you tell the story, pause briefly at those points where the word is used to "emphasize" it.

Step 2: Child Storytelling
Invite volunteers to tell a story in which the sight word displayed on the card is used. Tell students that both you and they will hold up the card containing the targeted sight word as it is used in the volunteer's story. Be an active listener and model for your students during this step.

Step 3: Scramble, Sort, and Find
Cut the targeted sight word into letters and scramble these letters on the student's table or desktop. The student's task is to unscramble the letters to create the word. Repeat the process three times.

Step 4: Take a Picture and Write It

Write the targeted word on the board. Ask children to pretend their eyes are the lens and shutter of a camera. Direct them to carefully look at the word on the board and close their eyes to take a picture of it in their minds. After several seconds, have them open their eyes to see if they correctly imaged the item in their minds. This can be repeated three times if necessary. Erase the word and have children write it on a card at their seats. Write the word on the board again for checking.

Step 5: Fill in the Blank

In a pocket chart, display several sentence strips containing a blank in the place of the word under study. Use sentences from previously read text in a big book or other enlarged text from shared reading. As you read the sentence strips and come to the missing word, invite a child to come forward and write the missing word on a card or strip and place it in the sentence strip at the correct location.

Step 6: New Text Close Reading

Using a new piece of enlarged text during shared reading, tell children to be on the lookout for the word under study. When they detect the word in the new text, they should make a signal or sound that the group predetermines before engaging in the shared reading.

Introduce Important Vocabulary. Introduce any new vocabulary that may not be familiar to students. There are three levels of vocabulary knowledge (National Reading Panel, 2000): unknown words, acquainted words, and established words. **Unknown words** are completely unfamiliar to students. **Acquainted words** are those students have some familiarity with, but which will require some kind of review. **Established words** are known to students when they hear them spoken or see them in print. Unknown and acquainted words that are important in the selection you plan to model are the ones you will need to introduce before reading aloud. In Chapter 4 dealing with vocabulary instruction, we go much more into detail on this point.

Introduce the Targeted Fluency Skill. Before reading the text, draw students' attention to the fluency skill you plan to emphasize. As noted earlier, the three main areas of fluency delineated in reading research are accuracy, rate, and expression. Name and describe the fluency skill you will be modeling, and then return to the skill after reading. Reread short portions of the selection, "thinking out loud" for students how you are using the fluency strategy. Thinking out loud (metacognition) is the essence of modeling and you should use many examples. Saturate students, if you will, with examples drawn from your reading.

One of the fluency skills you will want your students to develop is the ability to "chunk text"—read in meaningful phrases. **Scooping** (Hook & Jones, 2002) is a strategy useful in chunking phrases (see Figure 3.8).

Lesson Part II: Guided Oral Reading Practice

This part of the Fluency Formula provides students with repeated and monitored oral reading experiences. These **guided oral reading** sessions are at the heart of the Fluency Formula and are based on the very best reading research. The National Reading Panel (2000) noted:

> [Guided oral reading] encourages students to read passages orally with systematic and explicit guidance and feedback from the teacher. . . . Guided repeated

Figure 3.8   Scooping

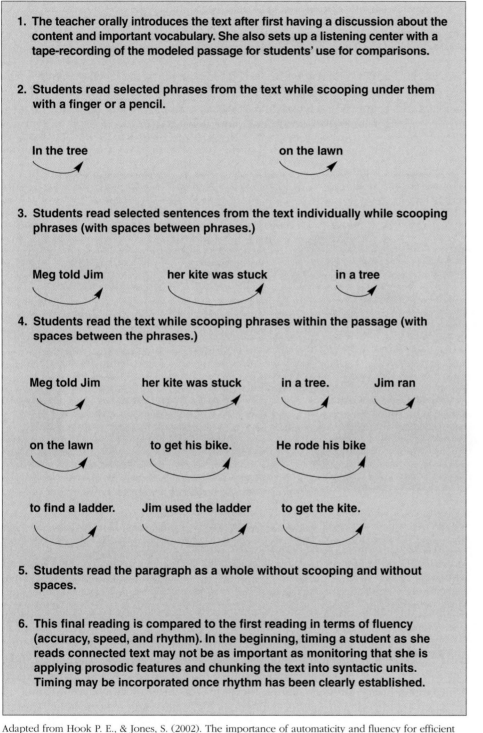

1. The teacher orally introduces the text after first having a discussion about the content and important vocabulary. She also sets up a listening center with a tape-recording of the modeled passage for students' use for comparisons.

2. Students read selected phrases from the text while scooping under them with a finger or a pencil.

   In the tree   on the lawn

3. Students read selected sentences from the text individually while scooping phrases (with spaces between phrases.)

   Meg told Jim   her kite was stuck   in a tree

4. Students read the text while scooping phrases within the passage (with spaces between the phrases.)

   Meg told Jim   her kite was stuck   in a tree.   Jim ran

   on the lawn   to get his bike.   He rode his bike

   to find a ladder.   Jim used the ladder   to get the kite.

5. Students read the paragraph as a whole without scooping and without spaces.

6. This final reading is compared to the first reading in terms of fluency (accuracy, speed, and rhythm). In the beginning, timing a student as she reads connected text may not be as important as monitoring that she is applying prosodic features and chunking the text into syntactic units. Timing may be incorporated once rhythm has been clearly established.

Adapted from Hook P. E., & Jones, S. (2002). The importance of automaticity and fluency for efficient reading comprehension. *Perspectives, 28*(1), 9–14.

oral reading procedures that included guidance from teachers, peers, or parents had a significant and positive impact on word recognition, fluency, and comprehension across a range of grade levels. These studies were conducted in a variety of classrooms in both regular and special education settings with teachers using widely available instructional materials. . . . These results . . . apply to all students—good readers as well as those experiencing reading difficulties. (p. 12)

Two kinds of guided oral reading are called for in Step II of the Fluency Formula. The first is done with the aid and guidance of the teacher. The second involves repeated readings with a peer. In each case, the student has ample practice rereading texts for fluency and for getting feedback from a more fluent reader.

Hope Madden/Merrill

Guided Oral Reading with Teacher Feedback. Guided reading is one means of providing oral reading practice that is guided by the teacher in small groups (Fountas & Pinnell, 1996; Mooney, 1990). Children are grouped by developmental levels that reflect a range of competencies, experiences, and interests. The strategy centers on developing the child's ability to successfully process text with limited teacher guidance and interaction.

Guided reading groups are composed of six to eight children who work together for a period of time under the direct guidance of the teacher. It is important to note that the membership in guided reading groups should change as children progress during the year. This is a crucial concern. Failure to modify groups as students progress can result in static ability groups much like the "Eagles, Bluebirds, and Buzzards" of earlier days. The static nature of ability groups in the past—particularly those comprised of struggling readers left in the "lower" developmental groups—caused children to suffer damage to their self-esteem and lowered academic expectations for them.

Getting to Know English Learners
Grouping for ELs must be modified during the year, too. Groups with same-language speakers who are more fluent readers are helpful, as are groups where English-speaking peers model read-alouds.

Success in fluency instruction during guided reading hinges on children working with texts appropriate to their reading level. Thus, the notion of **leveled books**—books categorized according to their difficulty so that they can be matched to students reading at that level—is an important one for fluency instruction. Before a guided reading group is begun, the teacher must take great care to match the level of text to the identified needs of a group of children to ensure that the group can enjoy and control the story throughout the first reading. Texts chosen for each leveled group should present children with a reasonable challenge, but also with a high degree of potential success.

Here is a listing of criteria typically used for leveling books for guided reading instruction (see Table 3.4).

Table 3.4   General Explanation of Criteria for Determining the Reading Levels of Texts

Levels 1–20 (A–K)

Levels 1–4 (A–D)

- Language patterns are repeated.
- Illustrations match and explain most of the text. Actions are clearly presented without much in the way of extraneous detail that might confuse the reader.
- The text is likely to match the experiences and conceptual knowledge common to most beginning readers.
- The language of the text developmentally matches the syntax and organization of most young children's speech.
- The sentences and books themselves are comparatively short (e.g., 10–60 words).
- Print is carefully laid out so that it consistently appears on the same place on the page throughout each book.

Assumption at this level: When students encounter an unknown word in print, they can easily use context from known words and illustrations along with language pattern cues and early word analysis skills for successful decoding.

Levels 5–8 (D–E)

- Reader often sees predictable, repetitive language patterns; however, the same pattern does not dominate the entire text.
- There is greater variation in language patterns, as opposed to one or two word changes.
- Words and phrases may express different meanings through varying sentence structures.
- By the end of these stages, the syntax is more typical of written or "book" language.
- Illustrations provide minimal support for readers' determination of exact language.

Levels 9–12 (E–G)

- Variation in sentence patterns is now the norm.
- There are longer sentences with less predictable text.
- Written language styles and genre become more prominent, including the use of some verb forms not often used by young children in oral settings.
- The average sentence length in text increases (double that found in levels 5–8).
- Events in a story may continue over several pages.
- Illustrations provide only moderate support to the meaning of the stories.

Levels 13–15* (G–H)

(*Consider these characteristics as enhancements to the description for levels 9–12.)
- There is a greater variety of words and the inclusion of more specialized vocabulary.
- Pictures provide some support for the overall meaning of the story, but cannot be used by the reader to interpret the precise message.

Levels 16–20 (I–K)

- Stories or sequences of events are longer.
- Story events are developed more fully than those in texts at lower levels.
- Vocabulary is progressively richer and more varied.
- Illustrations are used to help to create atmosphere and setting rather than to specifically depict content of the text.
- Full pages of print are now the norm.

Table 3.5   Guided Reading Leveling Comparisons

Here is a handy guide to help you translate books from publishers using Guided Reading ratings to leveling systems common in one-to-one tutorial programs (i.e., Reading Recovery, Cooter & Cooter's *BLAST* program, etc.).

Grade Level (Basal)	Guided Reading Level (Fountas-Pinnell)	One-to-One Tutoring Level	Stages of Reading
Kindergarten	A	A	Emergent
	B	1	Emergent
		2	Emergent
Pre-Primer			
	C	3	Emergent
	D	4	Emergent
	E	6–8	Emergent
Primer			Early
	F	10	Early
	G	12	Early
1st Grade			Transitional
	H	14	Transitional
	I	16	Transitional
2nd Grade			Transitional
	J–K	18–20	Fluent/Extending
	L–M	24–28	Fluent/Extending
3rd Grade			Fluent/Extending
	N	30	Fluent/Extending
	O–P	34–38	Fluent/Extending
4th Grade			Fluent/Extending
	Q–R	40	Fluent/Extending
5th Grade	—	44	Fluent/Extending
6th Grade	—	—	Fluent/Extending

In Table 3.5 we include a useful reading level cross-referencing guide comparing grade levels to guided reading levels, and then to Reading Recovery levels (a popular remedial reading program for first grade students), and then the stages of reading.

Lesson Planning for Guided Reading. The basic lesson pattern employed in guided reading lessons consists of seven phases, which are listed and explained in Figure 3.9.

Teacher Feedback During Instruction. Understanding the nature, quantity, and quality of teacher feedback during guided oral reading, as well as in other "coaching" situations, is a crucial part of helping students become fluent readers. The following self-assessment questions for teachers are provided to assist in this process.

1. Am I more often telling the word than providing a clue?
2. What is the average self-correction rate of my students?
3. Do I assist poor readers with unknown words more often than good readers? If so, why?
4. Am I correcting miscues even when they do not alter the meaning of the text? If so, why?

Figure 3.9   Guided Reading Lesson Overview

Picture Talk • Walk through a new book by looking at the pictures. Ask children, "What do you see?"

First Reading • Depending on the students' developmental levels, the first reading is initially done by the teacher with children following the lead. Later, the teacher gradually releases responsibility for the first reading to the children by sharing the reading role and then fading into one who encourages children to try it on their own.

Language Play • In this phase of the guided reading lesson, the teacher carefully analyzes the text to find specific elements associated with written language to teach children how language works. For early emergent readers, this may mean letter identification, punctuation, or directionality. In the fluency stage, children might identify text genre or compound words.

Rereading • Children read the text again with the assistance of the teacher, a peer, or a mechanical device such as a computer or tape. Novice readers are encouraged to point to the text as they read, whereas fluent readers are encouraged to "read the text with your eyes" or silently.

Retelling • Children retell what they have read to their teacher or to their peers. Typically we say, "Can you tell me what you've read?" Sometimes we probe children's retellings with other questions to prompt recall.

Follow-up • The most effective follow-up activity to a guided reading lesson is to invite children to take guided reading books home for demonstrating their ability to parents and siblings. This provides needed practice time and promotes increased confidence and self-esteem among young readers.

Extensions • Extending books through performances, murals, artwork, and even music helps children deepen their understandings and increase their interpretations of text.

Source: Adapted from "Teacher Interruptions During Oral Reading Instruction: Self-Monitoring as an Impetus for Change in Corrective Feedback," by M. Shake, *Remedial and Special Education, 7*(5), pp. 18–24.

5. Does one reading group tend to engage in more self-correction than other groups? If so, why?
6. Does one reading group have more miscues that go unaddressed than other groups?
7. What types of cues for oral reading errors do I provide and why?
8. What is my ultimate goal in reading instruction?
9. How do I handle interruptions from other students during oral reading? Do I practice what I preach?
10. How does my feedback influence the self-correction behavior of students?
11. Does my feedback differ across reader groups? If so, how and why?
12. Would students benefit more from a form of feedback different from that which I normally offer?
13. Am I allowing students time to self-correct (3–5 seconds)?
14. Am I further confusing students with my feedback?
15. Do I digress into "mini-lessons" mid-sentence when students make a mistake? If so, why?
16. Do I analyze miscues to gain information about the reading strategies students employ?
17. Does the feedback I offer aid students in becoming independent, self-monitoring readers? If so, how?
18. Do I encourage students to ask themselves, "Did that make sense?" when they are reading both orally and silently? If not, why not?
19. Do students need the kind of feedback I am offering them?

Adapted from Shake, M. (1986). Teacher interruptions during oral reading instruction: Self-monitoring as an impetus for change in corrective feedback. *Remedial and Special Education, 7*(5), 18–24.

Hope Madden/Merrill

Choral Reading. **Choral readings** of text can be done in at least three ways. Wood (1983) recommends **unison reading** and **echo reading.** In unison reading, everyone reads together. During echo (sometimes called *echoic*) reading, the teacher or a student reads a passage aloud, and then everyone else "echoes" by repeating it. A third method we have found useful is **antiphonal reading.** Derived from ancient monastic traditions, antiphonal reading involves two groups. The first reading group reads a passage aloud (usually a sentence or two), and the second group echoes the reading.

Getting to Know English Learners
Choral reading is a tried and true method of ELL instruction.

Student-Assisted Fluency-Building Strategies.

Partner or Paired Reading. **Partner** or **paired reading** ("buddy" reading) has a student reading aloud with a more fluent partner or one of equal fluency. The partner models fluent reading in place of the teacher, provides useful feedback, and helps with word recognition.

Usually partners take turns reading aloud an assigned passage to one another, with the more developed reader reading first, thus providing the model for fluent reading. The second reader then reads the passage in the same way as the first. The more fluent reader offers feedback on how his partner can read the passage more fluently, and the less-fluent reader rereads the passage until he can do so independently.

Readers of about the same ability are sometimes paired for this exercise. The difference is that both readers first hear the teacher reading the passage as the model, then the two "buddies" take turns reading to each other and offering feedback until they can each read the passage fluently.

The Neurological Impress Method. The **neurological impress method** (NIM) involves the student and a more fluent reader in reading the same text aloud simultaneously (Heckelman, 1966, 1969). Unlike partner reading examples described earlier, NIM has the student and more fluent model reading in unison at the same volume at first. The model's voice gradually fades as the student becomes more confident.

The use of multiple sensory systems during NIM is thought to "impress" upon the student the fluent reading patterns of the teacher through direct modeling. It is assumed that exposing students to numerous examples of texts (read in a more sophisticated way than struggling readers could achieve on their own) will enable them to achieve automaticity in word recognition more naturally. This assumption stands to reason when viewed in light of more recent advances in learning theory, especially those espoused by Vygotsky (1978).

Each NIM session is aimed at reading as much material as possible in 10 minutes. Reading material selected for the first few sessions should be easy, predictable, and make sense for the reader. However, other more challenging materials that are on the student's normal guided reading level can eventually be used.

To use NIM, the student sits slightly in front and to one side of his or her partner as they hold the text. The more fluent reader moves her finger beneath the words as both partners read in near-unison fashion. Both try to maintain a comfortably brisk and continuous rate of oral reading. The more fluent reader's role is to keep the pace when the less-proficient student starts to slow down. Pausing for analyzing unknown words is not permitted. The more fluent reader's voice is directed at her partner's ear so that words are seen, heard, and spoken simultaneously.

Because many struggling readers have not read at an accelerated pace before, their first efforts often sound like mumbling. Most less-fluent readers typically take some time to adjust to NIM; however, within a few sessions they start to feel more at ease. Many struggling readers say they enjoy NIM because it allows them to read more challenging and interesting material like "good" readers.

At first, the more fluent reader's voice will dominate oral reading, but in later sessions it should be reduced gradually. This will allow the less-fluent student to assume the vocal lead naturally. Usually three sessions per week are sufficient to obtain noticeable results. This routine should be followed for a minimum of 10 consecutive weeks (Henk, 1983).

NIM can also be adapted for group use (Hollingsworth, 1970, 1978). Here the teacher tape-records 10 minutes of his or her own oral reading in advance. Individual students can read along with the tape while following the text independently, or the tape can be used in a listening center to permit the teacher to spend individual time with each student as others read with the tape. Despite the convenience of the prerecorded tape format, teachers' and more fluent peers' one-to-one interactions with individual students result in a better instructional experience.

Technology-Assisted Reading Strategies: Read-Along Audio Cassettes and CDs. In technology-assisted reading, children read a book with the assistance of a fluently read model on an audiotape or a computer. Technology-assisted reading for fluency development is a solution to the problem teachers experience in arranging one-to-one learning activities for students.

During a first reading using an audiotape, children follow along in their own copy of the text. They are instructed to point to each word as the fluent reading model says it on the audiotape. Younger children reading short books then read aloud with the tape three to five times or until they can read the text fluently. Students who are reading longer texts listen to the entire piece once, and then select a passage (usually 150–300 words) for repeated practice. Once they have read the passage repeatedly (3–5 times), they read the passage to the teacher.

Teacher management of technology-assisted fluency centers is of great importance. For some students, listening to a tape presents an opportunity to engage in off-task behaviors—looking like readers but not engaging (Stahl, 2004).

In recent years, a number of computer-based programs such as *Read Naturally* (Ihnot & Ihnot, 1996) at *http://www.readnaturally.com/* and *Insights: Reading Fluency* (Adams, 2005) at *http://www.charlesbridge-fluency.com/* have been developed to provide students with repeated reading practice. Generally speaking, most of these computer programs use speech recognition software and immediate feedback as students read text aloud as it is presented on the computer screen. Computer-assisted reading has been found to be effective in improving fluency across a range of grade levels (National Reading Panel, 2000).

Lesson Part III: Independent Fluency Practice

A teacher who develops fluent readers is like a coach who develops Olympic swimmers. Numerous skills must be taught until the learner reaches the point of automaticity. If the student, or swimmer, is to become proficient, he or she must put in many hours of practice. You might say, then, that guided and independent reading practice opportunities are intended to develop Olympic readers—strong, capable, and fluent.

Three of the more productive strategies for independent practice are repeated readings (Dowhower, 1991; Samuels, 1979), wide oral reading (Kuhn, 2005b; Kuhn & Schwanenflugel, 2006), and modified sustained silent reading (Reutzel, Smith, & Fawson, in preparation).

Repeated Readings. **Repeated readings** engage students in reading interesting passages orally over and over again to enhance their reading fluency (Dowhower, 1987; Samuels, 1979). Although it might seem that reading a text again and again leads to boredom, it can actually have just the opposite effect.

In the beginning, texts selected for repeated readings should be short, predictable, and easy. When students attain adequate speed and accuracy with easy selections, the length and difficulty of texts can gradually be increased.

Repeated readings help students by expanding the total number of words they can recognize instantaneously. They also help improve students' comprehension and oral elocution (performance) with each succeeding attempt. Improved performance quickly leads students to improved confidence regarding reading aloud and positive attitudes toward the act of reading. Additionally, because high-frequency words (e.g., *the, and, but, was,* etc.) occur in literally all reading situations, the increase in automatic sight word knowledge developed through repeated readings transfers far beyond the practiced texts.

Research indicates that repeated readings are most effective when students are supported during independent reading. Audiotapes, tutors, or peer feedback are supports shown to be most effective during repeated reading practice sessions (National Reading Panel, 2000). For example, try providing a tape-recorded version of the story or poem to be practiced. Students can read along with an audiocassette tape to develop fluency similar to the model's. Also, students can tape record their oral reading for immediate feedback. If two audiocassette tape players are available, have the student listen and read along with the taped version of the text using headphones. At the same time, use the second recorder for recording the student's oral reading. The student can then replay his version simultaneously with the teacher-recorded version to compare, or simply listen to his own rendition alone. Either way, feedback can be both instant and effective.

You may use taped recordings of repeated readings for further analysis of each reader's improvement in fluency and comprehension. Also, using a tape recorder frees you to work with other students, thereby conserving precious instructional time and leaving behind an audit trail of student readings for later assessment and documentation. On occasion, listen to tapes with the reader present. During this time, you and your students can discuss effective ways of reducing word recognition errors and increasing reading rate.

Several excellent technology-based software packages are available to augment classroom fluency practice and assessment. These rely heavily on repeated oral readings. We recommend that teachers examine *Insights Reading Fluency* RFCL 3 Workstation License at *www.charlesbridge.com* and *Read Naturally* at *www.readnaturally.com*. Both of these software packages are research-based.

Wide Oral Reading. Wide oral reading involves students in reading different text types (narrative, expository, and poetic) across a range of genres (fantasy, fairy tales, myths, science fiction, historical fiction, series books, autobiographies, diaries, journals, logs, essays, encyclopedia entries, information books) rather than reading the same book or passage over and over again. To assure that students read widely, many teachers find a reading genre wheel useful. See Figure 3.10.

Children are required to read one of each type of genre represented on the wheel during a specified period of time determined by the teacher. Children usually color in each part of the genre wheel as they complete it. In wide oral reading, children read aloud and receive support, guidance, feedback, and monitoring from a peer, a tutor, or the teacher. Some teachers encourage children to read aloud quietly, using a PVC-pipe-constructed fluency phone (pictured earlier in this chapter).

Recent research studies conducted by Stahl, Bradley, Smith, Kuhn, Schwanenglugel and Meisinger (2003) and Kuhn (2005a, 2005b) suggest wide readings of different texts rather than repeated readings of the same text may be as effective or more so for second grade readers. Stahl et al. (2003) found that a wide-reading group significantly outperformed a repeated-reading group. In a separate study of small-group fluency instruction focused on struggling second grade readers, Kuhn (2005a, 2005b) found that wide oral reading of different titles and genres compared with repeated oral reading resulted in equivalent gains in fluency using several measures that included number of words read in isolation, correct words per minute in context, and expressive reading measures. In addition, the wide oral reading group performed better on answering text-implicit and -explicit questions to assess comprehension than did the oral repeated reading group.

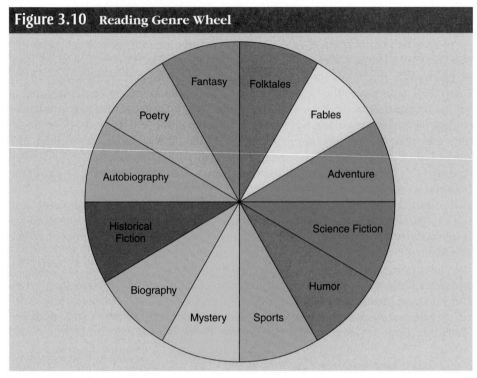

Figure 3.10 Reading Genre Wheel

From D. R. Reutzel & P. C. Fawson. *Your Classroom Library: Ways to Give It More Teaching Power.* New York: Scholastic Professional Books.

Scaffolded Silent Reading (ScSR). Silent sustained reading (SSR) or some related form of silent, independent reading practice such as DEAR time (Drop Everything and Read) is a very popular method of independent reading practice in our schools. However, educators have discovered that simply providing all students the time to self-select their own books and read silently does not guarantee that they will actually engage in silent reading practice. In fact, it is quite possible that such practices allow many children (and some teachers) time to take an "in-the-room field trip" using a book as a prop!

Advocates of SSR suggest that allowing students time for unfettered, self-selected silent reading practice will lead to increases in motivation and engagement as compared with other less-motivating reading practices such as round-robin oral reading and/or the writing of book reports. Despite these claims, there is growing recognition among classroom practitioners and in the reading research community that some students derive little benefit from, or fail to make good use of, independent silent reading time (Gambrell, 1978; Lee-Daniels & Murray, 2000; Moore et al., 1980; Robertson et al., 1996). In fact, some elementary and secondary schools have experienced so many challenges implementing SSR over the long term that they have decided to discontinue the program (Halpern, 1981; Moore et al., 1980). Another problem with SSR is that some children become bored with the routine (Gambrell, 1978; Lee-Daniels & Murray, 2000). Other children, particularly younger or struggling readers, find it difficult to conform to the requirement of staying quiet, prompting some early-grade teachers to modify the SSR acronym from "silent sustained reading" to "self-selected reading" (Reutzel & Cooter, 2000). Often, these younger, not-yet-independent students are in need of more—not less—assistance, guidance, and scaffolding to stay on task and to benefit from time allocated to reading practice (Robertson et al., 1996). Despite SSR's acceptance among some teachers, students, and reading researchers, many other educators and researchers, including members of the National Reading Panel, steadfastly maintain that more research needs to be conducted into the value of SSR and at what levels of reading development it may or may not be effective (Efta, 1984; Manning & Manning, 1984; Moore et al., 1980; National Reading Panel, 2000; Robertson et al., 1996).

One well-known concern associated with the implementation of SSR as described in the literature and as implemented in many classrooms across the nation is the conspicuous absence of interaction around the reading of texts or any accountability for whether or not students actually read during this allocated time.

It can be argued, and often has been argued, that teachers who themselves read silently during SSR time are, in fact, *teaching* by modeling the behaviors of a silent, engaged "reader." But no research has ever established the effect of teachers serving as "silent reading models" on either the achievement or the engagement of elementary-aged students. Conversely, we argue that modeling silent reading behaviors *without* discussion, interaction, and teacher explanation is often so transparent for many young students that it is entirely overlooked. Along this same line of criticism, Stahl (2004) notes that "Many SSR advocates do not allow teachers to check up on children or recommend that teachers read their own books during this time to be a model of a reader. . . . One failing of SSR is that teachers may not monitor their children's reading . . ." (p. 206). As a result, reading practice as found in the implementation of SSR may or may not be useful for children, but it is highly unlikely to be effective without the active monitoring, interaction, and guidance of a concerned teacher.

Recent research (Bryan, Fawson, & Reutzel, 2003) demonstrated that when classroom teachers randomly monitored their students during SSR through brief interactions and accountability conferences, even the most disengaged students in the class remained on task for up to three weeks without additional random monitoring visits. These findings seem to suggest that rather than reading silently to themselves, teachers ought to jettison the traditional SSR practice of modeling reading and instead engage in random monitoring of students' reading during SSR. Furthermore, the National Reading Panel (2000) asserted from their review of forms of reading practice that one prominent feature of effective time spent in reading practice was receiving feedback about one's reading. In this particular respect, the National Reading Panel (2000) also endorsed the need for teachers, and others, to monitor and interact with students around their reading. It is clear from these findings and criticisms that, without monitoring, teachers cannot be assured that children are in fact reading during traditional SSR time at all! As a result, we have designed and researched a modified silent sustained reading process that has been shown to equal the effects of the National Reading Panel's (2000) recommended approach of oral repeated readings (guided oral reading) with feedback among third-grade students.

The way Scaffolded silent reading (ScSR) works is simple. Students are encouraged to read widely from across a variety of genres using a reading genre wheel like that shown in Figure 3.10. Students are asked to read one self-selected book from each slice of the reading genre wheel before selecting another book from that genre to read. This approach assures that students are reading widely. Next, students self-select an independent-level book of interest to them from a collection of leveled books displayed by genre in the classroom library. For example,

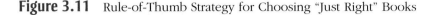

Figure 3.11 Rule-of-Thumb Strategy for Choosing "Just Right" Books

1. Choose a book that looks interesting.
2. Open the book to any page that has lots of words on it.
3. Begin reading aloud or silently. When you come to a word you do not know, hold up your small finger.
4. If you come to another word you do not know, hold up your next finger. If you use up all of your fingers on one hand (and come to your thumb) on one page, then the book is too hard and you should put it back. Find another book you like just as well and repeat the ROT exercise to make sure it is just right for you.

students wanting to read a fairy tale will go to the fairy tale section of the classroom library and select a book at their level by looking at the back of the book for a colored dot that indicates a match with their independent reading level. Alternatively, children can make sure the book they select will not be too hard for them using a strategy known as "Rule-of-Thumb," or ROT, that is taught to them by the teacher (see Figure 3.11). Many teachers like to use the chart above that shows the steps in ROT.

Once students have chosen their books, they are ready to read. The goal is for students to read a total of 20 minutes per day in a self-selected book chosen from among various genres. Younger students may need to have two 10-minute periods of ScSR time. Teachers often set a timer for the amount of MSSR time they have allocated; the children read while the teacher circulates among them, randomly stopping and asking students to read aloud the book they have chosen. The teacher may ask the student some questions to measure comprehension, or talk with the student about her or his goal for reading in the next few days. The teacher also discusses with each student monitored a way that she or he can share with others what she or he has been reading, including posters, oral or written book reports, sharing a favorite part of the book through a read-aloud performance, or other form of expression. Teachers often give prompts like the following.

> "I'd like you to draw me a picture of your favorite character when you finish reading this story."
>
> "Find five _____ (e.g., color, describing, number, etc.) words for me as you read."
>
> "I will want you to act out one of the characters when you finish and I'll see if I can guess which one it is!"

After completing the reading of a book, students color in the appropriate genre in their reading genre wheel and tell the teacher they are ready to share their book. Stahl (2004) has indicated that for ScSR to be effective, student reading practice must be monitored by the teacher regularly!

Step IV: Performance Reading for Fluency Assessment

Performance reading has students reading aloud for the teacher and/or an audience so that the teacher can monitor fluency growth. Students prepare for the exercise, regardless of format, by orally rereading the text to be performed until they can read it with maximum fluency. There are several ways this can be done that have found support in evidence-based research. Before we get to those, we will examine a very well-known approach that you should *not* use—round-robin reading.

Long ago, teachers commonly relied on round-robin reading as a means for listening to students read orally. Students would sit in a circle, and the teacher would call on a student to begin reading orally from a story in the basal reader while the other students would follow along. After the first student read a paragraph or two, the teacher would stop him or her and call on the next student to continue reading. This process was repeated until every child in the circle had a chance to read aloud.

Though the simplicity of round-robin is very appealing, research has revealed it to be far less effective than other available strategies for monitoring fluency development. The process can even have a negative impact on some children (Eldredge, Reutzel, & Hollingsworth, 1996). Round-robin fails to give children adequate opportunities for repeated readings before performing, defeats comprehension (i.e., when a student realizes the paragraph he'll be asked to read is three ahead of the current student in the "hot seat," he'll tend to look ahead and start silently reading his passage feverishly, hoping he won't "mess up" when it's his turn), and causes some students embarrassment when they are unable to read their paragraph fluently. Our advice? Do not use round-robin in your classroom; there are better alternatives that will help you monitor fluency development, improve comprehension, and protect fragile egos in the process. Following are several activities that can be used for performance reading found to be effective in classrooms.

Readers' Theatre. Perhaps the most successful performance reading strategy, in terms of the research (Sloyer, 1982; National Reading Panel, 2000, Griffith & Rasinski, 2004) is readers' theatre. **Readers' theatre** involves rehearsing and performing before an audience a script that is rich with dialogue. The script itself may be one from a book or, in the upper elementary or middle school grades, could be developed by a group of students working in collaboration as part of a literature response activity (Cooter & Griffith, 1989).

Stayter and Allington (1991) tell about a readers' theatre activity for which a group of heterogeneously grouped seventh graders spent five days reading, rehearsing, and performing short dramas. After a first reading, students began to negotiate about which role they would read. More hesitant students were permitted to opt for smaller parts, but everyone was required to participate. As time passed, students critiqued each others' readings and made suggestions as to how they should sound (e.g., "You should sound like a snob"). The most common response in this experience was how repeated readings through drama helped them better understand the text. One student said,

> The first time I read to know what the words are. Then I read to know what the words *say* and later as I read I thought about how to say the words. . . . As I got to know the character better, I put more feeling in my voice. (Stayter & Allington, 1991, p. 145)

Texts selected for readers' theatre are often drawn from oral traditions, poetry, or quality picture books designed to be read aloud by children. However, nonfiction passages can also be adapted for presentation. Selections should, whenever possible, be packed with action, have an element of suspense, and comprise an entire, meaningful story or nonfiction text. Also, texts selected for use in readers' theatre should contain sufficient dialogue to make reading and preparing the text a challenge as well as necessitate the involvement of several children as characters. Narrative texts we have seen used in readers' theatre include Martin and Archambault's *Knots on a Counting Rope* (1987), Viorst's *Alexander and the Terrible, Horrible, No Good, Very Bad Day* (1972), and Barbara Robinson's *The Best Christmas Pagent Ever* (1972).

Here is an easy procedure to follow. If a story is selected for reading, students should be assigned to read characters' parts. If poems are selected, students may read alternating lines or groups of lines. Readers' theatre in-the-round, where readers stand around the perimeter of the room surrounding their audience, is a fun and interesting variation for both performers and audience.

Students will often benefit from a discussion prior to reading a readers' theatre script for the first time. This discussion helps students make connections between their background experiences and the text to be read. Also, struggling readers usually benefit from listening to a previously recorded performance of the text as a model prior to their initial attempts at reading the script.

Hennings (1974) described a simplified procedure for preparing readers' theatre scripts for classroom performance. First, the text to be performed is read silently by individual students. Second, the text is read again orally, sometimes using choral reading in a group. After the second reading, readers either choose their parts, or the teacher assigns parts to them. We suggest that students be allowed to select their three most desired parts, write these choices on a slip of paper, and submit it to the teacher. Teachers should do everything possible to assign one of these three choices. The third reading is also an oral reading with students reading their parts with scripts in hand. There may be several rehearsal readings as students prepare for the final reading or performance in front of the class or other audience.

Readers' theatre offers students a unique opportunity to participate in reading along with other, perhaps more-skilled readers. Participating in the mainstream classroom with better readers helps students having reading problems feel a part of their peer group, provides them with ready models of good reading, and demonstrates how good readers, through practice, become even better readers. Working together with other readers fosters a sense of teamwork, support, and pride in personal and group accomplishment.

Radio Reading. **Radio reading** possesses all of the effective elements of practice in developing fluency we have just discussed. Radio reading (Greene, 1970; Optiz & Rasinski, 1998; Rasinski, 2003; Searfoss, 1975) is a variation on repeated reading and readers' theatre. We have found radio reading to be most

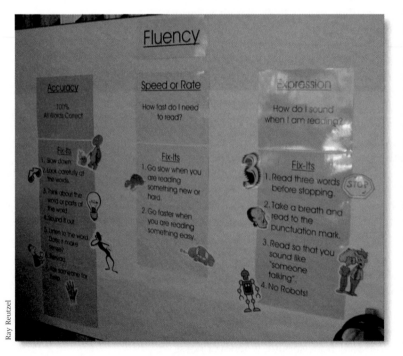

Ray Reutzel

effective with short selections from information texts threaded together into a single news broadcast performance script.

In radio reading, each student is given a script to read aloud. Selections can be drawn from any print media, such as newspapers, magazines, or any print source that can be converted into a news story, such as short selections from articles or sections in information books. One student acts as the news anchor, while other students act in the roles of various reporters presenting the weather, sports, breaking news, and so on. Only the radio readers and the teacher have copies of the scripts. Because other students have no script to follow, minor word recognition errors will go unnoticed if the text is well presented. Struggling students enjoy radio reading from *Know Your World*. This publication is well-suited for use in radio reading activities because the content and level of difficulty make it possible for older readers with fluency problems to read with ease and enjoyment. Short selections from information books on weather, volcanoes, spiders, sports figures, or any other topic can be presented as short reports by various reporters during the news broadcast. An example of a radio reading script is found in Figure 3.12 titled, "Mummies Made in Egypt." A script for the anchor may need to be written by students with help from the teacher to thread the various news reports together in a cohesive fashion. Once students have the radio reading script prepared for rehearsal, they gather materials for sound effects (police whistles, doors opening or shutting, people screaming, and others).

Before performing a radio reading for an audience, students should rehearse their parts with a partner or the teacher until they gain confidence and can read the script with proper volume, accuracy, rate, phrasing, and expression. Emphasis is first placed on the meaning of the text segments so that the students can paraphrase any difficult portions of the text if needed during the presentation. Students are encouraged to keep ideas flowing in the same way a reporter or anchor person does. After thorough rehearsal of the script with sound effects, the radio play is taped on cassette recorder and played over the school's public address system into other classrooms.

Step V: Goal Setting and Monitoring Student Progress

To conclude the Fluency Formula, students are taught to self-assess their fluency after reading using a simple assessment rubric containing the elements of oral reading fluency shown in Figure 3.13. Once students have self-assessed and identified areas of strength and weakness, they are taught to select an appropriate fluency "fix-up" strategy (see Figure 3.14) and apply this strategy in improving their fluency in future practice sessions.

Finally, children read aloud the passage or book they have been practicing for one minute for the teacher. After completing the one-minute sample, the teacher charts or graphs the words correct per minute (wcpm) for younger children. For children in grades 2–3 they chart or graph the number of words read correct per minute. Students set reasonable goals, usually two to four more words read correctly per minute the next week, trying to better their own reading rate and cut down on errors with each successive assessment. Also, students are encouraged to improve their prosody or vocal inflections, as fluent reading is not strictly confined to reading rate and accuracy (Dowhower, 1987; Hudson, Lane, & Pullen, 2005; Rasinski, 2006; Reutzel & Hollingsworth, 1993). Figure 3.15 illustrates a tracking graph for charting a student's progress across several one-minute reading samples.

Figure 3.12 Mummies Made in Egypt by Aliki

Radio reading script by
Dr. John A. Smith
Department of Elementary Education
Utah State University

Performers: Radio Newsperson #1 and Radio Newsperson #2

Radio Newsperson #1	We are here to report some very important information about mummies.
Radio Newsperson #2	We have learned that ancient Egyptians believed that a person would start a new life after he died. They believed that the person's soul would travel back and forth to a new world.
Radio Newsperson #1	They believed that the person's soul needed his body to come back to. That is why Egyptians preserved dead bodies as mummies.
Radio Newsperson #2	A mummy is a dead body, or corpse, that has been dried out so it will not decay. The earliest mummies were dried out naturally in the hot, dry sands of Egypt's deserts.
Radio Newsperson #1	Later, the Egyptians wrapped the mummies in cloth and buried them in wooden coffins or put them in tombs made of brick and stone.
Radio Newsperson #2	It took 70 days to prepare a mummy. First they took out the dead person's inner organs. They cut a hole in the mummy's side to remove the intestines. They pulled the dead person's brains out through the nose with metal hooks.
Radio Newsperson #1	The inner organs were kept in jars with a chemical called *natron* that dried out the body parts. After the inner organs were removed, embalmers also put natron inside the body to dry it out.
Radio Newsperson #2	After 40 days, the natron was removed from the body, and the body was cleaned with oils and spices.
Radio Newsperson #1	The body was packed with new chemicals to keep it dry. The mummy's eyes were closed, and the nose was stuffed with wax.
Radio Newsperson #2	The hole in the mummy's side was sewn up and the mummy was carefully wrapped with long strips of cloth.
Radio Newsperson #1	After the embalmers finished wrapping the mummy, they painted it to look like the person and then covered it with resin, a sticky substance that dried into a hard covering.
Radio Newsperson #2	When the mummy was finished, they made a coffin to put the mummy in for burial. The coffin was decorated with pictures of gods and magic spells to protect it. Jewels and other treasures were also put into the coffin.
Radio Newsperson #1	Finally, the mummy and its coffin were placed in a tomb made of brick and stone. The Egyptian pyramids are large tombs that are burial places for powerful Egyptian rulers.
Radio Newsperson #2	There would be an elaborate funeral parade. The mummy would be placed in the tomb, sometimes in a secret chamber. Then the tomb would be sealed shut for the mummy's eternal resting place.
Radio Newsperson #1	Thank you very much, and now back to our teacher.

Figure 3.13   **Assessment Rubric of the Elements of Oral Reading Fluency**

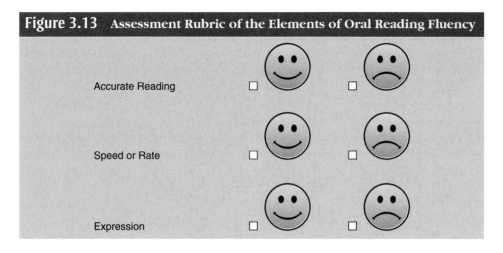

Figure 3.14   Fluency Fix-Up Strategies for Oral Reading Fluency Elements

Accuracy

1. Slow down your reading speed.

2. Look carefully at the words and the letters in the words you didn't read correctly on the page.

3. Think about if you know this word or parts of this word. Try saying the word or word parts.

4. Make the sound of each letter from left to right and blend the sounds together quickly to say the word.

5. Listen carefully to see if the word you said makes sense.

6. Try rereading the word in the sentence again.

7. After saying the word, use pictures to help you make sure you have the right word.

8. If the word still doesn't make sense, ask someone to help you.

Rate

1. Adjust your reading speed to go slower when the text is difficult or unfamiliar, or you need to read to get detailed information.

2. Adjust your reading speed to go faster when the text is easy or familiar, or you are reading to just enjoy the book.

Expression

1. Try to read three or more words together before pausing, stopping, or taking a breath.

2. Take a big breath and try to read to the comma or end punctuation without stopping for another breath.

3. Be sure to raise or lower your pitch when you see punctuation marks at the end of sentences.

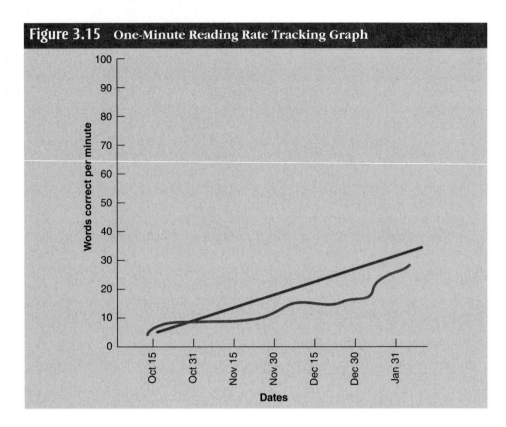

Figure 3.15 One-Minute Reading Rate Tracking Graph

Some teachers draw a blue line indicating the number of wcpm needed to maintain grade level reading rates and use red lines to indicate the student's actual performances. As an illustration of the power of graphing progress, one second-grade student recently remarked when he absorbed the fact that his red line was above the blue line: "Oh, I better slow down; I've gone over the blue line!" All students, especially struggling readers, find it greatly reinforcing to see visible evidence of their reading fluency improvement.

How Can Reading Fluency Instruction Be Adapted to Meet Diverse Student Needs?

Fluency Oriented Reading Instruction (FORI), based on repeated reading research, is an integrated lesson framework for providing differentiated instruction and practice in fluency (Stahl, Heuback, & Cramond, 1997; Kuhn & Schwanenflugel, 2006; Stahl 2004). FORI consists of three interlocking instructional steps: (1) a redesigned basal or core reading program lesson; (2) a free-reading period at school; and (3) a home reading program. Recent research on the effects of FORI showed that children receiving FORI instruction significantly outperformed a control group

(Stahl et al., 2003). To provide a FORI lesson, teachers need a core reading or basal reading program text, an adequately appointed classroom library for free reading at school and home, extension activities drawn from the core or basal reading program text, a teacher-prepared graphic organizer of the text in the core or basal program, and a teacher-prepared audiotape for tape-assisted reading practice.

Getting to Know English Learners
Reading at home also helps parents of ELs who may not yet be fluent in English.

On the first day of a FORI reading lesson, the teacher begins by reading the core reading program story or text aloud to the class. Following the reading by the teacher, the students and teacher interactively discuss the text to place reading comprehension upfront as an important goal to be achieved in reading any text. Following this discussion, the teacher teaches vocabulary words and uses graphic organizers and other comprehension activities focused around the story or text.

On the second day of a FORI reading lesson, teachers can choose to have students echo read the core reading program text with the teacher or have children read only a part of the story repeatedly for practice with a partner or with the teacher. Following this practice session on the second day, the core reading program story is sent home for the child to read with his/her parents, with older siblings, or with other caregivers.

On the third and fourth day of a FORI lesson, children receive additional practice as well as participate in vocabulary and comprehension exercises based on the story read in the core reading program. On these two days, children are also given decoding instruction on difficult words in the core reading story or text.

On the fifth and final day of the FORI lesson, children are asked to generate a written response to the story to cement their comprehension of the text.

In addition to the basal or core reading program instruction to develop fluency found in the FORI framework, the teachers provide additional in-school free reading practice with instructional level books that are read alone or with a partner for between 15 and 30 minutes per day. At the beginning of the year, the time allocated to this portion of a FORI lesson is closer to 15 minutes; as the year progresses, it increases to 30 minutes. As a part of their homework assignment in the FORI framework, children are expected to read at home 15 minutes a day at least four days per week. This outside reading is monitored through the use of weekly reading logs turned in to the teacher (Stahl, 2004).

What Can Families and Communities Do to Develop Children's Reading Fluency?

One very effective way to connect fluency practice from the school to the home is to recommend to parents to use closed-caption television (Koskinen, Wilson, & Jensema, 1985; Neuman & Koskinen, 1992). Closed-caption TV has been found to be a particularly effective tool for motivating students who are learning English as a second language to improve reading fluency. Closed-caption television, which uses written subtitles, provides students with meaningful and motivating reading material. Parents should carefully select high-interest television programs. They may even want to record and preview programs before making final selections for captioned TV practice at home (Koskinen et al., 1985).

One advantage of captioned TV fluency practice is that it does not require busy parents to sit and read daily with their children at home. However, if parents want to increase their involvement in captioned TV fluency practice, they can engage in a couple of different activities. First, parents and children can record and watch a part of the captioned TV program together. Then parents can stop the program and ask the child to predict what will happen next. They continue viewing the program so that the child can check his/her predictions. Second, after watching a closed-caption TV program, children can practice reading aloud along with the captions. If necessary, both the auditory portion and the closed captioning can be played simultaneously to provide children with support. At some later point, children should be allowed to practice reading the captioning without the auditory portion of the program. Koskinen et al. (1985) do "not recommend that the sound be turned off if this, in effect, turns off the children. The major advantage for using captioned television as fluency practice is the multisensory stimulation of viewing the drama, hearing the sound, and seeing the captions" (p. 6).

Summary

Fluency is the ability to read a text accurately, with appropriate intonation and phrasing, and at an age-appropriate speed. Fluency instruction, because it helps readers achieve automatic decoding, provides the opportunity for readers to turn more of their mental energies toward comprehending the message of text. Reading fluency can be developed through explicit teacher-led instruction, teacher modeling of fluency skills, and by having students participate in guided oral repeated reading sessions. Fluency is further strengthened by engaging children in generous amounts of daily reading practice. Struggling readers and, in fact, all others benefit most from practice reading that provides feedback and monitoring in appropriately challenging texts. Monitoring and assessing children's development of oral reading fluency is important in effecting needed improvements. Careful tracking of students' oral reading progress should lead to goal setting, which in turn leads to incremental improvements in students' oral reading fluency.

Classroom Applications

1. In groups of four, perform the following tasks regarding a selected grade level.
   a. Identify your state's standards for fluency instruction for the selected grade level. These can usually be located on the state's department of education Web site.
   b. For each element of reading fluency (accuracy, rate, expression, and phrasing), determine which are addressed in the state standards and which are not.

c. Outline the strategies named in this chapter that would be appropriate for improving reading fluency at this level, and match each to one of the state standards.

d. If you are using this book as part of a college course, present your findings to the whole class. Be sure to provide your classmates with a copy of your findings for future reference.

e. If you are a small group of teachers from a school working through this exercise, share your findings with another grade-level team and your principal. Determine together whether a renewed emphasis on reading fluency is warranted in your school based on current classroom practices.

Recommended Readings

Brown, K. J. (1999). What kind of text—for whom and when? Textual scaffolding for beginning readers. *The Reading Teacher, 53*(4), 292–307.

Dowhower, S. L. (1989). Repeated reading: Research into practice. *The Reading Teacher, 42*(7), 502–507.

Opitz, M. F., & Rasinski, T. V. (1998). *Good-bye round robin: 25 effective oral reading strategies*. Portsmouth, NH: Heinemann.

Osborn, J., Lehr, F., & Hiebert, E. H. (2003). *Focus on fluency*. Available at *www.prel.org*. Honolulu, HI: Pacific Resources for Education and Learning (PREL).

Rasinski, T. V. (2003). *The fluent reader: Oral reading strategies for building word recognition, fluency, and comprehension*. New York: Scholastic, Inc.

Rasinski, T. V., Blachowicz, C., & Lems, K. (2006). *Fluency instruction: Research-based best practices*. New York: Guilford Press.

Stahl, S. (2004). What do we know about fluency? In P. McCardle & V. Chhabra (Eds.), *The voice of evidence in reading research* (pp. 187–211). Baltimore, MD: Paul H. Brookes.

Increasing Reading Vocabulary

Chapter Questions

1. What does research tell us about vocabulary learning?

2. How can teachers effectively assess students' vocabulary knowledge?

3. What evidence-based strategies are used in vocabulary instruction?

4. What can be done to assist students with special needs in vocabulary learning?

5. How can "reading backpacks" be used to involve parents in their child's vocabulary learning?

Can You Hear Me Now?

(Authors' Note: Learn more about how to teach using Joint Productive Activities (JPA) and other innovative instructional techniques from the Center for Research on Education, Diversity & Excellence (CREDE) *free online at: http://crede.berkeley.edu/standards/ standards.html.)*

It is November, and Becky just arrived at Hillview School a week ago from Pennsylvania. She likes living on the West Coast and has made a new friend, Katy. Katy has been asked to be Becky's personal fourth-grade *docent* for a few weeks by their teacher, Mr. Garcia, to help Becky feel comfortable in her new surroundings. Today is a great day for Katy-the-docent for two reasons. For one thing it is a stormy day.

"I positively *love* a good gulley-washer!" says Katy to Becky rather theatrically. Not only that, today Mr. Garcia is having the students work in groups of four on a "joint productive activity" or JPA during science. Katy enjoys JPAs because she gets to work with a small group and they have a chance to solve a kind of puzzle as a team. When they finish, the group always gets to post their "findings" on chart paper for a Gallery Walk and see how the other students did the same task. Since Katy is Becky's docent they get to be in the same group. Katy and Becky are assigned to work with Alfred and Walker in their JPA group. Their task sheet is on the following page.

After their group work and Gallery Walk were finished and they were at lunch, Katy asked Becky what she liked best about the JPA.

"I have never done anything like it," replied Becky. "I'm not used to being allowed to *talk* in class like that. It was pretty great! I liked how we were able to decide together how to fill out the grid. Raymond had some ideas about cell phones I *never* would have thought of on my own. Also, Walker did a great job being our champion for the Gallery Walk. I think I'd like to try being champion sometime."

"No problem," said Katy. "Mr. Garcia makes sure everyone gets a turn. Just let the rest of the group know when you want to try it. We'll all help you!"

Joint Productive Activity

Can you hear me now?
Comparing and Contrasting Hi-Tech Vocabulary

Time Allowed: 45 minutes

Your Group's Task: Scan the article we have been reading together, "The Cell Phone Revolution," from *Invention & Technology* magazine to complete the "semantic feature analysis grid" below. In this chart you will compare and contrast the important ideas and characteristics of the words listed in the left-hand column. This activity should be done in the same way I modeled the example yesterday when we compared insects and animals.

Important things to remember from past JPAs:
1. All group members must agree on answers.
2. You should appoint a timekeeper to keep things moving. You will only have 45 minutes to complete this task. No exceptions.
3. Use a "six-inch voice" when you talk so you don't disturb the other groups.
4. No "sidebar" conversations. Listen as each person talks; you might learn something!
5. Observe "equity of voice"; let everyone talk at least two times.

When your work is done, copy your semantic feature analysis grid onto the chart paper provided using the colored markers at your table. Vote for one of your group members to be the "champion" for the group to do a one-minute presentation at the beginning of the Gallery Walk to explain your answers. If someone hasn't been champion for a group before, let them give it a go if they are ready.

Here is the semantic feature analysis grid for you to complete.

The Cell Phone Revolution

	Wireless	Makes this tool work	Early communications technology	People who use or have used this	Tool for two-way communication technology
cellular phone tower					
mobile phone					
transistor radio					
antenna					
silicon chip					
subscriber					
BlackBerry					
walkie-talkie					

Directions: After checking for the meanings of the vocabulary words in the left-hand column against the magazine article, "The Cell Phone Revolution," put a "0" in the appropriate box if the word and description do NOT go together, a "1" if the word partly matches, and a "2" if they go together well. If you have disagreement in your group, vote for a majority opinion before marking your response.

What Does Research Tell Us About Vocabulary Learning?

Understanding word meanings is essential to reading success. Indeed, unless students are able to understand the meanings of words as they read, the process is reduced to mindless decoding (Fountas & Pinnell, 1996). Children who come to school with thousands of words "in their head"—words they can hear, understand, and use in their daily lives—are already on the path to reading success (Allington & Cunningham, 1996). Conversely, children who have small listening, speaking, and reading vocabularies—who are from what could be termed "language-deprived backgrounds"—must receive immediate attention if they are to have any real chance at reading success (National Research Council, 1998; Johnson, 2001).

Words are the symbols we use to express ideas—*captions,* you might say, that describe our life experiences (Reutzel & Cooter, 2007). Vocabulary development is a process that goes on throughout life and can be enhanced in the classroom through enticing learning experiences. Except for the economically deprived or children with learning disabilities, most acquire a vocabulary of over 10,000 words during the first five years of their lives (Smith, 1987). Most school children will learn between 2,000 and 3,600 words per year, though estimates vary from 1,500 to more than 8,000 (Clark, 1993; Johnson, 2001; Nagy, Herman, & Anderson, 1985).

How Do Students Acquire New Vocabulary?

Truth is, there are many sources for learning new words. Some of them may surprise you—at least, just a bit. Students learn a great deal of their new vocabulary from conversations, independent reading, and even from the media. However, they do not learn new words from each source equally. To illustrate this point, Table 4.1 presents selected statistics revealing the sources of rare words (i.e., new or unfamiliar words) found in various language and text sources that are commonly accessed by children and adults (Cunningham & Stanovich, 1998; Rasinski, 1998).

Were you surprised by any of these findings? How about the number of rare words used by college graduates in their conversations with friends compared to the

Table 4.1   Sources of Rare Words in Children's and Adults' Vocabulary Acquisition

Source	Number of Rare (Uncommon) Words per 1,000
Adult speech (expert testimony)	28.4
Adult speech (college graduates to friends)	17.3
Prime time adult television	22.7
Mister Rogers and *Sesame Street*	2.0
Children's books—preschool	16.3
Children's books—elementary	30.9
Comic books	53.5
Popular magazines	66.7
Newspapers	68.3
Adult books	52.7
Scientific article abstracts	128.0

number commonly found in comic books!? Or, for that matter, the number of uncommon words found in comic books compared to elementary children's books? Perhaps there is a case to be made for daily reading for children in self-selected books—including comics and popular magazines!

In this section, we take a careful look—an *evidence-based* look—at how children learn new words and at the kinds of vocabulary they should learn.

Research on Vocabulary Learning

In reviewing recent research on vocabulary learning and its role in reading, one conclusion becomes crystal clear: Reading and writing activities are dependent on words. Indeed, all good readers have a large store of high-frequency words they can read and spell instantly and automatically (Allington & Cunningham, 1996). So what do we know about vocabulary learning? To partially answer this question, we discuss in the following section key findings supported by recent research (e.g., Adams, 1990a; Burns, Griffin, & Snow, 1999; Guthrie, 1982; Krashen, 1993; Johnson, 2001; McKeown, Beck, Omanson, & Pople, 1985; Nagy, Herman, & Anderson, 1985; National Reading Panel, 2000; National Research Council, 1998; Stahl, Hare, Sinatra, & Gregory, 1991; Templeton, 1995).

Getting to Know English Learners

Language acquisition is innate, but social interaction with adult caretakers is crucial for this acquisition to take place.

Vocabulary Is Built Through Language Interactions

Children who are exposed to vocabulary through conversations learn words they will need to recognize and comprehend while reading (K. Cooter, 2006c). Burns, Griffin, and Snow (1999) explain early language acquisition this way:

Vocalization in the crib gives way to play with rhyming language and nonsense words. Toddlers find that the words they use in conversation and the objects they represent are depicted in books—that the picture is a symbol for the real object and that the writing represents spoken language. In addition to listening to stories, children label the objects in books, comment on the characters, and request that an adult read to them. In their third and fourth years, children use new vocabulary and grammatical constructions in their own speech. Talking to adults is children's best source of exposure to new vocabulary and ideas. (p. 19)

Reading and being read to also increase vocabulary learning. Books give us challenging concepts, colorful description, and new knowledge and information

Hope Madden/Merrill

about the world in which we live. Children whose backgrounds are language-rich come to school with relatively expansive vocabularies that are fertile ground for beginning reading instruction. Conversely, children who come to school with limited vocabularies as a result of either second language learning or the effects of poverty (Cooter, 2003) struggle to take even their first steps in reading and understanding texts. Burns, Griffin, and Snow (1999) ask, "How can they understand a science book about *volcanoes, silkworms,* or *Inuits?* What if they know nothing of *mountains, caterpillars,* or *snow* and *cold climates?*" (p. 70). As teachers, we must make sure that no child is left behind because of inadequate vocabulary development.

Research Findings by the National Reading Panel. To determine how vocabulary can best be taught and related to the reading comprehension process, the National Reading Panel (NRP) examined more than 20,000 research studies identified through electronic and manual literature searches. The studies reviewed suggest that vocabulary instruction does not necessarily lead to gains in comprehension *unless the methods used are appropriate to the age and ability of the reader.* Several studies found that the use of computers in vocabulary instruction was more effective than some traditional methods, indicating that software programs are emerging as potentially valuable aids to classroom teachers in the area of vocabulary instruction.

Vocabulary also can be learned incidentally in the context of storybook reading or in listening to others read. Learning words before reading a text is also helpful. The technique of **repeated exposure** (having the student encounter words in various contexts) appears to enhance vocabulary development.

The Four Types of Vocabulary

Although we often speak of vocabulary as if it were a single entity, it is not. Human beings acquire *four* types of vocabulary. They are, in descending order according to size, listening, speaking, reading, and writing vocabularies. **Listening vocabulary,** the largest, is made up of words we can hear and understand. All other vocabularies are subsets of our listening vocabulary. The second-largest vocabulary, **speaking vocabulary,** is comprised of words we use when we speak. Next is our **reading vocabulary,** those words we can identify and understand when we read. The smallest vocabulary is our **writing vocabulary**—words we use in writing. These four vocabularies are continually nurtured in the effective teacher's classroom.

Levels of Vocabulary Knowledge

As with most new learning, new vocabulary words and concepts are mastered by degree. The Partnership for Reading (2001) described three levels of word knowledge, or degree of familiarity with words: in relation almost *unknown, acquainted,* and *established.* Definitions for these levels are presented in Table 4.2. Bear in mind that these levels of vocabulary knowledge apply to each of the four vocabularies: listening, speaking, reading, and writing; thus, helping children build strong reading and writing vocabularies can sometimes be a formidable task indeed.

We sometimes learn new meanings to words that are already known to us. The word *race,* for example, has many different meanings (to move with great speed, a group of people, a political campaign). One of the most challenging tasks for students can be learning the meaning of a new word representing an unknown concept. According to research, much of learning in the content areas involves this type of word learning. As students learn about *deserts, hurricanes,* and *immigrants,*

Go to the National Reading Panel Website at *www.nationalreadingpanel.org* to learn about their conclusions.

Table 4.2 Levels of Vocabulary Learning (Partnership for Reading, 2001)

Level of Word Knowledge	Definition
Unknown	The word is completely unfamiliar and its meaning is unknown.
Acquainted	The word is somewhat familiar; the student has some idea of its basic meaning.
Established	The word is very familiar; the student can immediately understand its meaning and use it correctly.

they may be learning both new concepts and new words. Learning words and concepts in science, social studies, and mathematics is even more challenging because each major concept often is associated with many other new concepts. For example, the concept *deserts* is often associated with other concepts that may be unfamiliar, such as *cactus, plateau,* and *mesa.* (Partnership for Reading, 2001, p. 43)

What Research Tells Us About Teaching Vocabulary

Most vocabulary is learned indirectly, but some vocabulary *must* be taught directly. The following conclusions about indirect vocabulary learning and direct vocabulary instruction are of particular interest and value to classroom teachers (National Reading Panel, 2000):

- *Children learn the meanings of most words indirectly, through everyday experiences with oral and written language.* Typically, children learn vocabulary indirectly in three ways. First, they participate in oral language every day. Children learn word meanings through conversations with other people; as they participate in conversations, they often hear words repeated several times. The more conversations children have, the more words they learn!

  Another indirect way children learn words is by being read to. Reading aloud is especially powerful when the reader pauses to define an unfamiliar word and, after reading, engages the child in a conversation about the book using the word. Conversations about books help children to learn new words and concepts and to relate them to their prior knowledge and experience (Partnership for Reading, 2001).

  The third way children learn new words indirectly is through their own reading. This is one of the reasons why many teachers believe that daily, independent reading practice sessions of 10–20 minutes are so critical (Krashen, 1993). Put simply, the more children read, the more words they'll learn. There is a caveat to mention on this point, however. Struggling readers are often incapable of sitting and reading on their own for extended periods of time. For best results, many readers get much more from their practice reading when working with a "buddy" who has greater ability.

- *Students learn vocabulary when they are taught individual words and word-learning strategies directly.* Direct instruction helps students learn difficult words (Johnson, 2001), such as those that represent complex concepts that are not part of students' everyday experiences (National Reading Panel, 2000).

We also know that when teachers preteach new words that are associated with a text students are about to read, better reading comprehension results.

- *Developing word consciousness can boost vocabulary learning.* **Word consciousness** learning activities stimulate an awareness of and interest in words, their meanings, and their power. Word-conscious students enjoy words and are zealous about learning them. In addition, they have been taught how to learn new and interesting words.

The keys to maximizing word consciousness are wide reading and use of the writing process. When reading a new book aloud to students, call their attention to the way the author chooses her words to convey particular meanings. Imagine the fun you can have discussing some of the intense words used by Gary Paulsen (1987) in his novel *Hatchet,* Shel Silverstein's (1974) clever use of rhyming words in his book of poetry *Where the Sidewalk Ends,* or the downright magical word selection employed by J. K. Rowling (1997) in *Harry Potter and the Sorcerer's Stone.* Encourage your students to play with words, by constructing puns or raps. Help them research a word's history and find examples of a word's usage in their everyday lives.

Which Words Should Be Taught?

McKeown and Beck (1988) have addressed an important issue in their research: Which vocabulary should be taught in elementary classrooms? They point out that one problem with traditional vocabulary instruction in basal readers has been the equal treatment of all categories of words. For example, a mythology selection in a basal reader about Arachne, who loved to weave, gives the word *loom* as much attention as the word *agreement.* McKeown and Beck point out that although the word *loom* may be helpful in understanding more about spinning, it is a word of relatively low use compared to the word *agreement,* which is key to understanding the story and of much higher utility as students move into adult life.

Not all words are created equal, especially in terms of difficulty in elementary classrooms. As McKeown and Beck (1988) explain:

> The choice of which words to teach and what kind of attention to give them depends on a variety of factors, such as importance of the words for understanding the selection, relationship to specific domains of knowledge, general utility, and relationship to other lessons and classroom events. (p. 45)

Why You Shouldn't Try to Teach *All* Unknown Words

There are several good reasons why you should not try to directly teach all unknown words. For one thing, the text may have far too many words that are unknown to students for direct instruction. Limit vocabulary teaching time to not more than 5 to 10 minutes so that students can spend the bulk of their time actually reading. Most students will be able to comprehend a fair number of new words, up to 5 percent, simply by using context clues in the passage. Students need many opportunities to practice and use the word-learning strategies you are teaching them for learning unknown words on their own.

Words You *Should* Teach

Realistically, you will probably be able to teach *thoroughly* only a few new words (8 to 10) per week, so you need to choose the words you teach carefully. Focus your

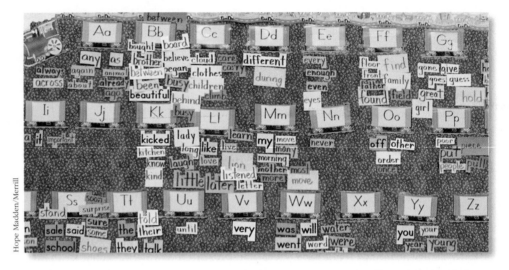

Hope Madden/Merrill

energy on high-utility words and words that are important to the meaning of the selections you will be reading in class.

Sight Words. **Sight words** occur frequently in most texts and account for the majority of written words. Understanding text relies, in part, on the immediate recognition of these high-frequency words. Studies of print have found that just 109 words account for upwards of 50 percent of all words in student textbooks, and a total of only 5,000 words accounts for about 90 percent of the words in student texts (Adams 1990b; Carroll, Davies, & Richman, 1971). Knowledge of high-frequency sight words can help readers manage text in a more fluent way. Many of these words, such as *the, from, but, because, that,* and *this,* sometimes called **structure words,** carry little meaning but do affect the flow and coherence of the text being read. The actual meaning of the text depends on the ready knowledge of less-frequent, or **lexical words,** such as *automobile, aristocrat, pulley, streetcar, Martin, Luther, King,* and *phantom.* Adams and her colleagues (1991) concluded that

Hope Madden/Merrill

. . . while the cohesion and connectivity of English text is owed most to its frequent words (e.g., *it, that, this, and, because, when, while*), its meaning depends disproportionately on its less-frequent words (e.g., *doctor, fever, infection, medicine, penicillin, Alexander, Fleming, melon, mold, poison, bacteria, antibiotic, protect, germs, disease*). (p. 394)

Because it is critical that all students learn to instantly recognize sight words, the teacher should have a reliable list of these words as a resource. Figure 4.1 presents the Fry (2000) list of the 1,000 most common words in print. The Fry list is widely regarded as the best-researched list of sight words in the English language.

Sight Words for Bilingual Classrooms (Spanish). Just as the most common sight words have been identified in English, high-frequency words have also been identified for Spanish (Cornejo, 1972). This popular word list is divided by grade and presented in Figure 4.2.

Key Vocabulary. Silvia Ashton-Warner, in her classic book *Teacher* (1963), described **key vocabulary** as "organic," or lexical words that emerge from the child's experiences. Ashton-Warner describes key vocabulary words as "captions" for important events in the child's life.

Children can be taught key vocabulary through a variety of direct instructional strategies. One such strategy is described here: The student meets with the teacher individually at an appointed time, or during a group experience, and indicates which words he or she would like to learn. The teacher might prompt: "What word would you like to learn today?" The child responds with a lexical word—*police, ghost, sing*. The teacher writes the word on an index card or a small piece of tagboard using a dark marker. The teacher directs the student to share the word with as many people as possible during the day. After the child has done so, the word is added to his or her writing folder or word bank for future use in writing.

Ashton-Warner found that the most common categories of key vocabulary children wanted to learn were (1) fear words *(dog, bull, kill, police);* (2) sex (as she called them) or affection words *(love, kiss, sing, darling);* (3) locomotion words *(bus, car, truck, jet);* and (4) a miscellaneous category that generally reflects cultural and other considerations *(socks, frog, beer, Disneyland, Dallas Cowboys).*

Ashton-Warner (1963) referred to key vocabulary as "one-look words" because one look is usually all that is required for permanent learning to take place. The reason that these words seem so easy for children to learn is that they usually carry strong emotional significance and, once seen, are almost never forgotten.

Discovery Words. During the course of a typical school day, students are exposed to many new words. These words are often discovered as a result of studies in the content areas. Words such as *experiment, algebra, social, enterprise, conquest, Bengal tiger, spider,* and *cocoon* find their way into students' listening and speaking vocabularies. Every effort should be made to add these **discovery words** to the word bank as they are discussed in their natural context. Such words often appear in student compositions. Developing vocabulary in content areas can help children discover words in their natural context.

Which Words Are the Most Difficult to Learn? Some words (or phrases) can be especially difficult for students to learn (National Reading Panel, 2000).

• **Words with multiple meanings** are quite challenging for students. They sometimes have trouble understanding that words with the same spelling and/or

Figure 4.1 Fry New Instant Word List

First Hundred				Second Hundred				Third Hundred			
1–25	26–50	51–75	76–100	101–125	126–150	151–175	176–200	201–225	226–250	251–275	276–300
the	or	will	number	over	say	set	try	high	saw	important	miss
of	one	up	no	new	great	put	kind	every	left	until	idea
and	had	other	way	sound	where	end	hand	near	don't	children	enough
a	by	about	could	take	help	does	picture	add	few	side	eat
to	words	out	people	only	through	another	again	food	while	feet	face
in	but	many	my	little	much	well	change	between	along	car	watch
is	not	then	than	work	before	large	off	own	might	mile	far
you	what	them	first	know	line	must	play	below	close	night	Indian
that	all	these	water	place	right	big	spell	country	something	walk	really
it	were	so	been	year	too	even	air	plant	seem	white	almost
he	we	some	call	live	mean	such	away	last	next	sea	let
was	when	her	who	me	old	because	animal	school	hard	began	above
for	your	would	am	back	any	turn	house	father	open	grow	girl
on	can	make	its	give	same	here	point	keep	example	took	sometimes
are	said	like	now	most	tell	why	page	tree	begin	river	mountain
as	there	him	find	very	boy	ask	letter	never	life	four	cut
with	use	into	long	after	follow	went	mother	start	always	carry	young
his	an	time	down	thing	came	men	answer	city	those	state	talk
they	each	has	day	our	want	read	found	earth	both	once	soon
I	which	look	did	just	show	need	study	eye	paper	book	list
at	she	two	get	name	also	land	still	light	together	hear	song
be	do	more	come	good	around	different	learn	thought	got	stop	being
this	how	write	made	sentence	farm	home	should	head	group	without	leave
have	their	go	may	man	three	us	America	under	often	second	family
from	if	see	part	think	small	move	world	story	run	later	it's

Source: Fry, Edward. (2000). *1000 Instant Words.* Westminster, CA: Teacher Created Materials.

Figure 4.2   Cornejo's High-Frequency Word List for Spanish (Graded)

Pre-Primer	Primer	1st	2nd	3rd	4th	5th
a	alto	bonita	ayer	amar	árbol	amistad
azul	flor	arriba	aqui	aquí	bandera	azucar
bajo	blusa	fruta	año	debajo	abeja	contento
mi	ella	globo	cerca	familia	escuela	corazón
mesa	ir	estar	desde	fiesta	fácil	compleaños
pan	leche	café	donde	grande	fuego	edad
mamá	más	letra	hacer	hermana	hacia	escribir
lado	niño	luna	hasta	jueves	idea	felicidad
la	padre	luz	hijo	lápiz	jardín	guitarra
papá	por	muy	hoy	miércoles	llegar	estrella
me	si	noche	leer	once	manzana	igual
no	tan	nombre	libro	quince	muñeca	invierno
esa	sobre	nosotros	martes	sábado	naranja	orquesta
el	sin	nunca	mejor	semana	saludar	primavera
en	tras	ojo	mucho	silla	sueño	recordar
cuna	color	pelota	oir	sobrino	señorita	respeto
dos	al	porque	papel	vivir	tierra	tijeras
mi	día	rojo	paz	zapato	traer	último
de	bien	té	quien	tarde	ventana	querer
los	chico	taza	usted	traje	queso	otoño

From Cornejo, R. (1972). *Spanish High-Frequency Word List.* Austin, TX: Southwestern Educational Development Laboratory.

pronunciation can have different meanings, depending on their context. For example, note the different uses of *run* in the following sentences:

> Molly complained when she found a *run* in her hose.

> Jeff Johnston plans to *run* for Congress.

Also note the different uses and pronunciations of the word *read* in the following sentences:

> I will *read* the story later today.

> I *read* the story yesterday.

For some students, choosing a context-specific definition from a list of possible definitions in a dictionary can be daunting.

  • **Idiomatic expressions** are combinations of words that have a meaning that is different from the meanings of the individual words. These can be especially problematical for language-deficient students and for students who are English language learners (ELL) (Cooter, 2003). Because idiomatic expressions do not convey the literal meanings of the words used, you may need to explain to students expressions such as "apple of my eye," "hell in a handbasket," or "like a chicken with its head cut off." A great book to use as a catalyst for discussing idioms is Fred Gwynne's (1976) *A Chocolate Moose for Dinner.*

Getting to Know English Learners
While urban students may have their own idiomatic expressions, or "slang" (that many "mainstream" students emulate and adapt), depending on one's culture and language, some idioms may be very foreign indeed!

How Can Teachers Effectively Assess Students' Vocabulary Knowledge?

As a teacher, you must consider ways of assessing reading vocabulary knowledge to plan and evaluate instruction (Blachowicz & Fisher, 2006). While everyone would surely agree that vocabulary knowledge is important to reading success, attempting to measure the extent of student vocabulary acquisition can be problematic. Dale Johnson (2001), a prominent researcher in the area of vocabulary learning, explains three problem areas: (1) choosing *which* words to test, (2) determining what it means for a student to actually "know" a word, and (3) deciding how to reliably test vocabulary knowledge. In this section, we take a look at ways classroom teachers can construct useful vocabulary assessments. We also examine commercially available assessment instruments sometimes used for diagnostic purposes.

Word Maps for Assessment and Teaching

A **word map** (Schwartz & Raphael, 1985) is a graphic rendering—a sketch—of a word's meaning. It answers three important questions about the word: What is it? What is it like? What are some examples? Answers to these questions are extremely valuable because they help children link the new word or concept to their prior knowledge and world experiences, a process known to have an effect on reading comprehension (Stahl et al., 1991). For this reason, word mapping can be used as an assessment tool to measure the depth of a student's understanding of a word. Mapping can also be used during instruction to help children construct new understandings of a word or concept. An example of a word map is shown in Figure 4.3.

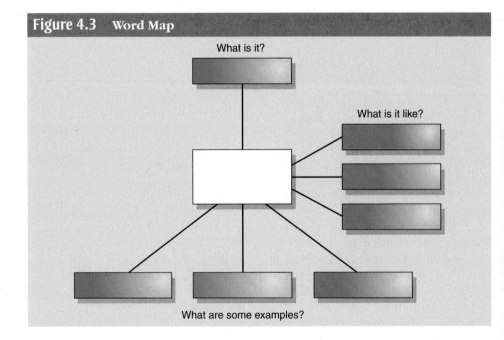

Figure 4.3 Word Map

What is it?

What is it like?

What are some examples?

Introducing this vocabulary assessment to students is a relatively easy task. First, the teacher presents the idea of using this kind of graphic organizer to understand new word meanings and models the word map with examples and think-alouds. Next, students work with the teacher using word maps featuring the target word(s) to be evaluated using the three key questions indicated earlier.

Simple concepts should be used in teacher modeling exercises to help students learn how to map. A practice map might be constructed using the word *car*. Answers for each of the word map questions that might be offered by elementary students follow:

Word: *car*

What is it? (Something that moves people and things from one place to another.)

What is it like? (It has four wheels, metal, glass, lights, seats, and a steering wheel.)

What are some examples? (Honda, station wagon, Thunderbird, convertible)

After working through several examples of word maps with the class, the teacher should give students opportunities to practice using the map before moving on to assessing word knowledge.

Before-and-After Word Knowledge Self-Ratings

Blachowicz and Fisher (2006) recommend the **before-and-after word knowledge self-rating** as an efficient way to survey student vocabulary knowledge. In introducing students to a new text, the teacher lists important vocabulary-building words in that text along the left-hand side of a before-and-after word knowledge self-rating form and distributes a copy of the form to students. Using the three-level self-rating on the form, students indicate whether they do not know a word (level 1), have heard the word (level 2), or can define and use the word (level 3). This rating system is congruent with research findings of the Partnership for Reading (2001) (alluded to earlier in this chapter) and the National Reading Panel (2000), which describe the three levels of vocabulary learning: unknown, acquainted, and established. Figure 4.4 features a completed before-and-after word knowledge self-rating form completed by a student before and after reading a text on the theme of transportation.

Teacher-Constructed Vocabulary Tests

Johnson (2001) summarized the common ways teachers construct effective vocabulary tests to fit their curriculum and students' learning needs. You can have students do one or more of the following:

- ✓ Read a target word in isolation (by itself) and select a picture that matches.
- ✓ Look at a picture and find the matching word.
- ✓ Read a target word in isolation and match it to its definition.
- ✓ Read a target word in isolation and find its synonym in a list.
- ✓ Read a target word in isolation and find its opposite (antonym) in a list.
- ✓ Read a target word in the context of a sentence or short paragraph and find a definition, synonym, or antonym in a list.

Figure 4.4　Before-and-After Word Knowledge Self-Rating Form

Before-Reading Word Knowledge			
Key Terms	**I can define and use this word in a sentence.** *(Established)* **3**	**I have heard this word before.** *(Acquainted)* **2**	**I don't know this word.** *(Unknown)* **1**
mileage	X		
freight		X	
GPS		X	
passenger	X		
fossil fuel			X
ethanol			X
route			X
express		X	
destination		X	
ETA			X
alternative fuels			X

After-Reading Word Knowledge				
Key Terms	**Self-Rating (3, 2, 1)**	**Define**	**Use in a Sentence**	**Questions I Still Have About This Term**
mileage	3	How far it is to a place you're going	The mileage from Salt Lake City to Provo is about 50 miles.	
freight	3	Things that are being shipped by a truck or by another way	Boxes on a truck are called freight.	
GPS	2	A kind of compass	A GPS can help me find my way home.	I can't remember what GPS means.
passenger	3	A person going somewhere in a vehicle	I was once a passenger in an airplane.	
fossil fuel	2	Makes a car run	Cars use fossil fuels to run the engine.	I don't know what *fossil* means.
ethanol	1			I can't remember anything about this. Did we really learn this?
route	3	How you are getting to a destination	I took a northern route to get to Canada.	
express	3	Getting something or someone to their destination quickly	I sent my package by FedEx overnight express.	
destination	3	Where you are going	My destination on my next trip is Boston.	
ETA	3	When you are getting somewhere	My estimated time of arrival or ETA is 9 A.M.	
alternative fuels	2	Like gas and diesel fuel	Some cars run on gas; others use diesel.	I think there may be other kinds, but I'm not sure.

✓ Read a sentence that has a target word left out. Fill in the blank with the missing word.

✓ Read a sentence and supply the missing target word orally.

✓ Read the target word and draw a picture of it. (Best used with young children.)

✓ Read the target word and place it in a category.

Modified Cloze Passages

Cloze passages, from the word *closure*, are short passages from books commonly used in the classroom in which certain words have been deleted (usually every fifth word) and replaced with a blank. For vocabulary assessment, teachers often use a **modified cloze passage** in which targeted vocabulary words have been deleted. Students are asked to read the cloze passages and fill in the missing words based on what they believe makes sense using context clues. In the modified cloze example (Figure 4.5), we have supplied in parentheses the target words selected by the teacher for this partial passage.

Cloze tests require that students use their background knowledge of a subject, their understanding of basic syntax (word order relationships), and their word and sentence meaning (semantics) knowledge to guess what a word missing from print might be (Cooter & Flynt, 1996). If students know the word and are reading effectively and with adequate comprehension, they are usually able to accurately guess the missing word—or, at least, a word of the same part of speech. This helps the teacher know whether the student has sufficient background knowledge and vocabulary to cope with a particular text. Materials needed to complete a cloze test include the textbook, a computer and word-processing program, and means by which to copy the cloze passage for students.

Maze Passages

The **maze passage** (Guthrie, Seifert, Burnham, & Caplan, 1974) is a modification of the cloze passage. Maze passages tend to be less frustrating to students than cloze passages because they are provided three possible answers to choose from in filling in the blank. Thus, students tend to get a greater percentage of items correct. The purpose and structure of maze passages are otherwise identical to those of cloze passages. You will need the textbook, a computer and word-processing program, and means by which to create the passage for students. Figure 4.6 features a partial maze passage.

Figure 4.5   Cloze Passage

There exists an old American Indian legend about an eagle that thought it was a chicken. It happens that a *(Hopi)* farmer and his only son decided to go to a nearby mountain to find an eagle's nest. The *(journey)* would take them all day so they brought along some *(rations)* and water for the trip. The man and the boy hiked the *(enormous)* fields of *(maize)* and beans into the day. Soon thereafter they were on the mountain and the climb became *(rigorous)* and hazardous. They eventually looked back toward their village and at the *(panoramic)* view of the entire valley.

Figure 4.6　Maze Passage

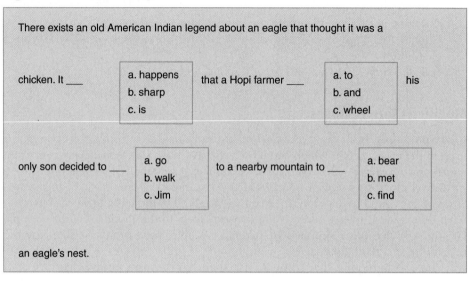

Vocabulary Flash Cards

A traditional way to conduct a quick assessment of a student's vocabulary knowledge uses flash cards. High-frequency words (those appearing most often in print) as well as other high-utility and specialized words for content instruction are printed individually in bold marker on flash cards and displayed to students for them to identify. Flash cards can also be produced with the computer and a word-processing program.

For recording purposes, you will also need a master list of the words to record each student's responses.

"Flash" each card to the student, one at a time, and ask him to name the word. Allow about five seconds for the student to respond. Circle any words that the student does not know or that he mispronounces on the student's record form.

This technique can be used to quickly assess vocabulary knowledge of an entire class. After you have shown the flash cards to all students, compile a list of troublesome words for whole-class or small-group instruction.

Published Diagnostic Vocabulary Tests

Several commercially published vocabulary tests are available. These are typically used by Title I reading specialists and special education faculty, but can be used by teachers who have appropriate training. We recommend three tests for assessing a student's word knowledge or **receptive vocabulary.** One is intended for native English speakers, and the other two are for students who speak Spanish as their first language and are learning to speak and read in English.

- *Peabody Picture Vocabulary Test, Third Edition* (PPVT–III) (Dunn & Dunn, 1997). The PPVT–III is a quickly administered instrument (11–12 minutes) that indicates how strong a student's vocabulary knowledge is compared to other students of the same age nationally. Results can help the teacher better understand the needs of students in terms of formal and informal vocabulary instruction.

- *Test de Vocabulario en Imágenes Peabody* (TVIP) (Dunn, Lugo, Padilla, & Dunn, 1986). This test is an adaptation of an early version of the previously described *Peabody Picture Vocabulary Test* for native Spanish speakers. It takes about 10 to 15 minutes to administer and measures Spanish vocabulary knowledge.

- *Woodcock–Muñoz Language Survey* (WMLS), English and Spanish Forms (Woodcock & Muñoz-Sandoval, 1993). Teachers, particularly in urban centers, often have a large number of students who are learning English as a second language (ESL). The extent to which students have acquired a listening and speaking vocabulary in English is an important factor in reading instruction because reading (a) is a language skill, and (b) depends on learners having a fairly strong English vocabulary. The WMLS is a widely respected instrument used throughout the United States. It takes about 20 minutes to administer. It features two subtests: Oral Language and Reading/Writing.

Another test used widely in schools for special diagnoses of reading ability, the *Woodcock Reading Mastery Tests–Revised* (Woodcock, 1997), includes a norm-referenced word identification subtest among its battery of six individually administered subtests. These subtests measure reading abilities from kindergarten through adult levels, and cover visual-auditory learning, letter identification, word identification, word attack, word comprehension, and passage comprehension. The Woodcock's design reveals a skills perspective of reading, and divides assessment into two segments according to age and ability levels: readiness and reading achievement. The WRMT–R/NU reports norm-referenced data for both of its forms and offers suggestions for remediation. Results may be calculated either manually or by using the convenient scoring program developed for personal computers.

What Are Examples of Research-Proven Strategies Used in Vocabulary Instruction?

An important question for teachers is this: How can we help students increase their vocabulary knowledge? In this section we present some of the most successful methods.

Principles of Effective Vocabulary Instruction

From the research cited previously, as well as that conducted by Stahl (1986) and Rasinski (1998), we have developed a list of principles for effective vocabulary instruction.

Principle 1: Vocabulary is learned best through explicit, *systematic instruction.* Context helps readers choose the correct meaning for multiple-meaning words. The old adage that "experience is the best teacher" is certainly true in vocabulary learning. The next best way to learn new vocabulary is through indirect, vicarious experience through daily reading in interesting and varied texts (Rasinski, 1998). Marilyn Jager Adams (1990a) put it this way:

The best way to build children's visual vocabulary is to have them read meaningful words in meaningful contexts. The more meaningful reading that children do, the larger will be their repertoires of meanings, the greater their sensitivity to orthographic structure, and the stronger, better refined, and more productive will be their associations between words and meanings. (p. 156)

Principle 2: Teachers should offer both definitions *and* context *during vocabulary instruction.* Children learn new words in two ways. First, they learn basic definitions or information that helps them connect the new word to known words (i.e., elaboration). This step can be accomplished by simply providing the definition, by building with students semantic maps linking the known with the new, and through examining the target word in terms of its synonym, antonym, classification, root, and affixes.

Context, which is the second foundation for building word knowledge, has to do with knowing the core definition of a word and understanding how that definition varies in different texts. For example, the word *run* is generally thought of as a verb meaning "to move swiftly." When looking for this simple word in the dictionary, one quickly realizes that the word *run* has approximately 50 definitions! Context helps the reader know which definition the author intends. In fact, without context, it is impossible to ascertain which meaning of a particular word is intended. Thus, it is important for teachers to help students understand both the definitional and contextual relations of words. Vocabulary instruction should include both aspects if reading comprehension is to benefit.

Principle 3: Effective vocabulary instruction must include depth of learning as well as breadth of word knowledge. Deep processing connects new vocabulary with students' background knowledge. Depth of learning, or **deep processing** of vocabulary, has two potential meanings: relating the word to information the student already knows (elaboration), and spending time on the task of learning new words (expansion). Stahl (1986) defines three levels of processing for vocabulary instruction:

1. *Association processing:* Students learn simple associations through synonyms and word associations.

2. *Comprehension processing:* Students move beyond simple associations by doing something with the association, such as fitting the word into a sentence blank, classifying the word with other words, or finding antonyms.

3. *Generation processing:* Students use the comprehended association to generate a new or novel product (sometimes called *generative comprehension*). This could be a restatement of the definition in the

student's own words, a novel sentence using the word correctly in a clear context, or a connection of the definition to the student's personal experiences. One caution relates to the generation of sentences by students: Sometimes students generate sentences without really processing the information deeply, as with students who begin each sentence with "This is a . . ." (Pearson, 1985; Stahl, 1986).

Principle 4: Students need to have multiple exposures *to new reading vocabulary words.* Multiple exposures to new vocabulary improve comprehension. Vocabulary learning requires repetition. To learn words thoroughly, students need to see, hear, and use words many times in many contexts (Rasinski, 1998). Providing students with multiple exposures in varied contexts appears to significantly improve reading comprehension. The amount of time spent reading these new words also seems to be a relevant factor in improving comprehension.

> **Getting to Know English Learners**
> Remember, ELs may apply their knowledge of cognates when they come across unfamiliar vocabulary words. (Refer to Chapter 2.)

In the remainder of this section we discuss some of the strategies we have found effective in vocabulary instruction.

Word Banks

Word banks are used to help students collect and review sight words. They can also be used as personal dictionaries. A word bank is simply a student-constructed box, file, or notebook in which newly discovered words are stored. Students review the words in their bank for use in their writing. In the early grades, teachers often collect small shoeboxes from local stores for this purpose. Students decorate the boxes to make them their own. In the upper grades, more formal-looking word banks—notebooks or recipe boxes—are used to give an "adult" appearance.

Alphabetic dividers can be used at all levels to facilitate the quick location of word bank words. Alphabetic dividers in the early grades help students rehearse and reinforce knowledge of alphabetical order. Figure 4.7 shows a sample word bank.

Specific Word Instruction

Specific word instruction can deepen students' knowledge of word meanings and, in turn, help them understand what they are hearing or reading (Johnson, 2001). It also can help them use words accurately in speaking and writing. Three ways of providing specific word instruction have been drawn from research evidence (National Reading Panel, 2000; Partnership for Reading, 2001): preteaching vocabulary, extended instruction, and repeated exposures.

What Specific Word Instruction Looks Like in the Classroom. The Partnership for Reading, a federally funded collaborative effort of the National Institute for Literacy, the National Institute of Child Health and Human Development, and the U.S. Department of Education, published in 2001 a booklet titled *Put Reading First: The Research Building Blocks for Teaching Children to Read.* This document was compiled to help disseminate data from the 2000 report of the

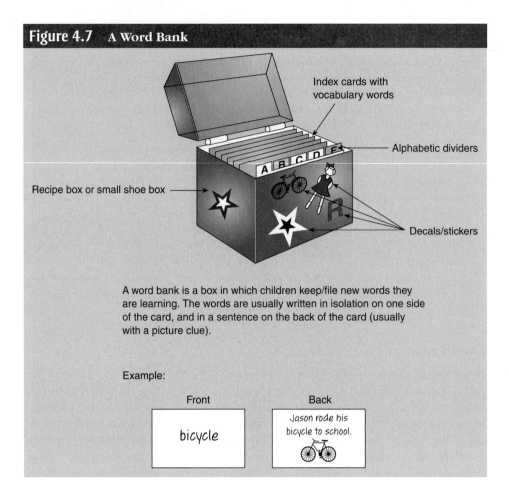

Figure 4.7 A Word Bank

Index cards with vocabulary words

Alphabetic dividers

Recipe box or small shoe box

Decals/stickers

A word bank is a box in which children keep/file new words they are learning. The words are usually written in isolation on one side of the card, and in a sentence on the back of the card (usually with a picture clue).

Example:

Front

bicycle

Back

Jason rode his bicycle to school.

You can order a free copy of *Put Reading First: The Research Building Blocks for Teaching Children to Read* (2001) online at *www.nifl.gov*. The report of the National Reading Panel titled *Teaching Children to Read: An Evidence-Based Assessment of the Scientific Research Literature on Reading and Its Implications for Reading Instruction* is also available at *www.nationalreadingpanel.org*.

National Reading Panel, and covers the topics of phonemic awareness instruction, phonics instruction, fluency instruction, vocabulary instruction, and text comprehension instruction. In order to help you better understand what each of the three specific word instruction components might look like in the classroom, we include examples after each definition borrowed from the *Put Reading First* booklet.

Preteaching Vocabulary. Teaching new vocabulary prior to students' reading of a text helps students learn new words and comprehend what they read.

AN EXAMPLE OF CLASSROOM INSTRUCTION

Preteaching Vocabulary*

A teacher plans to have his third-grade class read the novel *Stone Fox*, by John Reynolds Gardiner. In this novel, a young boy enters a dogsled race in hope of winning prize money to pay the taxes on his grandfather's farm. The teacher knows that understanding the concept of taxes is important to understanding the novel's plot. Therefore, before his students begin reading the novel, the teacher may do several things to make sure that they understand what the concept means and why it is important to the story. For example, the teacher may:

- engage students in a discussion of the concept of taxes
- read a sentence from the book that contains the word *taxes* and ask students to use context and their prior knowledge to try to figure out what it means.

To solidify their understanding of the word, the teacher might ask students to use taxes in their own sentences.

*From *Put Reading First: The Research Building Blocks for Teaching Children to Read* (2001). Non-copyrighted material published by the National Institute for Literacy. Available online at *www.nifl.gov.*

Extended Instruction. Students should be saturated (marinated!) with word-learning activities spread over an extended period of time. These should be activities that actively engage students as opposed to passive learning tasks.

AN EXAMPLE OF CLASSROOM INSTRUCTION

Extended Instruction*

A first-grade teacher wants to help her students understand the concept of jobs, which is part of her social studies curriculum. Over a period of time, the teacher engages students in exercises in which they work repeatedly with the concept of jobs. Students have many opportunities to see and actively use the word *jobs* in various contexts that reinforce its meaning.

The teacher begins by asking students what they already know about jobs and by having them give examples of jobs their parents have. The class also has a discussion about the jobs of different people who work at the school.

The teacher then reads the class a simple book about jobs. The book introduces the idea that different jobs help people meet their needs, and that jobs provide either goods or services. The book does not use the words *goods* and *services;* rather, it uses the verbs *makes* and *helps.*

The teacher then asks students to make up sentences describing their parents' jobs using the verbs *makes* and *helps* (e.g., "My mother is a doctor. She helps sick people get well.").

Next, the teacher asks students to brainstorm other jobs. Together, they decide whether the jobs are "making jobs" or "helping jobs." The job names are placed under the appropriate headings on a bulletin board. Students might also suggest jobs that do not fit neatly into either category.

The teacher then asks students to share which kind of job—making or helping—they would like to have when they grow up.

The teacher also asks students to talk with their parents about jobs. She tells students to bring to class two new examples of jobs—one making job and one helping job.

As students come across different jobs throughout the year (for example, through reading books, on field trips, through classroom guests), they add the jobs to the appropriate categories on the bulletin board.

*From *Put Reading First: The Research Building Blocks for Teaching Children to Read* (2001). Non-copyrighted material published by the National Institute for Literacy. Available online at *www.nifl.gov.*

Repeated Exposures to Vocabulary. You will find that the more students use new words in different contexts, the more likely they are to learn the words permanently. When children see, hear, and work with specific words, they seem to learn them better.

AN EXAMPLE OF CLASSROOM INSTRUCTION

Repeated Exposures to Vocabulary*

A second-grade class is reading a biography of Benjamin Franklin. The biography discusses Franklin's important role as a scientist. The teacher wants to make sure that her students understand the meaning of the words *science* and *scientist,* both because the words are important to understanding the biography and because they are obviously very useful words to know in school and in everyday life.

At every opportunity, therefore, the teacher draws her students' attention to the words. She points out the words *science* and *scientist* in textbooks and reading selections, particularly in her science curriculum. She has students use the words in their own writing, especially during science instruction.

She also asks them to listen for and find in print the words as they are used outside of the classroom—in newspapers, magazines, at museums, in television shows or movies, or on the Internet.

Then, as they read the biography, she discusses with students ways in which Benjamin Franklin was a scientist and what science meant in his time.

*From *Put Reading First: The Research Building Blocks for Teaching Children to Read* (2001). Noncopyrighted material published by the National Institute for Literacy. Available online at *www.nifl.gov.*

Making Words

Making Words (Cunningham & Cunningham, 1992) is an excellent word-learning strategy that helps children improve their phonetic understanding of words through invented or "temporary spellings" while also increasing their repertoire of vocabulary words they can recognize in print (Reutzel & Cooter, 2007). Making Words will be a familiar strategy to anyone who has played the popular crossword board game Scrabble.

Students are given a number of specific letters with which to make words. They begin by making two- or three-letter words in a given amount of time; they then must increase the number of letters in each word they make until they arrive at a specific word that uses all the letters. This final word is usually the main word to be taught for the day. By manipulating the letters to make words using temporary or "transitional" spellings, students have an opportunity to practice their phonemic awareness skills. Making Words is recommended as a 15-minute activity for first and second graders. In Figures 4.8 and 4.9, we summarize and adapt the steps in planning and teaching a Making Words lesson suggested by Cunningham and Cunningham (1992).

Figure 4.10 features directions for two more lessons suggested by Cunningham and Cunningham (1992) that may be useful for helping students learn the Making Words procedure. Examples of Making Words activities and another Cunningham favorite, word walls, are discussed in Chapter 7.

Figure 4.8   Planning a Making Words Lesson

1. Choose a word to be the final word to be emphasized in the lesson. It should be a key word that is chosen from a fiction or nonfiction selection to be read by the class, or it may simply be of particular interest to the group. Be sure to select a word that has enough vowels and/or one that fits letter-sound patterns useful for most students at their developmental stage in reading and writing. For illustrative purposes, we will use the word *thunder*, as is suggested by Cunningham and Cunningham (1992).

2. Make a list of short words that can be spelled using the letters in the main word to be learned. From the word *thunder*, one could derive the following words: *red, Ted, Ned, den, end, her, net, hut, herd, nut, turn, hunt, hurt, under, hunted, turned, thunder.*

   From the words you were able to list, select 12 to 15 that represent a variety of characteristics of written language: (a) words that contain a certain pattern, (b) big and little words, (c) words that can be made with the same letters in different positions (as with *Ned, end, den*), (d) a proper noun, if possible, to remind students about using capital letters, and (e) words that students already have in their listening vocabularies.

3. Write each word on a large index card and order the words from smallest to largest. Also, write each of the individual letters found in the key word for the day on a large index card. Make two sets.

4. Reorder the words one more time to group them according to letter patterns and/or to demonstrate how shifting around letters can form new words. Store the two sets of large single-letter cards in two envelopes—one for the teacher and one for students participating in the modeling activity.

5. Store the word stacks in envelopes and note on the outside the words/patterns to be emphasized during the lesson. Also note clues you can use with students to help them discover the words you desire. For example, "See if you can make a three-letter word that is the name of the room in some people's homes where they like to watch television." *(den)*

Figure 4.9   Teaching a Making Words Lesson

1. Place the large single letters from the key word in the pocket chart or along the chalkboard ledge.

2. For modeling purposes the first time you use Making Words, select one student to be the "passer"; this student will pass the large single letters to other designated students.

3. Hold up and name each of the letter cards and have students selected to participate in the modeling exercise respond by holding up their matching card.

4. Write the numeral 2 (or 3, if there are no two-letter words in this lesson) on the board. Next, tell student volunteers the clue you developed for the desired word. Direct them to put together two (or three) of their letters to form the desired word.

5. Continue directing students to make more words using the clues provided until you have helped them discover all but the final key word (the one that uses all the letters). Ask student volunteers if they can guess what the key word is. If not, ask the remainder of the class if anyone can guess what it is. If no one is able to do so, offer a meaning clue (e.g., "I am thinking of a word with _____ letters that means . . .").

6. Repeat these steps the next day with the whole group as a guided practice activity using a new word.

Function ("Four-Letter") Words

Many words are very difficult for students to learn because their meanings are abstract rather than concrete. Referred to as *structure words* (also *functors, glue words,* and *four-letter words*), these words are perhaps the most difficult to teach because

Figure 4.10   Making Words: Additional Examples

Sample Making Words Lessons (Cunningham & Cunningham, 1992)

Lesson Using One Vowel

Letter cards: *u, k, n, r, s, t*

Words to make: *us, nut, rut, sun, sunk, runs, ruts, rust, tusk, stun, stunk, trunk, trunks* (the key word)

Sort for: rhymes, *s* pairs *(run, runs; rut, ruts; trunk, trunks)*

Lesson Using Big Words

Letter cards: *a, a, a, e, i, b, c, h, l, l, p, t*

Words to make: *itch, able, cable, table, batch, patch, pitch, petal, label, chapel, capital, capable, alphabet, alphabetical* (the key word)

Sort for: *el, le, al, -itch, -atch*

Reprinted by permission of the International Reading Association.

they express concepts, functions, and relationships. Imagine trying to define or draw a picture of the word *what!*

Patricia Cunningham (1980) developed the **drastic strategy** to help teachers solve this difficult instructional problem. Here is her six-step process:

Step 1: Select a function word and write it on a vocabulary card for each child. Locate a story for storytelling, or spontaneously create a story, that features multiple repetitions of the word. Before you begin your story, ask students to hold up their card every time they hear the word printed on it. As you tell the story, pause briefly each time you come to the targeted word in the text.

Step 2: Ask for volunteers to make up a story using the word on their card. Listeners should hold up their card each time they hear their classmate use the function word.

Step 3: Have students study the word on their card. Go around to each child and cut the word into letters (or allow students to do it for themselves). Direct students to arrange the letters to make the word. Check each student's attempt for accuracy. Have students repeat this process several times before moving on to the next step. Put the letters into an envelope and write the word on the outside. Encourage students to practice making the word during their free time.

Step 4: Write the word on the chalkboard. Have students pretend their eyes are like a camera and to take a picture of the word and put it in their mind. Have them close their eyes and try to see the word in their mind. Next, have them open their eyes and check the board to see if they correctly imagined the word. Have them repeat this process three times. Finally, have them write the word from memory after the chalkboard has been erased, then check their spelling when it is rewritten on the chalkboard. This should be done three times.

Step 5: Write several sentences on the board containing a blank in the place of the word under study. Read each aloud. As you come to the missing word in the sentences, invite a student to come to the board and write the word in the blank.

The drastic strategy is useful for teaching "function words," those having little meaning.

Step 6: Give students real books or text in which the function word appears. Have them read the story, and whenever they find the word being studied, lightly underline (in pencil) the new word. When they have done this, read the text to them, and pause each time you come to the word so students can read it chorally.

We recommend adding one final step to the drastic strategy: Deposit the word under study to students' word banks for future use in writing.

There is one drawback to the drastic strategy: time. It is not always necessary to teach every step in the drastic strategy for all words. A careful assessment of your students' vocabulary knowledge and needs, coupled with years of classroom experience, will help you decide when certain steps can be omitted.

Teaching Word Functions and Changes

Synonyms **Synonyms** are words that have similar, but not exactly the same, meaning (Johnson & Pearson, 1984). No two words carry exactly the same meaning in all contexts. Thus, when teaching new words and their synonyms, teachers should provide numerous opportunities for students to see differences as well as similarities. As with all reading strategies, this is best done within the natural context of real books and authentic writing experiences.

Getting to Know English Learners
English is a very rich language as it has borrowed vocabulary from many languages, so synonym games are very useful in helping students see these relationships.

One very productive way to get students interested in synonyms in the upper elementary grades is to teach them how to use a thesaurus to add variety and flavor to their writing. This tool is best used during the revising and editing stages of the writing process when students sometimes have problems coming up with descriptive language. For example, let's say a character in their story was tortured by hostile savages (sorry to be so violent in our example!), but the child writes that the victim felt "bad." If this word is targeted for thesaurus research, then the student might come up with synonyms for *bad* such as *in pain, anguished, in misery, depressed,* or *desperate.*

Following are several common words that students overuse and their synonyms as listed in a thesaurus.

good	**big**	**thing**
pleasant	vast	object
glorious	grand	item
wonderful	enormous	gadget
delightful	huge	organism

One way to stimulate students' interest in synonyms is to develop a modified cloze passage using an excerpt from a favorite book. In preparing the passage, leave out targeted words. Have students fill in the blanks with synonyms for the words contained in the original text. The following excerpt from Eric Carle's *The Grouchy Ladybug* (1986) is well-suited to this strategy.

"Good morning," said the friendly ladybug.
"Go away!" shouted the grouchy ladybug. "I want those aphids."
"We can share them," suggested the friendly ladybug.
"No. They're mine, all mine," screamed the grouchy ladybug.
"Or do you want to fight me for them?"*

*From *The Grouchy Ladybug* by E. Carle, 1977, 1986. New York: HarperCollins. Reprinted by permission.

The teacher might delete the words *said, shouted, suggested,* and *screamed* and list them on the chalkboard along with possible synonyms, such as *hinted, greeted, growled, yelled, reminded, mentioned, pointed out,* and *offered.* Student rewrites might look something like the following:

"Good morning," *greeted* the friendly ladybug.
"Go away!" *growled* the grouchy ladybug. "I want those aphids."
"We can share them," *hinted* the friendly ladybug.
"No. They're mine, all mine," *yelled* the grouchy ladybug.
"Or do you want to fight me for them?"

Class discussions might relate to how the use of different synonyms can alter meaning significantly, thus showing how synonyms have similar meanings, but not the exact same meanings. For example, if we took the sentence

"Go away!" *shouted* the grouchy ladybug.

and changed it to read

"Go away!" *hinted* the grouchy ladybug.

it would be easy for children to understand how the author's message had been softened considerably. This "cross-training" with reading and writing experiences helps synonyms take on new relevance as a literacy tool in the hands of students.

Antonyms. **Antonyms** are word opposites or near opposites. *Hard–soft, dark–light, big–small* are examples of antonym pairs. Like synonyms, antonyms help students gain insights into word meanings. When searching for ideal antonym examples, teachers should try to identify word sets that are mutually exclusive or that completely contradict each other.

Several classes of antonyms have been identified (Johnson & Pearson, 1984) that may be useful in instruction. One class is referred to as *relative pairs* or *counterparts* because one term implies the other. Examples include *mother–father, sister–brother, uncle–aunt,* and *writer–reader.* Other antonyms reflect a complete opposite or reversal of meaning, such as *fast–slow, stop–go,* and *give–take.* Complementary antonyms tend to lead from one to another, such as *give–take, friend–foe,* and *hot–cold.*

Antonym activities, as with all language-learning activities, should be drawn from the context of familiar books and student writing samples. Interacting with familiar text and clear meanings, children can easily see the full impact and flavor of different word meanings. Remember, in classroom instruction involving mini-lessons, teaching from whole text to parts (antonyms in this case) is key. Thus, if the teacher decides to develop an antonym worksheet for students, it should be drawn from a book that has already been shared (or will be shared) with the whole class or group. A fun book for this exercise is *Weird Parents* by Audrey Wood (1990), which could yield sentences like the following for which students supply antonyms for the underlined words.

1. There once was a boy who had <u>weird</u> ( ) parents.
2. In the <u>morning</u> ( ), the weird mother always walked the boy to his bus stop.
3. At twelve o'clock when the boy <u>opened</u> ( ) his lunchbox, he'd always have a weird surprise.

From *Weird Parents,* by Audrey Wood, 1990. Used by permission of Dial Books for young Readers. A Division of Penguin Young Readers Group, A member of Penguin Group (USA) Inc. 395 Hudson Street, New York, NY 10014. All rights reserved.

Another activity providing practice with antonyms is to ask students to find words in their writing or reading for which they can think of antonyms. A student in sixth grade who reads *A Wrinkle in Time* (L'Engle, 1962) might create the following list of words from the novel and their antonyms.

Wrinkle Words	Antonyms
punishment	reward
hesitant	eager
frightening	pleasant

A student in third grade who writes a story about his new baby sister might select antonyms for some of the words he uses in his account.

Baby Story Words	Opposites
asleep	awake
cry	laugh
wet	dry

One way to assess students' ability to recognize antonyms is through multiple-choice and cloze exercises. The teacher should extract sentences from familiar text and have students select the correct antonym for a targeted word from among three choices. These choices might be (1) a synonym of the targeted word, (2) an unrelated word, and (3) the appropriate antonym. Following are two examples of this assessment technique that are based on *The Glorious Flight* (Provensen & Provensen, 1983).

1. Like a great swan, the *beautiful* (attractive, *homely*, shoots) glider rises into the air. . . .
2. Papa is getting *lots* (*limited*, from, loads) of practice.

Of many possible classroom activities, the most profitable will probably be those in which students are required to generate their own responses. Simple recognition items, as with multiple-choice measures, do not require students to think critically in arriving at a correct response.

Euphemisms. According to Tompkins and Hoskisson (1995), **euphemisms** are words or phrases that are used to soften language to avoid harsh or distasteful realities, usually out of concern for people's feelings. Euphemisms are certainly worth some attention in reading instruction that focuses on building vocabulary because interpreting them correctly contributes to reading comprehension.

Euphemisms can be *inflated* or *deceptive*. Inflated euphemisms tend to make something sound greater or more sophisticated than it is. For example, *sanitation engineer* is an inflated euphemism for *garbage collector*. Deceptive euphemisms are words and phrases intended to misrepresent. Students should learn that this language often is used in advertisements to persuade an uninformed public to purchase a good or service. Several examples of euphemisms based on the work of Lutz (cited in Tompkins & Hoskisson, 1991, p. 122) follow:

Euphemism	Real Meaning
dentures	false teeth
expecting	pregnant

funeral director	undertaker
passed away	died
previously owned	used
senior citizen	old person
terminally ill	dying

Onomatopoeia and Creative Words. **Onomatopoeia** is the imitation of a sound in a word *(buzz, whir, vrooom)*. Some authors such as Dr. Seuss and Shel Silverstein have made regular use of onomatopoeia and other creative words in their writing. One instance of onomatopoeia may be found in Dr. Seuss's *Horton Hears a Who!* (1954) in the sentence, "On clarinets, *oom-pahs* and *boom-pahs* and flutes." A wonderful example of creative language is found in Silverstein's (1974) poem "Sarah Cynthia Sylvia Stout Would Not Take the Garbage Out" in the phrase "Rubbery *blubbery* macaroni. . . ."

Students can be shown many interesting examples of onomatopoeia and creative words from the world of great children's literature. The natural extension to their own writing comes swiftly. Students may want to add a special section to their word banks for onomatopoeic and creative words to enhance their self-generated writing.

Shared Reading Experiences and Vocabulary Learning

Senechal and Cornell (1993) studied ways vocabulary knowledge can be increased through shared reading experiences—when adults and children read stories together. Methods investigated included reading the story verbatim (read-alouds), asking questions, repeating sentences containing new vocabulary words, and what has been referred to as "recasting" new vocabulary introduced in the selection.

Recasts build directly on sentences just read that contain a new word the teacher (or parent) may want to teach the child. The sentence is recast (changed) in some way to focus attention on a targeted word. For example, if a child says or reads, "Look at the *snake*," the adult may recast the statement by replying, "It is a large, striped *snake*." In this example, adjectives were added to enhance the learner's understanding of the word *snake*.

Interestingly, Senechal and Cornell concluded that teacher questioning and recasts were about as effective as reading a book aloud to a child as a word-learning tool. Thus, reading passages aloud to students can often be just as potent as direct teaching strategies. We need to do both: read aloud regularly *and* discuss passages containing new vocabulary with students in challenging ways.

Helping Students Acquire New Vocabulary Independently

The ultimate task for teachers is to help students become independent learners. The ongoing learning of new vocabulary throughout life is unquestionably a key to continued self-education. In this section, we feature ways students can become independent learners of new words.

Word-Learning Strategies

Students must determine the meaning of words that are new to them when these words are discovered in their reading. The teacher must help them develop effective **word-learning strategies** such as how to use dictionaries and other reference aids, how to use information about word parts to figure out the meanings of words in text, and how to use context clues to determine word meanings.

Using Dictionaries and Other Reference Aids. Students must learn how to use dictionaries, glossaries, and thesauruses to help broaden and deepen their knowledge of words. In preparation for using these tools, students must learn alphabetical order, ordinal language (i.e., first, second, third), and the function of guide words. The most helpful dictionaries and reference aids include sentences providing clear examples of word meanings in context.

> **Getting to Know English Learners**
> Native-language dictionaries are very helpful for ELs as well, and are often permitted for use during certain statewide assessments as an ESL accommodation.

Using Information About Word Parts. Structural analysis involves the use of word parts, such as affixes (prefixes and suffixes) and base words, to decode new words in print. Students can also use structural analysis independently as a meaning-based, word-learning tool. For example, learning the four most common prefixes in English *(un-, re-, in-, dis-)* can provide helpful meaning clues for about two-thirds of all English words having prefixes. Prefixes are relatively easy to learn because they have clear meanings (for example, *un-* means "not" and *re-* means "again") and they are usually spelled the same way from word to word. Suffixes can often be a bit more challenging to learn than prefixes. For one thing, quite a few suffixes have confusing meanings (e.g., the suffix *-ness,* meaning "the state of" is not all that helpful in figuring out the meaning of *tenderness*).

> **Getting to Know English Learners**
> English is a Germanic language in origin, but because of various influences, including the Battle of Hastings in 1066, most of our English vocabulary is indeed Latin in origin—stemming mainly from the Romance language of French.

Students should also learn about **word roots.** About 60 percent of all English words have Latin or Greek origins (Partnership for Reading, 2001). Latin and Greek word roots are common to the subjects of science and social studies, and also form a large share of the new words for students in their content-area textbooks. Teachers should teach the highest-frequency word roots as they occur in the texts students read.

> The four most common prefixes in English, *un-, re-, in-,* and *dis-,* provide helpful meaning clues for about two-thirds of all words having prefixes.

Using Context Clues to Determine Word Meanings. **Context clues** are meaning cues found in the words, phrases, and sentences that surround an unknown word. It is not an overstatement to say that the ability to use context clues is fundamental to reading success. This is because most word meanings will be learned indirectly from context. Following is another classroom example from the publication, *Put Reading First* (2001), this time demonstrating the use of context clues as a word-learning strategy.

AN EXAMPLE OF CLASSROOM INSTRUCTION

Using Context Clues*

In a third-grade class, the teacher models how to use context clues to determine word meanings as follows:

Student *(reading the text):* When the cat pounced on the dog, the dog jumped up, yelping, and knocked over a lamp, which crashed to the floor. The animals ran past Tonia, tripping her. She fell to the floor and began sobbing. Tonia's brother Felix yelled at the animals to stop. As the noise and confusion mounted, Mother hollered upstairs, "What's all that commotion?"

Teacher: The context of the paragraph helps us determine what *commotion* means. There's yelping and crashing and sobbing and yelling. And then the last sentence says, "as the noise and confusion mounted." The author's use of the words *noise* and *confusion* gives us a very strong clue as to what *commotion* means. In fact, the author is really giving us a definition there, because *commotion* means something that's noisy and confusing—a disturbance. Mother was right; there was definitely a commotion!

*From *Put Reading First: The Research Building Blocks for Teaching Children to Read* (2001). Noncopyrighted material published by the National Institute for Literacy. Available online at *www.nifl.gov.*

Encouraging Wide Reading

Wide reading is a powerful way for students to build vocabulary knowledge independently.

Reading involves cognitive skill development that in some ways mirrors physical skill development. As with physical skills, the more one practices reading, the more his or her reading ability increases. Over the years in our work with at-risk students, we have come to realize that if we can simply get children to read every day for at least 15 to 20 minutes, their reading ability will improve dramatically. In one study, Reutzel and Hollingsworth (1991c) discovered that allowing children to read self-selected books 30 minutes every day resulted in significantly improved scores on reading comprehension tests. These children performed as well as students who had received 30 minutes of direct instruction on the tested reading comprehension skills. Their results suggest that regular daily reading is probably at least as effective as formal reading instruction, and the students can do it on their own! Encouraging students to read books that match their interests can motivate them to read widely and independently, thereby nurturing vocabulary growth.

Scott Cunningham/Merrill

What Are Some Ways Teachers Can Encourage Wide Reading? How can teachers encourage students to read independently on a regular basis? The answer lies in helping students become aware of their interests and in finding books they can read. The interest issue can be resolved in two steps. First, the teacher can administer an **interest inventory** to the class at the beginning of the year (see Chapter 6 for ways of assessing student interest) to determine what types of books are indicated for classroom instruction. These results can be taken a little further. As the second step, we suggest that the teacher start an **individual interest sheet** (IIS) for each student based on inventory results. Students can review their IIS with the teacher during individual reading conferences (discussed more in later chapters). Besides listing topics that appear to be of interest to the student, the IIS can suggest books available in the school library that relate to those topics. Over time, students can list additional topics they discover to be of interest and can look for books in those areas. Figure 4.11 shows a sample IIS, with new interests written in by the student. A useful reference for teachers attempting to match students' interests with quality literature is Donna Norton's (1998) *Through the Eyes of a Child: An Introduction to Children's Literature.* Most high-interest topic areas are discussed in this text and are matched to several possible book titles. Book suggestions include brief descriptions of the main story line to help in the decision-making process.

> Surveying student interests with an individual interest sheet (IIS) helps teachers select free-reading materials.

> Describe two ways teachers can enhance vocabulary learning.

Computer-Assisted Vocabulary Learning

As computers become more accessible to students and teachers, the question arises: Can innovative computer applications help students learn new vocabulary? Reinking and Rickman (1990) studied the vocabulary growth of sixth-grade students who had computer-assisted programs available to them. They compared students who read passages on printed pages accompanied by either a standard dictionary or glossary (the traditional classroom situation) with students who read passages on a computer screen. These computer-assisted programs provided either optional assistance (on command) for specific vocabulary words or mandatory (automatic) assistance. Two very interesting things were learned from their research. First, students reading passages with computer assistance performed significantly better on vocabulary tests that focused on the words emphasized than did students in traditional reading groups. Second, students receiving automatic computer assistance with the passages also outperformed the more traditional reading group on a passage comprehension test relating to information read in the experiment. These results suggest that computer programs that offer students passages to read with vocabulary assistance can be helpful. Further, they suggest to

> Computer-assisted vocabulary instruction can provide highly motivating word-learning instruction in a classroom learning center.

Figure 4.11   Sample Individual Interest Sheet (IIS)

Individual Interest Sheet

Mrs. Harbor's Sixth Grade

Sunnydale School

Name: Holly Ambrose

Things I am interested in knowing more about, or topics that I like . . .

Topics	Books to consider from our library
horses	*The Red Pony* (J. Steinbeck)
getting along with friends	*Afternoon of the Elves* (J. Lisle)
romantic stories	*The Witch of Blackbird Pond* (E. Speare)
one-parent families	*The Moonlight Man* (P. Fox)

us another possible advantage of the computer: teaching students to use what might be termed a "vocabulary enhancer," such as a thesaurus program, with their writing, which could help students discover on their own new synonyms and antonyms for commonly used words. Most word processing programs, such as Microsoft Word, include a thesaurus.

Vocabulary Overview

Vocabulary overviews help students decide which words they will learn. In classroom settings, teachers can usually anticipate vocabulary that may be troublesome during reading and teach these words through brief mini-lessons. But when children read independently, they need to find ways to learn new words on their own. One activity that serves this purpose is the vocabulary overview. **Vocabulary overviews** help students select unfamiliar words in print and then use context clues and their background knowledge to determine word meaning.

One way of helping students develop their own vocabulary overviews is Haggard's (1986) **vocabulary self-selection strategy** (VSS). Our version of the VSS begins with a small-group mini-lesson during which the teacher explains the process. Students are asked to find at least one word they feel the class should learn. Next, they define the word to the best of their ability based on context clues and their background knowledge. On the day the words are presented for whole-class study, each student takes turns explaining (a) where he or she found his or her word, (b) his or her context-determined definition of the word, and (c) reasons why the class should learn the word.

What Can Be Done to Assist Students with Special Needs in Vocabulary Learning?

Students sometimes have particular needs in vocabulary learning. Students growing up in poverty circumstances and English language learners (ELL) are two key groups who may need special adaptations in vocabulary instruction to ensure learning. These two groups can benefit from many of the same instructional adaptations.

Peregoy and Boyle (1993), in their book *Reading, Writing, & Learning in ESL,* suggest guidelines for vocabulary development.

- Select words that you consider important to comprehending each assigned passage.
- Create several sentences loaded with context using these target words. This will give students an opportunity to use context to predict the meaning of the target words.
- Model prediction strategies using context.
- Follow modeling and guided practice sessions with discussion using excerpts from the text students will be assigned in which the target words appear.

Two vocabulary development activities are highly recommended for English learners (May & Rizzardi, 2002; Peregoy & Boyle, 1993; Reutzel & Cooter, 2003) that can also be helpful to children whose vocabularies are underdeveloped: the vocabulary cluster strategy and semantic maps.

The Vocabulary Cluster Strategy

It is especially important that students who struggle with reading use the context of the passage, their background knowledge, and the vocabulary they know to understand new words in print. This is true whether English is their second language or their first (as is the case with students from language-deprived backgrounds). With the vocabulary cluster strategy, students are helped to read a passage, gather context clues, and then predict the meaning of a new word targeted for learning. Here's how it works.

You will need multiple copies of the text students are to read, an overhead transparency and projector, and erasable marking pens for transparencies. Select vocabulary you want to teach from the text you will use; this text could be a poem, song, excerpt from a chapter book (novel), or nonfiction. Prepare a transparency containing an excerpt from this text with sufficient context to help students predict what the unknown word might be. Delete the target word(s) and replace them with a blank line, much the same as you would with a cloze passage. Figure 4.12 illustrates a passage prepared in this way along with a vocabulary cluster supporting the new word to be learned. This example is based on the book *Honey Baby Sugar Child*.

Through discussion, lead students into predicting what the unknown word might be. If the word is not already in students' listening vocabulary, you will be able to introduce the new word quite easily and effectively using the context and synonyms provided in the vocabulary cluster.

Semantic Maps

A **semantic map** is essentially a kind of blueprint in which students sketch out or map what is stored in their brain about a topic. Semantic maps help students relate new information to schemata and vocabulary already in the brain, integrate new information, and restructure existing information for greater clarity (Yopp & Yopp, 1996). Students who struggle with reading can use semantic maps prior to the act of reading to promote better recall (Sinatra, Stahl-Gemake, & Berg, 1984).

Semantic maps are useful in connecting new vocabulary with prior knowledge and related terms (Johnson & Pearson, 1984; Monroe, 1998; Reutzel & Cooter, 2003).

There are many ways to introduce semantic mapping to students, but the first time around it is best to use direct instruction followed up with a lot of teacher modeling and guided and independent practice.

The actual map is a form of graphic organizer in which a topic under discussion forms the center of a network of descriptors, concepts, and related categories. In introducing the process of mapping, begin with a topic familiar to the entire class, such as a state that is being studied. Write the topic on the board or an overhead transparency. Have students brainstorm categories of descriptors and concepts related to the topic. Record these. Connect these categories to the topic visually using bold or double lines. Then have students brainstorm details that relate to these major categories. Connect details to categories with single lines. Figure 4.13 shows a semantic map for the topic "Tennessee."

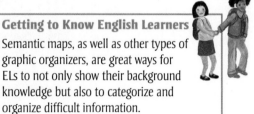

Getting to Know English Learners
Semantic maps, as well as other types of graphic organizers, are great ways for ELs to not only show their background knowledge but also to categorize and organize difficult information.

Semantic maps (also called webs) can also relate to a story or chapter book students are reading. Figure 4.14 features an example (Reutzel & Cooter, 2007) of a semantic map from a story in the book *Golden Tales: Myths, Legends, and Folktales from Latin America* (Delacre, 1996).

Any of the strategies found in this chapter can be adapted for struggling readers as long as you are direct and explicit in your teaching. Direct instruction helps

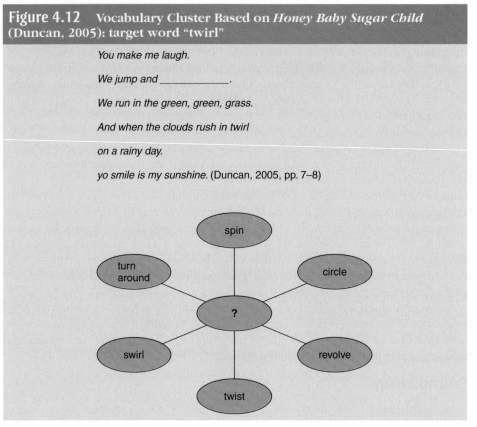

Figure 4.12 Vocabulary Cluster Based on *Honey Baby Sugar Child* (Duncan, 2005): target word "twirl"

You make me laugh.

We jump and _____.

We run in the green, green, grass.

And when the clouds rush in twirl

on a rainy day.

yo smile is my sunshine. (Duncan, 2005, pp. 7–8)

Source: Honey Baby Sugar Child by A. F. Duncan and illustrated by S. Keeter, 2005, New York, Simon & Schuster Children's Publishing. Used with permission.

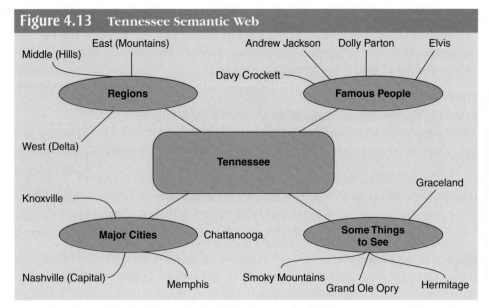

Figure 4.13 Tennessee Semantic Web

Source: From Reutzel, D. R., & Cooter, R. B. (2007). *Strategies for Reading Assessment and Instruction: Helping Every Child Succeed,* 3rd ed. Upper Saddle River, NJ: Merrill/Prentice-Hall.

Figure 4.14   Semantic Map: "Guanina"

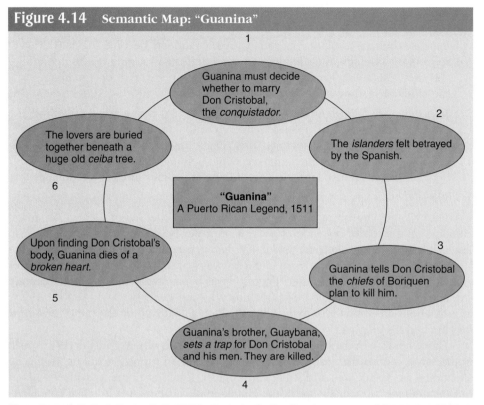

*From Reutzel, D. R., & Cooter, R. B. (2007). *Strategies for Reading Assessment and Instruction: Helping Every Child Succeed*, 3rd ed. Upper Saddle River, NJ: Merrill/Prentice-Hall. Used with permission.

less-proficient readers create mental scaffolding for support of new vocabulary and concepts.

Linking Multicultural Experiences with Vocabulary Development

Vocabulary development in spoken and written English is at the heart of literacy learning (Wheatley, Muller, & Miller, 1993). Because of the rich diversity found in U.S. classrooms, teachers need to consider ways of adapting the curriculum so that all students can learn to recognize and use appropriate and varied vocabulary. In this section, we consider three possible avenues proven to be successful in multi-cultural settings.

Link vocabulary studies to a broad topic or novel. We know that there is a limit to the number of words that can be taught directly and in isolation. Au (1993) tells us that students in multicultural settings learn vocabulary best if the new words are related to a broader topic. Working on vocabulary development in connection with students' exploration of content area topics is a natural and connected way to learn new words and explore their various meanings.

Getting to Know English Learners
Every human being actually speaks several dialects—depending on situation and audience, for example, and all of us have our own dialect or "idiolect," which is thought to be as unique as our own fingerprints!

Encourage wide reading at independent levels as a vehicle for vocabulary development. Reading for enjoyment on a daily basis helps students increase their vocabulary. Teachers can help students become regular readers by assessing their reading interests and then locating books that "fit" them. Matching books with students is a simple way of encouraging the kinds of reading behaviors that pay dividends.

Implement the Village English activity. Delpit (1988) writes about a method of teaching Native Alaskan students new vocabulary that works well in many other multicultural settings. The Village English activity respects and encourages students' home language while helping them see relationships between language use and social/professional realities in the United States (Au, 1993).

The Village English activity begins with the teacher writing "Our Language Heritage" at the top of one side of a piece of poster board and "Standard American English" at the top of the other side. The teacher explains to students that in the United States people speak in many different ways, and that this variety of languages makes our nation as colorful and interesting as a patchwork quilt. For elementary students, we think this would be a good time to share *Elmer* by David McKee (1990), a book about an elephant of many colors (called a "patchwork elephant") and how he enriched his elephant culture.

The teacher then explains that there are many times when adults need to speak in the same way so they can be understood, usually in formal situations. In formal situations, we speak Standard American English. When at home or with friends in our community, we usually speak the language of our heritage. It is like the difference between a picnic compared to a "dressed-up" formal dinner. The teacher writes phrases used in students' native dialect under the heading "Our Language Heritage," and notes and discusses comparative translations on the side labeled "Standard American English." These comparisons can be noted in an ongoing way throughout the year as part of a special word wall. The Village English activity can be an engaging way to increase vocabulary knowledge while demonstrating appreciation for language differences.

How Can Reading Backpacks Be Used to Involve Parents in Their Child's Vocabulary Learning?

During our respective careers, we have gone back and forth between teaching in the elementary classroom and in teacher education programs. Some may think we have suffered a series of identity crises (especially our spouses), but we never tire of working with children and their families. Because our better halves are teachers themselves, they humor us. Teaching is the greatest profession on earth!

One of the mainstays of our instruction is the **reading backpack** strategy (Cooter et al., 1999; Reutzel & Cooter, 2007; Reutzel & Fawson, 1990). The technique is straightforward: Have available a number of backpacks, perhaps with your school's name and mascot emblazoned on them, that you send home at least once a week containing reading or writing activities that can be completed by the child and his or her parent. Many homes are without printed text of any sort, and reading backpacks can bring fresh opportunities for enjoyment and learning into the family's evening. They can also help parents in their efforts to do something constructive for their child's literacy development. We have used backpacks to send home a supply of trade books on a variety of topics on different reading levels matching the child's ability (in both English and Spanish), easy activities written on laminated card stock so they can be reused, and materials for written responses to books (e.g., markers, colored paper, scissors, tape, etc.). Sometimes, if parents

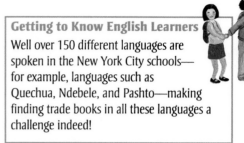

Getting to Know English Learners
Well over 150 different languages are spoken in the New York City schools—for example, languages such as Quechua, Ndebele, and Pashto—making finding trade books in all these languages a challenge indeed!

themselves are not literate, we have sent books accompanied by tape recordings and a tape player. Teacher-produced videotapes or DVDs demonstrating educational games parents can play with their children can be sent home for special occasions.

In this section, we share a few backpack ideas you might consider for drawing families into the circle for developing reading vocabulary. In most cases these ideas are easy and inexpensive.

Newspaper Word Race. In the backpack, send home:

- ✓ two out-of-date newspapers
- ✓ two copies of a list of target words you want the child to practice seeing and saying
- ✓ an egg timer
- ✓ two highlighting markers
- ✓ directions explaining the task

On a laminated instruction card to the parents, explain that they are to sit down at a table with their child and take one newspaper and highlighter for themselves and give one of each to the child. They should set the egg timer for one minute, and then have a race to see how many of the target words they can find and circle in the newspaper with their highlighter. When they are finished, they should share with each other the words they found and read the sentence in which they appear. For beginning readers, the parent will sometimes need to read the sentence to the child for words located by the student, then explain what the sentence means. This process encourages meaningful verbal interaction between parent and child—*very powerful!*

Garage Sale Books. If you enjoy garage sales (and many teachers do), look for bargain books having lots of pictures that seem to tell a story. Children's books are best. Cut out pictures from books you find, arrange them on card stock, and laminate them into place so they can be reused. Send these story cards home in the backpack with directions that the parent and child are to write a story that goes along with the pictures. Child and parent can rename the picture so that the character or depiction is in their family or a familiar environment. For instance, the odd-looking little puppy could be one the child found at the park across from her apartment. Be sure to include a word card with target vocabulary to be used in the student's story. Sometimes parents are willing to come to school and share with the class the story they have written with their student. This will often inspire other students to do the same with their parents when you send the backpack home with them. For this backpack strategy you will need to send home only a handful of supplies:

✓ a story card
✓ writing materials (pencils, paper)
✓ target words card
✓ directions explaining the task

Barbie and G.I. Joe. We know of a teacher who purchased old Barbie dolls at (where else?) a garage sale for pennies on the dollar. In her center, this teacher placed catalogs where the little girls in her class could select clothes for Barbie and write about them. She also found a Barbie car and had students write about places she traveled. The center became so popular with the girls that boys complained that they wanted something similar—an argument for equity?! So, she went garage saling again, bought G.I. Joe action figures for the boys, and set up similar centers.

We recommend Barbie and G.I. Joe backpack activities in which you include:

✓ a doll or action figure that is appropriate to the child's gender
✓ a target words vocabulary card with words to be used in writing
✓ a catalog, map of the country, or other stimulus that may be used for inspiring joint writing between the child and parent
✓ directions explaining the task
✓ writing supplies (paper, pencils)

Catalog Interviews. In this backpack activity, the parent is given an imaginary $5,000 to spend in a shopping spree. The student interviews the parent about what she or he will purchase and why. After the interview, the student should write a short summary of what he or she learned from the interview.

This activity can also be carried out by supplying the student with a large, artificial "million dollar bill." The student is to interview family members to find out what they would do with such a fantastic sum. The student then writes about their responses.

The point here is to inspire real dialog between the parent and student in which words are exchanged and discussed. As we saw earlier in this chapter, students add words to their listening and speaking vocabularies when they are engaged in two-way discussions (K. Cooter, 2006c), and this activity helps make that happen. For this backpack activity you will need:

✓ a target words vocabulary card with words to be used in writing
✓ a catalog that may be used for inspiring joint writing between student and parent
✓ directions explaining the task
✓ writing supplies (paper, pencils)

Mona Lisa. In this backpack strategy, the teacher sends home a photocopy of a famous painting or some other work of art. Abstract art works well for this activity. In your directions, ask the parent and student to describe what is going on in the painting or piece of art. For example, if you send home a copy of DaVinci's *Mona Lisa*, you might ask, "What do you suppose the young woman in Da Vinci's painting is smiling about?" This activity is especially powerful when you send along a list of target words that must be used in the written summary the student and parent co-produce (e.g., descriptive words, artistic terms the children may be learning, etc.). For this backpack activity you will need:

✓ a picture of a work of art (color is best)
✓ a target words vocabulary card with words to be used in writing
✓ directions explaining the task
✓ writing supplies (paper, pencils)

Scrabble. If you are lucky in your garage sale junkets you may come across an old edition of the perennial favorite *Scrabble* for your reading backpacks. This is the quintessential vocabulary game, of course, and having students play Scrabble with their family will provide a splendid opportunity for word talk. A variation would be to send home with the board game a target words vocabulary card and indicate that every target word used by anyone playing the game earns an extra five points. For this backpack activity you will need:

✓ a Scrabble game
✓ a target words vocabulary card with words to be used for bonus credit
✓ directions explaining the task

Summary

Dale Johnson (2001, pp. 41–48), an eminent researcher in the field of vocabulary development, provided valuable insights in his book entitled *Vocabulary in the Elementary and Middle School.* He wonderfully encapsulates information presented in this chapter. First, we know that word knowledge is essential for reading comprehension. Evidenced-based research tells us that vocabulary instruction should utilize activities (like the ones found in this chapter) that link word learning to concept and schema development. We should also teach specific word learning strategies to our students, as well as strategies they can use on their own to understand unfamiliar words in print.

Wide reading should be encouraged and made possible in the classroom. Literally thousands of words are learned through regular and sustained reading. Time should be set aside each day for this crucial learning activity. As an example, Johnson (2001) advocated the use of a program called "Read-a-Million-Minutes" which was designed to foster wide reading throughout Iowa. All students set their own in-school and out-of-school reading goal that contributes to the school's goal.

Direct instruction should be used to teach words that are necessary for passage comprehension. Considering how critical some words are for comprehending a new passage, teachers should not leave vocabulary learning to incidental encounters, but rather plan regular direct instruction lessons to make sure that essential words are learned. Active learning activities yield the best results. According to research conducted by Stahl (1986), vocabulary instruction that provided only definitional information (i.e., dictionary activities) failed to significantly improve comprehension. Active learning opportunities; such as creation of word webs, playing word games, and discussing new words in reading groups or literature circles, are far more effective in cementing new knowledge and improving comprehension.

We also know that students require a good bit of repetition to learn new words and integrate them into existing knowledge (schemas). In some cases, students may require as many as forty encounters to fully learn new vocabulary. To know a word well means knowing what it means, how to pronounce it, and how its meaning changes in different contexts. Repeated exposures to the word in different contexts is the key to successful learning.

Students should be helped to develop their own strategies for word learning from written and oral contexts. This includes the use of context clues, structural analysis (word roots, prefixes, suffixes), and research skills (use of the dictionary, thesaurus, etc.).

Finally, parents can help their children succeed in expanding concept and vocabulary knowledge by exposing them to new experiences and helping them to read about and discuss new ideas in the home.

In this chapter we have gained some important insights into ways children can be helped to expand their vocabulary knowledge. First, we know that word knowledge is essential for reading comprehension. Evidence-based research tells us that vocabulary instruction should utilize activities (like the ones found in this chapter) that link word learning to concept and schema development. We should also teach specific word learning strategies to our students as well as strategies they can use on their own to understand unfamiliar words in print.

Classroom Applications

1. Design a lesson plan introducing a word-learning strategy to third-grade students. Be certain that the lesson includes rich literature examples, teacher-student interaction, student-student interaction, modeling, and ample guided practice.
2. Review a local school district's curriculum guide (or curriculum map) for a specific grade level, and select two topics or themes of study in either science or social studies. Locate in the college or university's curriculum library the textbook adopted by the school for that grade level for the selected subject area(s). With a partner, construct a before-and-after word knowledge self-rating form for each topic you selected. Present your form to your class or group. Use the suggested vocabulary words in the curriculum guide as a start, but consider the typical background knowledge of your learners as well in your thinking.
3. Prepare a lesson plan for second-year (not the same as second grade) EL students introducing one of the vocabulary learning strategies discussed in this chapter. Identify the age of the students as well as their first language, and consider the background knowledge they might have to help them use the new strategy. As always, be certain that the lesson includes rich literature examples, extensive dialogue, teacher modeling, and ample guided practice for students. Remember that children need to interact with the teacher or with each other using language to truly make it their own.
4. Conduct an interest inventory with five students at a local elementary school. Next, prepare an IIS that matches at least four of their interests to popular children's literature. Books might be recommended by the school librarian or

drawn from D. Norton's (2007) *Through the Eyes of a Child: An Introduction to Children's Literature* (7th ed.). Finally, present the IIS forms to the students and explain how they are to be used. Turn a copy of both forms in to your instructor, along with a journal entry explaining how each child reacted.

5. Prepare and teach a mini-lesson demonstrating the VSS for diverse classrooms. Develop a simple handout for students containing helpful hints about collecting new words for investigation.

6. With two partners, fully develop five reading backpack family activities. Work with your cooperating classroom teacher to distribute your backpacks to five students. Once the backpacks return, interview the students to discover what happened at home and what they thought of the backpack activity. Send home a brief survey to parents as well if time permits.

Recommended Readings

Blachowicz, C., & Fisher, P. J. (2006). *Teaching vocabulary in all classrooms* (3rd ed.). Upper Saddle River, NJ: Pearson/Merrill/Prentice Hall.

Cooter, K. S. (2006). When mama can't read: Counteracting intergenerational illiteracy. *The Reading Teacher, 59*(7), 698–702.

Cunningham, P. M., & Cunningham, J. (1992). Making words: Enhancing the invented spelling–decoding connection. *The Reading Teacher, 46*(2), 106–116.

Fry, E. B., Kress, J. E., & Fountoukidis, D. L. (1993). *The reading teacher's book of lists* (3rd ed.). Upper Saddle River, NJ: Prentice Hall.

Johnson, D. D. (2001). *Vocabulary in the elementary and middle school.* Boston, MA: Allyn and Bacon.

Norton, D. (2007). *Through the eyes of a child: An introduction to children's literature* (7th ed.). Upper Saddle River, NJ: Pearson/Merrill/Prentice Hall.

Peregoy, S. F., & Boyle, O. F. (2001). *Reading, writing, & learning in ESL.* New York: Longman.

5

Teaching Reading Comprehension

Chapter Questions

1. What is reading comprehension?

2. How do children develop reading comprehension?

3. What does research say about reading comprehension instruction?

4. How is reading comprehension assessed effectively?

5. What are evidence-based instructional practices or strategies for developing reading comprehension?

6. How can comprehension instruction be adapted to meet the needs of diverse learners?

7. How can can families and communities support children's reading comprehension development?

Breakthroughs to Comprehension

Since the beginning of the school year, Ms. Dewey has taught seven comprehension strategies to her students. She has taught these strategies one at a time, using clear explanations and think-aloud modeling, and has scaffolded her instruction so each student can use the strategies independently. But now, after the winter holiday break, Ms. Dewey decides to teach her second graders how to use the seven comprehension strategies altogether—as a "strategy family"—while reading and discussing texts. To start this process, she produces seven posters, one for each strategy in the set of seven. She refers to these posters when she models for her students how to select comprehension strategies and use them during reading. Her posters are shown in the photo on the next page.

Ms. Dewey loves to read science books with her students, especially big books. And her students particularly enjoy reading science big books and participating in lessons using the "family" of seven comprehension strategies.

One day while videotaping a lesson for later review, Ms. Dewey records one little boy, Juan, saying enthusiastically, "I just love this stuff!" The class is reading a book about different frogs.

It has taken several years for Ms. Dewey to reshape comprehension instruction in her classroom and to see students achieve on much higher levels. In fact, she is always making adjustments to her teaching as she learns more about comprehension instruction and, most important, her students. As she listens to Juan's excited pronouncement, she echoes it, whispering to herself, "I love this stuff, too!"

Comprehension is the very heart and soul of reading. Although learning to translate letters into words is extremely important, teachers must never lose sight of the ultimate goal of reading instruction—comprehending text! From the very beginning, teachers should help students apply meaning to print by providing effective comprehension instruction in listening and reading. But what is it that teachers like Ms. Dewey know that help them to provide students with reading comprehension instruction that is effective?

What Is Reading Comprehension?

Research on reading comprehension has been carefully summarized by two major "blue ribbon" panels, the National Reading Panel (2000) and the RAND Reading Study Group (2001). The National Reading Panel (NRP) (2000, pp. 4–5) described reading comprehension as follows:

> Comprehension is a complex process . . . often viewed as 'the essence of reading.' Reading comprehension is . . . *intentional thinking* [emphasis added] during which meaning is constructed through interactions between text and reader. Meaning resides in the intentional, problem-solving, thinking processes of the reader that occur during an interchange with a text. The content of meaning is influenced by the text and by the reader's prior knowledge and experience that are brought to bear on it.

Similarly, the RAND Reading Study Group (2001) described reading comprehension (Sweet & Snow, 2003, p. 1) as "the process of simultaneously extracting and constructing meaning." This process of comprehending entails four essential components: (1) the reader, (2) the text, (3) the activity, and (4) the situational context. The first three essential components of reading comprehension, the reader, the text, and the task, occur within the fourth essential component of reading comprehension, the situational context. Obviously, the reader is the one doing the comprehending in reading, and the text is the reading material (e.g., fiction/narrative text, nonfiction/expository text) the reader is approaching. The "activity" refers to what kind of comprehension task the reader is attempting. The National Reading Panel (2000) recommended eight comprehension strategies that provide a firm scientific basis for instruction:

1. comprehension monitoring
2. cooperative learning
3. graphic organizers
4. question answering
5. question generating
6. story structure/text structure
7. summarizing
8. multiple-strategy instruction

Ray Reutzel

The situational context of reading comprehension can be thought of in at least two ways. First, there is the actual location or setting in which the reading of a text occurs—the home, the school classroom, the library, a church, under a blanket at bedtime, and so on. There is little doubt that one's purpose for reading a text is influenced by the setting in which one reads.

Second, there is a social context associated with reading comprehension. In some cases, reading comprehension is a solitary activity in which the reader constructs meaning using the author's ideas in the text. This is, of course, a very limited social setting. In other cases, however, reading comprehension can be a vibrant social activity in which people—teachers, parents, and children—read a text together and jointly construct meaning through discussion.

The *Report of the National Reading Panel* (2000) found that lively discussion about a text in the company of others seems to be the optimal situational context to enhance students' reading comprehension. Classroom discussion, then, seems to provide the best context for children to improve their reading comprehension.

How Do Children Develop Reading Comprehension?

Research occurring in the past 25 to 30 years has contributed greatly to our collective understanding of the cognitive processes involved in reading comprehension, but little or no research has focused on the development of young children's comprehension (National Reading Panel, 2000; Reutzel, Smith, & Fawson, 2005). Pressley (2000) described the development of reading comprehension as a two-stage process. Reading comprehension begins with lower processes focused at the word level—word recognition (phonics, sight words), fluency (rate, accuracy, and expression), and vocabulary (word meanings). Several previous chapters in this book have focused on efficient and effective processing of text at the word level; thus, our focus in this chapter will be on how higher-order reading comprehension processes develop.

> **Getting to Know English Learners**
> Of course, ELs have their own sets of schemata, or background knowledge, matched to their unique, perhaps, language, cultural, and background experiences.

The second stage of reading comprehension development focuses on higher-order processing—activating and relating prior knowledge to text content, and consciously learning, selecting, and controlling the use of several cognitive strategies to assure remembering and learning from text. Reading comprehension research has been profoundly influenced in the past by **schema theory,** a theory that explains how information we have stored in our minds helps us gain new knowledge.

A **schema** (the plural is *schemata* or *schemas*) can be thought of as a kind of file cabinet of information in our brains containing related (1) concepts (chairs, birds, ships), (2) events (weddings, birthdays, school experiences), (3) emotions (anger, frustration, joy, pleasure), and (4) roles (parent, judge, teacher) drawn from our life experiences (Anderson & Pearson, 1984; Rumelhart, 1981). Researchers have represented the total collection of our schemas as neural networks (i.e., "brain networks") of connected associated meanings (Collins & Quillian, 1969; Lindsay & Norman, 1977). Each schema is connected to other related schemas, forming a vast, interconnected network of knowledge and experiences. The size and content of one's schemas are influenced by one's experiences, both direct and vicarious. Thus, younger children typically possess fewer, less-well-developed schemas about a great many things than do mature adults.

One of the most important findings from the past three decades of comprehension research, from our point of view, is that readers can *remember* a text without *learning* from it. For instance, a reader might remember learning the definition of *photosynthesis* in a biology class. He might be able to recite the definition, but have no understanding of a related concept, *semipermeable membrane,* which is important to a full understanding of photosynthesis.

Perhaps even more important, readers can *learn* from a text without *remembering* much of what they learned for a very long time (Kintsch, 1998). When readers successfully comprehend what they read, they construct meaning that is interrelated, establishing a logical, integrated understanding that they can draw from memory in the future to help them understand and learn from reading new texts.

Kintsch (1998) developed **construction-integration theory** to explain the complex cognitive processes used by readers to successfully comprehend a text. We will briefly illustrate how this construction-integration process works using the story *The Carrot Seed* by Ruth Krauss (1945). We begin with a familiar series of statements from the text:

> A little boy planted a carrot seed.
> His mother said, "I'm afraid it won't come up."
> His father said, "I'm afraid it won't come up."
> His big brother said, "It won't come up."
>
> © 1945 by Ruth Krauss. Used by permission of HarperCollins Publishers.

To understand these lines, we draw from our previous experiences with family members—parents and siblings. We also call up our specific situational recollections for planting seeds or growing a garden. Next we read:

> Every day the little boy pulled up the weeds around
> the seed and sprinkled the ground with water.

At this point, we focus in on the meaning of the actions taken by the little boy: pulling weeds and sprinkling the ground with water. This connects with our previous experiences of planting seeds and growing things. Next we read:

> But nothing came up.
> And nothing came up.

These two sentences lead us to make the prediction that, in this case, the outcome of planting a seed might be different than expected. Our motivation is to find out why, in this story, the seed is not coming up—or to think, "Maybe it will."

The **surface code,** or printed text as shown above, preserves in the reader's memory for an extremely short period of time the exact letters, words, and grammar or syntax of the text. This image is like the one you see quickly fading after turning off a television in a dark room. Once the text information is registered, it is quickly moved from a mental picture or *iconic* memory and processed through short-term or *working* memory in the brain. In long-term working memory in the brain, the image is transformed, using one or more strategies, into a text base that preserves the meaning of the text. A text base in long-term working memory might include connective inferences, for example, the inference that sometimes when seeds are planted, they do not grow (the microstructure). A text base in long-term working memory might also include important or gist ideas such as the fact that the little boy has done everything he can to get the seed to grow (the macrostructure). A constructed text base in long-term working memory is usually retained for several hours, but may also be forgotten in a few days. As a text base is formed and placed into long-term memory, these same memory processes and strategies are employed to integrate the details of the text base to form a situation model.

The **situation model,** according to Kintsch (1998), is what the text is really all about: ideas, people, objects, processes, or world events. And it is the situation model that is remembered longest—days, months, or even years. In the case of *The Carrot Seed,* the process of planting, nurturing, and harvesting as well as persevering in the face of doubt are the information and messages that are stored as the situation model(s) for this story.

Processing of a text by a reader occurs in cycles, usually clause by clause (just as we presented and discussed the story of *The Carrot Seed*), and it involves multiple, simultaneous cognitive processes. The cognitive processes involved in eventually creating a situation model are influenced by (a) the reader's knowledge about the text topic or message, (b) the reader's goals and motivations, (c) the reader's strategy selection and use, (d) the genre, type, and difficulty of the text, (e) the processing constraints of the reader's memory (Kintsch, 1998; van Dijk, 1999), and (f) the reader's ability to learn in and from a sociocultural context (group, classroom) if it is available when a text is processed.

Two phases of mental processing occur, then, for each clause the reader encounters in a text: (1) a construction phase and (2) an integration phase. In the construction phase, lower-level processes, such as activating prior knowledge and experiences, retrieving words meanings, examining the surface and grammatical structure of the printed text, and analyzing each clause into idea units called propositions occur. Propositions include text elements, connecting inferences, and generalizations, which are formed into a coherent network of connected meanings. For example, a sentence like "The student placed a tack on the teacher's chair" could be reduced in memory to a generalization that the student played a prank on his teacher (Zwann, 1999). In the construction phase of processing, other closely associated ideas also are activated, including irrelevant and even contradictory ideas. All of these activated elements are initially part of the coherence network of meaning under construction.

During the second phase of processing meaning, the integration phase, the ideas from the text that are strongly interconnected with our prior knowledge are strengthened; those associated concepts that do not fit with the meaning context of the story or text are deactivated and deleted from the network of integrated knowledge.

From this two-phase process, one first constructs meaning from text and then integrates it with prior knowledge to make what Kintsch (1998) calls the "situational model" that is stored in and retrieved from long-term memory. In the case of Krauss's (1945) *The Carrot Seed,* the situational model categorizes this story as being about how to grow things and how perseverance in the face of doubts expressed by others can lead to success. It is this situation model that is stored with other such instances in long-term memory.

What Does Research Say About Reading Comprehension Instruction?

During the late 1960s and throughout the 1970s, reading comprehension was largely taught by asking students questions following reading, or by assigning skill sheets as practice for reading comprehension skills such as getting the main idea, determining the sequence, following directions, noting details, and recognizing cause-and-effect relationships. In 1978, Dolores Durkin reported findings from reading comprehension studies conducted in public school classrooms. After observing a variety of "expert" teachers engaged in reading instruction in both reading and social studies classrooms, Durkin concluded that these teachers spent very little time actually teaching children how to understand text. *In fact, less than 1 percent of total reading or social studies instructional time was devoted to the teaching of reading comprehension.* Unfortunately, many researchers have concluded that the situation in today's schools has not improved appreciably over the past 25 years (Collins-Block, Gambrell, & Pressley, 2002). Durkin (1978) also suggested that effective comprehension instruction includes such teacher behaviors as helping, assisting, defining, demonstrating, modeling, describing, explaining, providing feedback, thinking aloud, and guiding students through learning activities. Simply asking students to respond to a worksheet or to answer a list of comprehension questions is not teaching and does nothing to develop comprehension strategies, concepts, or skills.

Getting to Know English Learners
Research among ELs indicates that a combination of activities or connecting to prior knowledge by the use of graphic organizers are effective strategies in EL instruction.

Past early literacy research has been directed toward the issues of word identification, particularly phonemic awareness and phonics instruction (National Reading Panel, 2000; RAND Reading Study Group Report, 2001; Snow, Burns, & Griffin, 1998). This is so much the case that "the terms *comprehension instruction* and *primary grades* do not often appear in the same sentence" (Pearson & Duke, 2002, p. 247). More recently, leading reading authorities, corporately sponsored study groups (RAND Reading Study Group), and federal government agencies have concluded that young children can and should be taught reading comprehension strategies from the onset of reading instruction.

As a result of this research, teachers are increasingly aware that they need to explicitly teach comprehension strategies to children (Pressley, 2000). Research has shown that reading comprehension improves most when teachers provide explicit comprehension strategy instruction to children (Bauman & Bergeron, 1993; Brown, Pressley, Van Meter, & Schuder, 1996; Dole, Brown, & Trathen, 1996; Morrow, 1985; National Reading Panel, 2000). From the work of the National Reading Panel, the evidence base supports the effectiveness of teaching the following reading comprehension strategies: (1) graphic organizers, (2) comprehension monitoring, (3) answering questions, (4) generating questions, (5) story structure, and (6) summarization. The National Reading Panel (2000) also examined the evidence for teaching the following comprehension strategies, but did not find sufficient numbers of studies disclosing the same findings: (1) activating or connecting to prior knowledge, (2) inferences, (3) visual imagery, and (4) listening actively. These findings do not imply that teachers should stop teaching these comprehension strategies, but rather suggest that more research is needed before we can know how effective these strategies are when taught. We suggest that teachers continue to include these latter strategies in their repertoire for comprehension strategy instruction, but give special emphasis to those that have proven their effectiveness. The National Reading Panel also found that comprehension instruction is most effective when there is a great deal of text-focused talk set in vibrantly interactive and collaborative classroom contexts (National Reading Panel, 2000; Pressley, 2006). And finally, research as reported by the National Reading Panel (2000) indicates that teaching children how to coordinate the use of a set or package of comprehension strategies as they read and discuss what they've learned with peers and with teacher support yields particularly strong results for improving children's reading comprehension. Examples of multiple-comprehension-strategy instruction include Palincsar and Brown's (1984) *Reciprocal Teaching* and Pressley's (2002) *Transactional Strategies Instruction*. When teaching multiple comprehension strategies, the goal is to teach children a "routine" for working through texts using a set of comprehension strategies. Recent research has also determined that teaching a combination of comprehension strategies as a set is, in some ways, preferable to teaching a series of single strategies one at a time (Reutzel, Smith, & Fawson, 2005).

Paris, Carpenter, Paris, and Hamilton (2005) have carefully examined correlates (things that seem to be related) of children's reading comprehension. They found that some correlates or relationships between reading comprehension and other variables are spurious (false) while other relationships are genuine. For example, oral reading fluency and print awareness are highly correlated with reading comprehension among very young readers. However, the relationship between oral reading fluency, print awareness, and reading comprehension is transitory in that it decreases with age and ability. Thus, oral reading fluency and print awareness are regarded as spurious or false correlates with comprehension because they do not continue to hold up over time. On the other hand, there are genuine correlates of children's reading comprehension, including (a) general oral language, (b) vocabulary, and (c) narrative text structure awareness. These correlates remain highly related with reading comprehension regardless of the age or experience of the reader. Implications for teaching reading comprehension from this research is that building children's understanding of text structure and store of word meanings is strongly predictive of the ability to comprehend text at all points of a child's reading development.

Other research evidence points clearly to the need for teachers to support students' ability to use comprehension strategies when reading a variety of text types (narrative and expository) and genres (fairy tales, realistic fiction, almanacs, encyclopedias, etc.) (Donovan & Smolkin, 2002; Duke, 2000). The key to successful reading comprehension instruction is for teachers to design and deliver carefully structured learning activities that support children while they are developing the ability to become self-regulated readers who can use multiple comprehension strategies to understand what they read (Pressley, 2006).

A Sequence for Reading Comprehension Instruction in Grades K–3

It is important that teachers know and understand the minimum expected outcomes, or **benchmark standards,** for comprehension development at each grade level, especially in the early years. This information becomes an essential roadmap for teachers to use in assessing each student's level of comprehension development. With this knowledge, you can plan instruction that best fits the needs of every child and that lays the groundwork for appropriate "next steps" in comprehension development. Of course, in the classroom you will discover students are at different places in their comprehension development, and you will need to plan small-group sessions each day for students having common needs. In this way, you can help all students continue learning in a systematic fashion.

Figure 5.1 lists the benchmark standards for reading comprehension for grades K through 3 (Cooter, 2004).

Figure 5.1   End-of-Year Reading Comprehension Benchmarks: K–3

Kindergarten End-of-Year Benchmarks

✓ Uses new vocabulary and language in own speech
✓ Distinguishes whether simple sentences do or don't make sense
✓ Connects information and events in text to life experiences
✓ Uses graphic organizers to comprehend text with guidance
✓ Retells stories or parts of stories
✓ Understands and follows oral directions
✓ Distinguishes fantasy from realistic text
✓ Demonstrates familiarity with a number of books and selections
✓ Explains concepts from nonfiction text

First-Grade End-of-Year Benchmarks

✓ Reads and comprehends fiction and nonfiction that is appropriate for the second half of grade one
✓ Notices difficulties in understanding text
✓ Connects information and events in text to life experiences
✓ Reads and understands simple written directions
✓ Predicts and justifies what will happen next in stories
✓ Discusses how, why, and what-if questions in sharing nonfiction text
✓ Describes new information in own words
✓ Distinguishes whether simple sentences are incomplete or don't make sense
✓ Expands sentences in response to what, when, where, and how questions
✓ Uses new vocabulary and language in own speech and writing
✓ Demonstrates familiarity with a number of read-aloud and independent reading selections including nonfiction
✓ Demonstrates familiarity with a number of types or genres of text like storybooks, poems, newspapers, phone books, and everyday print such as signs, notices, and labels
✓ Summarizes the main points of a story

Second-Grade End-of-Year Benchmarks

✓ Reads and comprehends both fiction and nonfiction that is appropriate for the second half of grade two
✓ Rereads sentences when meaning is not clear
✓ Interprets information from diagrams, charts, and graphs
✓ Recalls facts and details of text
✓ Reads nonfiction materials for answers to specific questions
✓ Develops literary awareness of character traits, point of view, setting, problem, solution, and outcome
✓ Connects and compares information across nonfiction selections
✓ Poses possible answers to how, why, and what-if questions in interpreting nonfiction text
✓ Explains and describes new concepts and information in own words
✓ Identifies part of speech for concrete nouns, active verbs, adjectives, and adverbs
✓ Uses new vocabulary and language in own speech and writing
✓ Demonstrates familiarity with a number of read-aloud and independent reading selections including nonfiction
✓ Recognizes a variety of print resources and knows their contents like joke books, chapter books, dictionaries, atlases, weather reports, *TV Guide,* etc.
✓ Connects a variety of texts to literature and life experiences (language to literacy)
✓ Summarizes a story including the stated main idea

Third-Grade End-of-Year Benchmarks

✓ Reads and comprehends both fiction and nonfiction that is appropriate for grade three
✓ Reads chapter books independently
✓ Identifies specific words or wordings that are causing comprehension difficulties
✓ Summarizes major points from fiction and nonfiction text

Figure 5.1   (Continued)

> ✓ Discusses similarities in characters and events across stories
> ✓ Discusses underlying theme or message when interpreting fiction
> ✓ Distinguishes between cause and effect, fact and opinion, and main idea and supporting details when interpreting nonfiction text
> ✓ Asks how, why, and what-if questions when interpreting nonfiction text
> ✓ Uses information and reasoning to examine bases of hypotheses and opinions
> ✓ Infers word meaning from roots, prefixes, and suffixes that have been taught
> ✓ Uses dictionary to determine meanings and usage of unknown words
> ✓ Uses new vocabulary and language in own speech and writing
> ✓ Uses parts of speech correctly in independent writing (nouns, verbs, adjectives, and adverbs)
> ✓ Shows familiarity with a number of read-aloud and independent reading selections, including nonfiction
> ✓ Uses multiple sources to locate information (tables of contents, indexes, available technology)
> ✓ Connects a variety of literary texts with life experiences (language to literacy)

How Is Reading Comprehension Assessed?

Reading comprehension assessment is currently a topic of focused debate and some concern (Paris & Stahl, 2005). Reading comprehension, as we have already learned, is composed of several essential components: the reader, the text, the activity, and the social context. Because reading comprehension is multifaceted, it cannot be adequately measured with any single approach, process, or test (Paris & Stahl, 2005). However, one of the most effective processes for finding out if children understand what they read is to ask them to retell what they have read (Brown & Cambourne, 1987; Gambrell, Pfeiffer, & Wilson, 1985; Morrow, 1985; Morrow, Gambrell, Kapinus, Koskinen, Marshall, & Mitchell, 1986). Asking children to retell a story or information text involves reconstructing the entire text structure, including the major elements, details, and sequence. In stories, children retell using story structure, including the story sequence and the important elements of the plot; in addition, they make inferences and note relevant details. Retelling can be used to assess children's memory for story and information text.

You will need the following supplies for capturing students' oral retellings of texts they have read:

- blank audiotape
- portable audiocassette recorder with internal microphone
- brief story or information text

Because the processes for eliciting and scoring oral retellings are different for narrative and expository text types, we will discuss each separately.

Eliciting and Scoring Narrative Oral Retellings

For the sake of example, let us assume that we selected *The Carrot Seed* by Ruth Krauss (1945) as a story text for oral retelling. Type the text of the story onto a

Figure 5.2   Story Grammar Parsing of *The Carrot Seed*

Setting

A little boy planted a carrot seed.

Problem (getting the seed to grow)

His mother said, "I'm afraid it won't come up."

His father said, "I'm afraid it won't come up."

And his big brother said, "It won't come up."

Events

Every day the little boy pulled up the weeds around the seed and sprinkled the ground with water.

But nothing came up.

And nothing came up.

Everyone kept saying it wouldn't come up.

But he still pulled up the weeds around it every day and sprinkled the ground with water.

Resolution

And then, one day, a carrot came up just as the little boy had known it would.

---

separate piece of paper for parsing. Parsing, in this instance, refers to dividing a story into four major and somewhat simplified story grammar categories: setting, problem, events, and resolution. These are shown in Figure 5.2.

Oral story retellings may be elicited from children in a number of ways. One way involves the use of pictures or verbal prompts related to the story. As pictures of the story are flashed sequentially, the child is asked to retell the story as remembered from listening or reading. Morrow (1985, 2005) suggested that teachers prompt children to begin story retellings with a statement such as: "A little while ago, we read a story called [name of story]. Retell the story as if you were telling it to a friend who has never heard it before." Other prompts during the oral story retelling may be framed as questions:

- "How does the story begin?" Or, "Once upon a time. . . ."
- "What happens next?"
- "What happened to [the main character] when . . . ?"
- "Where did the story take place?"
- "When did the story take place?"
- "How did the main character solve the problem in the story?"
- "How did the story end?"

Getting to Know English Learners

Because beginning language learning is receptive, and not necessarily productive, it may make sense to elicit oral story retellings from ELs by assigning a more capable peer who can translate the EL's understandings into English.

Morrow (2005) recommends that teachers offer only general prompts such as those listed previously rather than ask about specific details, ideas, or a sequence of events from the story. Remember that when asking questions such as those previously listed, you are moving from free recall of text to a form of assisted recall of text information. Incidentally, you should know that assisted recall of story text information is especially useful with struggling readers.

Figure 5.3 Oral Story Retelling Coding Form

Student's name: _____ Grade: _____

Title of story: _____ Date: _____

General directions: Give 1 point for each element included, as well as for "gist." Give 1 point for each character named, as well as for such words as *boy, girl,* or *dog.* Credit plurals (*friends*, for instance) with 2 points under characters.

Setting

    a. Begins with an introduction   _____

    b. Indicates main character   _____

    c. Names other characters   _____

    d. Includes statement about time or place   _____

Objective

    a. Refers to main character's goal or problem to be solved   _____

Events

    a. Number of events recalled   _____

    b. Number of events in story   _____

    c. Score for "events" (a/b)   _____

Resolution

    a. Tells how main character resolves the story problem   _____

Sequence

    Summarizes story in order: setting, objective, episodes, and resolution. (Score 2 for correct order, 1 for partial order, 0 for no sequence.)   _____

Possible score: _____   **Student's score:** _____

Reutzel, D. Ray; Cooter, Robert B. *Strategies for Reading Assessment and Instruction: Helping Every Child Succeed,* 3rd Edition, © 2007. Reprinted by permission of Pearson Education, Inc.

A second way to elicit oral story retellings from students is to use unaided recall, in which students retell the story without picture or verbal prompts. Asking the child to tell the story "as if she were telling it to someone who had never heard or read the story before" begins an unaided oral story retelling. To record critical elements of the story structure included in the child's oral story retelling, use an audiotape recording and oral story retelling coding sheet like the one shown in Figure 5.3.

The information gleaned from an oral story retelling may be used to help you, the teacher, focus future instruction on enhancing students' understanding of narrative parts or story structure.

Eliciting and Scoring Expository Oral Retellings

Several researchers have found that children in the elementary grades are aware of and can be taught to recognize expository text structures (McGee, 1982; Williams, 2005). One of the most effective ways to find out if a child understands expository text is to use oral retellings (Duke & Bennett-Armistead, 2003). Asking children to retell an expository text involves reconstructing the contents of the expository text into its major, main, or superordinate ideas and its minor or subordinate details, both within the underlying organization of the text (compare/contrast, cause-effect, description, list, enumeration, etc.) Thus, oral expository text retellings assess both content comprehension and text structure knowledge in holistic, sequenced, and organized ways.

Begin an expository text oral retelling by selecting a brief, information trade book or textbook chapter for students to listen to or to read either aloud or silently, depending on the grade level and development of the student. We recommend that children in grades K–1 listen to the text read aloud, that children in grades 2–3 read aloud, and that students in grade 4 and beyond read silently. *Is It a Fish?* by Cutting and Cutting (2002) from the *Wright Group Science Collection* might be selected for the assessment. The teacher should type the text onto a separate piece of paper for parsing. Parsing, in this instance, refers to dividing a text into main or superordinate ideas and subordinate ideas as shown in Figure 5.4, *Oral Expository Text Retelling Coding Form.*

Expository text oral retellings may be elicited from children in a number of ways. One way involves the use of pictures or verbal prompts from the text. As pictures in the text are flashed sequentially, students are asked to retell what they remember from listening or reading about this picture. This approach is modeled after the work of Beaver (1997) in the *Developmental Reading Assessment* and the work of Leslie and Caldwell (2001) in the *Qualitative Reading Inventory–3.* Morrow (1985, 2005) suggests that teachers prompt children to begin oral retellings with a statement such as: "A little while ago, we read a book or text called [name the text or book]. Retell the text or book as if you were telling it to a friend who has never heard about it before." Other prompts during the recall may include the following:

- Tell me more about. . . .
- You said _____. Is there anything else you can tell me about. . . .
- Tell me about gills.
- Tell me about fins.
- Tell me how fish move, look, or breathe.

Asking students to retell what they remember using these types of prompts is a form of assisted recall and, as previously mentioned, may be especially useful with struggling readers.

A second way to elicit expository text oral retellings from students is to use unaided recall, in which students retell the content and order of the content in a book or text structure without pictures or verbal prompts. Asking the student to retell the information read "as if she were telling it to someone who had never heard or read the content of the book or text before" is used to begin an unaided expository text oral retelling. To record critical elements of the expository text oral retelling included in the child's oral retelling, use an audiotape recording. To make judgments about the quality of an unaided expository text oral retelling you might use a rating guide sheet like the one shown in Figure 5.5, which is based on the work of Moss (1997).

As you develop the ability to listen to expository text oral retellings, you may no longer need to use an audio recording and may simply make notes on the scoring sheet as to the features you hear the child include in his or her oral retelling.

Figure 5.4   Oral Expository Text Retelling Coding Form

Put a check mark by everything the child retells from his or her reading of the text.

_____ **Big Idea: A fish is an animal.**

_____ Detail: It has a backbone (skeleton inside).
_____ Detail: Most fish have scales.
_____ Detail: It is cold-blooded.

_____ **Big Idea: All fish live in water.**

_____ Detail: Some live in salt water.
_____ Detail: Some live in fresh water.
_____ Detail: Salmon and eels live in salt and fresh water.
_____ Detail: Salmon leave the sea to lay eggs in the river.

_____ **Big Idea: All fish breathe with gills.**

_____ Detail: All animals breathe oxygen.
_____ Detail: Some get oxygen from the air.
_____ Detail: Fish get oxygen from the water.
_____ Detail: A shark is a fish.
_____ Detail: Gills look like slits.
_____ Detail: A ray's gills are on the underside of its body.
_____ Detail: Rays breathe through holes on top of their head when they rest.

_____ **Big Idea: Most fish have fins to help them swim.**

_____ Detail: A sailfish has a huge fin that looks like a snail on its back.
_____ Detail: A (sting) ray waves its pectoral fin up and down.

Scoring:

Tally the marks for the big ideas and details. Place the total number in the blanks shown below.

Big Ideas _____ /4   Details: _____ /16   # of Prompts _____

Sequentially Retold (Circle One):   Yes   No

Other ideas recalled including inferences: _____

The information gleaned from an expository text oral retelling may be used to help you, the teacher, focus instruction on enhancing students' understanding of expository text structures. It will also be useful as you teach students strategies for sorting out the main ideas from details, sequencing, and summarizing information.

Figure 5.5　A Qualitative Assessment of Student Expository Text Oral Retellings*

Rating Level	Criteria for Establishing a Level
5	Student includes all main ideas and supporting details, sequences properly, infers beyond the text, relates text to own life, understands text organization, summarizes, gives opinion and justifies it, and may ask additional questions. The retelling is complete and cohesive.
4	Student includes most main ideas and supporting details, sequences properly, relates text to own life, understands text organization, summarizes, and gives opinion. The retelling is fairly complete.
3	Student includes some main ideas and details, sequences most material, understands text organization, and gives opinion. The retelling is fairly complete.
2	Student includes a few main ideas and details, has some difficulty sequencing, may give irrelevant information, and gives opinion. The retelling is fairly incomplete.
1	Student gives details only, has poor sequencing, gives irrelevant information. The retelling is very incomplete.

*Moss, B. (1997). A qualitative assessment of first graders' retelling of expository text. *Reading Research and Instruction, 37*(1), 1–13.

What Are the Characteristics of Effective Comprehension Instruction?

Pressley (2000) is quick to remind us that reading comprehension instruction begins with teaching decoding skills. Research shows there is a strong predictive relationship between well-developed word recognition skills and reading comprehension. Both the ability to decode unfamiliar words and recognize a core group of words by sight in the primary grades predicts good comprehension in the later elementary grades (Juel, 1988). Once students can recognize a word, they should be taught to use context—the surrounding print meaning or pictures—to evaluate whether the word has been properly recognized.

Students should be taught word meaning (vocabulary) if we are serious about improving their reading comprehension. This is especially true when students are taught word meanings that are related to reading selections (Beck, Perfetti, & McKeown, 1982; McKeown, Beck, Omanson, & Pople, 1985). As a part of extending children's vocabulary development and reading fluency, research clearly recommends extensive reading of a wide range of reading materials (National Reading Panel, 2000; Pressley, 2000; Stahl & Nagy, 2006). Within this environment of extensive reading of a variety of texts, children must be taught to activate their relevant background knowledge to understand and remember texts (Pearson & Anderson, 1984). They must also be explicitly taught comprehension strategies (National Reading Panel, 2000; Pressley,

2000). Teaching what comprehension strategies are and how to use each one independently is necessary; however, they are insufficient for effective, evidence-based comprehension strategy instruction. Children need to be taught how to orchestrate or self-regulate their selection and use of multiple comprehension strategies to remember and learn from text (Kintsch, 1998, 2004; National Reading Panel, 2000; Reutzel, Smith, & Fawson, 2005).

Another characteristic of evidence-based reading comprehension strategy instruction is assuring that students are guided to practice the application of comprehension strategies across a variety of text types—narrative and expository—as there is some indication that students do not spontaneously transfer their ability to select and use comprehension strategies across these text types (Donovan & Smolkin, 2002; Duke, 2000). Finally, students need to receive teacher-guided practice and feedback in using comprehension strategies in collaborative, highly interactive settings that stress student motivation and collaboration (National Reading Panel, 2000).

In summary, effective, evidence-based reading comprehension instruction recognizes the early need for children to learn to efficiently, effortlessly, and fluently recognize words. Children need to read extensively and receive expert and explicit reading comprehension instruction from teachers that is focused on vocabulary (see Chapter 4) and comprehension strategy acquisition. At some point, children need to be helped, through teacher-guided instruction, to select and use multiple comprehension strategies to process a variety of texts (National Reading Panel, 2000; Pressley, 2000). And finally, the conditions that support effective classroom comprehension instruction include rich interactions and collaborations among teachers and children around a variety of interesting texts (National Reading Panel, 2000; Pressley, 2000).

What Are Effective Reading Comprehension Strategies We Should Teach?

The answer to this question is organized around the four essential components of the RAND Reading Study Group's (2002) description of reading comprehension: (1) the reader, (2) the text, (3) the activities or strategies, and (4) the situational context. We begin our discussion of effective reading comprehension strategies with a focus on helping the reader prepare for and succeed in reading comprehension.

> **Getting to Know English Learners**
> Activating background knowledge for ELs follows the same rules—storytelling, particularly in the form of fairy tales or fables, is a universal, cross-cultural phenomenon.

The Reader

Activating Student Background Knowledge: Theme or Topic? Activating students' background knowledge in preparation for reading is critical for promoting reading comprehension. Many core reading program or basal reader teacher's guides contain a section titled "Building Background for the Story," or "Building Background Knowledge." Unfortunately, the guidance offered in many core reading program teacher's editions for building students' background knowledge is often misleading.

Analyses of several basal teachers' manuals show instances of problems in the pre-reading component. Some manuals suggest that teachers focus on tangential concepts that are irrelevant to the upcoming selection; sometimes the suggestion for presenting the concepts would encourage far-ranging discussions that could distract children from what is important. Even under the best conditions, the teacher's manuals may suggest concepts inappropriate for a specific group of children. (Beck, 1986, p. 15)

Some teacher's manuals make no distinction between activating students' prior knowledge for story texts as compared with information texts. For example, in presenting the story *The Ugly Duckling,* one teacher's manual focused background knowledge activation on a discussion of the differences between ducks and swans. Although such a concept may be appropriate for an information text dealing with the topic of ducks and swans, it was totally misdirected for the story *The Ugly Duckling.* Background knowledge activation for stories should focus discussion on the message or theme rather than on a topic. For example, one might ask students to respond to the question, "Have any of you ever experienced what it feels like to have someone not want to play with you? How did you feel when you were left out of a game?" These questions would be much more likely to evoke the necessary background knowledge to guide the interpretation of the story of the ugly duckling than would a study of the difference between ducks and swans. If the teacher determines the text is story (fiction or narrative), background knowledge activation should focus on evoking knowledge related to the theme or message of the story, e.g., exclusion or being left out because you are different.

On the other hand, if the text is informational (nonfiction or expository), background knowledge activation should focus on evoking knowledge from the particular domain or topic associated with the content of the text, e.g., migratory waterfowl or land formations.

Activating Student Background Knowledge: K-W-L. One well-known, highly used, but inadequately researched strategy for activating background knowledge is called K-W-L (Ogle, 1986; Stahl, 2004). Although this strategy may in fact be useful, it can be misused in light of what we have just discussed about activating students' background knowledge. Before using this strategy, teachers must determine the type of text to be read and then shape the questions to guide the K-W-L process so that the appropriate knowledge is activated to act as the interpretive framework for reading the text. Ogle (1986), the originator of K-W-L, asserts that this strategy is best suited for use with information texts, although with appropriate guidance and questioning, teachers can adapt K-W-L for use with narratives as well.

Step K: What I Know. K-W-L strategy lessons begin with step K, *What I Know.* This step is composed of two levels of accessing prior knowledge: (a) brainstorming and (b) categorizing information. Ask children to brainstorm about a particular topic (in the case of a narrative, brainstorm a particular theme or message). For instance, you might ask children what they know about bats. A list of associations is formed through brainstorming. When students make a contribution, Ogle (1986) suggests asking them where or how they got their information to challenge them to use higher levels of thinking.

Next, ask students to look for ways in which the brainstorming list can be reorganized into categories of information. For example, you may notice that the brainstorming list shows three related pieces of information about how bats navigate. These can be reorganized into a "navigation" category. Encourage students to look at the list and think about other categories represented in the brainstorming list.

Step W: What Do I Want to Learn? During step W, students recognize gaps, inaccuracies, and disagreements in their prior knowledge to decide what they want to learn. You, the teacher, can play a central role in pointing out these problems and helping students frame questions for which they would like to have answers.

Questions can be framed by using the stem "I wonder." After children generate a series of questions to be answered from the reading, they are to write down questions for which they would like answers. These are often selected from those questions generated by the group.

Step L: What I Learned. After reading, ask students to write down what they learned. This can take the form of answers to specific questions they asked or a concise written summary of their learning. These questions and answers may be discussed as a group or shared between pairs of students. In this way, other students benefit from the learning of their peers as well as from their own learning.

In summary, K-W-L has been shown to be effective in improving reading comprehension by causing students to activate, think about, and organize their prior knowledge as an aid to reading comprehension (DeWitz & Carr, 1987).

Motivation and Engagement

Turner and Paris (1995) discuss six "C's" of motivation that promote student engagement in the act of reading and comprehending a text: (1) choice, (2) challenge, (3) control, (4) collaboration, (5) constructing meaning, and (6) consequences. Choice does not mean that students are free to select any text or to make up what they have read when asked about it. Choices are never unlimited; instead they are bounded or limited. To offer choice may mean choosing to read from two different information books on rocks and rock formations. However, when children have the sense that they can make some choices about what to read and for which purposes, they are more willing to persist and remain intellectually engaged while reading.

> **Getting to Know English Learners**
> Collaboration is also key to language acquisition as students discuss, share, listen to, and negotiate with language.

Challenge is the second way in which we can encourage increased reading motivation and engagement to increase reading comprehension. Turner and Paris (1995) suggest that the common wisdom that children like "easy" reading texts and tasks more than more difficult or challenging reading texts or tasks is not supported by research. In fact, students enjoy challenge. Of course, here again the level of challenge associated with the text or task must not become excessive to the point of frustration. But giving children appropriately challenging texts and tasks has been shown to positively impact reader motivation to read for comprehension.

Control is the third motivational factor associated with increasing students' reading comprehension. Sharing the control of texts and tasks in the classroom with the teacher or other students is associated with greater engagement while reading. Students need to feel that they have an integral role to play while reading a text in order to take sufficient control of their own thinking processes to be successful in reading for comprehension.

Collaboration has been shown to be one of eight comprehension strategies for which there is sufficient scientific evidence of efficacy. The National Reading Panel (2000) recommends collaboration for implementation into classroom practice to improve students' reading comprehension. Collaboration requires that students discuss, interact, and work together with each other and their teachers to construct the meaning of texts. Collaboration results in students obtaining greater insights into the thinking processes of others around a text. Collaborative discussions and interactions also elaborate the outcomes of the reading comprehension process by adding to one another's memories for and meanings constructed from the reading of a text.

Constructing meaning is the very essence of reading comprehension instruction. This requires the conscious selection, control, and use of various cognitive comprehension strategies while engaged in reading text.

Consequences are the final factor that leads students to increased motivation and reading comprehension. This concept refers to the nature of the outcomes expected when comprehending. If the outcome expected is completing or participating in an open-ended rather than a closed-ended task, such as contributing to a discussion rather than getting the "right" answers to questions on a worksheet, students interpret their failures in comprehension differently. When seeking correct or "right" answers, they often feel that they just do not have enough ability (Turner & Paris, 1995). On the other hand, if through discussion they detect that they failed to pick up on some element in the text, they often view this failure as the result of insufficiently or improperly selecting or applying effective comprehension strategies rather than just that they are not "smart enough" or "don't have the ability."

In conclusion, when preparing to teach reading comprehension, teachers must carefully consider how they can increase students' motivation to actively engage in and take control of their own thinking processes while reading texts. The six Cs mentioned earlier—choice, challenge, control, collaboration, constructing meaning, and consequences—can be considered when building motivation.

The Text

The quality of the text examples children experience in the books or texts we use in teaching comprehension is a consideration of principal importance. Text that is well-presented, well-written, and well-organized has been shown by many researchers to have a positive impact on all students' comprehension (Donovan & Smolkin, 2002; McKeown, Beck, & Worthy, 1993; Seidenberg, 1989). As a teacher, you must select and use those texts that provide clear examples of the text features and structures you are intent upon teaching children to recognize and use to improve their comprehension.

Text Structure and Using Graphic Organizers. A model for teaching children to use text structure is found in Figure 5.6.

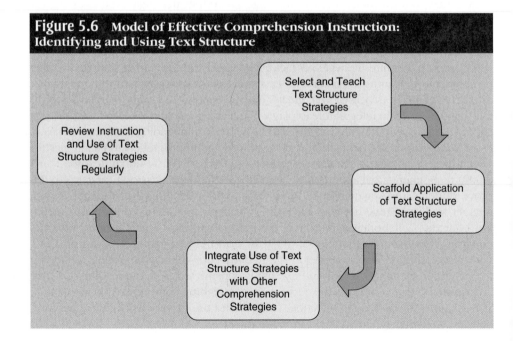

Figure 5.6 Model of Effective Comprehension Instruction: Identifying and Using Text Structure

Select and Teach Text Structure Strategies

Scaffold Application of Text Structure Strategies

Integrate Use of Text Structure Strategies with Other Comprehension Strategies

Review Instruction and Use of Text Structure Strategies Regularly

To begin, text structure instruction should focus on the physical features that help students understand the way that an author has organized a text including the table of contents, chapter headings and subheadings, paragraph organization such as topic sentence location and signal words, typographic and spacing features, and visual insets or aids. Next, students can be helped to recognize and use the way the author has organized the text. For narrative texts, this means teaching explicitly the parts of a narrative or story structure (NRP, 2000). For young children, this may begin with the concepts of story to include *beginning, middle,* and *end.* Older children should be taught that a story has prototypical parts organized in a predictable sequence, including the *setting, problem, goal, events,* and *resolution.* Because our lives are stories, stories mirror lived experiences for which we all eventually acquire an internal context into which we can place story structure. Young children are relatively adept at working with and understanding narrative text structures.

Teaching the organization or structure of expository texts means explicitly teaching different text structures of time order, cause and effect, problem and solution, comparison, simple listing/enumeration, and descriptions. Among information texts, it appears that sequence text structures are the easiest for younger students to understand. Examples of sequence text structures include counting books, days of the week, months of the year, step-by-step instruction, seasons, and so on. These books typically follow an established order or sequence familiar to younger children from their everyday lives. Another sequence text structure is the question–answer format. In these types of expository structures, authors typically ask a question and then proceed immediately to answer the question in the very next sentence, paragraph, or page. After this type of text structure, in a developmental progression of difficulty, come information books that describe single topics such as frogs, sand, or chocolate. Another information book structure that is closely aligned with descriptive structures enumerates or lists a category of related concepts or objects for description such as reptiles, dogs, or information about the Pueblo Indians. In listing/enumerative text structures, different types, examples, and aspects of a category are described as a collection. Compare and contrast or cause-effect expository text structures are the most challenging for young readers.

Effective text structure instruction requires that teachers provide short, frequent review opportunities for application of the text structure strategies taught. We have listed the characteristics of effective text structure instruction in Figure 5.7.

We have chosen two types of text structures, narrative and expository, as examples to illustrate the kind of effective text structure instruction we describe in Figure 5.7. We begin by focusing on effective text structure instruction with a selected narrative text.

Effective Narrative Text Structure Instruction. We begin by selecting an excellent example of a narrative text.

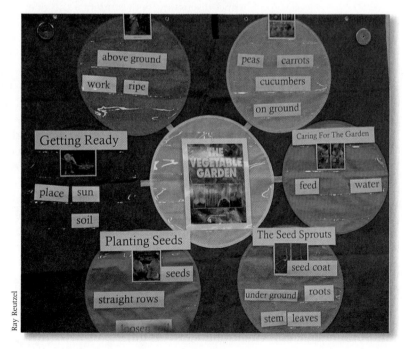

Ray Reutzel

Figure 5.7 Characteristics of Effective Text Structure Instruction

- Select exemplars of varying text types.
- Focus initial instruction on physical features of text that help students understand organization:
  - table of contents
  - chapter headings
  - subheadings
  - paragraph organization
    - main idea and topic sentence location
    - signal words
    - typographic features
    - spacing features
    - visual insets
- Teach children how to determine the way the author has organized or structured the text.
- Teach children how to think about and visually represent the way the author has implicitly organized the text using graphic organizers.
- Provide scaffolding or gradual release.
- Activate and use text feature and text structure knowledge in regular review cycles.

This means we want to find a story text that exemplifies the clear and traditional use of story structure. For a text to qualify for selection, it must possess the traditional elements and follow the traditional sequence of elements in a story grammar: setting, characters, problem, goal, events, and resolution. The familiar story *The Tale of Peter Rabbit* (Beatrix Potter, 1986) is well-suited to our purpose.

Next, we carefully examine the physical features of our text. We note several important physical features in *The Tale of Peter Rabbit* that we make a point of showing and discussing with students: the title, the author, the illustrator, the title page, and how many stories begins with "Once upon a time" and end with "The End." Although not as rich in physical features as some narrative texts, *The Tale of Peter Rabbit* does evidence clear paragraph structure. For example, when Peter saw Mr. McGregor, he was very frightened and the details of the paragraph clearly relate to actions and events that would support this major idea—the character's rushing all over, forgetting his way out, losing something in the tussle, and so on. This storybook also makes use of a great many signal words: *first, after, after a time, presently, suddenly,* and *at last.* The book also makes good use of spacing and print arrangements. On the first page, ONCE UPON A TIME is printed in all capitals, as is THE END. Also on the first page, the four little rabbits' names—Flopsy, Mopsy, Cottontail, and Peter—are printed one name to a line with an increasing paragraph indent as each name is added to the list, resulting in a four-stair, step-shaped list. This print arrangement is used several times throughout the book as a visual indicator of a list.

The Tale of Peter Rabbit is a narrative with traditional story structure. The setting is clearly stated in this story, including mention of the characters of Flopsy, Mopsy, Cottontail, Peter, and Mother. The problem is described when Mother Rabbit tells the children to stay away from Mr. McGregor's garden because their father had been caught and ended up in Mr. McGregor's pie. Peter, of course, decides he will test fate by straying away from his siblings into Mr. McGregor's garden. Once Peter has eaten his fill, he is spotted by Mr. McGregor. The story chronicles Peter's many close calls and his multiple attempts to escape Mr. McGregor. In the process, Peter loses his coat and his shoes. The resolution occurs when Peter escapes from Mr. McGregor and goes home to his waiting Mother, who gives him chamomile tea to settle his upset stomach.

For younger children, a simple graphic organizer with beginning, middle, and end of story components can be used to convey implicit story structure. Older students can be presented with a more complex graphic organizer that includes setting, characters, location, time, problem, goals, events, and resolution. Two examples of graphic organizers are shown in Figures 5.8 and 5.9. Figure 5.8 shows *The Tale of Peter Rabbit* graphic organizer for teaching younger children story structure. Figure 5.9 shows *The Tale of Peter Rabbit* graphic organizer for teaching older students story structure.

Once story structure is explicitly and thoroughly explained and modeled by the teacher, we turn our attention to the issue of scaffolding narrative text structure instruction effectively in the classroom. *Scaffolding* refers to the gradual release of control and responsibility for selecting and using text structure comprehension strategies like graphic organizers, beginning with high teacher control and involvement, moving to shared control and involvement between teachers and students, and finally to students' independent control over strategy selection and use. This release requires multiple lessons such as the one just described, perhaps using a variety of storybooks such as *The Little Red Hen, The Three Pigs,* or *Jack and the Beanstalk.*

In the first lesson, the teacher would do most of the explaining, thinking aloud, and representing of the elements of story structure in the graphic organizer. In the

Figure 5.8 Simple Story Structure Graphic Organizer

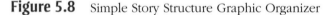

> **The Tale of Peter Rabbit**
> **Beatrix Potter**
>
> ---
>
> **Beginning:** **Once upon a time. . . .**
> *Mother, Flopsy, Mopsy, and Peter*
> *Mother goes to market and children are warned not to go into Mr. McGregor's garden.*
>
> *Children go out to gather blackberries.*
>
> ---
>
> **Middle:** *Peter eats his fill. Mr. McGregor sees Peter and tries to catch him. Peter gets lost, is nearly caught, and becomes very frightened. Peter loses his jacket and shoes in escaping Mr. McGregor.*
>
> ---
>
> **End:** *Peter finally returns home. He doesn't feel well. His mother gives him chamomile tea.*
> **The End**

Figure 5.9 Complex Story Structure Graphic Organizer

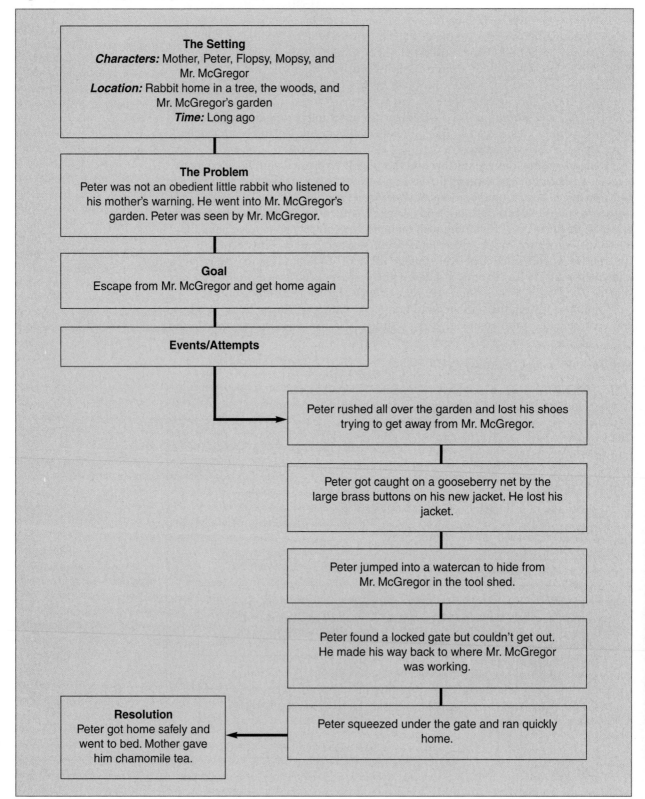

The Setting
Characters: Mother, Peter, Flopsy, Mopsy, and Mr. McGregor
Location: Rabbit home in a tree, the woods, and Mr. McGregor's garden
Time: Long ago

The Problem
Peter was not an obedient little rabbit who listened to his mother's warning. He went into Mr. McGregor's garden. Peter was seen by Mr. McGregor.

Goal
Escape from Mr. McGregor and get home again

Events/Attempts

Peter rushed all over the garden and lost his shoes trying to get away from Mr. McGregor.

Peter got caught on a gooseberry net by the large brass buttons on his new jacket. He lost his jacket.

Peter jumped into a watercan to hide from Mr. McGregor in the tool shed.

Peter found a locked gate but couldn't get out. He made his way back to where Mr. McGregor was working.

Peter squeezed under the gate and ran quickly home.

Resolution
Peter got home safely and went to bed. Mother gave him chamomile tea.

second and third lessons, the teacher might share the explaining of story structure, thinking aloud, and representing of the elements of story structure in the graphic organizer with students. Finally, in remaining lessons, students would do most of the explaining, thinking aloud, and representing of the elements of story structure in the graphic organizer with the expert guidance of the teacher. Later on, students would be encouraged to make and use graphic organizers of story structure independently to help them understand and remember the narrative texts with which they engage.

Effective Expository Text Structure Instruction. Here again, we begin by selecting an exemplary expository text, perhaps one within the information text genre. This means we want to find an expository text that exemplifies the clear and simple use of only one of the many expository text structures, such as problem–solution or question–answer. For a text to qualify for selection, it must utilize one and only one expository text structure throughout rather than a mix or variety of expository text structures, as many do. A simple information text, *Sand* (Clyne & Griffiths, 2005), serves as our example. This information book is published by Dorling-Kindersley/Celebration Press, part of the Pearson Education Group, and is found in the *I Openers* information text series. This book features an attractive appearance, clear layout, and interesting content for younger and even some older children.

To begin, we consider carefully the physical features of this expository text. We note several important physical features that we make a point of showing to and discussing with children, namely the title, the author, and post-reading follow-up questions at the end of the book. Although not as rich in physical features as some expository books, *Sand* does evidence the use of a single text structure—question–answer—throughout. For example, the book begins with the question "What is sand?" The book also makes good use of spacing, print arrangements, and typographic features. "What is sand?" is printed on a single line at the top of the first page in bold typeface. The answer to the question is at the bottom of the page in regular typeface.

Every question in *Sand* appears at the top of the page in isolation in bold typeface. Answers are all placed on the bottom of the page in regular typeface and relate to an illustrative photograph that helps answer the question. The book also uses black versus white type, depending on the background, color of the page. This use of color leads readers' attention to the answers to the questions in physically obvious ways.

For younger children, a simple graphic organizer using icons along with print can be helpful. For older students, a more complex graphic organizer may include student-generated questions for which they will seek and retrieve answers through reading across a variety of other information texts on the topic of sand, rocks, and soil. Two examples of question–answer graphic organizers for the book *Sand* are shown in Figures 5.10 and 5.11. Figure 5.10 shows a *Sand* graphic organizer for teaching younger students this expository text structure. Figure 5.11 shows a *Sand* graphic organizer for teaching older students about question–answer expository text structure.

Similar to our narrative example, we turn our attention to the issue of scaffolding expository text structure instruction effectively in the classroom. As mentioned earlier, scaffolding refers to gradually releasing the control and responsibility for selecting and using text structure comprehension strategies, beginning with high teacher control and involvement, moving to shared control and involvement between teachers and students, and finally relinquishing to students' independent control over strategy selection and use. This would require multiple lessons such as the one just described using a variety of expository books that implement question–answer text structure, such as *Bridges* (Ring, 2003), *How Do Spiders Live?* (Biddulph & Biddulph, 1992), and others. In the first

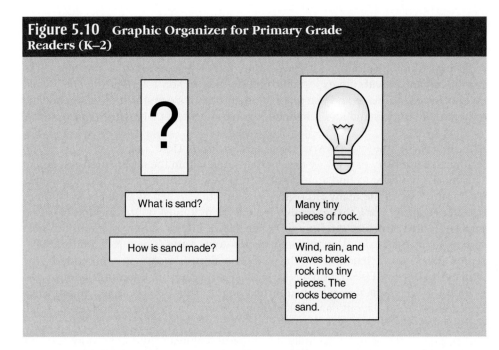

Figure 5.10 Graphic Organizer for Primary Grade Readers (K–2)

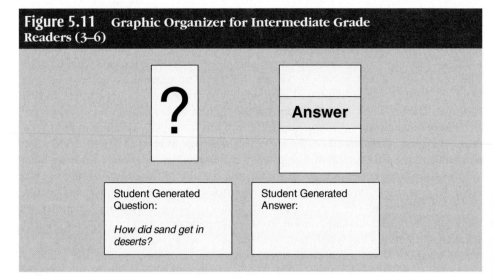

Figure 5.11 Graphic Organizer for Intermediate Grade Readers (3–6)

lesson, the teacher would do most of the explaining, thinking aloud, and representing of the elements of question–answer structure in the graphic organizer. In the second and third lessons, the teacher might share the explaining of question–answer expository text structure, the thinking aloud, and the representing of the elements of question–answer expository text structure in the graphic organizer with students. In subsequent lessons, students would do most of the explaining, thinking aloud, and representing of the elements of question–answer expository text structure in the graphic organizer with the expert guidance of the teacher. Later on, students would be encouraged to make and use graphic organizers of question–answer expository texts independently to help them understand and remember the expository texts they read.

The Activity or Strategies

The third essential component in the RAND Reading Study Group's (2002) definition of reading comprehension is the activity. One of the chief comprehension activities for young readers is learning how to use comprehension strategies to improve their understanding and memory for text. We begin our discussion of comprehension strategies by focusing on one strategy that has long been a mainstay in elementary school classrooms: question asking and answering.

Questions are an integral part of life both in and out of school. From birth, we learn about our world by asking and answering questions. In school, teachers ask questions to guide and motivate children's reading comprehension and to assess the quality of their reading comprehension after reading. Because questions are so much a part of teaching reading comprehension successfully, all teachers must know how to use questioning effectively. We begin with some basic information about the levels of thought required by different kinds of questions.

Asking Questions at Differing Levels of Thinking

During the past several decades, a variety of questioning taxonomies—ordered lists of questions that tap different levels of human thought, such as Bloom's (1956), Barrett's (1972), and Taba's (1975) taxonomies—were published along with impassioned appeals for teachers to ask students more higher-level questions. Figure 5.12 illustrates Bloom's taxonomy.

In addition to simplifying the task of teaching reading comprehension to the act of asking questions at differing levels of thinking, taxonomies were thought to help teachers develop sensitivity to the levels of thinking students would need to use to answer the questions they ask of students.

Others have challenged the idea that asking higher-level questions leads to higher-level thinking abilities (Gall et al., 1975). While much can be and will be argued about asking higher-level questions for some time into the future, the fact is that students will need to answer a great many questions throughout their school life and beyond. Unfortunately, many students are not helped to develop effective strategies for answering or asking their own questions to improve their reading comprehension. Raphael and Pearson (1985) developed a strategy for teaching students how to answer questions asked of them called **Question–Answer Relationships** (Raphael, 1982).

Question–Answer Relationships

Raphael (1982, 1986) and Raphael and Au (2005) describe four question–answer relationships (QARs) that help children identify the connection between the type of question asked and the information sources necessary and available for answering it: (a) right there, (b) think and search, (c) author and you, and (d) on my own.

Instruction using QARs begins by explaining that when students answer questions about reading, there are basically two places they can look for information: in the book and in their head. This concept should be practiced with students by reading aloud a text, asking questions, and having students explain or show where they would look to find their answers. Once students understand the two-category approach, expand the *in the book* category to include *right there* and *think and search*. The distinction between these two categories should be practiced under the guidance of the teacher using several texts and gradually releasing responsibility to students.

Figure 5.12 Bloom's Taxonomy

LITERAL (LOW LEVEL)

KNOWLEDGE – Identification and recall of information

Who, what, when, where, how?
Describe . . .

COMPREHENSION – Organization and selection of facts and ideas.

Retell _____ in your own words.
What is the main idea of _____?

INFERENTIAL LEVEL (HIGHER ORDER THINKING)

APPLICATION – use of facts, rules, principles

How is _____ an example of _____?
How is _____ related to _____?
Why is _____ significant?

ANALYSIS – Separation of a whole into component parts

What are the parts or features of _____?
Classify _____ according to _____.
Outline/diagram/web _____.
How does _____ compare/contrast with _____?
What evidence can you list for _____?

SYNTHESIS – Combinations of ideas to form a new whole

What would you predict/infer from _____?
How would you create/design a new _____?
What might happen if you combined _____ with _____?
What solutions would you suggest for _____?

EVALUATIVE LEVEL (HIGHER ORDER THINKING)

EVALUATION – Development of opinions, judgments, or decisions

Do you agree _____?
What do you think about _____?
What is the most important _____?
How would you prioritize _____?
How would you decide about _____?
What criteria would you use to assess _____?

Raphael (1986) suggests that older students be shown specific strategies for locating the answers to *right there* questions. These include looking in a single sentence or looking in two sentences connected by a pronoun. For *think and search* questions, students can be asked to focus their attention on the structure of the text (cause–effect, problem–solution, listing–example, comparison–contrast, and explanation).

Next, instruction is directed toward two subcategories in the *in my head* category: (a) *author and me,* and (b) *on my own.* Here again, these categories can be practiced as a group by reading a text aloud, answering the questions, and discussing the sources of information. To expand this training, students can be asked to identify the types of questions asked in their basal readers, workbooks, content area texts, and tests as well as to determine the sources of information needed to answer these questions.

Students may be informed that certain types of questions are asked before and after reading a text. For example, questions asked before reading typically require that students activate their own knowledge. Therefore, questions asked before reading will usually be *on my own* questions. However, questions asked after reading will make use of information found in the text. Therefore, questions asked after reading will typically focus on the *think and search* and *author and me* types of questions.

Using the QAR's question–answering training strategy is useful for at least two other purposes. First, it can help teachers examine their own questioning with respect to the types of questions and the information sources students need to use to answer their questions. Second, some teachers may find that by using QARs to monitor their own questioning behaviors, they are asking only *right there* types of questions. This discovery should lead teachers to ask questions that require the use of other information sources.

Students can use QARs to initiate self-questioning before and after reading. They may be asked to write questions for each of the QAR categories and answer these questions. Finally, posters displaying the information in Figure 5.13 can heighten children's and teachers' awareness of the types of questions asked and the information sources available for answering those questions.

Raphael and Pearson (1982) provided evidence that training students to recognize these question–answer relationships resulted in improved comprehension and question–answering behavior. In addition, evidence also shows that teachers find the QAR strategies productive for improving their own questioning behaviors. More recently, Raphael and Au (2005) have shown that training in QARs can have positive effects on students' performance on a variety of local, state, and national reading assessments.

Questioning the Author

Research has shown that many students construct very little meaning from the information they read in expository books and textbooks. Several features in expository texts

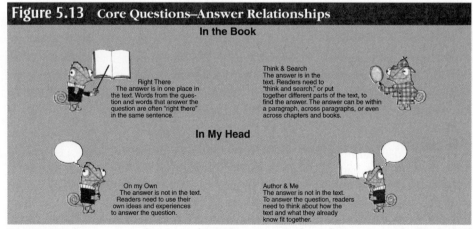

Figure 5.13   Core Questions–Answer Relationships

In the Book

Right There
The answer is in one place in the text. Words from the question and words that answer the question are often "right there" in the same sentence.

Think & Search
The answer is in the text. Readers need to "think and search," or put together different parts of the text, to find the answer. The answer can be within a paragraph, across paragraphs, or even across chapters and books.

In My Head

On my Own
The answer is not in the text. Readers need to use their own ideas and experiences to answer the question.

Author & Me
The answer is not in the text. To answer the question, readers need to think about how the text and what they already know fit together.

From "QAR Enhancing comprehension and test taking across grades and content areas" by T.E. Raphael and K.H. Au. *The Reading Teachers, 59*(3), pp. 206–221. Used by permission of the publisher, McGraw-Hill/Wright Group.

combine to create a number of obstacles for young readers' comprehension of information text. These include (1) incoherence, (2) lack of clear descriptions and explanations, (3) assumption of an unrealistic level of background knowledge, (4) the objective nature of the language used, and (5) the "authority" that places it above criticism (McKeown, Beck, & Worthy, 1993). These "inconsiderate" features of a textbook's organization and content inhibit comprehension, and the textbook's authority causes students to attribute their difficulty in understanding text to their own inadequacies. As a result, some students are reluctant to persist in using their natural problem-solving abilities in the face of these perceptions (Anderson, 1991; Schunk & Zimmerman,1997).

Questioning the author lessons attempt, in a sense, to "'depose' the authority of the book or textbook through actualizing the presence of an author" (McKeown, Beck, & Worthy, 1993, p. 561). Recent research has shown that questioning the author results in increased length and complexity of recalled ideas from text and answers comprehension questions as compared with other forms of book discussions (Sandora, Beck, & McKeown, 1999).

To begin, students are shown examples in information books and textbooks where someone's ideas may not be written as well or as clearly as they might be. Next, the teacher prompts students as they read a book or textbook using a series of questions like the following:

- What is the author trying to tell you?
- Why is the author telling you that?
- Is it said so that you can understand it?

Asking children to search out answers to these questions encourages them to actively engage with the ideas in the text. As children encounter difficulties in understanding the text they are encouraged, again through teacher questioning, to recast the author's ideas in clearer language. Questions used for this purpose include:

- How could the author have said the ideas to make them easier to understand?
- What would you say instead?

Asking children to restate the author's ideas causes them to grapple with the ideas and problems in a text. In this way, children engage with text in ways that successful readers use to make sense of complex ideas presented in texts.

Elaborative Interrogation

Elaborative interrogation is a student-generated questioning intervention. It is especially well-suited to generating and answering questions in information texts. By helping students generate their own "why" questions, active processing of factual reading materials is promoted (National Reading Panel, 2000; Wood, Pressley, & Winne, 1990). By asking and answering their own questions, students link information together into a network of relationships improving both understanding and memory for text information.

It is important that "why" questions be asked about the text in such as way as to orient students to search their prior knowledge for supporting the facts they need to learn—otherwise such questions will not enhance comprehension and memory for text. We apply the elaborative interrogation student-generated questioning strategy to a trade book titled *Ways of Measuring: Then and Now* (Shulman, 2001), in the model lesson shown in Figure 5.14.

Figure 5.14 Example of an Elaborative Interrogation Lesson

Purpose for Learning the Strategy: This strategy will help students relate their own experiences and knowledge to what they read in information texts. By using this strategy, they will improve their understanding of and memory for text information.

Objective: To learn to respond to statements in text as if they were stated as "why" questions.

Teacher Explanation and Modeling: This strategy is begun by the teacher reading a section of text aloud and modeling. The teacher reads the title of the book: *Ways of Measuring: Then and Now.* She asks herself: "Why are ways of measuring today different than in the past?" Her answer might include ideas about in the past people not having scales, rulers, and measuring cups. Next, she reads the sentence: "Long ago, people used their bodies to measure the length of things." She asks herself the "why" question: "Why did people use their bodies to measure things instead of something else?" She reads on: *"Arms and hands were always around when you needed them, and they couldn't get lost. But you can't weigh flour with a hand span, or measure oil with a cubit. For thousands of years, people used stones to weigh things. They used hollow gourds and shells to measure out amounts."* She asks herself: "Why did people in the old days use stones and gourds to measure?"

Guided Application: The teacher says: "Now let's use this strategy together. Manny, please read this statement aloud for the class." Manny reads: "'The old ways of measuring had some problems.'" The teacher forms a "why" question based on the statement. Then she says, "Mariann, please read this statement." Mariann reads: "'The metric system is used almost everywhere in the world except in the United States.'" The teacher generates a "why" question based on the statement: "Why doesn't the United States use the metric system?" She then invites students to use their background knowledge to respond to her question. The teacher says: "Now let's reverse roles." She reads aloud the next statement from the text. "'Using these measurement systems solves a lot of problems.' Who can put together a good "why" question based on this statement?" Benji raises his hand. He asks, "Why do measurement systems solve problems?" Discussion ensues.

Individual Application: The teacher says: "I want you to read the rest of this book. When you get to the end of each page, pick one statement and write a "why" question about it in your notebooks. See if you can answer the question from your own knowledge or experiences. If not, try using the book to answer your question. If neither source can answer your question, save it for our discussion of the book when we are all finished reading. Now, go ahead and read. If you forget what I want you to do, look at this poster for step-by-step directions." The teacher points to the poster at the front on the room on the board.

> *Using the Elaborative Interrogation Strategy*
>
> • Read each page carefully.
> • Stop at the end of each page and pick a statement.
> • Write a "why" question for the statement you pick in your reading notebooks.
> • Think about an answer to the "why" question using your own knowledge and experiences.
> • If you can, write an answer to your "why" question.
> • Read the pages again looking for an answer. Read on to another page to look for the answer.
> • If you can, write an answer to your "why" question.
> • If you can't write an answer to your "why" question, save it for our group discussion after reading.

(continued)

Figure 5.14 (Continued)

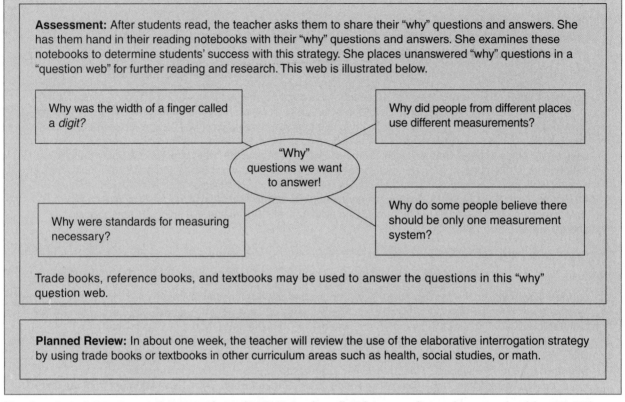

Assessment: After students read, the teacher asks them to share their "why" questions and answers. She has them hand in their reading notebooks with their "why" questions and answers. She examines these notebooks to determine students' success with this strategy. She places unanswered "why" questions in a "question web" for further reading and research. This web is illustrated below.

Why was the width of a finger called a *digit*?

Why did people from different places use different measurements?

"Why" questions we want to answer!

Why were standards for measuring necessary?

Why do some people believe there should be only one measurement system?

Trade books, reference books, and textbooks may be used to answer the questions in this "why" question web.

Planned Review: In about one week, the teacher will review the use of the elaborative interrogation strategy by using trade books or textbooks in other curriculum areas such as health, social studies, or math.

*Based on: Reutzel, D.R., Camperell, K., & Smith, J.A. (2002). Hitting the wall: Helping struggling readers comprehend (pp. 321–353). In C. Collins-Block, L. B. Gambrell, & M. Pressley (Eds.) *Improving comprehension instruction: Advances in research, theory, and classroom practice*. San Francisco, CA: Jossey-Bass.

Menke and Pressley (1994) state that, "answering 'why' questions is as good as constructing images to boost memory for facts, providing the questions are well focused" (p. 644). The elaborative interrogation strategy has been shown to improve readers' comprehension of factual material ranging from elementary school ages to adult. It is recommended that teachers use elaborative interrogation to train students to begin asking their own questions to guide their search for and construction of meaning from information and other expository texts and textbooks.

Comprehension Monitoring and Fix-Ups

The National Reading Panel (2000) found that teaching students to monitor the status of their own ongoing comprehension to determine when it breaks down is one of a handful of scientifically supported, evidence-based comprehension instructional strategies. The act of monitoring one's unfolding comprehension of text is called **metacognition,** or sometimes **metacomprehension.** The ability to plan, check, monitor, revise, and evaluate one's unfolding comprehension is of particular importance in reading. If a reader fails to detect comprehension breakdowns, then she or he will take no action to correct misinterpretations of the text. However, if a reader

Hope Madden/Merrill

expects that text should make sense and has the ability to strategically self-correct comprehension problems, then reading can progress as it should.

Click or Clunk. To help students develop the ability to monitor their own comprehension processes, Carr (1985) suggested a strategy called "click or clunk." This strategy urges readers to reflect at the end of each paragraph or section of reading by stopping and asking themselves if the meaning or message "clicks" for them or goes "clunk." If it clunks, the reader asks what is wrong and what can be done to correct the problem.

Fix-Ups. Although the ability to detect when comprehension breaks down is important, it is equally important to know which strategies to select in repairing broken comprehension and when to use them. Children should be introduced to the options available to them for repairing broken comprehension. Collins and Smith (1980) suggest the following repair strategies for use by readers who experience comprehension failure:

- Ignore the problem and continue reading.
- Suspend judgment for now and continue reading.
- Form a tentative hypothesis, using text information, and continue reading.
- Look back or reread the previous sentence.
- Stop and think about the previously read context; reread if necessary.
- Seek help from the environment, reference materials, or other knowledgeable individuals.

To help students develop a sense for when to select these strategies, teachers may consider using a think-aloud modeling procedure. The teacher begins by reading part of a text aloud, and as she proceeds, comments aloud on her thinking. By revealing to students her thinking, the hypotheses she has formed for the text, and anything that strikes her as difficult or unclear, the teacher demonstrates for students the processes successful readers use to comprehend a text (Duffy, 2003). Next, the teacher reminds students of the click or clunk strategy. Gradually, she releases the responsibility for modeling metacognitive strategies to students during follow-up lessons on metacognitive monitoring. She displays the fix-up or repair strategies listed above along with the click-or-clunk strategy on a wall chart or poster in a prominent place in the classroom and draws students' attention to these strategies throughout the year.

Summarizing

The purpose of summarizing is to extract and succinctly organize the "gist" of a text. Summarizing is important because it helps readers select and store relevant main ideas and details from their reading to form memory structures for text. Many readers do not spontaneously summarize their reading and, as a result, have poor understanding and recall of what they read (Brown, Day, & Jones, 1983).

To begin a lesson on summarizing, we recommend using an information trade book, a story book, or content area textbook along with a chart displaying the steps for producing a summary based on the work of Hare and Borchordt (1984) featured in Figure 5.15.

Distribute sufficient numbers of copies of the text to be read by the group. Have the students silently read the first few passages. Next, on an overhead transparency,

Figure 5.15   Steps for Producing a Summary

1. *Collapse lists.* If there is a list of things, supply a word or phrase for the whole list. For example, if you saw *swimming, sailing, fishing,* and *surfing,* you could substitute *water sports.*
2. *Use topic sentences.* Sometimes authors write a sentence that summarizes the whole paragraph: If so, use that sentence in your summary. If not, you'll have to make up your own topic sentences.
3. *Get rid of unnecessary detail.* Sometimes information is repeated or is stated in several different ways. Some information may be trivial and unnecessary. Get rid of repetitive or trivial information. Summaries should be short.
4. *Collapse paragraphs.* Often, paragraphs are related to each other. For example, some paragraphs simply explain or expand on other paragraphs in a selection. Some paragraphs are more important than others. Join the paragraphs that are related. Important paragraphs should stand alone.
5. *Polish the summary.* When you collapse a lot of information from many paragraphs into one or two paragraphs, the resulting summary sometimes sounds awkward and unnatural. There are several ways to remedy this: add connecting words such as *like* or *because,* or write introductory or closing statements. Another method is to paraphrase the material, this will improve your ability to remember what you read and enable you to avoid plagiarism—using the exact words of the author.

Source: From "Direct Instruction of Summarization Skills" by V. C. Hare and K. M. Borchordt, 1984, *Reading Research Quarterly 20*(1), pp. 62–78. Copyright 1984 by the International Reading Association.

model for students how you would use the five summary rules in Figure 5.14 to produce a summary. After modeling, direct students to finish reading the entire text. Divide the chalkboard into four sections. For example, if you are learning about an animal (say, alligators), your subcategories might be "Description," "Food," "Home," and "Interesting Facts." As the groups read, have students write facts on the chalkboard in each of the four sections.

Next, organize students into groups of five to work on summarizing together. Each student in the group is assigned to take charge of one of the five summary-writing rules shown in Figure 5.15. Circulate around the classroom to assist groups as needed. After reading the selection and working in their groups, students responsible for the topic statement rule in each group should read their topic statement aloud to the other students in the group. Next, have students discuss the facts they have listed at the board, erase duplicates, and restate the remaining main ideas and detail facts in complete sentences. You may want to have students use different colored transparency pens for each of the five summary rules to record their work in the groups. For example, green may be used for lists, red for eliminating unnecessary details, and so on. Share each group's summarizing processes and their summary statement(s) with the entire class on the overhead projector. Be sure to provide additional practice on summarizing throughout the year with other books and gradually release the task of summarizing using all five rules to students for independent use.

If students encounter difficulties initially using the five rules in Figure 5.15, we have found the following procedure by Noyce and Christie (1989) to be helpful. The teacher will need to model this process and then guide students as they apply it in their work. Noyce and Christie (1989) use the four easy steps listed here.

Step 1: Write a topic sentence, that is, one that summarizes the content in general terms. You need to either select one that the author has written or write your own.

Step 2: Delete all unnecessary or irrelevant sentences, words, and other information from the entire passage.

Step 3: After sorting all terms into categories, think of a collective term(s) for those things that fall into the same category.

Step 4: Collapse paragraphs on the same subject down to one when they are largely redundant.

Strategy instruction on how to summarize text has been reported by the National Reading Panel (2000) to be highly effective in promoting children's reading comprehension and as such should be a part of regular comprehension strategy instruction in classrooms from kindergarten on.

The Situational Context

The National Reading Panel (2000) found four conditions that support effective comprehension instruction. First, when teachers provide explicit comprehension strategy instruction by explaining, modeling, guiding, and scaffolding, students are helped toward independence and self-regulated use of comprehension strategies. Research has shown for nearly three decades that explicit or formal comprehension strategy instruction has led to improved student understanding of text and use of information. Second, comprehension strategy instruction works well when readers work together to learn strategies in the context of reading, discussion, and interaction around a variety of text types and genres. Third, children comprehend text more readily when they are motivated to engage in reading. Finally, research indicates that comprehension strategy instruction is optimally effective when readers are taught to orchestrate or coordinate the use of a "set" or "family" of several reading comprehension strategies in interaction with the teacher over multiple texts over extended periods of time. In what follows, we discuss each of the three conditions of effective comprehension instruction.

Explicit Comprehension Strategy Instruction

The primary purpose of an explicit comprehension strategy lesson on comprehension monitoring is twofold: (1) to teach students to clearly understand what is meant by *comprehension monitoring,* and (2) to teach students, through guidance and practice, how to self-monitor, evaluate, self-regulate, and otherwise independently "fix up" their own comprehension problems.

> Some students struggle with reading because they lack information about what they are trying to do and how to do it. They look around at their fellow students who are learning to read [fluently and well] and say to themselves, "How are they doing that?" In short they are mystified about how to do what other students seem to do with ease. (Duffy, 2003, p. 9)

It is typically very difficult for teachers to provide explicit cognitive comprehension strategy explanations on how to monitor one's own construction of meaning from a text. To do so, teachers must become aware of the processes *they* use to monitor their own reading comprehension processes. However, because teachers are already readers who comprehend what they read, they often do not think deeply or systematically about the processes they use to do so (Duffy, 2003). Both information and story texts should be selected for providing explicit comprehension strategy instruction on comprehension monitoring. It is best if books can also be selected that can be read and discussed in a single sitting.

To teach an explicit comprehension strategy lesson such as comprehension monitoring, a framework lesson plan template is needed. Reutzel and Cooter (2007) have developed an explicit lesson framework called **EMS—*E*xplanation, *M*odel, *S*caffold.** Explanations include what is to be learned, where and when it is to be used, and why it is important. Modeling requires teachers to demonstrate, often through think-alouds with a text, how an aspect of comprehension monitoring, like using fix-ups, is to be done. Finally, teachers gradually release through a series of guided practice experiences the reading of a text to individual student application through a process we call "Me (teacher model)—You and Me (teacher and student share the monitoring task, reading with the whole class or with partners)—and Me (student monitors reading comprehension independently)." A template explicit cognitive comprehension strategy lesson on comprehension monitoring is found in Figure 5.16. This model demonstrates each of the parts of the EMS explicit cognitive comprehension strategy lesson.

Remember, as unpopular as what we are about to say is with many teachers, to begin the process of becoming an explicit comprehension strategy teacher one must write out a lesson plan. In fact, this is the *only* way for you to become an explicit comprehension strategy teacher! Doing so helps you in at least three different ways. Writing a lesson plan helps you to (1) think through what to say and how to say it, (2) internalize the lesson template for explicit instruction, and (3) internalize the language necessary for explicit instruction.

Cooperative/Interactive Comprehension Discussions. Research reported by the National Reading Panel (2000) found that cooperative, collaborative, and highly

Figure 5.16   Explicit Comprehension-Monitoring Strategy Lesson Plan Template

Objective *Children will monitor their own comprehension processes and use fix-up strategies to repair broken comprehension processes when necessary.*

Supplies
- Exemplary story or information text

Explain

What
- Today, boys and girls, we are going to be learning about how to monitor or check our understanding or comprehension as we read. The first step in learning to monitor our understanding or comprehension as we read is to learn to stop periodically and ask ourselves a few simple questions like "Is this making sense? Am I getting it? Do I understand what this is about?"

Why
- We need to monitor our comprehension or understanding when we read because what we read should make sense to us. If it doesn't make sense, there is no point in continuing to read. Monitoring our comprehension while reading helps us to be aware of whether or not we understand or are making sense of what we read. We can just keep on reading if we understand, or stop and do something to help us understand if the text is not making sense to us.

When/Where
- Whenever we read, we should monitor or think about whether or not we are understanding or comprehending what we are reading.

Model
- I am going to read aloud the first two pages of our book *Volcano!* (Jewell Hunt, 2004). After reading the first two pages, I am going to stop and monitor my comprehension. I will think out loud about the questions I should ask when I stop to monitor my comprehension: "Is this making sense? Am I getting it? Do I understand what this is about?" I've written these monitoring steps (stop and question) on a poster to help me remember. I have also written the three comprehension-monitoring questions on the poster to help me remember. After thinking about these questions for a minute, I will answer the question with a yes or no. If my answer is yes, I will continue to read. If my answer is no, I will have to stop for now because I don't yet know what I should do when it doesn't make sense to me. Notice that I have also put YES and NO on our poster to help me know what to do when I answer yes or no to the three comprehension-monitoring questions. Okay. Here I go.

Volcano!*
There are many volcanoes in the world.
About 1,500 of them are active.
That means that they are erupting, or they might erupt someday.
An erupting volcano is quite a sight!
Rocks and ash shoot up.
Lava races down.
Smelly gases fill the air.
(STOP!)

"Am I getting it? Is it making sense? Do I understand what this is about?" Yes, I think I do. There are loads of volcanoes all over. Some of them are active, meaning they might erupt. An example of an active volcano is Mt. Etna. When volcanoes erupt they send rocks, ash, lava, and gases into the air. So, if what I have read makes sense and I answer yes, I just keep on reading. After I read a few more pages, I should STOP to monitor my comprehension again.
> (Repeat this cycle with a few more pages and one or two more stopping points for modeling.)

(continued)

Figure 5.16 (Continued)

Scaffolding (ME, YOU & ME, YOU)

Whole Group (Me & You)

- Now that I have shown you how I STOP and monitor my comprehension, I want to share this task with you. Let's read three more pages. At the end of the three pages, I want you to call out, "STOP!" After I stop, I want you to ask me the three monitoring questions on our poster: "Is this making sense? Am I getting it? Do I understand what this is about?" I will answer YES or NO. If I answer yes, tell me what to do. If I answer no, then tell me I will have to quit reading until we learn what to do tomorrow. Okay. Here we go.

Volcanoes come in different sizes and shapes. Some volcanoes have steep sides. They rise high above the land around them.
Other volcanoes are very wide.
Their sides are not so steep.
This type of volcano may look like a regular mountain. But it isn't!
(STOP!)

Small Group/ Partners/Teams (Me & You)

- Now that we have shared the process of STOPPING and monitoring our comprehension as a group when we read, I want you to share this monitoring process with a partner. I am going to give you either the number 1 or the number 2. Remember your number. (Count heads by one and two.) We are going to read three more pages in our story. At the end of the three pages, I want partner #1 to call out, "STOP!" Then I want partner #2 to ask partner #1 the three monitoring questions on our poster: "Is this making sense? Am I getting it? Do I understand what this is about?" Then partner #1 will answer the questions asked by partner #2 with a yes or no. If partner #1 answers yes, partner #2 tells him/her to keep on reading. If partner #1 answers no, then partner #2 tells him/her to quit reading until we learn what to do tomorrow. Okay, ready.

Volcanoes can change the land quickly.
In 1980, a volcano in the state of Washington erupted. Its top blew off with a roar.
Mud raced down its sides.
Trees crashed, and animals fled.
But the land was not bare for long.
The ash from volcanoes helps things grow.
Today, Mount St. Helens is full of new life.
(STOP!)

Individual (You)

- Today we have learned that when we read we should STOP every few pages and monitor our comprehension or understanding by asking ourselves three questions. Today, during small-group reading or in paired reading, I would like for you to practice monitoring comprehension with a friend and/or by yourself as you read. STOP every few pages and ask yourself the three questions on our poster. Then decide if you should keep on reading or quit reading and wait until tomorrow, when we will learn about what to do when what you read isn't making sense.

Assess

- Pass out a bookmark that reminds students to stop every few pages while reading and ask the three questions. List the three questions on the bookmark to remind students about them.

Reflect

- What went well in the lesson?
- How would you change the lesson?

---

* Excerpted with permission from *Volcano!* from Reading Power Works by Sundance/Newbridge Educational Publishers, L.L.C.

interactive discussions where readers work together to learn comprehension strategies while interacting with each other and the teacher around a variety of texts is highly effective. There are multiple ways to create and sustain a cooperative and interactive classroom conducive to discussing texts. One effective approach for carrying on cooperative, collaborative, and highly interactive discussions of text to support reading comprehension instruction is called *text talk*.

Text Talk. Effective reading comprehension instruction, at least in the primary grades, is also dependent upon developing younger children's oral language vocabularies and language structures. Beck and McKeown (2001) have adapted their questioning-the-author strategy for intermediate grades for use in the early grades. They refer to this adaptation for simultaneously developing younger children's reading comprehension and oral language as **text talk.** Beck and McKeown (2001) recommend that teachers of younger students read aloud books that have stimulating and intellectually challenging content. Doing so allows younger students to grapple with difficult and complex ideas, situations, and concepts in text even when their word recognition abilities are quite limited. Talk around texts should give students a chance to reflect, think, and respond beyond simple answers to simple questions. Talk should be analytic, requiring that students think deeply about the content of the text and the language (Dickinson & Smith, 1994).

When they observed children talking about texts read aloud to them, Beck and McKeown (2001) found that children often talked about the pictures or related something from their background knowledge rather than focusing their attention and talk on the content of the text or the language in the text. Similarly, teachers' talk during read-aloud experiences in the classroom often focused on clarifying unfamiliar vocabulary by asking a question such as, "Does anyone know what a tsunami is?" The other practice among teachers talking with children about text was to ask a question directly from the language, such as, "When the little red hen asked the goose, the dog, and the cat for help, what did they say?" These types of interactions constrain children's construction of meaning for the whole text to local issues of understanding. Text talk was developed to help teachers further students' comprehension as well as to promote greater use of oral language in elaborated responses to text during discussion.

Text talk has six components: (1) selection of texts, (2) initial questions, (3) follow-up questions, (4) pictures, (5) background knowledge, and (6) vocabulary. For our discussion here, we will use the book *White Socks Only* by Evelyn Coleman (1996). This book has a challenging story line that centers on the theme of racial discrimination. When reading this book, we can focus on several important text-related concepts, including fairness, equality, and social justice. To begin our text talk, we will construct a series of open-ended questions that we can use to initiate discussion with students at several points in the story:

- When Grandma was telling her story, she said, "I had two eggs hid in my pockets. Not to eat mind you. But to see if what folk said was true." What do you think she was going to do with those eggs in her pocket?
- What is a "chicken man" in this story?
- When Grandma got to the courthouse, she broke the egg against the horse's leg. Why do you think she did this?
- What do you think "frying an egg on cement" means?

- There was a sign on the water fountain that read, "Whites only." What do you think Grandma thought this sign meant?

Next, we need to think of a few follow-up questions that will help children elaborate on their answers to our initial, open-ended questions:

- Grandma couldn't understand why the white man pushed her away from the water fountain and asked her if she couldn't read. After all, she was wearing her white socks when she stepped up to the fountain to get a drink. Why was the white man mad at Grandma?
- What does "whites only" mean?
- Why did people move aside when the chicken man came into town?
- What was the fight about between the white man and the black people in the town?

After reading each page in the book displaying the drinking fountain with the sign "Whites Only," we would draw students' attention to the picture on these pages, asking them to explain what the sign means. We might ask questions like: Why were the black people in this story ignoring the sign and stepping up to the drinking fountain to take a drink? Why did the white man whip the black people with his belt? What happened to Grandma when the chicken man showed up? Why did they take the sign "Whites Only" down? Remember that rich, text-related discussions occur *before* showing pictures in text talks. Seeing the pictures after reading and discussing the text will take some getting used to for younger children, but they will soon come to expect it and pay greater attention to the linguistic and meaning content of the text.

When children bring up their background knowledge in response to questions, teachers have found it best to acknowledge their comments by repeating back or rephrasing what the child has said, and then moving discussion back to the text content. For example, a child might respond to the question "What does 'whites only' mean" with the comment "My grandpa says he eats only the whites from the eggs because it's better for his heart." The teacher might say, "Yes, I have heard that eating egg whites can be better for your heart. But why do you think they would put a sign that reads, "Whites Only" on a drinking fountain in the middle of town?"

An integral part of an effective text talk lesson is developing children's oral language vocabulary. Beck and McKeown (2001) recommend that vocabulary words be selected from the text that seem likely to be unfamiliar to young readers but that represent concepts they can identify with and use in normal conversation (p. 18). Words from our story, *White Socks Only*, that meet these criteria include *slinking, prancing, bandanna, fumbled,* and *snorted.* What seems to work best for vocabulary instruction is to create a chart of the words from the story along with their meanings, examples, and attributes. Then the teacher can keep track of the times during the day students read, say, or hear the words on the chart. Points can be awarded to individual students or teams for finding, saying, or hearing the words on the chart to create motivation for learning and using new vocabulary.

In summary, the keys to a successful text talk lesson are to (1) keep important ideas in the text as the focus of the discussion, (2) monitor length and quality of students's responses during the discussion, (3) scaffold the ideas of students toward constructing the meaning of the whole text, and (4) encourage students to extend their use of oral language to express the meanings they have gained from the read-aloud experience. Reading aloud can be done by most literate adults, but taking full advantage of the read-aloud experience to develop children's comprehension and use of language is demanding and complex. We have found that it is best to write out a lesson plan for initial text talk lessons. After writing and implementing several lessons, the format, content, and questioning routines will become a more natural and regular part of your teaching repertoire.

Affective Responses: Interpreting and Elaborating Meaning

Discussion and dialog are critical aspects of effective comprehension instruction (Gambrell & Almasi, 1996). One widely recognized and recommended approach to discussion of and dialog about text is called **reader response,** which invites students to take a much more active role (Bleich, 1978; Rosenblatt, 1978, 1989, 2004). Reader response theories suggest there are many possible meanings in a text, depending on the reader's background and interpretation of that text. Rosenblatt's (1978) transactional theory describes reading as a carefully orchestrated relationship between the reader and the text.

Rosenblatt (1978) also described two stances readers may choose in focusing their attention during reading: efferent and aesthetic. When readers focus their attention on information to be remembered from reading a text, they are taking an efferent stance. When readers adopt an aesthetic stance, they draw on past experiences, connect these experiences to the text, often savor the beauty of the literary art form, and become an integral participant in the unfolding events of the text.

> **Getting to Know English Learners**
> Reader response techniques along with literature circles and other "alternative" ways of interpreting and elaborating meaning give ELs a chance to express their understandings in unique ways, such as making a "wanted poster" or illustrating a book.

Discussion of or dialog about texts in small groups often takes place in **literature circles** or **book clubs** that lead students into **grand conversations** about books (Daniels, 1994; McMahon & Raphael, 1997; Peterson & Eeds, 1990; Tompkins, 2006). Grand conversations about books motivate students to extend, clarify, and elaborate their own interpretations of the text as well as to consider alternative interpretations offered by peers.

To initiate a literature circle, begin by selecting four or five books that will engender interest and discussion among students. Next, give a book talk on each of the four or five titles selected, enthusiastically presenting and describing each book to the students. Then, ask students to individually select their top three book choices they want to read. Give each student her first choice. If too many students want the same title, go to each student's second choice as you compile the assignments list. This system works well, because students always know that they get to read a book of their own choosing. After books are distributed the next day, give the students a large block of uninterrupted reading time in class to read. At the beginning of the year, students can read about 20 minutes without undue restlessness. However, later in the year children can often sustain free reading for up to one full hour.

As students complete several hours of independent reading, each literature circle meets on a rotating basis for about 20 minutes with the teacher. Group members discuss and share their initial reactions to the book. We have found that meeting with one to two literature circles per day—with a maximum of two days independent reading between meetings—works quite well.

Based on the group discussion, an assignment is given to the group to extend the discussion of the book into their interpretive media (i.e., writing, art, drama, and so on). Each member of the literature circle works on this assignment before returning to the group for a second meeting. This sequence of reading and working on an extension response assignment repeats until the entire book is completed. We recommend that the first extension assignment focus on personal responses and connections with the book. Subsequent assignments can focus on understanding literary elements (i.e., characterization, point of view, story elements, role of the narrator, and so on). At the conclusion of the book, the literature circle meets to determine a culminating project (Reutzel & Cooter, 2000; Zarillo, 1989). This project captures the group's interpretation and feelings about the entire book as demonstrated in a mural, story map, diorama, character wanted posters, and so on.

There are many ways to invite students to respond to texts they read. One of the most common is to ask children to write in a response journal (Parsons, 1990). We have developed a listing of affective responses to text that represent both aesthetic and efferent stances as described by Rosenblatt (1978) in Figure 5.17.

Figure 5.17   Alternative Affective Responses to Books

1. Prepare a condensed or simplified version of the text to read aloud to younger readers.
2. Draw a map of the journey of characters in a story.
3. Talk to your teacher or a peer about the book.
4. Make a "Wanted" poster for a character in the text.
5. Make a poster based on an information book.
6. Select a part of the book to read aloud to others.
7. Send a letter to your parents, a friend, or your teacher telling about a book and why they should read it.
8. Write a classified newspaper ad for a book.
9. Rewrite a story or part of a story as a Reader's Theater.
10. Make overhead transparencies about the story to use on the overhead projector.
11. Make a PowerPoint slide computer presentation about an information book.
12. Make a character report card on your favorite character.
13. Make a passport application as your favorite character.
14. Write a "Dear Abby" column as your favorite character.
15. Write a missing persons report about a story character.
16. Draw a part of the book and ask others to tell about what part of the story is illustrated.
17. Write a newspaper headline for a book or story.
18. Write a newspaper report for a story character or about information you have learned in an information book.
19. Write to the author to describe your responses to a book.
20. Illustrate a book using a variety of art media or techniques.
21. Write a letter to the librarian suggesting why he or she should or should not recommend a book to someone.
22. Study about the author and write a brief biography.
23. Compose a telegram about the book to tell someone why he or she must read this book.
24. Write a TV commercial and videotape it.
25. Plan a storytelling session for kindergarten children.
26. Interview a story character and write the interview.
27. Compare and contrast characters, settings, or facts in a book using a Venn diagram.
28. Construct a game of Trivial Pursuit using facts in an information book.
29. Construct a game of Password using clues about characters or events in a story.
30. Compose an imaginary diary that might be kept by a book character.

Multiple-Strategies Reading Comprehension Instruction

Although teaching comprehension strategies one at a time explicitly to students has been shown to be effective (Duffy, 2003; National Reading Panel, 2000), students also need to learn how to effectively orchestrate, coordinate, and self-regulate the application of many comprehension strategies to construct meaning when reading a variety of texts (El-Dinary, 2002; National Reading Panel, 2000; Pressley, 2002; Reutzel, Smith, & Fawson, 2005). Real readers do not use comprehension strategies one at a time; they do not use a single strategy for weeks at a time, as these are sometimes taught to students; and they do not apply a single comprehension strategy while reading an entire text. Teaching children to self-regulate their comprehension through the coordination and use of multiple comprehension strategies is exceedingly rare in U.S. classrooms, especially in the primary grades (El-Dinary, 2002; Pearson & Duke, 2002; Stahl, 2004). The rarity of collaborative multiple-strategies-comprehension instruction is largely the result of the difficulty and complexity of providing such instruction. Descriptive research by El-Dinary (2002) and Pressley et al. (1991) showed that acquiring the ability to teach the simultaneous use of multiple comprehension strategies required up to three years of practice before competency was achieved. Regardless of when or where teachers help students to self-regulate the application of multiple comprehension strategies during reading and discussion of texts, there are three important conditions that need to be in place (El-Dinary, 2002; Palincsar, 2003).

> **Getting to Know English Learners**
> Again, a highly interactive setting in the classroom is an ideal place for ELs to acquire language.

First, teaching for self-regulation requires teachers to gradually scaffold the responsibility and authority for determining what is worth knowing in a text or how the text might be interpreted, starting with the teacher's total control, moving to a shared control between teacher and students, and finally progressing to students' independent control. Second, multiple-comprehension-strategies instruction focuses on the *process* of constructing meaning from text rather than on the *product* of that construction. This means that teachers make explicit for students, usually through using think-aloud modeling, how one goes about making decisions about what is worth knowing in a text or how a text might be interpreted. The teacher must then make sure that students actually begin to adopt, adapt, and apply these reading comprehension strategies in their own reading. Finally, teachers must model for students in a collaborative, highly interactive setting how to strategically orchestrate, coordinate, and apply a collection of reading comprehension strategies to the comprehension of text. It is important for teachers to understand and convey to students that learning reading comprehension strategies is a means to an end and not an end in and of itself. Reading comprehension strategies are essential tools for constructing meaning with text, checking on one's own understanding, and prompting one to take certain actions when experiencing difficulty in understanding a text (Palincsar, 2003). In summary, teaching multiple reading comprehension strategies requires a highly interactive, collaborative social setting for discussing text. Teachers need to promote independence through explicitly showing students how to select and apply each and every reading comprehension strategy in the set of multiple strategies. This means starting by teaching each strategy explicitly and then quickly moving to combine the use of the entire set of strategies when reading a text. This means that teachers need to explicitly and interactively model how to strategically coordinate multiple strategies while interacting around texts over time. And finally, teachers gradually release the responsibility and authority for using multiple strategies in collaborative settings to the students themselves while interacting over texts (El-Dinary, 2002; Palincsar, 2003).

In order to illustrate how to teach multiple reading comprehension strategies, let us consider the case of Mr. Summo, a fifth-grade teacher, who has taught for seven years in a low-achieving, low-income school in a southeastern city using reciprocal teaching.

Reciprocal Teaching. In 1984, Palincsar and Brown designed an instructional procedure called **reciprocal teaching (RT)** for students who struggled with comprehending text. RT makes use of a set of four reading comprehension strategies to enhance students' reading comprehension. The RT instructional process typically involves teachers and students in a discussion or dialog about text. The purpose of the discussion is for teachers and students to work together to co-construct the meaning of the text (Palincsar, 2003). Any discussion between teachers and students is supported by the consistent application of the four RT comprehension strategies: (1) predicting, (2) question generating, (3) clarifying, and (4) summarizing. When first using RT in the classroom, teachers explain and model the application of the four RT comprehension strategies while reading and thinking aloud over small text segments, usually paragraphs. Over time, however, teachers gradually progress to larger units of text and release the responsibility for using the four RT strategies independently to students. Prior to providing a classroom example of reciprocal teaching, we describe in a bit more detail the four RT strategies.

Predicting requires that students hypothesize or make a "best guess" based on their background knowledge of the topic, theme, text type, or other cursory information available to them from previewing a text. This information includes such variables as reading headings, chapter titles, pictures, or illustrations, boxed items, and so on. When predicting, students usually anticipate what might happen next, the order that events may take, or even the knowledge or information they expect to be able to learn from reading a text. Using a graphic organizer to facilitate predictions has also been shown to have positive effects on students' predictions and comprehension of text (Meyers, 2006; Oczkus, 2003, Reutzel & Fawson, 1989, 1991).

Question generating reinforces the summarizing strategy, according to one of RT's authors (Palincsar, 2003). Formulating appropriate questions is difficult, as we have previously discussed.

Clarifying, according to Palincsar (2003), is a particularly important strategy for working with children who have come to believe that reading is all about saying the words correctly and who do not monitor their understanding of text. When children are taught to clarify the meaning of text, their attention is directed toward unknown vocabulary words, unclear referent terms, and unfamiliar concepts or text organizations. When they encounter difficulty understanding a text or term, they are taught to identify what is causing the problem and take affirmative steps to "fix up" their comprehension difficulties.

Summarizing involves students in identifying, in proper sequence, the important ideas found within a text. They are asked to sort through many details and come up with the most important ideas through paraphrasing and integrating important ideas in sentences, paragraphs, and across the entire text. For example, if students have read a narrative text, they may summarize it by using story structure—setting, problem, events, and resolution. On the other hand, if students have read an expository text, they may summarize the important ideas by using headings, subheadings, and important related details in the proper sequence. Students need to pay attention to the most important ideas in the text as well as the order in which those ideas are presented. Research by Rinehart, Stahl, and Erickson (1986) has shown that summarizing improves students' reading comprehension of fiction and nonfiction texts.

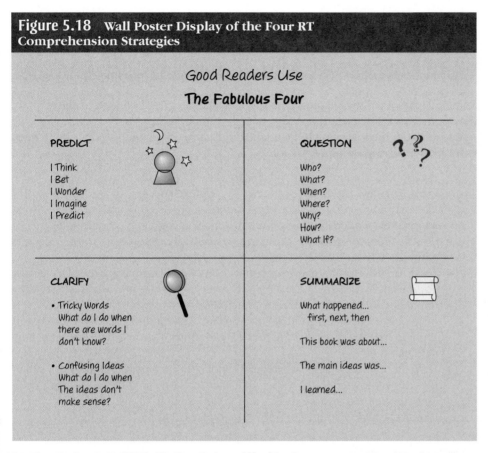

Figure 5.18 Wall Poster Display of the Four RT Comprehension Strategies

Good Readers Use
The Fabulous Four

PREDICT

I Think
I Bet
I Wonder
I Imagine
I Predict

QUESTION

Who?
What?
When?
Where?
Why?
How?
What If?

CLARIFY

• Tricky Words
  What do I do when
  there are words I
  don't know?

• Confusing Ideas
  What do I do when
  The ideas don't
  make sense?

SUMMARIZE

What happened...
  first, next, then

This book was about...

The main ideas was...

I learned...

Based on Oczkus, L. D. (2003). *The Four Reciprocal Teaching Strategies*. In Reciprocal Teaching at work (pp. 13–28). Newark, DE: *International Reading Association*.

We recommend that a poster or wall chart be produced and displayed showing the four RT comprehension strategies. (See Figure 5.18).

Research on the effects of using reciprocal teaching has been summarized in a meta-analysis by Rosenshine and Meister (1994). These researchers analyzed 16 studies where RT was compared with traditional basal reader instruction, explicit instruction in reading comprehension, and reading to answer questions. These researchers found that using RT produced generally superior outcomes when compared to the other comprehension or reading instructional conditions. Effects favoring RT ranged from about 10 percent to 30 percent difference in students' comprehension performance. They also determined that neither the number of RT sessions nor the number of students in the groups seemed to significantly affect the positive outcomes of using RT on students' reading comprehension performance. And finally, Palincsar and Brown (1984) found that the collection of four strategies improved students' comprehension more than the use of any single strategy selected and used in isolation from among the four RT strategies. Hence the collection or set of four RT comprehension strategies taught was more powerful than teaching any single strategy drawn from among the four RT comprehension strategies for the same length of time.

How Can Reading Comprehension Instruction Be Adapted to Meet Diverse Student Needs?

Some adaptation of the reading comprehension strategies discussed in this chapter may be necessary to meet the varied needs of students in your classroom. We urge you to consider the following recommendations for working with students who need extra help in reading comprehension:

- Ensure that students can read the text fluently to allow availability of sufficient cognitive processing capacity for comprehension.
- Use dialog, discussion, pictures, diagrams, charts, and graphics liberally to supplement understanding of text materials and strategy applications.
- Use flexible, cooperative grouping to allow all children to learn from and with others.
- Focus on developing deep conceptual knowledge domains as well as literary appreciation.
- Capitalize on students' interests and abilities.
- Make connections to students' background knowledge and experiences.
- Provide increased scaffolding and extended instructional time for struggling students.
- Help all readers achieve self-regulation of comprehension, motivation, strategies, and knowledge through explicit instruction, modeling, selecting challenging but achievable tasks and texts, setting goals and performance standards, and engaging in self-evaluation.

What Can Families and Communities Do to Develop Children's Reading Comprehension?

Although families usually do not have the expertise to provide explicit reading comprehension strategies instruction and guided practice, they can do a great deal to facilitate children's reading comprehension. For years now, Allington (2006) has insisted that children need to read a lot to get good at reading! Families are in an ideal position to facilitate wide reading and discussion of text. As teachers, we can provide families with both access to reading materials and structure for facilitating discussion and interaction around texts.

Richgels and Wold (1998) have designed the *Three for the Road* program to involve parents in choosing one or more books to read and discuss with their children at home from among three "leveled" books. These leveled books are placed in a backpack that is sent home to parents with their children. The three books selected in each backpack represent a variety of themes, including fantasy, comedy, math mania, adventure, ABCs, and sing-along. The three levels of books included in each backpack are at the "easiest," "in-between," and "most challenging" levels for the student's grade level. The backpack includes a letter to parents as shown in Figure 5.19. This letter may be easily adapted to suit the needs of parents and children in grades other than first.

Getting to Know English Learners

Where possible, provide the letter in multiple languages to meet the needs of ELs' parents.

Figure 5.19 Parent Letter from *Three for the Road*

Dear First-Grade Parents,

Beginning next week, the first graders will be taking home our "Three for the Road" backpacks. The packs are designed to foster enjoyment of children's literature and to nurture lifelong reading habits. We encourage your partnership in reading by sharing these stories and your responses together.

During the year, the A-B-C Pack, Adventure Pack, Comedy Pack, Fantasy Pack, Math Mania Pack, and Sing-Along Pack will rotate in the first grades. Your child will take a pack home once in the next 4 to 5 weeks. Please return the pack to school the next morning after you have helped your child recheck all of the contents on the inside pocket list. In this way, every child will have a chance to take home a class pack once each month.

Since your child may choose to read all or only some of the books included, please try to set aside a special reading time. First graders love to make choices about their reading and may ask a parent to read aloud, to read along with them, or to listen to them read alone. A black journal is also included for students' and parents' written comments and illustrations about meaningful characters or preferred story parts. Check the inside cover of the journal for parent and child response ideas. You may also choose how you would like to respond. Sock puppets are furnished to support language and literacy development. To encourage story responses, you may consider asking, "Which character seems most like the purple puppet?" Or your child may want to "role play" a favorite person or animal by making the puppet "talk" like the story character.

Whatever activities you choose, make this a relaxed and enjoyable experience in reading, from parent read-alouds to rereading children's favorite parts.

We thank you for your support and hope you enjoy our Three for the Road packs!

Your Partners in Reading at _____ School.

Printed with Permission. Richgels, D. J., & Wold, L. S. (1998). Literacy on the road: Backpacking partnerships between school and home. *The Reading Teacher, 52*(1), pp. 18–29.

Parents are given several ways to respond to and discuss the books with their children within each themed backpack. Child responses include writing or drawing about (1) whatever they wanted in relation to the book, (2) their favorite part, (3) how the book reminded them of something else, and (4) how these three books were alike or different. Parents can also respond by writing and drawing about (1) something of interest to them in the books, and (2) something they learned with their child from this activity.

The *Three for the Road* parent involvement program as described by Richgel and Wold is an easy-to-implement approach to extending students' opportunities to read widely, to interact meaningfully with their parents or caregivers, and to choose how many books to read and how to respond at home. When put into use in one Illinois school, the *Three for the Road* program was widely accepted and used by parents to partner with schools and teachers in providing reading materials and text talk in the home.

Summary

Comprehension is intentional thinking during which meaning is constructed through interactions between texts and readers. Comprehending a text involves two phases, a construction and an integration phase. In phase one of this process, one constructs meaning from text and in the second phase one integrates this newly constructed knowledge into the existing prior knowledge network. Monitoring and assessing children's development of comprehension is an important activity to help you, the teacher, select appropriate comprehension strategy instruction and other comprehension instructional supports. Reading comprehension is developed through activating and adding to students' background knowledge, explicit teacher-led comprehension strategy instruction, and by helping students coordinate a set or family of comprehension strategies to construct meaning through rich discussions and interactions around a variety of text structures and genres. Struggling readers and, in fact, all young readers benefit from increased scaffolding to support comprehension development including demonstrations, pictures, diagrams, charts, collaborating with other students, deepening students' breadth and depth of conceptual knowledge, and capitalizing on students' interests and motivations. Finally, families and communities can read and discuss appropriately challenging, themed books of interest as found in the *Three for the Road* program to add to children's background knowledge and develop their abilities to think and talk about a variety of texts.

Classroom Applications

1. Make a poster showing steps students can take to produce a text summary.
2. Select a popular children's story. Parse the story into its story structure parts: setting, characters, problem, goal, events, and resolution. Make a story map like the one shown in this chapter.
3. Summarize the Report of the National Reading Panel (2000) describing its findings on text comprehension. Make a poster displaying these major findings.
4. In small groups, examine several narrative and expository texts. With your peers, discuss how to activate or build students' background knowledge before reading these texts.
5. Organize into literature circle groups. Examine a set of children's books to read as a group. Use reciprocal teaching strategies to discuss one chapter of the book during class.

Recommended Readings

Almasi, J. F. (2003). *Teaching strategic processes in reading.* New York: Guilford Press.

Blachowicz, C., & Ogle, D. (2001). *Reading comprehension: Strategies for independent learners.* New York: Guilford Press.

Boyles, N. N. (2004). *Constructing meaning through kid-friendly comprehension strategy instruction.* Gainesville, FL: Maupin House.

Bransford, J. D., Brown, A. L., & Cocking, R. R. (2000). *How people learn: Brain, mind, experience, and school.* Washington, DC: National Academy Press.

Carr, E., Aldinger, L., & Patberg, J. (2004). *Teaching comprehension: A systematic and practical framework with lessons and strategies.* New York: Scholastic, Inc.

Collins-Block, C., Rodgers, L. L., & Johnson, R. B. (2004). *Comprehension process instruction: Creating reading success in grades K–3.* New York: Guilford Press.

Israel, S. E., Collins-Block, C., Bauserman, K. L., & Kinnucan-Welsch, K. (2005). *Metacognition in literacy learning: Theory, assessment, instruction, and professional development.* Mahwah, NJ: Lawrence Erlbaum Associates.

McLaughlin, M. (2003). *Guided comprehension in primary grades.* Newark, DE: International Reading Association.

McLaughlin, M., & Allen, J. B. (2002). *Guided comprehension: A teaching model for grades 3–8.* Newark, DE: International Reading Association.

Ockzus, L. (2004). *Super 6 comprehension strategies: 35 lessons and more for reading success.* Norwood, MA: Christopher-Gordon.

Owocki, G. (2003). *Comprehension: Strategic instruction for K–3 students.* Portsmouth, NH: Heinemann.

Paris, S. G., & Stahl, S. A. (2005). *Children's reading comprehension and assessment.* Mahwah, NJ: Lawrence Erlbaum Associates.

Pinnell, G. S., & Scharer, P. L. (2003). *Teaching for comprehension in reading: Grades K–2.* New York: Scholastic, Inc.

Spiegel, D. L. (2005). *Classroom discussion.* New York: Scholastic, Inc.

Sweet, A. P., & Snow, C. E. (2003). *Rethinking reading comprehension.* New York: Guilford Press.

6

Assessment

Chapter Questions

1. What are the principles of effective classroom reading assessment?

2. What are the four purposes of classroom reading assessment? What is an example of each?

3. What commercial reading tests are available for classroom use?

4. What is *student* and *classroom profiling*? How is profiling used to form needs-based reading groups?

5. What is meant by "IF–THEN Thinking"?

Great Teaching Begins with Assessment!

When I was in my second year of teaching, I moved to a new school in order to teach third grade—my dream job. The other three third-grade teachers at Mt. Juliet Elementary School were smart and welcoming as we began planning for our new year. One problem, they explained, was that we would have almost 120 students and little, if any, assessment information about our students' reading abilities and needs. One teacher asked, "Bob, since you're still fresh from college, what did they teach you about beginning-of-the-year reading assessment?"

I broke into a cold sweat as I wracked my brain for some semblance of an intelligent thought. Then I remembered something. "One thing I have used is an informal reading inventory. It's a published reading test that teachers can use to determine students' overall reading level, how well they comprehend what they read, and how well they deal with phonics and other word attack skills."

"Have you got one with you?" asked Ms. Holden, a veteran teacher whom everyone seemed to admire.

"Yes," I responded, "and I had a chance to use it with quite a few of my fourth-grade children last year, and during summer school."

That did it. Before I knew it, my colleagues had elected me to screen *all* third graders at Mt. Juliet Elementary using my trusty informal reading inventory and chart their strengths and needs so that we could plan small-group instruction. (They agreed, as their part of the bargain, to take my students into their classes mornings of the first week of school so that I could test each child one at a time.)

In the end, the plan worked as a starting point for our reading instruction. The data from my initial screening helped us group children according to their reading needs *across* all of our classrooms. This experience was an epiphany for me. I saw first-hand the power assessment gives us to provide every child, from the first days of school, the reading instruction he or she needs.

—*RBC*

Reading assessment is the tool that informs your teaching. In Chapter 1 we identify classroom reading assessment as one of the "pillars" of effective reading programs. In Chapters 2 through 5 we explain how key assessment strategies are used to plan instruction in such areas as phonics, vocabulary, reading comprehension, fluency, and so forth. These assessment strategies help teachers know which reading skills each child already has and which he or she has yet to develop. Assessment happens in effective classrooms before, during, and after instruction has taken place. It is essential for making sure every student receives appropriate instruction, and then verifying that learning has taken place. With the array of data teachers are able to assemble through classroom reading assessment, they are able to analyze and plan "just-in-time" instruction that meets the need of every student.

In this chapter, we add to what you have learned about classroom reading assessment in earlier chapters. The focus here is on the guiding principles of effective reading assessment, school-wide assessment concerns, important assessment terminology for teachers to know, and national issues surrounding reading assessment. We also provide wide-ranging assessment strategies not discussed in earlier chapters, but that are quite useful. Let's begin at the beginning with a brief summary of the governing principles and fundamental purposes of reading assessment.

Principles and Purposes of Reading Assessment

The following **principles of classroom assessment** are intended to help teachers decide which strategies should be adopted to improve their classroom instruction. They are based on our own classroom experiences, current research in the field, and expert opinions expressed to us by successful classroom teachers.

Principle 1: Assessment should inform and improve teaching. When considering whether or not to perform any sort of reading assessment, the teacher should ask, "Will this procedure help me make important instructional decisions regarding my students' reading needs?" The procedure should yield rich insights as to materials and ways of offering instruction (e. g., skills to be learned next, grouping based on student needs, etc.) that can positively affect students' reading growth. The process begins with an understanding of required state standards, and careful survey of what is known about students using available information (home surveys, cumulative records, informal assessments, student self-assessments, and the like).

Next, the teacher forms hypotheses about where each student is in his or her reading development (Bintz, 1991; Flippo, 2003; McKenna & Stahl, 2003; Rathvon, 2004). The task is to select assessment procedures that will help the teacher better understand student abilities and confirm or reject earlier hypotheses. Armed with information obtained from these processes, the teacher teaches lessons aimed at helping the student improve in reading proficiency. Figure 6.1 depicts this assessment–teaching process.

Principle 2: Assessment procedures should help teachers discover what children can *do, not just what they cannot do.* Rather than spending

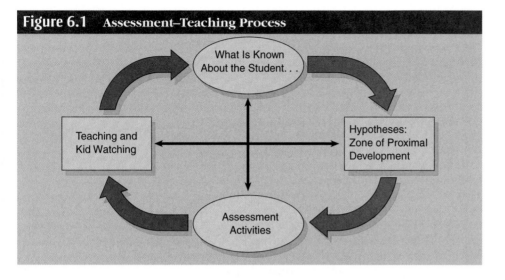

Figure 6.1   Assessment–Teaching Process

precious classroom time trying to identify the myriad skills students *do not* possess, many teachers focus on determining the skills they *do* possess, and then deciding what students are ready for next in reading development, i.e., building on students strengths to help them develop new skills. Once teachers understand student strengths in reading, it becomes much easier to decide which learning experiences should be offered to help them develop further.

Principle 3: Every assessment procedure should have a specific purpose. Sometimes we can fall into the habit of giving reading tests just because they are our "standard operating procedure" rather than selecting assessment activities as an integral part of providing high-quality instruction. For instance, it is common practice in many schools for students identified by their teacher as having reading problems to be given a "battery" of tests (i.e., a preselected set of tests) to discover what the problem seems to be. This one-size-fits-all approach fails to take into account what is already known about the student's reading ability, and the specific *purpose* of the assessment experience (e.g., for diagnosis, for provision of data for progress reports, for information to be given to parents, etc.). We need to enter into student assessment with a clear purpose.

There Are Four Purposes of Reading Assessment

Because reading assessment removes children from precious instructional time in the classroom, we should be mindful of the **four purposes of reading assessment.** These purposes, by the way, are embedded in the federal Reading First and No Child Left Behind legislation and are built on principles of valid and reliable measurement (see principle 7 in this list). These purposes are depicted metaphorically in Figure 6.2 as a chalice.

At the open end or broadest part of the chalice, since it involves the whole class, is **outcome assessment.** Outcomes are the results of our reading program in terms

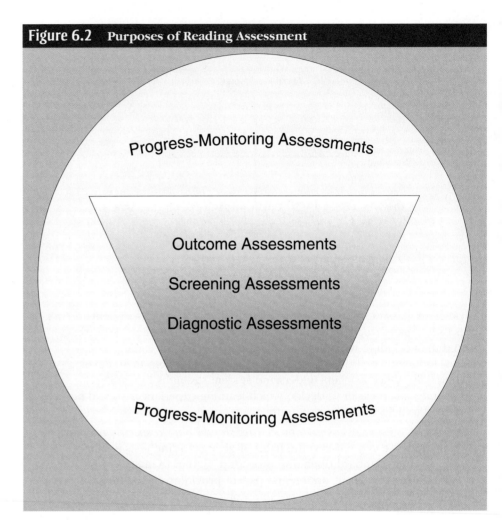

Figure 6.2   Purposes of Reading Assessment

Progress-Monitoring Assessments

Outcome Assessments

Screening Assessments

Diagnostic Assessments

Progress-Monitoring Assessments

of student test scores and other hard data. The main purpose of outcome assessment is to survey the reading achievement of the class as a whole. It provides a snapshot of the reading program's effectiveness when compared to established end-of-year reading benchmarks (standards) for each grade level.

In order for differentiated instruction to occur, the focus of assessment shifts to individual students. **Screening assessments** provide initial information about students' reading development. These assessments should be quick but also provide reliable and valid data. These assessments should help teachers place students into preliminary instructional groups based on their general reading abilities and needs. They provide an especially critical "first look" at students who may be at-risk and in need of special instructional services.

Invariably, teachers notice that some students are having unusual difficulty with tasks during small-group instruction. Parents also might bring their child's reading problem to the teacher's attention. **Diagnostic assessments** provide in-depth information about each student's particular strengths and needs. These assessments are a bit more involved and take longer to administer. Sometimes an educational psychologist, a certified diagnostician, or a bilingual specialist may be needed to administer a diagnostic test because of the time investment involved or because special training is needed. Students requiring special education or who are enrolled in Title I programs for reading often undergo diagnostic testing for initial placement or for retention in the program.

Encircling the chalice in Figure 6.2 are **progress-monitoring assessments.** These are an essential part of every reading teacher's daily plan, which is why they surround all other assessments (and students) represented in the chalice. Progress-monitoring assessments provide ongoing and timely feedback as to how well individual students are responding to teaching, referred to today as **Response to Intervention,** or **RtI.** This allows the teacher to continually reevaluate her or his instruction and make adjustments as needed.

Principle 4: Classroom assessment should be linked to accountability standards *and provide insights into the* process *of reading.* Passage of the No Child Left Behind Act and other state and federal legislation in reading has generated a pervasive emphasis on classroom assessment. **Accountability standards** established by the individual states and professional organizations, such as the International Reading Association (IRA) and the National Council of Teachers of English (NCTE), describe evidence-based reading skills that are typically mastered by the end of each school year. These **benchmark skills** (as they are often referred to) should be monitored on a regular basis.

Principle 5: Assessment procedures should help identify zones of proximal development. Vygotsky (1962, 1978), a Russian educator, discussed the notion of a zone of proximal development, or the area of potential growth in reading that can occur with appropriate instruction. To identify students' zones of proximal development, teachers need to determine accurately what children can already do, and thus, which new skills they may be ready to learn next. For example, in a kindergarten or first-grade classroom, children who can create story lines for wordless picture books and who have been doing so for some time should be ready for books containing simple and predictable text.

David Mager/Pearson Learning Photo Studio

Principle 6: Assessment should not supplant instruction. State and locally mandated testing sometimes seems to overwhelm teachers and take over the classroom. In Texas, for example, a state that has had high-stakes testing since the early 1980s, many principals complained to us that some teachers virtually stop teaching from January until April in order to drill students on practice tests. If a teacher loses sight of the purpose of classroom assessment—to inform and influence instruction—then he or she may well move into the role of teacher as manager rather than teacher

as teacher (Pearson, 1985). The assessment program should complement the instructional program and grow naturally from it.

Getting to Know English Learners

Issues of reliability and validity are important for choosing assessment measures for ELs, as poor test scores on some measures may really reveal an EL's struggle with learning a new language and culture, not with learning to read and write.

Principle 7: Effective classroom assessment makes use of both valid *and* reliable *instruments.* Although master teachers are comfortable using many informal assessment processes to gather information about students' reading progress, instruments that possess validity and reliability evidence are sometimes necessary. These assessment tools give teachers consistent and trustworthy feedback for adapting or modifying their teaching to meet individual needs.

Reliability evidence demonstrates whether student performance will be measured in a stable and consistent manner (Jennings, Caldwell, & Lerner, 2006). In other words, a reliable test is one that provides the same results for the same children with repeated testing no matter who administered the test. Reliability is reported numerically with a coefficient (a perfect reliability score for a test would be 1.0). Salvia and Ysseldyke (2004) believe that if a test is used for screening it should have a reliability of 0.80 or better. If a test is to be used for decisions about individual students, such as placement in Title I or special education, the test's reliability should be 0.90 or higher.

Measures of **validity** indicate the degree to which tests measure what their developers claim they measure (Jennings, Caldwell, & Lerner, 2006). If a test measures reading, then it should measure the complete reading act, or at least the area of reading specified by the test-makers (e.g., phonics, reading comprehension), not some other skill, ability, or construct.

The Reliability-Validity Caveat

Though the selection of reading tests that are both reliable and valid is our goal, finding one that meets our highest standards in each category is problematic. There is an important caveat commonly understood in assessment circles (Cooter, 1990): *As test reliability increases, validity usually decreases, and vice versa.* For example, informal reading inventories (IRIs) are widely used and respected as *valid* measures of reading ability, but they are also notorious for being rather unreliable (i.e., two teachers giving an IRI to the same child can come to substantially different conclusions about the student's reading needs). Conversely, the *Stanford Diagnostic Reading Test* (SDRT) is considered to be a very reliable test, but not very valid (i.e., the multiple-choice format for measuring reading comprehension is very *unlike* normal reading behavior). A number of tests are now available that report both validity and reliability estimates, but you will discover that the validity-reliability caveat is evident: if the test is high in reliability, it is probably weak in the validity department, or vice versa.

How does a teacher overcome the validity-reliability caveat? You will need to develop a *comprehensive* approach to reading assessment, one that includes some tests and procedures that are extremely valid and others that are highly reliable.

Where Do We Begin? A Classroom Teacher's Perspective

In the remainder of this chapter we take a closer look at reading assessment, adding special reading assessment strategies to those presented in Chapters 2 through 5. It seems logical to us that we should start with the kinds of assessments you might use every day. Screening assessments useful for the first days and weeks of school and progress-monitoring assessments used daily to check the effectiveness of your teaching are the daily bread and butter assessment tasks you will use to validate teaching and learning. Because these assessments—screening and progress-monitoring—may be used more or less interchangeably, we group them together in the upcoming sections. How will you know which assessment tool is best for screening or progress-monitoring? Not to worry. Early in the next section we provide you with a handy chart that helps you decide.

Screening and Progress-Monitoring Assessments

Screening Assessments

The first day of school is always magical. It is a day filled with hope, expectation, and, for some, even fear. Your young charges walk slowly into your classroom—some tall and gangly, some short, some smiling, some moving very cautiously. It is the day when you begin to establish classroom management routines and get to know each student a little. It is also the day they begin to form opinions about *you!*

The first week of school should include a basketweave of assessment activities that are quick and efficient and that yield a lot of important information about reading. They should also be pleasant and nonthreatening, since some of your students will have had repeated experience with failure and you don't want to lose them.

It is essential to use screening assessments during the first days of school, or for students who come to you after the school year has begun. These assessments are easy to administer and yield extremely useful information. You may actually decide to use many of these same tools for progress-monitoring.

> **Getting to Know English Learners**
> Often, necessary screening assessments are conducted for you by the ESL teacher in your school or district, as required by law. ELs, unlike students with special needs, do not have IEPs, so be prepared to ask your ESL teacher to help plan an appropriate reading/writing program for your ELs.

Progress-Monitoring in the Reading Classroom

Progress-monitoring is an essential part of teaching. As you learn more about your students, you plan instruction that you believe will best meet their needs. In essence, you try to find the zone of proximal development for each reading skill area for each student—not a simple task. Thus, as you offer targeted instruction in small groups, you constantly reassess each student's growth to see if learning is occurring and then tailor your instruction based on what you discover.

So, how do you decide which of the tests or strategies that follow in this section should be used, either for screening or progress-monitoring? In Figure 6.3 we offer a kind of "IF–THEN" chart to help you choose. IF–THEN thinking works like this: IF you have a particular need that is represented by one of the assessments listed along the left-hand column, THEN you determine the particular test or assessment

Figure 6.3 Selected Screening and Progress-Monitoring Assessment Strategies

	Appropriate for SCREENING? (First days/weeks)	Appropriate for PROGRESS-MONITORING?
CATEGORY: Interests and Self-Perception		
Comprehensive Reading Inventory	YES	NO
Burke Interview	YES	YES
Self-Rating Scale–Subject Areas	YES	YES
Background Knowledge	YES	YES
Family Survey	YES	NO
Kid Watching	NO	YES
Screening Checklists	YES	YES
Concepts About Print	YES	YES (for emergent readers only)
CATEGORY: Phonemic Awareness (PA) and Alphabet Knowledge (AK)		
PA- Recogn. Rhyming Words	YES (in small groups)	YES
PA- Oddity Task	YES (in small groups)	YES
PA- Same-Different Word Pairs	YES (in small groups)	YES
PA- Syllables and Counting Syll.	YES (in small groups)	YES
PA- Auditory Sound Blending	YES (in small groups)	YES
PA- Segmenting Sounds	YES (in small groups)	YES
AK- Alphabet Identification	YES (in small groups)	YES
AK- Letter Production	YES (in small groups)	YES
CATEGORY: Decoding and Word Attack		
Running Records	YES (first three weeks)	YES
CATEGORY: Vocabulary		
Oral Reading Assessment	NO	YES
Vocabulary Flash Cards	YES	YES
CATEGORY: Comprehension		
Questioning (Bloom)	YES	YES (use mainly higher levels)
Retelling–Story Grammars (Oral)	YES (in small groups)	YES
Retelling–Using Graphic Organizers	YES (in small groups)	YES
Retelling–Written Summaries	NO	YES
Expository Text Frames	YES (in small groups)	YES
Cloze	YES	YES
Maze	YES	YES
Content Area Reading Inventory (CARI)	YES (in small groups)	YES
CATEGORY: Fluency		
Multidimensional Fluency Scale (MFS)	YES (in small groups)	YES
Rubric for evaluation	NO	YES
CATEGORY: Commercial Tools		
Informal reading inventories	YES (in first three weeks)	YES (quarterly)
Curriculum-based measurements (CBM)	YES (in first month)	YES (quarterly)

strategy that is appropriate for screening or progress-monitoring by checking the appropriate row to the right. Following Figure 6.3 is a detailed description of many of these strategies (others may be found in Chapters 2–5). Let's get started!

Kid Watching

For many teachers, the most basic assessment strategy is systematic observation of children engaged in the reading act, or **kid watching.** Clay, in her classic book *The Early Detection of Reading Difficulties* (1985), explains her philosophy concerning observations:

> I am looking for movement in appropriate directions. . . . For if I do not watch what [the student] is doing, and if I do not capture what is happening in records of some kind, Johnny, who never gets under my feet and who never comes really into a situation where I can truly see what he is doing, may, in fact, for six months or even a year, practice behaviours that will handicap him in reading. (p. 49)

Observation and systematic data collection during observation are critical tool at the teacher's disposal for the early assessment of students and their abilities.

***But Do You Know** What to Look For?* One semester a young student teacher was busily making anecdotal notes on a clipboard as she watched second graders working away. The students were engaged in activities such as reading, planning writing projects, working at a computer station, listening to books on tape while following along in small books, and several other reading–learning tasks. When the student teacher was asked by the visiting college supervisor what she was working on, she said, "I'm trying to figure out where the children are in their reading development." The supervisor responded, "That's great! How do you know what to watch for?" The student teacher appeared bewildered, so the supervisor said, "If you have time later, I'd like to share with you information about reading milestones. They are observable learning stages that can be noted as part of your assessment profiling system." The student teacher quickly accepted the offer and welcomed the information enthusiastically.

To be an effective "kid watcher," you must gain an understanding of end-of-year benchmark reading skills (Cooter, 2003), or the reading milestones through which children grow. Knowing which of these skills students have and have not acquired will help you construct a classroom profile and plan whole-class, small-group, and individualized instruction. We have provided benchmark skills by grade level in Chapters 2 through 5 in the sections titled "Classroom Assessment" to assist you with your kid watching. Most state departments of education also have a listing of reading and language arts skills that should be learned by grade level. The effective teacher will have a copy of his or her state's reading standards (benchmarks) and use it to monitor the full range of readers he or she is likely to have in his or her classroom. (Note: State standards are provided online on the Web page for each state's department of education. You can link to your own state's standards from the Teacher Prep site that accompanies this text.)

Assessing Reading Interests and Self-Perception

On the most basic level, we need to know what kinds of books and materials will be of interest to our students. This helps us choose (or avoid) certain topics of interest for small-group instruction, as interest can have a powerful effect on student reading performance (Guthrie, Hoa, Wigfield, Tonks, & Perencevich, 2006). We also want to be sure and ask the obvious question: Are you a good reader? Why?

Hope Madden/Merrill

In this section, we share some essential tools for screening students in the areas of interest and self-perception.

Attitude/Interest Inventories. Getting to know students is critical if the teacher is to have insights into their background knowledge and oral language abilities. It is also useful in selecting reading materials that will be of interest to students. An interest inventory that is administered either one-to-one or in small groups is a great tool for getting to know students. However, there are many inventories from which you can choose, and all interest inventories are not created equally. Further, not all questions on the inventory can tell you what is helpful in choosing appropriate reading materials for instruction.

Figures 6.4 and 6.5 feature two interest inventories developed by Flynt and Cooter (2004) that we find to be helpful. The primary form is appropriate for students in kindergarten through grade 2, and the upper-level form is to be used with students from grade 3 and above.

Getting to Know English Learners
When possible, provide all these forms in English learners' native languages for use with beginning EL students and newcomers to the country.

The Burke Reading Interview. The *Burke Reading Interview* (Burke, 1987) provides some initial insights into how students see themselves as readers and the reading task in general. The following questions have been adapted from the Burke procedure:

1. When you are reading and come to a word you don't know, what do you do? What else can you do?
2. Which of your friends is a good reader? What makes him/her a good reader?
3. Do you think your teacher ever comes to a word she doesn't know when reading? What do you think she does when that happens?
4. If you knew that one of your friends was having problems with his or her reading, what could you tell your friend that would help?

Figure 6.4   The Flynt–Cooter Interest Inventory: Primary Form

---

PRIMARY FORM

Student's Name _____ Age _____

Date _____ Examiner _____

Introductory Statement: *[Student's name],* *before you read some stories for me, I would like to ask you some questions.*

Home Life

1. Where do you live? Do you know your address? What is it?

2. Who lives in your house with you?

3. What kinds of jobs do you have at home?

4. What is one thing that you really like to do at home?

5. Do you ever read at home? [*If yes, ask:*] When do you read and what was the last thing you read? [*If no, ask:*] Does anyone ever read to you? [*If so, ask:*] Who, and how often?

6. Do you have a bedtime on school nights? [*If no, ask:*] When do you go to bed?

7. Do you have a TV in your room? How much TV do you watch every day? What are your favorite shows?

8. What do you like to do with your friends?

9. Do you have any pets? Do you collect things? Do you take any kinds of lessons?

10. When you make a new friend, what is something that your friend ought to know about you?

School Life

1. Besides recess and lunch, what do you like about school?

2. Do you get to read much in school?

3. Are you a good reader or a not-so-good reader?

   [*If a good reader, ask:*] What makes a person a good reader?

   [*If a not-so-good reader, ask:*] What causes a person to not be a good reader?

4. If you could pick any book to read, what would the book be about?

5. Do you like to write? What kind of writing do you do in school? What is the favorite thing you have written about?

6. Who has helped you the most in school? How did that person help you?

7. Do you have a place at home to study?

8. Do you get help with your homework? Who helps you?

9. What was the last book you read for school?

10. If you were helping someone learn to read, what could you do to help that person?

Figure 6.5   The Flynt–Cooter Interest Inventory: Upper-Level Form*

UPPER LEVEL FORM

Student's Name _____ Age _____

Date _____ Examiner _____

Introductory Statement: *[Student's name]*, *before you read some stories for me, I would like to ask you some questions.*

Home Life

1. How many people are there in your family?

2. Do you have your own room or do you share a room? [*Ask this only if it is apparent that the student has siblings.*]

3. Do your parent(s) work? What kinds of jobs do they have?

4. Do you have jobs around the house? What are they?

5. What do you usually do after school?

6. Do you have a TV in your room? How much time do you spend watching TV each day? What are your favorite shows?

7. Do you have a bedtime during the week? What time do you usually go to bed on a school night?

8. Do you get an allowance? How much?

9. Do you belong to any clubs at school or outside school? What are they?

10. What are some things that you really like to do? Do you collect things, have any hobbies, or take lessons outside school?

School Environment

1. Do you like school? What is your favorite class? Your least favorite class?

2. Do you have a special place to study at home?

3. How much homework do you have on a typical school night? Does anyone help you with your homework? Who?

4. Do you consider yourself a good reader or a not-so-good reader?

   [*If a good reader, ask:*] What has helped you most to become a good reader?

   [*If a not-so-good reader, ask:*] What causes someone to be a not-so-good reader?

5. If I gave you the choice of selecting a book about any topic, what would you choose to read about?

6. What is one thing you can think of that would help you become a better reader? Is there anything else?

7. Do you like to write? What kind of writing assignments do you like best?

8. If you went to a new school, what is one thing that you would want the teachers to know about you as a student?

9. If you were helping someone learn to read, what would be the most important thing you could do to help that person?

10. How will knowing how to read help you in the future?

---

*From: Flynt, E. S., & Cooter, R. B. (2004). *The Flynt/Cooter Reading Inventory for the Classroom* (5th ed.). Upper Saddle River, NJ: Merrill/Prentice Hall. ISBN: 0-13-112106-5. Used with permission.

Table 6.1   Class Interests Profile Sorting Table

Student Names	Q1	Q2								

5. How would a teacher help your friend with reading problems?
6. How do you think you learned to read?
7. Are you a good reader?
8. What would you like to be able to do better as a reader?

Sorting Out Student Interests. After you have collected student responses to the *Flynt/Cooter Interest Inventory,* create a grid for your class like the one shown in Table 6.1. List student names along the left hand column, and question numbers along the top row (i.e., "Q1" for question number 1, "Q2" for question number 2, and so on). You may decide that some questions provide more information than others; if so, only list the numbers you plan to survey.

After the entire class has been surveyed, compile the individual responses into a class profile. Record abbreviated answers to each question for each student in the class interests profile. Look over the responses to each question by all of the children for categories of interests to be observed in your teaching and for choosing reading materials. Make any changes on the class profile sheet you discover throughout the year. This updated information about your students' reading interests will help you adjust your selection of topics and reading materials as the year progresses.

Self-Rating Scales for Subject-Area Reading

No one knows better than the reader how he or she is doing in reading. A teacher carrying out an assessment agenda should never overlook the obvious: Ask kids how they're doing! Although this is best achieved in a one-to-one discussion setting, large class sizes frequently make it a prohibitive practice. A good alternative to one-to-one interviews for older elementary children is a student self-rating scale, in which students complete a questionnaire tailored to obtain specific information about the reader from the reader's point of view. One example is illustrated in Figure 6.6 for a teacher interested in reading and study strategies used with social studies readings. Whichever reading skills are to be surveyed, remember to keep self-rating scales focused and brief.

Assessing Background Knowledge

Children's background knowledge and experiences are among the most important contributors (or inhibitors) of comprehension. Researchers have determined that students who possess a great deal of background information about a subject tend to recall greater amounts of information more accurately from reading than do students with little or no background knowledge (Carr & Thompson, 1996; Pearson, Hansen, & Gordon,

Figure 6.6 Self-Rating Scale: Reading Social Studies

Reading Social Studies

Name _____ Date _____

1. The first three things I usually do when I begin reading a chapter in social studies are (number 1, 2, 3):

   _____ Look at the pictures.

   _____ Read the chapter through one time silently.

   _____ Look at the new terms and definitions.

   _____ Read the questions at the end of the chapter.

   _____ Read the first paragraph or introduction.

   _____ Skip around and read the most interesting parts.

   _____ Skim the chapter.

   _____ Preview the chapter.

2. What is hardest for me about social studies is . . .

3. The easiest thing about social studies is . . .

4. The thing(s) I like best about reading social studies is (are) . . .

Getting to Know English Learners

Background knowledge and experience may vary widely with an EL's linguistic and cultural background and may include often overlooked important facts like whether or not the EL came from a rural or urban setting.

1979; Pressley, 2000). It is also a well-known fact that well-developed background information can inhibit the comprehension of new information that conflicts with or refutes prior knowledge and assumptions about a specific topic. Thus, knowing how much knowledge a reader has about a concept or topic can help teachers better prepare students to read and comprehend successfully. One way that teachers can assess background knowledge and experience is to use a procedure developed by Langer (1981) for assessing the amount and content of students' background knowledge about selected topics, themes, concepts, and events.

Here's the procedure you will follow. Select a story for students to read. Construct a list of specific vocabulary terms or story concepts related to the topic, message, theme, or events to be experienced in reading the story. For example, you might have students read the story *Stone Fox* by John R. Gardiner (1983), which is about a boy named Willy who saves his grandfather's farm from the tax collector. Construct a list of 5 to 10 specific vocabulary terms or concepts related to the story, such as those presented here:

broke

taxes

tax collector

dogsled race

samoyeds

Figure 6.7   Checklist of Levels of Prior Knowledge

Phrase 1   What comes to mind when . . . ?
Phrase 2   What made you think of . . . ?
Phrase 3   Have you any new ideas about . . . ?

_____

Stimulus used to elicit student background knowledge _____
(Picture, word, or phrase etc.)

Much (3)	Some (2)	Little (1)
category labels	examples	personal associations
definitions	attributes	morphemes
analogies	defining characteristics	sound alikes
relationships		personal experiences

Student name

	Much (3)	Some (2)	Little (1)
Maria	____	__X__	____
Jawan	__X__	____	____
____	____	____	____
____	____	____	____
____	____	____	____

Source: Reutzel, D. R., & Cooter, R. B. (2007). _Strategies for Reading Assessment and Instruction: Helping Every Child Succeed,_ (3rd ed.). Upper Saddle River, NJ: Merrill/Prentice Hall. Used with permission.

Ask students to respond to each of these terms in writing or through discussion. This is accomplished by using one of several stem statements (see Figure 6.7) such as, "What comes to mind when you think of paying bills and you hear the word _broke?_" Once students have responded to each of the terms, score responses to survey the class's knowledge (Figure 6.7). Assign the number of points that most closely represents the level of prior knowledge in the response is used to score each item. Divide the total score by the number of terms or concepts in the list to determine the average knowledge level of individual students. Compare these average scores against the Checklist of Levels of Prior Knowledge in Figure 6.7 for each student. By scanning the Xs in the checklist, you can get a sense of the entire class's overall level of prior knowledge. You can easily use information thus gathered to inform both the content and nature of your whole-group comprehension instruction.

Family Surveys of Reading Habits

We recently observed a friend of ours who has a heart condition going through his normal daily activities with a small radio-like device attached to his belt. When asked what this gadget was, he indicated that it was a heart monitor. He went on to say that the device constantly measured his heart rate for an entire day to provide the doctor with a reliable account of his normal heart rhythms in the real world of daily activity.

Traditional reading assessment has often failed to give teachers such a "real-world" look at students' reading ability by restricting the assessment to school settings. So the question posed here is, "How do we acquire information about a student's reading habits and abilities

Getting to Know English Learners
Again, where possible, provide the family surveys in the native language of the ELs' parents or have local translators help you make phone calls to the home where you can then conduct the home survey information orally.

Figure 6.8 Family Survey

September 6, 200____

Dear Adult Family Member:

As we begin the new school year, I would like to know a little more about your child's reading habits at home. This information will help me provide the best possible learning plan for your child this year. Please take a few minutes to answer the questions below and return in the self-addressed stamped envelope provided. Should you have any questions, feel free to phone me at XXX–XXXX.

Cordially,

Mrs. Shelley

_____

1. My child likes to read the following at least once a week (check all that apply):

Comic books _____   Sports page _____

Magazines (example: *Highlights*) _____   Library books _____

Cereal boxes _____   Cooking recipes _____

T.V. Guide _____   Funny papers _____

Others (please name):

2. Have you noticed your child having any reading problems? If so, please explain briefly.

3. What are some of your child's favorite books?

4. If you would like a conference to discuss your child's reading ability, please indicate which days and times (after school) would be most convenient.

away from the somewhat artificial environment of the school?" One way is to assess what is happening in the home using family surveys.

Family surveys are brief questionnaires (too long and they'll never be answered!) sent to adult family members periodically to maintain communication between the home and school. They also remind parents of the importance of reading in the home to support and encourage reading growth. When taken into consideration with other assessment evidence from the classroom, family surveys enable teachers to develop a more accurate profile of the child's reading ability. An example of a family survey is provided in Figure 6.8.

Screening Checklists and Scales

Teachers often create their own screening checklists using the reading benchmarks for their grade level. Lamme and Hysmith (1991) developed a scale that can be used to identify key developmental behaviors in emergent readers. It describes 11 levels often seen in the elementary school and can be used in tandem with the much more comprehensive reading benchmarks previously discussed. Following is an adaptation of that scale:

Level 11: The student can read fluently from books and other reading materials.

Level 10: The student seeks out new sources of information. He or she volunteers to share information from books with other children.

Level 9: The student has developed the ability to independently use context clues, sentence structure, structural analysis, and phonic analysis to read new passages.

Level 8: The student reads unfamiliar stories haltingly (not fluently), but requires little adult assistance.

Level 7: The student reads familiar stories fluently.

Level 6: The student reads word-by-word. He or she recognizes words in a new context.

Level 5: The student memorizes text and can pretend to "read" a story.

Level 4: The student participates in reading by doing such things as supplying words that rhyme and predictable text.

Level 3: The student talks about or describes pictures. He or she pretends to read (storytelling). He or she makes up words that go along with pictures.

Level 2: The student watches pictures as an adult reads a story.

Level 1: The student listens to a story but does not look at the pictures.

Many teachers find that checklists that include a **Likert scale** (a five-point scale) can be useful in student portfolios because many reading behaviors become more fluent over time. One example, developed by Deborah Diffily (1994), is shown in Figure 6.9.

Assessing Students' Reading of Nonfiction Texts

The key to effective expository (i.e., nonfiction) text instruction lies in the accurate identification of the types of nonfiction texts that students are able to read effectively, as well as the forms of expository writing that are difficult for them to comprehend. We have discovered that several rather common forms of reading assessment are easily adaptable to expository texts and can help teachers plan instruction. Offered in this section are some examples of each for your consideration.

Expository Text Frames. **Expository text frames** are useful in identifying types of expository text patterns that may be troublesome for students. Based on the "story frames" concept (Fowler, 1982; Nichols, 1980), expository text frames are completed by the student after reading an expository passage. Instruction can be focused much more precisely, based on student needs, as a result of this procedure.

To develop your own expository text frames for classroom assessment, you will need a reading selection from the adopted content textbook, a personal

Figure 6.9 Diffily's Classroom Observation Checklist

Student's Name _____ Date _____

Literacy Development Checklist

	Seldom				Often
Chooses books for personal enjoyment	1	2	3	4	5
Knows print/picture difference	1	2	3	4	5
Knows print is read from left to right	1	2	3	4	5
Asks to be read to	1	2	3	4	5
Asks that story be read again	1	2	3	4	5
Listens attentively during story time	1	2	3	4	5
Knows what a title is	1	2	3	4	5
Knows what an author is	1	2	3	4	5
Knows what an illustrator is	1	2	3	4	5
In retellings, repeats 2+ details	1	2	3	4	5
Tells beginning, middle, end	1	2	3	4	5
Can read logos	1	2	3	4	5
Uses text in functional ways	1	2	3	4	5
"Reads" familiar books to self/others	1	2	3	4	5
Can read personal words	1	2	3	4	5
Can read sight words from books	1	2	3	4	5
Willing to "write"	1	2	3	4	5
Willing to "read" personal story	1	2	3	4	5
Willing to dictate story to adult	1	2	3	4	5

Gratefully used by the authors with the permission of Deborah Diffily, Ph.D., Alice Carlson, Applied Learning Center, Ft. Worth, TX.

Figure 6.10 Expository Text Frames: Description

Decimals are another way to write fractions when _____
_____
_____
_____

Source: Reutzel, D. Ray; & Cooter, R. B. (2007). *Strategies for Reading Assessment and Instruction: Helping Every Child Succeed,* (3rd ed.). Upper Saddle River, NJ: Merrill/Prentice Hall. Used with permission.

computer, and a printer or photocopier. Abbreviated examples of expository text frames for each of the primary expository text patterns are shown in Figures 6.10 through 6.14.

Before asking students to read the targeted selection, list the major vocabulary and concepts. Discuss what students already know about the topic and display it on the chalkboard or on chart paper. Next, have students read an expository selection

Figure 6.11 Expository Text Frames: Collection*

Water Habitats

Freshwater habitats are found in _____, _____, _____, and rivers. Each freshwater habitat has special kinds of _____ and _____ that live there. Some plants and animals live in waters that are very _____. Others live in waters that are _____. Some plants and animals adapt to waters that flow _____.

Figure 6.12 Expository Text Frames: Causation*

America Enters the War

On Sunday, December 7, 1941, World War II came to the United States. The entry of the United States into World War II was triggered by _____. Roosevelt said that it was a day that would "live in Infamy." *Infamy* (IN·fuh·mee) means remembered for being evil.

Figure 6.13 Expository Text Frames: Problem/Solution*

Agreement by Compromise

Events that led to the Civil War

For a while there were an equal number of Southern and Northern states. That meant that there were just as many senators in Congress from slave states as from free states. Neither had more votes in the Senate, so they usually reached agreement on new laws by compromise. One way that the balance of power was maintained in Congress was _____

_____.

Figure 6.14 Expository Text Frames: Comparison*

Segregation

Many people said that the segregation laws were unfair. But in 1896, the Supreme Court ruled segregation legal if _____

_____. "Separate but equal" became the law in many parts of the country.

But separate was not equal. One of the most serious problems was education. Black parents felt _____

_____. Sometimes the segregated schools had teachers who were not _____ as teachers in the white schools. Textbooks were often _____ if they had any books at all. But in many of the white schools the books were _____. Without a good education the blacks argued their children would not be able to get good jobs as adults.

* *Source:* Reutzel, D. Ray; & Cooter, R. B. (2007). *Strategies for Reading Assessment and Instruction: Helping Every Child Succeed,* (3rd ed.). Upper Saddle River, NJ: Merrill/Prentice Hall. Used with permission.

similar to the one you will ask them to read in class. Once the passage has been read, model the process for completing expository text frames using examples. Finally, have students read the actual selection for the unit of study and complete the expository text frame(s) you have prepared for this passage.

Content Area Reading Inventory (CARI). A **content area reading inventory (CARI)** (Farr, Tully, & Pritchard, 1989; Readence, Bean, & Baldwin, 1992) is a teacher-made informal reading inventory used to assess whether students have learned sufficient reading/study strategies to succeed with content materials. Constructing a CARI can be quite time consuming, but is well worth the effort.

A CARI can be administered to groups of students, and typically includes three major sections (Farr et al., 1989) that assess the following:

- Student knowledge of and ability to use common textbook components (i.e., table of contents, glossary, index) and supplemental research aids (card catalog, reference books, periodicals)
- Student knowledge of important vocabulary and skills such as context clues
- Comprehension skills important to understanding expository texts

For the last two sections of a CARI assessment, students are asked to read a selection from the adopted text. Readence et al. (1992) suggest contents of a CARI assessment.

Suggestions for Content in a CARI

Part I: Textual Reading/Study Aids

1. Internal aids
2. Table of contents
3. Index
4. Glossary
5. Chapter introduction/summary
6. Information from pictures
7. Other aids included in the text
8. Supplemental research aids
9. Online card catalog searches
10. Periodicals
11. Encyclopedias
12. Other relevant resources that lead students to access additional information related to the content (e.g., online search engines like Google.com, video libraries, online university periodicals)

Part II: Vocabulary Knowledge

1. Knowledge and recall of relevant vocabulary
2. Use of context clues

Part III: Comprehension Skills and Strategies

1. Text-explicit (literal) information
2. Text-implicit (inferred) information
3. Knowledge of text structures and related strategies

To develop a CARI, follow this process.

Step 1: Choose a passage of at least three to four pages from the textbook(s) to be used. The passage selected should represent the typical writing style of the author.

Step 2: Construct about 20 questions related to the text. Readence et al. (1992) recommend 8 to 10 questions for Part I, 4 to 6 questions for Part II, and 7 to 9 questions for Part III. We urge the use of questions based on writing patterns used in the sample selection; they should reflect the facts, concepts, and generalizations in the selection.

Step 3: Explain to students that the CARI is not used for grading purposes, but is useful for planning teaching activities that will help them succeed. Be sure to walk students through the different sections of the CARI and model appropriate responses.

Step 4: Administer Part I first, then Parts II and III on separate day(s). It may take several sessions to work through a CARI. We recommend devoting only about 20 minutes per day to administering parts of a CARI so that other class needs are not ignored during the assessment phase.

Readence et al. (1992) suggest the following criteria for assessing the CARI.

Percent Correct	**Text Difficulty**
86%–100%	Easy reading
64%–85%	Adequate for instruction
63% or below	Too difficult

From careful analysis of this assessment, teachers can plan special lessons to help students cope with difficult readings and internalize important information. Students can be grouped according to need for these lessons and practice strategies leading to success.

Published Reading Tests for Screening and Progress-Monitoring Assessments

A number of products are available commercially to help teachers survey their students. While these may be helpful, they can also be somewhat expensive. In this section, we present products that have been useful in our own classroom practices and meet with our general approval. We begin with the most valid of them all, informal reading inventories, or IRIs.

Informal Reading Inventory

The **informal reading inventory** (IRI) is an individually administered test (though some can be given to groups of children), and often has graded word lists and story passages. The IRI is one of the best tools for observing and analyzing reading performance and for gathering information about how a student uses a wide range of reading strategies (Jennings, Caldwell, & Lerner, 2006). Emmett A. Betts is generally considered to be the first developer of the IRI; however, several other individuals contributed to its development as far back as the early 1900s (Johns & Lunn, 1983).

The Teacher's Guide to Reading Tests (Cooter, 1990) lists several advantages and unique features of IRIs that help explain why teachers continue to find them useful.

One benefit is IRIs provide authentic assessments of the reading act: (i.e., an IRI more closely resembles real reading). Students are better able to "put it all together" by reading whole stories or passages. Another advantage of IRIs is that they usually provide a systematic procedure for studying student miscues or reading errors.

IRIs are rather unusual when compared to other commercial reading tests. First, because they are "informal" most IRIs do not offer norms, reliability data, or validity information, though a few have begun offering validation information in recent years (see *The Comprehensive Reading Inventory* later in this chapter). Second, IRIs are unusual (in a positive way) because they provide a great deal of information that is helpful to teachers in making curricular decisions, especially teachers who place students into needs-based or guided reading groups (Fountas & Pinnell, 1996). IRIs supply an estimate of each child's ability in graded or "leveled" reading materials, such as basal readers and books used for guided reading. IRIs usually offer student performance data in several key areas of reading: word identification via a running record (see Chapter 2 for details about running records), passage comprehension, and reading fluency.

IRIs tend to be somewhat different from each other. Beyond the usual graded word lists and reading passages, IRIs vary a great deal in the subtests offered (e.g., silent reading passages, phonics, interest inventories, concepts about print, phonemic awareness, auditory discrimination) and in the scoring criteria used to interpret reading miscues. Some argue (us included) that the best IRIs are those constructed by classroom teachers themselves using reading materials from their own classrooms. Several examples of IRIs now used in many school systems follow:

- *The Comprehensive Reading Inventory: Measuring Reading Development in Regular and Special Education Classrooms (CRI)* (R. Cooter, Flynt, E.S., & Cooter, K.S., 2007) is a modern version of the traditional IRI concept, and has both English and Spanish forms under one cover. The authors apply National Reading Panel (2000) and other more recent research on "alphabetics" (i. e., phonemic awareness, letter-naming, phonics, etc.), vocabulary knowledge, comprehension processes, running records, fluency, and miscue analysis into an effective authentic reading assessment.

  Unlike most commercial IRIs on the market today, the *CRI* also includes validity and reliability data, a feature required by many states for tax-supported adoption by school districts. The authors include such research-based procedures as unaided/aided recall and story grammar comprehension evaluation, high-interest selections, appropriate length passages, both expository and narrative passages, and a time-efficient miscue grid system for quick analyses of running records.

- *Developmental Reading Assessment (DRA)* (Beaver, 2001). An informal reading inventory offering graded reading passages for students to read, rubrics for evaluating students' oral reading, and a handy box in which to store student portfolios.

- *The English–Español Reading Inventory* (Flynt & Cooter, 1999). This easy-to-use tool offers complete informal reading inventories for pre-kindergarten through grade 12 students in both Spanish and English. The Spanish passages were carefully developed and field-tested with the aid of native Spanish-speaking teacher-researchers from the United States, Mexico, and Central and South America to avoid problems with dialect differences and to maximize their usefulness in United States classrooms.

Curriculum-Based Measurement

Curriculum-based measurement (CBM) is a tool for measuring student skill development in the areas of reading fluency, spelling, math, and written language. CBM uses "probes" developed from each school district's curriculum; thus, it measures what students are taught.

Curriculum-based measurement looks at three different areas that pertain to reading.

- Reading fluency measures how many words a student correctly reads in one minute. In practice, three reading probes are given and the middle or median score is reported.
- The spelling measure presents 10 words (at first grade) or 17 words (second through fifth grades). Spelling lists are scored for words spelled correctly.
- For the written expression task, students are presented with a story starter and given three minutes to write a story. Student work is scored for total words written, words spelled correctly, and correct writing sequences.

CBM procedures are usually used to screen for students who may be at risk for reading difficulty and to monitor student progress and response to instructional interventions. Screenings are conducted three times each year in many school districts for all students: fall, winter, and spring. If a student receives additional support in reading, CBM might be administered several times weekly to evaluate the effects of the intervention. Similarly, CBM is often used for decision making when determining if a student should receive special education services.

Outcome Assessments

Outcome assessments help us determine how effective our reading program and our teaching is in helping students attain grade level standards or benchmarks. These kinds of tests are usually given to whole groups of students at once, but may be given individually when necessary. The following two measures are used nationally and are considered to be exemplars in this emerging area of reading assessment.

Dynamic Indicators of Basic Early Literacy Skills (DIBELS)

The *Dynamic Indicators of Basic Early Literacy Skills* or DIBELS are a set of four standardized, individually administered measures of early literacy development. DIBELS was specifically designed to assess three of the "five big ideas" of early literacy development: phonological awareness, alphabetic principle, and oral reading fluency (measured as a corrected reading rate) with connected text. Another test not directly linked to the three of five big ideas in early literacy but used as a risk indicator is the *Letter Naming Fluency* (LNF) measure. These short, efficient, and highly predictive measures are designed to be one minute, timed indicators used to regularly monitor the development of pre-reading and early reading skills. A full description was presented in Chapter 2.

Texas Primary Reading Inventory (TPRI)

The *Texas Primary Reading Inventory* or TPRI is an assessment tool that provides a picture of a student's reading progress in kindergarten, first, and second grades. Originally developed to help teachers in Texas in measuring the state's "essential knowledge and skills" in reading, this instrument is suitable for outcome assessment as well as for screening and progress-monitoring assessment purposes. A quick screening section is designed to work together with a more detailed inventory section to help teachers identify strengths and problem areas as well as to monitor students' progress.

TPRI covers all five of the "big ideas" in early reading development: phonemic awareness, phonics, fluency, vocabulary, and comprehension strategies. The TPRI also provides an *Interventions Activities Guide* directly linked to students' performance of each on the parts of TPRI.

The TPRI is administered individually by the classroom teacher. In the screening section of the TPRI, three assessment measures are provided: (1) graphophonemic knowledge, (2) phonemic awareness, and (3) word reading. In the graphophonemic measure, students are assessed on their ability to recognize letters of the alphabet and their understanding of sound-to-symbol relationships. In the phonemic awareness measure, students are assessed on their ability to identify and manipulate individual sounds within spoken words so that letters can be linked to sounds. In the word reading measure of the screening portion of the TPRI, students are asked to identify a list of high-frequency words.

In the inventory section of the TPRI, students are assessed across seven measures: (1) book and print knowledge, (2) phonemic awareness, (3) listening comprehension, (4) graphophonemic knowledge, (5) reading accuracy, (6) reading fluency, and (7) reading comprehension. The TPRI, unlike the DIBELS, addresses the important role of concepts about print in the development of early reading.

The TPRI is based on longitudinal data on over 900 English-speaking students. More recently, the TPRI has also become available in Spanish, which, like DIBELS, has yet to be shown to be a valid and reliable indicator of reading development in this population. For a more extensive review of the TPRI, we recommend that you consult: *www.tpri.org*.

Diagnostic Assessments

Diagnostic assessments are used to gather in-depth information about students' particular strengths and needs and are typically used for struggling readers. Diagnostic assessments probe deeper than other assessments and take extra time to conduct. An educational psychologist, certified diagnostician, or a bilingual specialist is sometimes needed to administer certain tests due to time constraints or required special training. Students in special education or Title I programs for reading often require diagnostic testing.

Diagnosing Vocabulary Knowledge

When teachers notice students who seem to struggle with reading, it is logical for them to want to know the extent to which these students' vocabulary has developed. We recommend three tests for assessing a student's word knowledge or **receptive vocabulary.** One is intended for native English speakers, and the other two are for students who speak Spanish as their first language and are learning to speak and read in English.

- *Peabody Picture Vocabulary Test, Third Edition* (PPVT-III) (Dunn & Dunn, 1997). The PPVT-III is a quickly administered test (11–12 minutes) that indicates how strong a student's vocabulary knowledge is compared to other students of the same age nationally. Results can help the teacher better understand the needs of students in terms of formal and informal vocabulary instruction.
- *Test de Vocabulario en Imágenes Peabody* (TVIP), (Dunn, Lugo, Padilla, & Dunn, 1986). This test is an adaptation of an early version of the previously described *Peabody Picture Vocabulary Test* for native Spanish speakers. It takes about 10 to 15 minutes to administer and measures Spanish vocabulary knowledge.
- *Woodcock-Muñoz Language Survey* (WMLS), English and Spanish Forms (Woodcock & Muñoz-Sandoval, 1993). Teachers, particularly in urban centers, often have a large number of students who are learning English as a second language (ESL). The extent to which students have acquired a listening and speaking vocabulary in English is an important factor in reading instruction because reading (a) is a language skill, and (b) depends on learners having a fairly strong English vocabulary. The WMLS is a widely used instrument used throughout the United States (García, McKoon, & August, 2006) that takes about 20 minutes to administer. It features two subtests: Oral Language and Reading/Writing.

Individual Diagnostic Reading Tests

Teachers sometimes believe it necessary to assess an individual student's reading ability using norm-referenced measures. This often happens when new students move into a school district without their permanent records, or when struggling readers are being considered for extra assistance programs such as Title 1 or special education services provided in inclusive classrooms. Following is an example of a commonly used test:

- *Woodcock Reading Mastery Tests—Revised* (Woodcock et al., 1987, 1997). The Woodcock Reading Mastery Tests—Revised (WRMT-R/NU) is a battery of six individually administered subtests intended to measure reading abilities from kindergarten through adult levels. Subtests cover visual-auditory learning, letter identification, word identification, word attack, word comprehension, and passage comprehension. Its design reveals a skills perspective of reading, and divides the assessment into two sections according to age and ability levels: *readiness* and *reading achievement.* The WRMT-R/NU reports norm-referenced data for both of its forms, as well as insights into remediation. Results may be calculated either manually or using the convenient scoring program developed for personal computers (PCs). This WRMT-R/NU is frequently used by teachers in special education and Title 1 reading programs.

Individually Administered Achievement Tests

It can be informative to know how well a student has developed over a wide range of academic subjects. Achievement tests are often given to whole groups of students at scheduled grade levels, but you may need this information right away to better understand a troubled reader's knowledge and abilities. Following is a description of our preferred wide range achievement test that can be individually administered as a diagnostic tool.

- *Kaufman Test of Educational Achievement* (K-TEA/NU) (Kaufman & Kaufman, 1997). Sometimes teachers require norm-referenced data to determine how a child is progressing compared to other children nationally, such as when teachers are working with a population of students who are performing at atypically high or low levels. That is, working with either struggling readers or gifted students over a long period of time may give teachers a distorted view of what "normal" achievement looks like. The Kaufman Test of Educational Achievement (K-TEA/NU), available in both English and Spanish forms, can provide useful insights in these situations.

The K-TEA/NU is a norm-referenced test yielding information in the areas of reading, mathematics, and spelling. Intended for students in grades 1 to 12, the K-TEA/NU is available in a brief form for quick assessments (when only standardized data are needed) and a comprehensive form, which provides both standardized data and insights into classroom remediation. Alternate forms are not available, but the authors suggest that the two versions may be used as pretest–posttest measures.

Getting Organized: Profiling Your Class

The assessment ideas presented in this chapter and in the classroom assessment section in Chapters 2 through 5 provide a means of measuring the development of various reading skills. But that is only one part of the reading teacher's job. Organizing and analyzing the assessment data—first for each child individually and then for the entire class—constitute an extremely important next step in instructional planning. Charting the reading skills students have learned and still need to acquire, both individually and as a class, is what we refer to as **profiling.**

Valerie Schultz/Merrill

Two Documents Needed for Profiling

Teachers need two profiling documents: a **student profile document** to record individual strengths and needs in some detail, and a **class profile document** to help organize the entire class's data for the formation of needs-based reading groups. A profiling system should be driven either by the state's reading standards or the school district's scope and sequence skills list. These are usually provided in a curriculum guide to all teachers upon assignment to a school.

Student Profiling Document. In Figure 6.15 you will find a partially completed student profiling document. Note that each skill has a blank space to note

Figure 6.15   A Partially Completed Student Profile Form (Fall, Third Grade)

STUDENT PROFILE FORM—READING

Student: **Molly H.**

Teacher: **Ms. K. Spencer**

KEY: Reading Skill Development Rating

E = Emergent (not observed)
D = Developing (some evidence, but not fully competent)
P = Proficient (fully competent)

Date of Observation	Category	Benchmark Skill	Student Skill Level
October 14	**Phonics**	Uses phonic knowledge and structural analysis to decode words.	Proficient
December 5	**Fluency**	Reads aloud with fluency any text that is appropriately designed for grade level.	Developing (Molly read at 71 wcpm)
September 12	**Comprehension**	Summarizes major points from fiction and nonfiction texts.	Fiction—Proficient
	Comprehension	Summarizes major points from fiction and nonfiction texts.	
August 15	**Comprehension**	Discusses similarities in characters and events across stories.	Proficient
	Comprehension	Discusses underlying theme or message when interpreting fiction.	

(a) the date the teacher observed the student performing the specified skill, and (b) the degree (rating) to which the student was able to demonstrate the skill. For the latter, a three-point rubric is provided: "E" for students who are just *emerging* with an awareness of the skill or who have not demonstrated any competency with the skill; "D" for students who are in the midst of *developing* competency in the skill; and "P" for students who have attained *proficiency* (i.e., mastery) of the skill. These designations are important because they help the teacher differentiate the needs of students in the class. The designations can also be useful for informing parents about how their child is developing as a reader.

Note that in the example provided in Figure 6.15, the child has skills at each level of development, as well as some with no designation at all. (This means that the child has not been tested for the skill.)

Class Profiling Document

Accompanying the student profile is the class profile. (Always have both.) This document lists the same reading standards as the student profile only in abbreviated form. Figure 6.16 features a partial classroom reading profile for third grade. Notice that the skills listed match those found in the individual student profile.

To demonstrate how individual student data can be collated into a class profile, we provide an example in Figure 6.17. This example is for decoding and word recognition, as well as spelling and writing skills assessment. It is easy to see how the teacher can begin forming reading groups based on student needs. For instance, the teacher not only might form a group of students who need to develop revising and editing skills, but also recognize that two groups are actually needed—one for those who are emerging in this ability (E-level students), and another for those who are a little further along, or developing (D-level students).

IF–THEN Thinking

An absolutely essential key to success in reading instruction is the teacher's ability to analyze reading assessment data and translate this information to a plan for instruction to meet students' learning needs. Earlier in this chapter, we referred to "IF–THEN" reasoning in analyzing reading data. IF–THEN thinking (Flynt & Cooter, 2004; Reutzel & Cooter, 2007; R. Cooter, Flynt, & K. S. Cooter, 2007) works like this in relation to student and classroom assessment data:

> **If** you have identified specific learning needs in reading for a student(s), **then** which reading skills and strategies are appropriate to offer the student(s) next in your classroom instruction?

Said another way by Cooter and his colleagues (2007), the teacher must first collect a good bit of information through valid classroom assessments that begin to paint a picture of where the student is in his or her reading development. Once that picture begins to take shape and the teacher has an educated impression of what the student is able to do independently in reading and what the student needs to learn, then she might think . . .

> **If** the student has this reading need, **then** I should teach the reading skill _____ using the _____ teaching strategy.

R. Cooter et al. (2007), in order to guide your instruction in using IF–THEN thinking, have offered examples of which we provide two in Tables 6.2 through 6.4 on the following pages. They describe a few common reading needs along with selected instructional strategies from a variety of sources.

Figure 6.16 Partial Class Profiling Instrument

CLASS PROFILE (BLAST™): THIRD-GRADE LITERACY MILESTONES

Teacher: _____ **Date/Grading Period Completed:** _____

> **Instructions:** Record the degree to which each milestone skill has been achieved by each student (**E** = Emergent, **D** = Developing Skill, **P** = Proficient) in each box corresponding to the student and skill in the grid.

Decoding and Word Recognition

3.D.1	Context clues, phonic knowledge, and structural analysis

Spelling and Writing

3.SW.1	Uses studied words and spelling patterns
3.SW.2	Uses the dictionary to check spelling
3.SW.3	Uses these aspects of the writing process:
3.SW.3.1	Combines information/multiple sources
3.SW.3.2	Revises and edits
3.SW.3.3	Variety of written work
3.SW.3.4	Graphic organizational tools
3.SW.3.5	Descriptions and figurative language
3.SW.3.6	Variety of formal sentence structures
3.SW.4.S.1	Orthographic patterns and rules (Spanish only)
3.SW.5.S.2	Spells words with three or more syllables using silent letters, dieresis marks, accents, verbs (Spanish only)

Oral Reading

3.OR.1	Reads aloud with fluency

(continued)

Figure 6.16 (Continued)

Reading Fluency														
3.F.1	Very few word-by-word interruptions													
3.F.2	Reads mostly in larger meaningful phrases													
3.F.3	Reads with expression													
3.F.4	Attends consistently to punctuation													
3.F.5	Rereads to clarify or problem-solve													
3.F.6	Reads sixty (60) words per minute (minimum)													
Language Comprehension and Response to Text														
3.C.1	Comprehends both fiction and nonfiction on level													
3.C.2	Reads chapter books independently													
3.C.3	Identifies problem words or phrases													
3.C.4	Summarizes fiction and nonfiction text													
3.C.5	Similarities: characters/events across stories													
3.C.6	Theme or message: interpreting fiction													
3.C.7	Nonfiction:													
	3.C.7.1 Cause/effect													
	3.C.7.2 Fact/opinion													
	3.C.7.3 Main idea/details													
3.C.8	Evaluation: Uses information/reasoning													
3.C.9	Word meaning from roots and affixes													
3.C.10	Dictionary: Determine meanings/usage													
3.C.11	Uses new vocabulary in own speech and writing													
3.C.12	Writing: Basic grammar/parts of speech													
3.C.13	Familiar w/read-aloud, indep. reading, nonfiction													
3.C.14	Locates information using:													
	3.C.14.1 Tables of contents													
	3.C.14.2 Indexes													
	3.C.14.3 Internet search engines													
3.C.15	Connects literary texts with life experiences													

Figure 6.17 Needs-Based Groups

CLASS PROFILE (BLAST™): THIRD-GRADE LITERACY MILESTONES

Teacher: **K. Spencer**   Date/Grading Period Completed: **12 – 14**

Instructions: Record the degree to which each milestone skill has been achieved by each student (**E** = Emergent, **D** = Developing Skill, **P** = Proficient) in each box corresponding to the student and skill in the grid.

Skill	Dora	Paula	Ameenah	Jason	Rosa María	Harry	James	Dirk	Sybonia	Alicia	Johnny	Anna
Decoding and Word Recognition												
3.D.1 Context clues, phonic knowledge, and structural analysis	P	P	P	D	D	P	P	D	P	D	P	P
Spelling and Writing												
3.SW.1 Uses studied words and spelling patterns	D	D	E	E	D	D	E	D	P	E	E	P
3.SW.2 Uses the dictionary to check spelling	D	D	D	D	D	D	P	D	D	D	E	P
3.SW.3 Uses these aspects of the writing process:												
3.SW.3.1 Combines information/multiple sources	E	E	E	E	E	E	E	E	E	E	E	E
3.SW.3.2 Revises and edits	D	D	D	E	E	E	E	D	D	E	E	P
3.SW.3.3 Variety of written work	E	D	P	E	D	P	E	E	E	E	E	P
3.SW.3.4 Graphic organizational tools	E	D	E	D	E	E	D	D	E	D	P	D
3.SW.3.5 Descriptions and figurative language	E	E	D	P	E	E	D	P	E	E	E	P
3.SW.3.6 Variety of formal sentence structures	D	D	D	D	D	D	D	D	E	D	D	P
3.SW.4.S.1 Orthographic patterns and rules (Spanish only)	D	P		D	D		D					
3.SW.5.S.2 Spells words with three or more syllables using silent letters, dieresis marks, accents, verbs (Spanish only)	P	P		P	P		D					

231

Table 6.2 IF–THEN Chart for Phonemic Awareness (PA)

IF a Student Has This Learning Need . . .	THEN Try Using a Strategy Like . . .	Resources for These and Other Strategies
Initial Sounds	• Word families (same/different beginning sounds) • Songs and poetry • Word rubber-banding • Tongue twisters	*Selected Internet Resources* *http://www.songsforteaching.com* *http://www.literacyconnections.com* *http://www.nifl.gov/partnershipforreading/* *http://www.readingrockets.org* *http://reading.uoregon.edu/pa/pa_features.php* *Books* Blevins, W. (1999). *Phonemic Awareness Songs and Rhymes* (Grades PreK-2). New York: Scholastic.
Phonemic Segmentation of Spoken Words	• Word rubber-banding • Add/take a sound from spoken words • Environmental print/logos • Songs, chants, raps, poetry	Opitz, M. (2000). *Rhymes and Reasons: Literature and Language Play for Phonological Awareness.* Portsmouth, NH: Heinemann.
Blending Sounds into Spoken Words	• Add/take a sound • Word rubber-banding • Environmental print/logos • Songs, chants, raps, poetry • Odd word out	Reutzel, D. R., & Cooter, R. B. (2007). *Strategies for Reading Assessment and Instruction* (3rd ed.). Upper Saddle River, NJ: Merrill/Prentice-Hall.
Rhyming	• Songs, chants, raps, poetry • Alphabet books • Tongue twisters	

Table 6.3 IF–THEN Chart for Phonics and Other Word Attack Skills

IF a Student Has This Learning Need . . .	THEN Try Using a Strategy Like . . .	Resources for These and Other Strategies
Letter Sounds	• Explicit phonics instruction • Word boxes • Tongue twisters • Letter–sound cards • Making words • Nonsense words	Selected Internet Resources "Between the Lions" (PBS)-*http://pbskids.org/lions/games/* "BBC Schools" *http://www.bbc.co.uk/schools/wordsandpictures/index.shtml* *http://www.adrianbruce.com/reading/* *http://cwx.prenhall.com/bookbind/pubbooks/literacy-cluster/* *http://toread.com/*

Table 6.3 (Continued)

IF a Student Has This Learning Need . . .	THEN Try Using a Strategy Like . . .	Resources for These and Other Strategies
"C" Rule	• Explicit phonics instruction • Word boxes • Letter–sound cards • Making words • Nonsense words	***Books*** Rycik, M., & Rycik, J. (2007). *Phonics and Word Identification: Instruction and Intervention K-8:1/e.* Upper Saddle River, NJ: Merrill/Prentice-Hall. Lucht, L. (2006). *The Wonder of Word Study: Lessons and Activities to Create Independent Readers, Writers, and Spellers.* Portsmouth, NH: Heinemann.
"G" Rule	• Explicit phonics instruction • Word boxes • Letter–sound cards • Making words • Nonsense words	Cunningham, P. (2005). *Phonics They Use* (4th ed.). Boston: AB/Longman. Reutzel, D. R., & Cooter, R. B. (2007). *Strategies for Reading Assessment and Instruction* (3rd ed.). Upper Saddle River, NJ: Merrill/Prentice-Hall.

Table 6.4 IF–THEN Chart for Reading Fluency

IF a Student Has This Learning Need . . .	THEN Try Using a Strategy Like . . .	Resources for These and Other Strategies
Reading Rate	• Repeated readings • Choral reading • Buddy reading • Reading television captions	***Selected Internet Resources*** *http://pbskids.org/readingrainbow/*
Reading Accuracy/Automaticity	• Oral recitation lesson • Assisted reading • Guided oral reading	***Books*** Opitz, M., & Rasinski, T. (1998). *Good-bye Round Robin: Effective Oral Reading Strategies.* Portsmouth, NH: Heinemann.
Quality/Prosody	• Repeated readings • Choral reading • Guided oral reading • Oral recitation lesson	Reutzel, D. R., & Cooter, R. B. (in press). *Strategies for Reading Assessment and Instruction* (3rd ed.). Upper Saddle River, NJ: Merrill/Prentice-Hall.

Summary

Assessment exists to inform and improve classroom teaching. When employed properly, assessments help teachers chart individual students' learning and proficiency with essential reading skills. Put another way, assessment helps teachers understand what each child *can* do in reading, and what they are ready to learn next. Once teachers know where students are in their reading development they are able to plan appropriate "next steps" in instruction, select appropriate reading materials with which to teach, and plan small-group instruction according to the mutual needs of students.

Four purposes of reading assessment have been described that are derived from two federal initiatives: the *No Child Left Behind* initiative, and *Reading First*. *Outcome assessments* are intended to survey the reading achievement of teacher's class as a whole and provide a kind of snapshot of the reading program's effectiveness. *Screening assessments* provide initial (beginning of the year, or the beginning of a new part of the reading curriculum) or "first look" information about each student's ability. *Diagnostic assessments* provide more in-depth information about students' individual strengths and needs. *Progress-monitoring assessments* are an extremely valuable tool for teachers as they provide ongoing and timely feedback as to how well individual students are responding to instruction currently in motion—"real time" feedback. Examples of commonly used assessment tools and strategies for each of these assessment purposes were described in some detail to augment other strategies shared throughout our text.

A number of commercially published reading assessments commonly used in schools were presented. We grouped these according to the four purposes just summarized for your convenience. These included informal reading inventories, curriculum-based measurements (CBM), DIBELS, the *Woodcock Reading Mastery Tests Revised,* and many more. While a school psychologist often administers some of these tests, all may be given by classroom teachers with minimal training.

Once student data has been gathered, the next phase of reading assessment requires interpretation of results. We described ways teachers can create student and classroom profiling documents to sort data and make decisions about small-group instruction. We also shared a way of selecting evidence-based teaching strategies that meet each students' needs called "IF–THEN thinking." This is a classroom-proven method that is both quick and effective in selecting best teaching practices. In this way we can ensure that every child receives the reading instruction needed.

Classroom Applications

1. With a partner (or two), conduct a library search of professional journals (e.g., *Educational Leadership, Phi Delta Kappan*) and education periodicals (e.g., *Education Week*) and prepare a response to this question: What are some of the issues regarding reading assessment? Be sure to take a look at the literature relating to No Child Left Behind and Reading First legislation.

Start with the year 2000 to get a good chronology of issues. Present a poster session of your findings to your classmates.

2. Develop a schedule for your classroom (name the grade level) that includes time for the daily assessment of at least four students. What will be the typical assessment tools you will probably use during this time period? (Identify at least four.) Justify your choices.

3. Develop three evaluation checklist forms that could be used in your classroom or a grade level you specify for reading comprehension, word identification, and content reading strategies. Include a suggested rubric with a rationale for each item.

Recommended Readings

Cooter, R. B., Flynt, E. S., & Cooter, K. S. (2007). *The comprehensive reading inventory.* Upper Saddle River, NJ: Merrill/Prentice Hall.

Dunn, L., & Dunn, L. M. (1997). *Peabody Picture Vocabulary Test–Third Edition* (PPVT-III). Circle Pines, MN: American Guidance Service.

Dunn, L., Lugo, D. E., Padilla, E. R., & Dunn, L. M. (1986). *Test de Vocabulario en Imágenes Peabody* (TVIP). Circle Pines, MN: American Guidance Service.

Reutzel, D. R., & Cooter, R. B. (2007). *Strategies for reading assessment and instruction: Helping every child succeed* (3rd ed.). Upper Saddle River, NJ: Merrill/Prentice Hall.

chapter 7

Programs and Standards for Reading Instruction

Chapter Questions

1. What is meant by "standards" for reading instruction?

2. What is a core reading program?

3. What are the supplemental reading programs for helping struggling readers succeed?

4. Which reading programs have been shown to be effective with English learners (ELs)?

5. How can teachers help parents and interested stakeholders better understand reading standards?

Which Reading Program Is Best?

It's Friday morning, 8:00 a.m. You are attending a meeting of the new Textbook Adoption Committee for your school district. The committee's task is to choose a new reading program. Just one month into your first year as a teacher, you and your teammates must review a plethora of basal reading programs, supplemental materials for reading instruction, and sundry other kits and manipulatives. The 40' by 40' conference room is absolutely packed with the latest offerings from major- and minor-league publishers, and properly coiffed sales representatives are waiting in the hallway like obedient soldiers to retrieve any needed information at a moment's notice. Great food and beverages are provided. The state's reading standards have been made available for your convenience as you match required skills to appropriate materials.

It all sounds straightforward, but where do you begin? Some of your colleagues feel strongly that a program that best matches the state standards should be selected. Others think that materials that supposedly help teachers teach to the state test are imperative. Still others like the programs with lots of "free stuff," like classroom libraries and technology support. As a new teacher, this latter option is especially appealing; you don't have much to work with beyond the relatively few supplies and materials you inherited from your predecessor. However, you admit that the other arguments may make better sense. After all, you will be judged by how well your students perform on the state standards and test.

But you also know that you are there to represent those who have no voice—the students. What should you do?

Many programs for reading instruction are available to teachers. While many publishers claim to offer comprehensive curriculums, in our view, no reading instructional program has ever been designed—or ever will be designed—that meets the needs of all learners. Therefore, it is important for teachers to know their learners' current developmental levels, the fundamentals of reading instruction, state reading standards, and reading instruction programs and materials that meet the needs of their students.

Our focus, as we discuss reading instruction standards and reading instruction programs, are the "Big Five" instructional strands drawn from the report of the National Reading Panel (2000): phonemic awareness, phonics, vocabulary, comprehension, and fluency. In this chapter, we look at how each of the Big Five is treated at each grade and developmental level of literacy learning according to scientifically-based reading research (SBRR).

First, we want to acquaint you with a summary of the standards-based movement in the United States and how it has impacted the development of reading programs.

What Is Meant by "Standards" for Reading Instruction?

In our opening vignette, our new teacher was caught between the horns of a dilemma: how to balance her need for high-quality books and materials with state demands for standards-based teaching and the omnipresent high stakes tests. In the past decade or so, standards-based curriculums and assessments have been prescribed as a cure for the poor performance and accountability of many public schools (Watt, 2005; Zuzovsky & Libman, 2006). Billions of dollars have been spent on programs and state tests, in part so that federal and state agencies can rank schools in terms of student achievement (Baines & Stanley, 2006).

Overview of the Standards-Based Movement

According to Watt (2005), the **standards-based movement** in the United States began as an outgrowth of a growing public debate on the rather tepid performance of school children on measures of reading, not to mention in other academic areas like mathematics and science. Concern for the effectiveness of U.S. education was heightened following the release of a number of national studies in the 1980s, most especially the report of the National Commission on Excellence in Education in 1983. In general, these reports sparked calls for the reform of public education by either decentralizing authority to local communities or, conversely, by giving more authority to state and federal agencies.

In 1989, then-governor George W. Bush convened the Charlottesville Education Summit involving President Clinton and the nation's 50 governors. The goal was to identify ways to make the U.S. more internationally competitive by 2000. Watt (2005, pp. 3–4) described the outcome thus:

> They reached agreement to establish a process for setting national education goals, seeking greater flexibility and accountability in using federal resources to meet the goals, undertaking a state-by-state effort to restructure the education system, and reporting annually on progress in achieving the goals (Vinovskis, 1999). . . . The six National Education Goals became the foundation for America 2000 and later

Goals 2000, and provided the impetus for defining national standards based in academic disciplines.

A multiplicity of trends in U.S. education had concurred [sic] by this time leading conservatives and liberals to forge a consensus about focusing on what students should know and be able to do. Policy-makers set nationally recognized groups in key disciplines [with] the task of developing national standards consisting of content, performance, and opportunity-to-learn standards. **Content standards** refer to broad descriptions of knowledge and skills that students should achieve in particular subject areas. **Performance standards** are examples and definitions of knowledge and skills in which students need to demonstrate proficiency. **Opportunity-to-learn standards,** which address conditions necessary at each level of the education system to provide all students with opportunities to master content standards and meet performance standards, provide criteria covering six elements. These elements refer to the quality and availability of curricula, materials and technology, the capability of teachers to meet learning needs, the availability of professional development, the alignment of the curriculum to content standards, the adequacy of school facilities for learning, and the application of non-discriminatory policies.

It seems fair to conclude that when Bush was elected president in 2000 he used the outcomes generated by the Charlottesville Education Summit to form the basis of the No Child Left Behind (NCLB) legislation. Approved by Congress with near-unanimous support, NCLB in effect federalized the standards-based movement and required all states to conform or risk losing tax dollars. NCLB also caused the producers of reading programs, tests, and support materials to conform to mandated "evidence-based" standards. If they did not do so, then their products would likely not be adopted by state or local education agencies. Regardless of where one stands on the philosophy of the standards-based movement and its implementation, it is nevertheless a matter of current law that dramatically influences the types and quality of reading instruction materials available.

Where Can I Find My State's Reading Standards and the Tools to Assess Them?

In Chapters 2 through 5, we present evidence-based standards for each skill area of reading. These are based on the most comprehensive and scientific research studies available, and make up the skeletal framework for most state standards in reading. But don't stop there. You should also seek out the specific standards articulated by your own state department of education and the state-mandated tests for measuring their acquisition by students. This information is available to teachers online. For your convenience, we present a listing of all state agencies that provide this important information.

In the next section, we turn our attention to the most prevalent type of reading materials. These are basal reading programs, also known as core reading programs.

Getting to Know English Learners
The standards for ELs are produced by the Teachers of English to Speakers of Other Languages (TESOL) based in Washington, DC. Its mission is to advocate for the education of ELs and for the profession of teaching ELs. Its standards may be found on its Web site: *http://www.tesol.org*

What Are Basal or Core Reading Programs?

Basal readers in one form or another have played an integral role in U.S. reading instruction for centuries and are likely to continue to do so well into the future (Giordano, 2001; Hoffman, 2001; McCallum, 1988; Reutzel, 1991; Robinson, in press). According to *The Literacy Dictionary,* a **basal reading program** is "a collection of student texts and workbooks, teachers' manuals, and supplemental materials for developmental reading and sometimes writing instruction, used chiefly in the elementary and middle school grades" (Harris & Hodges, 1995, p. 18). Simmons and Kame'enui (2003) explain that basal reading programs are the primary instructional tool that teachers use to teach children to learn to read and to ensure that they reach reading levels that meet or exceed grade-level standards. Historically, these programs have been termed "basal" because they serve as the "base" for reading instruction. These programs are also referred to as **core reading programs;** however, for our purposes, we will use the term "basal reader."

Understanding the Basal Reader

Research indicates that basal readers are used daily in 92 to 98 percent of primary classrooms in the United States (Flood & Lapp, 1986; Goodman, 1987; Wade & Moje, 2000). Recent data suggest that 85 percent of intermediate grade classrooms continue to rely on basal reader instruction to some degree (Shannon & Goodman, 1994; Wade & Moje, 2000).

Anatomy of the Basal Reading Approach

Basal readers are typically composed of a set of foundation materials. These include: (1) the student text, (2) the teacher's edition (TE), (3) student workbooks, (4) a teacher's edition workbook, (5) supplemental practice exercises, (6) enrichment activities (usually the latter two are in the form of masters that can be duplicated), (7) big books, (8) leveled readers, (9) phonic or decodable readers, and (10) end-of-unit and end-of-book tests. Other supplemental materials can be acquired at additional cost: picture cards, picture-with-letter cards, letter cards, word cards for display on word walls, pocket charts, classroom trade-book libraries, big books, and

© Ellen B. Senisi/Ellen Senisi

technology resources such as videotapes, CDs, DVDs, and publisher World Wide Web sites on the Internet. In addition, many basal reading series provide a system for record keeping, management of the reading skills taught and mastered, and assessments. Because many teachers will employ a basal series in a school reading program, we will describe each of the most basic basal components and provide examples.

The Basal Teacher's Edition (TE). For teachers, perhaps the most important part of the basal reading program is the **teacher's edition** or **TE** because it contains instructional guidance and support (see Figure 7.1). For many new teachers, the TE is an important resource for initial professional development.

Within the pages of the teacher's edition, one usually finds three important features: (a) the scope and sequence chart of the particular skills taught in the basal reading program, (b) a reduced version or facsimile of the student text, and (c) recommended lesson plans (see Figures 7.2 and 7.3). A **scope and sequence chart** describes in great detail the *range* of skills and/or concepts to be taught in a basal program as well as the *sequence* in which these are to be presented during the school year. The entire student text, shown as a reduced facsimile, is included for convenience in the teacher's edition. Lesson plans in the basal reader are included to save the teacher preparation time. Current basal readers typically design reading lessons around a modified sequence of the directed reading thinking activity (Stauffer, 1969).

It is important that teachers and administrators understand that the teacher's edition (TE) is a resource to be used discriminatingly—not a script to be followed rigidly. Teachers and administrators should not allow the basal teacher's edition

Figure 7.1 **Example of a 2000 Teacher's Edition for *Scott Foresman Reading* Basal Series**

From *Scott Foresman Reading: Take Me There* (Teacher's ed., Grade 1, Volume 5), Glenview, IL: Scott Foresman Company. Copyright 2000 by Scott Foresman Company. Reprinted by permission.

Figure 7.2 A Scope and Sequence Chart Showing the Range of Skills to Be Taught in a Basal Program

From *Scott Foresman Reading, Take Me There* (Teacher's ed., Grade 1, Volume 5, pp. 228–229), 2000, Glenview, IL: Scott Foresman Company. Copyright 2000 by Scott Foresman Company. Reprinted by permission.

Figure 7.3 Example of the Internal Pages from a 2002 Teacher's Edition for *SRA Open Court Reading* Basal Series

From *SRA Open Court Reading: Things That Go* (Teacher's ed., Level 1, Unit 3), 2002, Columbus, OH: SRA/McGraw-Hill. Copyright 2002 by SRA/McGraw-Hill. Reprinted by permission.

to dictate the reading program. Rather, teachers should be encouraged to decide what is and what is not appropriate in the TE for use with a particular group of children.

The Student Basal Text. The student basal text is an anthology of original contemporary and classic stories, poems, news clips, and expository text selections. Some reading selections have been created expressly for inclusion in the student basal reader. Other selections have been adapted from contemporary and classic children's literature or trade books. High-quality artwork generally accompanies the selections. Interspersed throughout the student text, one may also find poems, jokes, riddles, puzzles, informational essays, and special skill and/or concept lessons. Some basal student texts contain questions children should be able to answer after reading the selections. Upper-level basal readers often contain a glossary of words that students can refer to when decoding new words or that they can use to determine the meaning of unfamiliar or new words found in the text.

Changes in basal student texts have resulted in a "more engaging basal" than those of two decades ago as judged by students, teachers, and reading experts (Hoffman et al., 1994; McCarthey et al., 1994).

Inclusion of Authentic Trade Literature. A close examination of quality children's literature included in the more recent basal reader revisions reveals few, if any, alterations of the authors' language or word choice. However, one disturbing publishing practice relates to cropping or cutting original artwork in children's picture book stories. Because of costs involved in the reproduction and permission for use of original artwork, basal publishers have sometimes cut the beautiful artwork that supports and sustains the text in many children's books (Reutzel & Larsen, 1995). The practice of cropping or cutting support artwork may be even more damaging than altering the text for young, emergent readers who may rely more heavily on the pictures for support throughout their initial readings of a new or unfamiliar text.

Information Texts. **Information texts,** those that are factual or nonfiction in nature, are important for helping children increase their vocabulary and concept knowledge—much more so than fiction texts (i.e., stories). Duke (2000) explains that information texts have several distinct features: (a) a function to communicate information about the social or natural world; (b) factual content; (c) technical vocabulary; (d) classificatory or definitional material; (e) graphic

> **Getting to Know English Learners**
> The five general TESOL standards are a blend of many disciplines and include wording on the necessity for ELs to engage successfully with informational texts across disciplines such as math, science, and social studies.

elements like maps, graphs, and diagrams; (f) varying text structures (e.g., cause and effect, problem and solution, compare and contrast, etc.); and (g) repetition of topical themes. Duke (2000) reviewed the reading experiences offered to children in 20 first-grade classrooms selected from very low and very high socioeconomic-status school districts with reading information texts. She found a scarcity of informational texts available in these classrooms—particularly in low-socioeconomic-status schools. To compound the scarcity of information texts found in the classrooms, there were relatively few informational texts available in school libraries and on classroom walls and other display surfaces in the schools. As a result, young children in low socioeconomic classrooms read information texts only 3.6 minutes per day on average.

In a more recent study, Moss and Newton (2001) investigated the amount of information text available in current second-, fourth-, and sixth-grade basal reading series. These researchers found that only 16–20 percent of all selections in current basal readers could be classified as information texts. The preponderance of selections found in current basal readers continues to be narrative or fictional (66 percent). Thus, one shortcoming of many basal programs is a lack of informational texts necessary for increasing student word knowledge and vocabulary. It is critical that you ensure that all students are exposed to a great deal of informational text, even if that means supplementing heavily your core or basal reading program. At least one-half of the reading curriculum, if not more, should involve informational texts.

Beginning Reading Texts

Controlling Word Difficulty and Frequency. Control over word difficulty in beginning reading texts presumably allows for the systematic introduction of a predetermined number of unfamiliar words in each story (Hiebert, 1999; Hoffman, 2001). Control of word difficulty is typically achieved by using simpler words or words with fewer syllables in place of longer words and by shortening sentences. Basal publishers have for many years controlled the language of beginning reading texts by using simple, one-syllable words. Town and Holbrook (1857), in the *Progressive Reading* basal reading series, are perhaps the earliest educators to explain the use of controlled texts in beginning reading materials:

> The authors, satisfied that the most simple language is best adapted to the class of pupils for whom this Reader is designed, have adhered, as strictly as possible, to the one-syllable system. They have departed from it only when necessary to avoid any stiffness of style, or weakness of expression, which might arise from too closely following it in every instance.

Compare the text from the following 1865 and 2000 basal readers beginning text.

1865

John stands by his father.
"I will be a good boy, father."

2000

Bob went to the barn for Dad.
Dad asked Bob to feed the pigs.

Controlling the difficulty of words encountered in basal reader stories supposedly renders text less difficult to read. However, research by Pearson (1974) challenged the idea that shorter sentences are easier to read. Pearson found that short, choppy sentences are actually more difficult to read because explicit connecting or sequencing words such as *because, and, so, then, before,* and *after* are deleted from the text and consequently must be inferred by the reader in order for her or him to comprehend the text.

Controlling Decoding Difficulty. In some basal reader programs, the earliest books, or **primers,** often contain reading selections known as **decodable text** (Adams, 1990a; Beck, 1997; Foorman, Francis, Fletcher, Schatschneider, & Mehta, 1998; Grossen, 1997; Hiebert, 1999). Decodable texts are designed to reinforce the teaching of particular phonic elements, such as short *a,* by using highly controlled vocabulary in their selections (e.g., *Nan* and *Dan*). Decodable texts are frequently sold as supplemental books to school districts to augment basal reader instruction.

A decodable text example is shown in the following excerpt (*Scholastic,* Book 14, Phonics Readers, pp. 2–7; Schreiber & Tuchman, 1997).

The Big Hit

Who hid? Pig.
Who had a mitt? Pig.
Who did not sit?
Who did hit?
Up. Up. Up.
Who had a big hit? Pig.
Who slid? Pig did!

From SCHOLASTIC PHONICS READERS, Book 14 by Schreiber and Tuchman. Copyright © 1997 by Scholastic Inc. Reprinted by permission of Scholastic Inc.

Although decodable texts can be useful for teaching phonics, children seldom encounter such contrived texts outside of school. As a consequence, the practice of controlling vocabulary to this extent continues to be questioned on the grounds that it tends to result in senseless or "inconsiderate" texts, and tends to cause children to think that reading is primarily a decoding task rather than a search for meaning (Allington, 1997; Armbruster, 1984; Hiebert & Martin, 2001). The lack of real content or a discernable story line in these decodable texts—particularly if they are over-used—is suspected to cause children to quickly lose interest in reading.

Controlling Language Patterns in Texts. Predictable texts are characterized by the repetition of a syntactic unit that can range from a phrase to a group of sentences, e.g., "Run, run, as fast as you can. You can't catch me, I'm the Gingerbread Man." Perhaps one of the best-known examples of patterned trade books are those authored and advocated by Bill Martin (1990), such as *Brown Bear, Brown Bear, What Do You See?* These books have been found to decrease the control over new or unique words and feature engaging illustrations. Other patterned books have been published as part of a total reading program. For example, those published by Wendy Pye Publishing that began in New Zealand have been well accepted in the United States. Books in the *Sunshine Series* begin with simple repetitious phrases accompanied by strong picture or illustration supports such as is found in the story titled *Look.*

Look said the birds, cats.
Look said the birds, dogs.
Look said the birds, bread.
Look said the birds, children.

From *Look* from the Sunshine Series. Wendy Pye Publishing. Used with permission.

You can clearly see that the difficulty of the language found in patterned beginning readers is still controlled as in the past. The major difference is that the control is exerted at larger levels of text—phrases and sentences. This approach to beginning reading has produced some interesting research findings. Children who read patterned texts learned a group of sight words as quickly as children who read controlled word difficulty and frequency texts (Bridge, Winograd, & Haley, 1983). However, more recently, Johnston (1998) found that learning new words in first grade was improved when words were learned separate from the text than in the context of predictable texts. It seems that controlling text patterns also presents some limitations in providing the texts needed for effective beginning reading instruction.

The Workbook

In years past, the most used part of any basal reading series was the workbook (Osborn, 1985). In fact, if any part of the basal reading lesson was neglected, it was seldom the workbook pages (Durkin, 1984; Mason, 1983). Although clearly less frequently the case today, workbook exercises remain firmly entrenched in many classrooms. It appears that some teachers, administrators, and publishers, as evidenced by their continued inclusion of workbook pages or worksheets as part and parcel of basal reading series, still see seatwork as the real "work" of the school literacy program (Allington & Cunningham, 1996).

Workbook exercises are not intended to supplant time for structured, well-planned reading instruction or independent reading. Rather, workbook exercises are intended for use by students to independently practice skills, strategies, and literary understandings previously taught by the teacher. Also, workbook exercises are often used as a type of formative or on-going "paper-and-pencil" assessment. In addition to these twin purposes, many teachers also use workbook exercises to manage, direct, or focus student activity in independent learning centers when the teacher is actively working with small groups of children in teacher-guided reading groups. Used in these ways, workbook exercises play at least three distinct roles in classrooms: practice, assessment, and management.

Research has revealed that primary grade students spend up to 70 percent of the time allocated for reading instruction—or 49 minutes per day—in independent practice or completion of worksheets, whereas less than 10 percent of total reading instructional time—or about 7 to 8 minutes per day—is devoted to silent reading. In fact, publishers indicate that there is an insatiable demand for worksheets (Anderson, Hiebert, Scott, & Wilkinson, 1985). Other studies (Knapp, 1991) indicate that many teachers assign or provide time for only small amounts of real reading and writing—in some cases less than 5 minutes per day! Jachym, Allington, and Broikou (1989) and Allington and Cunningham (1996) reported that seatwork (independent completion of worksheets) is displacing many of the more important aspects of reading instruction, such as the acquisition of good books and time spent in actual reading. Based on these findings, it seems obvious that workbooks have been misused and overused. However, when teachers judiciously select workbook exercises to support and reinforce concepts and skills provided during teacher-guided instruction, students benefit from valuable practice and feedback on their progress in relation to specific reading skills, strategies, and literary understandings. Dole, Osborn, and Lehr (1990, pp. 8–15) provide six guidelines for assessing the worth of workbook and worksheet-type reading tasks in the Workbooks subtext for the Basal Reading Programs: Adoption Guidelines project.

Standards and Guidelines for Analyzing Workbook Tasks

1. When analyzing the content of workbook tasks, look for tasks that
   - Are integrated with the lessons in the teacher's manual and with the student textbook
   - Relate to the most important (and workbook-appropriate) instruction in the lessons
   - Are based on the reading selections
   - Use vocabulary that is from current or previous lessons
   - Increase in difficulty as grade level increases

Hope Madden/Merrill

2. When analyzing the content of workbook task design, look for tasks for which
   - The student must read all of the possible choices before selecting an answer
   - Student responses can be judged correct or incorrect
   - Student responses indicate to the teacher what the student knows
   - Students can successfully complete part two of the task without successfully completing part one
3. When analyzing the practice and review tasks, look for tasks that provide
   - Sufficient practice
   - Independent practice

Hope Madden/Merrill

- Extra practice
- Systematic review
4. When analyzing instructional language, look for tasks that
   - Use language consistent with the rest of the program
   - Are accompanied by brief explanations of purpose or explanatory titles that students understand
   - Have clear and easy-to-follow instruction, with attention to consistency, sentence length, and directional steps
5. When evaluating reading and writing responses, look for tasks that
   - Provide opportunities for students to respond in their own words
   - Provide opportunities for students to apply several comprehension strategies or decoding skills in one task
6. When evaluating the considerateness to students, look for
   - Repeated use of task formats
   - Consistent responses
   - Occasional tasks that are fun
   - Few or no nonfunctional tasks

From Dole, J. A., Osborn, J., & Lehr, F. (1990). *A guide to selecting basal reading programs.* Urbana, IL: Center for the Study of Reading.

Workbooks can be a valuable resource for teachers and students when used correctly. On the other hand, when they are misused or overused, workbook exercises can be a debilitating deterrent to students' reading progress.

Assessment

Although workbook exercises can be used for formative assessment of reading skill, strategy, and literary understandings development, most basal reading series provide end-of-unit or end-of-book tests for summative evaluation of student learning. These tests are generally criterion-referenced tests, which means that the items measured are directly related to the specific skills, strategies, or literary concepts taught in that unit, level, or book. Most basal readers now provide suggestions for designing individual assessment portfolios for each student, including the use of running records. Teachers who want to present students' reading demonstrations to their parents will need to obtain audiotapes of students' reading and analyze them using something like running records analysis (see Chapter 2 for details about running records). As the stakes are raised higher and higher in terms of standardized assessment measures, many basal readers are correlating skills, strategies, and literary understandings with nationally published standardized tests (See Figure 7.4).

> **Getting to Know English Learners**
> Workbooks can be a valuable tool for ELs, especially if they include visual learning aids such as maps, photos, pictures, diagrams, graphs, and/or tables.

Just as workbook exercises can be abused, so can tests. Tests should provide teachers with information about the quantity and quality of children's literacy learning to inform, shape, and direct future instructional choices and selection of interventions. Test results should not be used to label children or embarrass teachers. Two poignant examples of the misuse of test data are found in the books *First Grade Takes a Test* (Cohen, 1980) and *Testing Miss Malarkey* (Finch, 2003). No single test score should ever form the basis for making important decisions about children's learning or their teachers' competence. Administrators and teachers must be extremely cautious in the use and interpretation of single literacy (reading and writing) test scores.

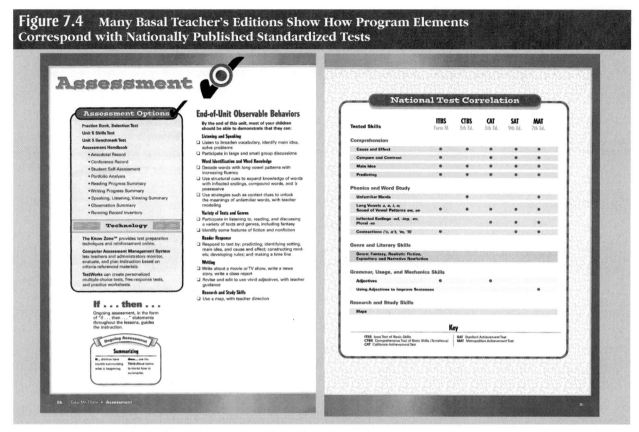

Figure 7.4 Many Basal Teacher's Editions Show How Program Elements Correspond with Nationally Published Standardized Tests

From *Scott Foresman Reading: Take Me There* 2000, (Teacher's ed., Grade 1, Volume 5, pp. 8h–8i), Glenview, IL: Scott Foresman Company. Copyright 2000 by Scott Foresman Company. Reprinted by permission.

Record Keeping

An **instructional management system** allows teachers to keep accurate records from year to year regarding each child's progress through the adopted basal reading program's scope and sequence of skills. Maintaining records to document teaching and learning is an important part of accountability. Most basal reading series provide a means for keeping records on children's progress through the skills outlined in the scope and sequence chart of the basal. Most often, the methods of assessment specified are paper-and-pencil testing or worksheet administration. The scores obtained on these exercises are entered into a master list or record available today in CD-ROM form, which follows students throughout their elementary years.

Unfortunately, some teachers spend inordinate amounts of time keeping records of this kind, which leads to a most undesirable condition as captured by Pearson in 1985 when he stated:

> The model implicit in the practices of [this teacher] was that of a manager—[a] person who arranged materials, texts, and the classroom environment so learning could occur. But the critical test of whether learning did occur was left up to the child as s/he interacted with the materials.

> Children practiced applying skills; if they learned them, fine; we always had more skills for them to practice; if they did not, fine; we always had more worksheets and duplicating sheets for the same skill. And the most important rule in such a mastery role was that practice makes perfect, leading to the ironic condition that children spent most of their time on precisely that subset of skills they performed least well. (p. 736)

To this we would like to add the comment that, disturbingly, teachers under this model spent the bulk of their time duplicating, assigning, correcting, and recording worksheets rather than guiding, demonstrating, or interacting with children or books. Although increasingly elegant with the addition of CD-ROM technology, record keeping should go well beyond keeping track of worksheet-type evaluations. Fortunately, many basal readers now recognize this fact and include process and product measures of children's reading and reading habits.

In summary, basal reading series are typically composed of a core of three elements—teacher's edition, student text, and workbooks—as well as a host of supplementary kits, charts, cards, tests, technology, additional practice exercises, and assessment/record-keeping systems. In an effort to compete with trade book publishers, basal publishers are also producing big books to complement the already expansive list of purchasable options listed previously. Teachers should be careful not to accept these new "basal" big books without careful examination. In some cases, big books published by basal companies are not big books at all—they are big basals!

Although the basal reader approach offers a resource for helping teachers provide systematic and sequenced reading instruction throughout the elementary and middle grades, teachers must nonetheless be careful to supplement this core program with trade books, silent reading time, group sharing, extensions of reading into writing, speaking, drama, music, and so on. In addition, they must take care to provide individual assessment of children's reading progress, behaviors, and attitudes. When this goal is understood and achieved, basal readers are valuable literacy tools and resources for schools, administrators, teachers, and children. In addition, basals provide a safety net for many teachers, novice and experienced, because they help teachers make personal and professional growth toward implementing balanced, comprehensive reading instruction.

Production and Organization of Basal Readers

Basal reading series are owned by large, diversified corporations and are produced by a variety of publishing houses from coast to coast. A chief editor oversees the production of a basal reader with the assistance of a senior author team, a group of individuals in the field of reading who are known and respected as experts.

Basal reading programs are often recognized and known by the name of the publishing houses that produce them. Over the past 20 years, the number of basal publishing companies that have survived intense competition, demanding and sometimes invasive state standards, and the vicissitudes of change has dwindled from over 20 to a half dozen or fewer.

Harcourt

Houghton Mifflin

National Geographic School Publishing

SRA/McGraw Hill

Scholastic

Scott Foresman

Minor revisions of basal readers occur every few years; major revision cycles occur every 5 or 6 years. Major revisions are usually slated for completion during the same year Texas and California consider basal readers for statewide adoption. Consequently, the "Texas and California" effect is known to exert considerable influence on the content and quality of new basal readers (Farr, Tulley, & Powell, 1987; Keith, 1981). In reading circles, one often hears the axiom, "As Texas and California go, so goes the nation."

Organization of the Basal Reader

Basal readers are designed to take children through a series of books, experiences, and activities toward increasingly sophisticated reading behaviors. Each basal series typically provides several readers or books of reading selections at each level. For example, the *Scott Foresman: Reading 2000* basal provides the following books organized by theme for each grade level:

Grade 1

Good Times We Share
Take a Closer Look
Let's Learn Together
Favorite Things Old and New
Take Me There
Surprise Me!

Grade 2

You + Me = Special
Zoom In!
Side by Side
Ties Through Time
All Aboard!
Just Imagine

Grade 3

Finding My Place
The Whole Wide World
Getting the Job Done
From Past to Present
Are We There Yet?
Imagination.kids

Grade 4

Focus on Family
A Wider View
Keys to Success
Timeless Stories
Other Times, Other Places
Express Yourself!

Grade 5

Relating to Others
My World and Yours
A Job Well Done
Time and Time Again
Traveling On
Think of It!

Grade 6

Discovering Ourselves
The Living Earth
Goals Great and Small
The Way We Were—The Way We Are
Into the Unknown
I've Got It!

Important features to be found in current teacher's editions include (1) philosophical statements, (2) a skills overview for each unit, (3) classroom routines, (4) suggestions for accommodating special needs, (5) assessment ties to national standards and tests, (6) technology information, (7) themes, (8) projects, (9) assessment benchmarks, (10) a glossary, (11) a bibliography, and (12) a scope and sequence chart. The scope and sequence chart is a year-by-year curricular plan, usually in chart form, that includes the instructional objectives and skills associated with a specific basal reading program. Objectives and skills are arranged in the scope and sequence chart by categories and grade levels. It is in the scope and sequence chart that teachers learn about the objectives of the basal program and the sequence of lessons designed to accomplish the objectives.

Most contemporary basal readers are organized into **themed units,** with several selections organized around a selected theme or topic; still others are organized into arbitrarily divided units of instruction. Most basal readers follow a somewhat modified version of the directed reading thinking activity (DRTA) format developed by Stauffer in 1969. This format can be represented in nine discrete parts or steps in the lesson.

1. Activating prior knowledge and building background
2. Delivering skill lessons in phonics, spelling, vocabulary, and comprehension
3. Previewing and predicting
4. Setting the purpose
5. Guiding the reading
6. Confirming predictions
7. Responding to comprehension discussion questions
8. Providing skill instruction and practice in oral language, writing, grammar, phonics, handwriting, comprehension, and fluency
9. Ideas and projects for enrichment

Lessons are arranged for teachers into a daily planner. It is intended that teachers will not use all of the resources of the basal reader teacher's edition, but rather will select those resources on a daily basis that best suit the needs of the students in the classroom. We remind our readers emphatically that basal teachers' editions are resources to augment the teacher's knowledge of the reading process and the needs of his or her students. They are not scripts to be followed without judgment, skill, and decision making.

Standards for Evaluating and Adopting Basal Readers

Few professional decisions deserve more careful attention than evaluating and adopting a basal reading series for a school district. Because you will probably be asked to evaluate one or more basal reading series during your professional career, you need to understand how to evaluate and select basal reading programs effectively. Learning about this process will also empower you to help reform, restructure, and strengthen future revisions, editions, and basal reading adoption processes.

Ways of Evaluating Basal Readers

Only after teachers are sufficiently well informed about the characteristics of effective basal reader programs can they act to correct or adjust the use of the basal to benefit their students. Dole, Rogers, and Osborn (1987) recommend that the evaluation of basal readers should focus on the following:

1. Identify the facets of effective reading instruction to be identified in each program.
2. Delineate criteria related to effective reading instruction to be analyzed in the basal readers.
3. Provide a means for carefully recording how well basal readers measure up to the established criteria.

Because many reading teachers are concerned with curriculum changes that reflect a decided move toward evidence-based comprehensive reading instructional practices in basal readers, we strongly recommend that classroom professionals obtain the materials, worksheets, and procedures found in Dole, Osborn, and Lehr's "Adoption Guidelines Project" *(A Guide to Selecting Basal Reading Programs)*. These can be obtained by sending requests to the Center for the Study of Reading, University of Illinois-Guide, P.O. Box 2121, Station A, Champaign, IL 61825-2121.

A Consumer's Guide to Evaluating a Core Reading Program

Recently, Simmons and Kame'enui (2003) developed an instrument to help educators evaluate basal reading programs called *A Consumer's Guide to Evaluating a Core Reading Program*. It particularly focuses on grades K through 3 and offers guidelines for evaluating the Big Five in reading instruction: phonemic awareness, phonics, vocabulary, comprehension, and fluency. You can obtain *A Consumer's Guide to Evaluating a Core Reading Program* free online at *http://reading.uoregon.edu/curricula/con_guide.php*. Figure 7.5 features several excerpts from *A Consumer's Guide to Evaluating a Core Reading Program* at the grade 1 level. Many other states have also developed core reading program evaluation instruments as part of justifying reading interventions for the Reading First legislation. Kentucky and Ohio are two that provide good examples available on the Internet. To see Ohio's basal evaluation instrument online, go to *http://www.readingfirstohio.org/assets/pdf/Eval_Guide_for_Supplemental_&_Intervention.pdf*.

Figure 7.5 Excerpts from *A Consumer's Guide to Evaluating a Core Reading Program*

Phonemic Awareness *is the ability to hear and manipulate the sound structure of language. It is a strong predictor of reading success. Phonemic awareness is an auditory skill and consists of multiple components.*

High-Priority Items—Phonemic Awareness Instruction

Rating	Criterion	Evidence		
		Initial Instruction	Week ___	Week ___
○ ●	1. Allocates appropriate amount of daily time to blending, segmenting, and manipulating tasks until proficient. *(w)* [NRP, pg. 2–41]			
○ ●	2. Incorporates letters into phonemic awareness activities. *(w)* [NRP, pg. 2–41]			

First-Grade Phonemic Awareness Instruction—High Priority
Tally the number of elements with each rating.

● ———— ○ ———— ○

High-Priority Items—Phonics Instruction

Rating	Criterion	Evidence		
		Initial Instruction	Week ___	Week ___
○ ●	1. Progresses *systematically* from simple word types (e.g., consonant-vowel-consonant) and word lengths (e.g., number of phonemes) and word complexity (e.g., phonemes in the word, position of blends, stop sounds) to more complex words. *(ss)* [NRP, pg. 2–132]			
○ ●	2. Models instruction at each of the fundamental stages (e.g., letter–sound correspondences, blending, reading whole words). *(w)* and *(ss)*			

Figure 7.5 Continued

High-Priority Items—Phonics Instruction

Rating	Criterion	Evidence			
		Initial Instruction	Week ____	Week ____	Week ____
○ ○ ●	3. Provides teacher-guided practice in controlled word lists and connected text in which students can apply their newly learned skills successfully. **(w)**				
○ ○ ●	4. Includes repeated opportunities to read words in contexts in which students can apply their knowledge of letter–sound correspondences. **(w)** and **(ss)** [NRP, pg. 3–28]				
○ ○ ●	5. Uses decodable text based on specific phonics lessons in the early part of the first grade as an intervening step between explicit skill acquisition and the students' ability to read quality trade books. Decodable texts should contain the phonics elements and sight words that students have been taught. **(w)** and **(ss)**				

First-Grade Phonics and Instruction—High Priority
Tally the number of elements with each rating.

● ____ ○ ____ ○

High-Priority Items—Connected Text and Fluency Instruction

Rating	Criterion	Evidence			
		Initial Instruction	Week ____	Week ____	Week ____
○ ○ ●	1. Introduces passage reading soon after students can read a sufficient number of words accurately. **(w)**				

(continued)

Figure 7.5 Continued

High-Priority Items—Connected Text and Fluency Instruction

Rating	Criterion	Evidence			
		Initial Instruction	Week____	Week____	Week____
○ ○ ●	2. Contains regular words comprised of letter-sounds and word types that have been taught. *(w)* and *(ss)*				
○ ○ ●	3. Contains only high-frequency irregular words that have been previously taught. *(ss)*				
○ ○ ●	4. Uses initial stories/passages composed of a high percentage of regular words (minimum of 75–80% decodable words). *(w)*				
○ ○ ●	5. Builds toward a 60-word-per-minute fluency goal by end of grade. *(ss)* [NRP, pg. 3–4]				
○ ○ ●	6. Includes sufficient independent practice materials of appropriate difficulty for students to develop fluency. *(w)* and *(ss)* [NRP, pg. 3–28]				

First-Grade Connected Text and Fluency Instruction—High Priority
Tally the number of elements with each rating. ____

● ○ ○

High-Priority Items—Vocabulary Instruction

Rating	Criterion	Evidence	
		Initial Instruction	Week____
○ ○ ●	1. Provides direct instruction of specific concepts and vocabulary. *(w)*		

Figure 7.5 Continued

High-Priority Items—Vocabulary Instruction

Rating	Criterion	Evidence		
		Initial Instruction	Week ___	Week ___
○ ●	2. Provides repeated and multiple exposures to critical vocabulary. (w) and (st)			
○ ●	3. Integrates words into sentences and asks students to tell the meaning of the word in the sentence and to use it in a variety of contexts. (w)			

First-Grade Vocabulary Instruction—High Priority
Tally the number of elements with each rating.   ● ___ ○ ___ ○ ___

High-Priority Items—Reading Comprehension Instruction

Rating	Criterion	Evidence		
		Initial Instruction	Week ___	Week ___
○ ●	1. Guides students through sample text in which teachers think out loud as they identify the components of story structure. (w) [NRP, pg. 4–122]			
○ ●	2. Provides plentiful opportunities to listen to and explore narrative and expository text forms and to engage in interactive discussion of the messages and meanings of the text. (ss) [NRP, pg. 4–109]			
○ ●	3. Explicitly teaches critical comprehension strategy (e.g., main idea, literal, inferential, retell, prediction). (w) and (ss)			

First-Grade Reading Comprehension Instruction—Discretionary
Tally the number of elements with each rating.   ● ___ ○ ___ ○ ___

(continued)

Figure 7.5 Continued

Summary of First-Grade Ratings

High-Priority Items

Item	Rating
Phonemic Awareness Instruction (2)	● ○ ○
Phonics Instruction (5)	● ○ ○
Irregular Words Instruction (2)	● ○ ○
Connected Text and Fluency Instruction (6)	● ○ ○
Vocabulary Development (3)	● ○ ○
Reading Comprehension Instruction (3)	● ○ ○

First-Grade High-Priority Totals ● ○ ○

Discretionary Items

Item	Rating
Phonemic Awareness Instruction (5)	● ○ ○
Phonics Instruction (4)	● ○ ○
Irregular Words Instruction (2)	● ○ ○
Connected Text and Fluency Instruction (2)	● ○ ○
Vocabulary Development (3)	● ○ ○
Reading Comprehension Instruction (3)	● ○ ○

First-Grade Discretionary Totals ● ○ ○

First-Grade Design Features

	Feature
● ○	1. Aligns and coordinates the words used in phonics/word recognition activities with those used in fluency building.
● ○	2. Provides ample practice on high-priority skills.
● ○	3. Provides explicit and systematic instruction.
● ○	4. Includes systematic and cumulative review of high-priority skills.
● ○	5. Demonstrates and builds relationships between fundamental skills leading to higher-order skills.

Additional Comments

Table 7.1   The Oregon Reading First Center (ORFC) Review of Reading Programs in the Areas of Phonemic Awareness, Phonics, and Fluency*

Basal/Core Program	Ranking: Phonemic Awareness Instruction	Ranking: Phonics Instruction	Ranking: Fluency	Overall Ranking
Houghton Mifflin	1	1	2	1
Open Court (McGraw Hill)	4	4	1	2
Harcourt	2	2	3	2
Scott Foresman	5	3	4	4
Macmillan (McGraw Hill)	3	5	5	5
Wright Group	6	6	6	6
Rigby	7	7	7	6

*Retrieved from *http:reading.uoregon.edu/curricula/or_rfc_review.php*

Recent Evaluations of Basal (Core) Reading Programs: Phonemic Awareness, Phonics, and Fluency

A number of evaluations of prominent basal/core reading programs and supplemental reading programs have been conducted in recent years by various state departments of education (SDE). Florida, Oregon, Maryland, Indiana, Ohio, Kentucky, California, Utah, and Texas are just a few of the states conducting such reviews in connection with Reading First funding. In many cases, the SDEs have opted to use Simmons and Kame'enui's (2003) *A Consumer's Guide to Evaluating a Core Reading Program* to aid them in this process.

One such evaluation that seems to reflect a consensus of findings on basal reader effectiveness is the *Oregon Reading First Center (ORFC): Review of Comprehensive Programs* (ORFC Curriculum Review Panel, 2004). Two rather severe limitations of the report is that it only considers reading programs for grades K–3, and only three of the Big Five areas of reading: phonemic awareness, phonics, and fluency. Reading comprehension and vocabulary development are ignored. Nevertheless, the report is very useful indeed for examining the strengths of each program in the three areas of reading considered. In Table 7.1 we offer a summary of the reading programs reviewed and their relative rating in each of the three areas reviewed. Our rankings summary from the ORFC reflects the mean score on "high priority" skills for all grade levels reviewed. Also, please note that we are only including the ORFC findings for what we consider to be basal/core reading programs. We will examine their findings for two other supplemental reading programs *(Reading Mastery, Success for All)* later in this chapter.

What Programs Are Available for the Struggling Reader?

In 1998, Pikulski reviewed the effectiveness of several national reading programs designed to prevent reading failure. Later, similar reviews of the effectiveness of supplemental programs were published by other researchers, committees, and state departments of education (e.g., St. John & Loescher, 2001; ORFC Curriculum Review Panel, 2004; Maryland Evaluation Committee, 2006) to help us better understand their relative merits. Although basal readers remain the predominant form of reading instruction in most classrooms, several of these national programs are worth noting.

Reading Recovery

Reading Recovery, developed by clinical child psychologist Marie Clay, is an early intervention program designed to reduce reading failure in the first grade for the lowest performing 20 percent of students. The aim of the program is to help low-achieving children catch up to the level of their age-related peers. Reading Recovery was imported to the United States by faculty at the Ohio State University (Allington, 1992). Reading Recovery (RR) trained teachers enroll in a yearlong course of graduate studies with regular follow-up professional development seminars to keep one's training current and approved (Lyons & Beaver, 1995). Teachers trained in RR must receive training from an approved RR teacher trainer and at one of several approved sites throughout the nation.

The average RR student is recovered from below-grade-level performance in an average of 12 to 14 weeks. Discontinued children show normal development after release from the program. Students in New Zealand and in the United States demonstrate the substantial positive effects this invention has on young children's reading and writing development (Clay, 1990a; DeFord, Lyons, & Pinnell, 1991; Pinnell, DeFord, & Lyons, 1994).

Children selected for the RR program receive one-to-one, intensive, daily reading instruction for 30 minutes. During this instructional period, teachers and children engage in five major activities in a sequenced and structured format. The first activity is the rereading of at least two familiar books or "familiar rereads" of books students have read previously with the assistance and guidance of the RR teacher taking a daily "running record" of the student's oral reading. During a running record, the teacher notes which words are read accurately or inaccurately and analyzes the inaccuracies for the cue system the student used or neglected to use to inform upcoming instructional emphasis and planning. Third, teacher and students work with letters and words. A typical activity is word-making using plastic magnetic letters on a cookie sheet. The teacher might show a child the word *ran* and ask him or her to blend the sounds to pronounce the word. Then the teacher might remove the *r*, substitute *f*, and ask the child to blend the new sound to get the word *fan*. In the fourth activity, the child dictates a sentence or two; this is called a "story" in RR terminology. The teacher helps the child write the "story" by stretching words with the child, encouraging him or her to write the letter for each sound to form each word. After each word is written, the teacher asks the student to reread the word(s) until the entire sentence is written. After reading the entire sentence, the teacher cuts the sentence into words strips and asks the student to re-order the word strips into the sentence. The fifth and final activity in an RR lesson is the introduction of a new story. The teacher has pre-read the story and noted challenges and obstacles the child might face in his or her reading. The teacher walks the student through the "pictures," introducing new vocabulary, sounding out "tricky" words with the student (often using a small, white board and marker), and discussing any unfamiliar concepts or language. Then the child reads the book with careful guidance, support, and feedback from the teacher.

Getting to Know English Learners

ELs always benefit from programs such as Reading Recovery, Success for All, and Early Steps because of the one-to-one intensive daily reading instruction and individual tutoring sessions. Providing bilingual or culturally different basal textbooks as well as picture and trade books will also help ELs feel welcome and succeed more quickly.

Some educators have suggested that RR may be too expensive to realistically implement on a wide scale in the United States, where the reading failure rate exceeds 20 percent. However, with over 80 percent of children in RR moving to discontinuance and grade level performance in less than a semester of intensive instruction and continuing to make acceptable progress, it seems that RR is substantially more cost effective than are many of the commonly tried remedial options, including special education, for addressing the needs of low-performing children (Dyer, 1992).

In their 2007 review of the Reading Recovery Program, the What Works Clearinghouse (WWC) rated it as highly effective in assisting struggling readers in improving general reading achievement. Reading Recovery received their highest or next to highest ratings for alphabetic (phonics and word attack skills), reading fluency and comprehension.

Success for All

Success for All (SFA) is a total school reform program for grades K–3. Originally developed for struggling readers, the goal of the SFA program is to have all children reading on grade level by third grade, with no retentions and referrals to special education for reading problems. Robert Slavin, Director of the Center for Research and Effective Schooling for Disadvantaged Students at Johns Hopkins University, and his colleagues developed the SFA program. The SFA program is grounded on three premises. First, the primary-grade classroom is the best place to work on ensuring children's school success. Second, additional instruction should be provided to students as soon as they are identified as needing it. Third, educators need to think creatively about the use of school resources, personnel, and instructional time.

SFA focuses on providing quality reading instruction in grades K–3 as well as providing supplementary support in the form of individual tutoring sessions. Students are placed into heterogeneous classroom groupings for most of the day, but when the 90-minute reading instructional block is begun, children are regrouped into "ability" groups of 15 to 20 students across the three grade levels 1–3. Regrouping according to reading levels allows whole group, direct instruction of children and is intended to eliminate the overreliance on seatwork and worksheets found in many classrooms.

For students who are not responsive to whole-class instruction in their reading groups, supplementary individual tutoring for 20 minutes per day is provided in the SFA program. Tutoring sessions focus on the same strategies and skills taught in the whole class sessions and, whenever possible, the classroom teacher is freed up by the use of classroom aides to provide the tutoring sessions. SFA also recommends that children attend half-day preschool and full-day kindergarten to accelerate progress in learning to read successfully. Multiple evaluations have shown that SFA is an effective program for reducing referrals to special education and grade-level retentions. However, studies indicate that SFA has not achieved its stated goal of helping every child read on grade level by the end of third grade (Slavin et al., 1990, 1992, 1996).

In the report *Oregon Reading First Center (ORFC): Review of Comprehensive Programs* (ORFC Curriculum Review Panel, 2004), SFA was fairly weak in the areas of phonemic awareness (6th), phonics (7th), and fluency (6th) when compared to eight other leading core programs.

Four Blocks

The **Four Blocks (FB)** program implemented in Winston-Salem, North Carolina, by P. Cunningham is a program of first-grade reading instruction. The FB program organizes daily reading instruction around four 30-minute blocks of instruction: (1) Basal Block, (2) Writing Block, (3) Working with Words Block, and (4) Self-Selected Reading Block. During Basal Block, the teacher and students selectively use materials and suggestions provided in the school's or district's adopted basal reading program. This means that students read stories, essays, articles, and other text found in the anthology (student's text) of the basal reader program. The activities found in the basal reader are used during this instructional time block.

During Writing Block, the teacher typically begins with a 5- to 10-minute mini-lesson on a writing convention, style, or genre. Following this mini-lesson, students engage in individually selected writing projects, taking these projects through the typical stages and activities of a writer's workshop—drafting, revising, editing, and publishing. The Working with Words Block of instructional time consists of reading words from the word wall and making words. Word wall words are high-frequency, phonically irregular words posted on a wall that students learn to read and spell by sight rather than through pattern analysis or decoding. The word-making activities consist of using groups of letters to make as many words as possible. The teacher usually issues a clue as to the words that can be made by using two or more letters in various combinations. This activity concludes with students using all of the letters in the group to make a single word known as the "secret" word. During the final 30-minutes time block, Self-Selected Reading, students read books of their own choosing. They complete projects and responses to the books they read to share their experiences and knowledge with other children. Results reported by Cunningham, Hall, and Defee (1998) indicate that the program has been successful with students of a wide range of literacy levels without the use of ability or leveled grouping.

Early Steps

Early Steps (ES) developed by Darrell Morris (Morris, Shaw, & Perney, 1990), is an early intervention program designed to reduce reading failure in the early years. Children selected for the ES program receive one-to-one, intensive, daily reading instruction for 30 minutes. During this 30-minute daily instructional period, teacher and students engage in four major activities in a sequenced and structured format. To begin a lesson, students reread familiar leveled books for 8 to 10 minutes. In the second activity, the teacher takes the student through a series of word sort activities for 5 to 6 minutes. The teacher places three words (for example, *hat, man, cap*) horizontally across the table or desktop. After watching the teacher demonstrate the task of sorting the words that remain in the deck, the student completes the task. Sorting tasks focus initially on sorting words according to phonograms, word families, or rimes. For the next 5 to 8 minutes of the lesson, the child writes a sentence from his or her own experience. After a short dialogue with the teacher, the student writes while saying aloud each word, stretching the word, and recoding the letter for each sound segmented from the stretched word. After the student is finished writing, the teacher writes the sentence on a sentence strip and cuts it apart for the student to put together and reread. The fourth and final step in the ES lesson is the introduction of a new book the child is expected to read the next day without much help. Books are selected in ascending levels of difficulty, thus pushing the student's reading progress forward. Before reading, the teacher helps the student look at the pictures, talk about the unfamiliar vocabulary words, and situate the book in a meaningful frame of reference. During the reading, the teacher coaches the student to use strategies and self-correct. When the student finishes this book, it is used the next day for familiar rereading.

In many ways, Early Steps is very much like Reading Recovery, only with a more systematic approach to the teaching of phonic decoding strategies. Research by Santa and Hoien (1998) showed Early Steps intervention in grades 1 and 2 helped the most at-risk students to approach the average performance level of their peers within one academic year of instruction. Early Steps boosted scores in decoding, spelling, word recognition, and reading comprehension.

Reading Mastery

Reading Mastery is a supplemental reading program best suited to students having severe reading problems, and for whom traditional programs and methods have failed. It may also be useful as a supplemental reading program for students at high risk of reading failure, and or for English language learners (Gunn, Biglan, Smolkowski, & Ary, 2000; Gunn, Smolkowski, Biglan, & Black, 2002). The What Works Clearinghouse (WWC) (see WWC online at: *http://www.whatworks.ed.gov/*) describes the program as follows:

> Reading Mastery is a direct instruction program designed to provide explicit, systematic instruction in English language reading. Reading Mastery is available in two versions, Reading Mastery Classic levels I and II (for use in grades K–3) and Reading Mastery Plus, an integrated reading-language program for grades K–6. The program begins by teaching phonemic awareness and sound-letter correspondence and moves into word and passage reading, vocabulary development, comprehension, and building oral reading fluency. Later lessons continue to emphasize accurate and fluent decoding while teaching students the skills necessary to read and comprehend and to learn from expository text. Lessons are designed to be fast-paced and interactive. Students are grouped by similar reading level, based on program placement tests. The program includes placement assessments and a continuous monitoring system.

Reading Mastery was originally developed by Siegfried Engelmann under the title *Distar® Reading* for use in Project Follow Through as part of the direct instruction teaching model, and is marketed by SRA/McGraw-Hill.

In the report *Oregon Reading First Center (ORFC): Review of Comprehensive Programs* (ORFC Curriculum Review Panel, 2004), Reading Mastery ranked highest in high-priority standards of all nine programs reviewed in the areas of phonemic awareness, phonics, and fluency. There is no extant impartial evidence we can find as to Reading Mastery's benefits to vocabulary learning or comprehension development. The What Works Clearinghouse rated Reading Mastery as having "potentially positive effects," though this evaluation is based on only one recorded study with English learners.

Reading Expeditions: Language, Literacy, & Vocabulary!

The National Geographic Society, a nonprofit organization famous for high-quality publications, has introduced a new informational text series called ***Language, Literacy, & Vocabulary!* (LLV).** The Reading Expeditions component of *Language, Literacy,*

& Vocabulary! for students in grades 3 through 8 uses a powerful "sheltered-instruction approach" that combines essential science and social studies content with nonfiction reading skills and strategies. This affordable program features the following:

- 48 high-interest, age-appropriate science and social studies titles
- Key vocabulary repeated and applied in different contexts
- Content broken down into manageable units
- Limited text loads; simple text layouts and sentence patterns
- Academic vocabulary with on-page definitions
- Comprehension strategies and fluency practice
- Research and writing opportunities
- Rich instructional support and tools based on latest research
- Differentiated instruction for various stages of English language proficiency and reading development
- Alignment with national and state standards

McNabb (2006) summarized a recent study of the effectiveness of *Language, Literacy, & Vocabulary!* as follows:

> The study was conducted in urban Illinois public schools with 259 students in 4 schools, 90 students in the treatment groups and 169 students in the control groups. . . . A thorough analysis of the data collected indicates that the students in treatment groups made statistically significant gains in their content area literacy development compared with students who did not use the *Language, Literacy, & Vocabulary!* curriculum. In each curriculum group, the mean improvement from pretest to posttest was substantially higher for the students in the treatment groups.

Language, Literacy, & Vocabulary! has been adopted as a key supplemental program in the Memphis research study in the federal Striving Readers project because of its infusion of scientifically-based reading research (SBRR) in an appealing informational text format. For online information about this innovative product, go to *www.ngschoolpub.org.*

Waterford Early Reading Program

The Florida Center for Reading Research (online at *www.fcrr.org*) describes the **Waterford Early Reading Program** as

> a comprehensive early intervention curriculum designed to develop literacy for kindergarten through third grade students. The three levels of the program are for emerging, developing, and fluent readers and include multimedia technology to provide daily, research-based, individualized instruction for every student in the classroom. Each of the three levels contains one school year's worth of instructional material so students work at their instructional level regardless of the grade level in which they are placed. Waterford provides all the materials necessary for implementation including the teacher guides (teacher-led or center-based off-line activities), CDs, videotapes, audiotapes, student materials, parent resources, hardware, software (curriculum that students engage in on the computer), and earphones with microphones. The computers can be in a lab setting or at a center in the classroom that contains three to four computers. Guidelines for teachers to follow in order to place students at appropriate levels of the program are also delineated in the Waterford "Getting Started Guide." For the software component, engaging tutorials regarding how to use the mouse are available for young children.

The only independent scientific-based reading research study available at this point on Waterford seems to be one showing disappointing results with an urban population. Paterson and colleagues (2003) conducted a one-year study of the effectiveness of the Waterford Early Reading Program on kindergarten and first grade children in a large urban school district. They concluded that Waterford classrooms failed to outperform non-Waterford classrooms in part because the program did not encourage the social interactions necessary for growth in early emergent reading and writing.

Supplementing Your Reading Program with Leveled Books

There is no such thing as a "one-size-fits-all" reading program. Any program will need to be supplemented if the needs of all learners are to be met. Sometimes a program lacks strength in one or more of the Big Five areas. Other times the core program, as we have seen, may lack sufficient nonfiction/informational reading selections. A common solution is to supplement the reading program with trade books. The problem here is knowing the reading level (difficulty level) of the different selections to be used; this is critical knowledge for matching "just right" books to each learner.

Fountas and Pinnell (1999), in their book *Matching Books to Readers: Using Leveled Books in Guided Reading, K–3,* describe a way to "level" reading materials in the classroom. Reutzel and Cooter (2007) have summarized key attributes of the Fountas and Pinnell leveling system for books as well other comparison information. We share this in Figure 7.6.

Many teachers in the primary grades rely heavily on a system for leveling books to match students with texts that meet their instructional needs. Although leveled books can be an enormously helpful tool in beginning reading instruction, Szymusiak and Sibberson (2001) in their book *Beyond Leveled Books: Supporting Transitional Readers in Grades 2–5,* warn against the dangers of a "steady diet" of reading in leveled books. They state:

> When students' reading diet is exclusively a leveled one, their purpose for reading disappears. They read for us. They become eager to reach the next level instead of being eager to earn more from what they are reading. (pp. 15–16)

We know the leveling mania has gone too far when students must read only from leveled materials, when teachers will only purchase materials for reading based on levels, and when students and teachers no longer seek the goal of independence in reading through instruction in self-selection of appropriately challenging and interesting reading materials!

Figure 7.6 Reading Level Translations

Reading Levels (traditional designations)	Guided Reading (GR) Levels (Extrapolated from Fountas & Pinnell, 1996, 2001)	Common Text Attributes	Exemplars Books and Publishers (using GR levels)	Approximate Level of Reading Development
Preschool-Kindergarten (Readiness)	A	Wordless picture books	**A** = *Dog Day!* (Rigby)	**Emergent**
	B	Repeated phrases; text-picture matching; experiences common to readers; short (10–60 words)	**B** = *Fun with Hats* (Mondo)	
PP (preprimer)	C D E	Same as above for B, but repeating phrases don't dominate the book; more language variation; by level E, syntax becomes more like regular "book language"	**C** = *Brown Bear, Brown Bear* (Holt) **D** = *The Storm* (Wright Group) **E** = *The Big Toe* (Wright Group)	**Emergent → Early**
P (primer)	F G	Longer sentences/less predictable text; new verb forms appear; story grammar elements continue over multiple pages; pictures provide only a little support.	**F** = *A Moose Is Loose* (Houghton Mifflin) **G** = *More Spaghetti I Say* (Scholastic)	**Early**
Grade 2 (early) Grade 2 Grade 2 (late)	J K L M	Longer stories with more complicated story grammar elements; varied vocabulary with rich meanings; common to have whole pages of text; more content (nonfiction) selections are in evidence	**J** = *The Boy Who Cried Wolf* (Scholastic) **K** = *Amelia Bedelia* (Harper & Row) **L** = *Cam Jansen and the Mystery of the Monster Movie* (Puffin) **M** = *How to Eat Fried Worms* (Dell)	**Transitional → Fluent**

(continued)

Figure 7.6 (Continued)

Grade 3	N–P	Fewer illustrations; more complex nonfiction; complex sentences and challenging vocabulary; higher order thinking begins here	**N** = *Pioneer Cat* (Random House) **O** = *Whipping Boy* (Troll) **P** = *Amelia Earhart* (Dell)	**Fluent (Basic)**
Grade 4	Q–S	Few illustrations; more complex language and concept load; higher order thinking is deepened; appearance of metaphor; topics are farther from student experiences; historical fiction is common; complex ideas are presented	**Q** = *Pony Pals: A Pony for Keeps* (Scholastic) **R** = *Hatchet* (Simon & Schuster) **S** = *Story of Harriet Tubman, Conductor of the Underground Railroad* (Scholastic)	**Fluent →** **Extending to** **Content Texts**

From D. R. Reutzel & R. B. Cooter. (2007). *Strategies for Reading Assessment and Instruction: Helping Every Child Succeed* (3rd ed.). Upper Saddle River, NJ: Pearson Merrill Prentice Hall. Reprinted by permission.

On the other hand, to abandon some controls on text difficulty seems to be, as Holdaway (1979) puts it, "sheer madness." Holdaway reminds us that many children continue to struggle to read authentic texts that are far too difficult for them to handle independently. It is clear that basal readers need to provide a balance of text types, including decodable, leveled, patterned, informational, and authentic story texts in quantities that allow teachers to choose what works best with each child at various levels of reading development. Hiebert (1999) makes an impassioned call for authors to produce a new kind of beginning reading text modeled after the creations of Dr. Seuss in books such as *Green Eggs and Ham*. She states:

> Over a decade ago, Anderson et al. (1985) called for inventive writers to use Dr. Seuss as a model for creating engaging texts for beginning readers. This call needs to be extended again but, this time, with a clearer mandate—one that derives from a strong vision of what beginning readers need to learn. Such texts require thought to word density ratios and to the repetitions across as well as within texts of words that share phonetic elements (p. 565).

Finding Leveled Books. Many Web sites provide information about leveled books using the Fountas and Pinnell (1999) and Pinnell and Fountas (2002) A–Z leveling approach. Some of these are listed here:

http://www.fountasandpinnellleveledbooks.com/

http://registration.beavton.k12.or.us/lbdb/

http://www.pps.k12.or.us/curriculum/literacy/leveled_books/

http://www.leveledbooks.com/

http://www.readinga-z.com/

http://www.readinglady.com/gr/Leveled_Books/leveled_books.html

The Internet site *www.readinga-z.com* provides many choices—at our last count, 1,300 downloadable leveled books—that can be easily used as "benchmark books" for assessment purposes.

How Can Basal Reading Programs Be Adapted to Assist the Struggling Reader?

Historically, the basal reader has not served very successfully as a tool for assisting struggling readers. There are several reasons for this situation. First, some teachers find the stories in basal readers to be bland and uninviting, especially for problem readers. What is needed most is literature that "turns on" the "turned-off" learner—an order too tall for many basals to fill. Second, if a student is failing to achieve success using one approach to reading instruction, in this case the basal reader, then common sense tells us that what is needed is an alternative strategy—not just more of the same. Finally, basal reader systems frequently do not allow students enough time for real reading. The multifarious collection of skill sheets and workbook pages tends to be so time-consuming that little time is left for actual reading. In Chapter 1, we discuss principles for encouraging literacy, some of which are most pertinent when using basal readers to help students with special needs. Three direct applications of these principles follow.

Reading the Basal Straight Through

Teachers working with special needs students recognize that what these children need most is regular and sustained reading. We suggest that skill sheets and workbook pages be used judiciously, or even avoided, to allow for more time spent reading. Students should be allowed to read basals straight through as an anthology of children's stories. The teacher may wish to skip stories that offer little to the reader in this setting.

Repeated Readings

In repeated readings, the teacher typically introduces the story as a shared book or story experience, then students attempt to read the book alone or with a friend (Routman, 1988). If the story has rhyme or a regular pattern, it may be sung or chanted. Repeated readings of stories help children achieve a sense of accomplishment, improve comprehension, and build fluency.

Supported, or Buddy, Reading

Many times, at-risk readers are very reluctant to become risk takers. Teachers simply must find ways of breaking the ice for them and create classroom safety nets.

Supported, or "buddy," reading allows students to read aloud basal stories together, either taking turns or in unison. By rereading these supported selections, students' fluency and comprehension improve. Another variation is for teacher–student combinations to read together. Similar to the procedure known as *neurological impress* (Hollingsworth, 1978), the student and teacher read aloud in unison at a comfortable rate. For first readings, the teacher usually assumes the lead in terms of volume and pace. In subsequent repeated readings, the student is encouraged to assume the lead.

Master teachers continually search for ways they can enhance the reading and writing environment as they begin making the transition from basal-only teaching to more balanced literacy perspectives and practices. In the process, teachers discover numerous opportunities for assisting students with special needs within the elementary classroom.

What Programs Are Available for Helping Students with Diverse Cultural or Language Needs Succeed?

Students who do not possess reading and writing ability in a first language should be taught to read and write in their native or first language to support and validate them as worthwhile individuals. In addition, reading instruction in the first language helps students capitalize on what they already know about their primary language and culture to build concepts that can facilitate the acquisition of English (Freeman & Freeman, 1992; Krashen & Biber, 1988). In any case, teachers must be sensitive to these students' special needs, which include (a) a need for safety and security, (b) a need to belong and be accepted, and (c) a need to feel self-esteem (Peregoy & Boyle, 1993).

Teachers should help English as a second language (ESL) or English learners (EL) feel at ease when they arrive in the classroom by assigning them a "personal buddy" who, if possible, speaks the language of the newcomer. This buddy is assigned to help the new student through the school day, routines, and so on. Another approach is to avoid changes in the classroom schedule by following a regular and predictable routine each day, which creates a sense of security. To create a sense of belonging, assign the student to a home group for an extended period of time. A home group provides a small social unit of concern focused on helping the newcomer adapt to everyday life. Finally, self-esteem is enhanced when an individual's worth is affirmed. Opportunities for the newcomer to share her or his language and culture during daily events in the classroom provide a useful way to integrate her or him into the ongoing classroom culture.

To help ESL or ELL students succeed in classrooms where basal readers are the core of instruction, Law and Eckes (1990, p. 92) recommend the following:

- Supplement the basal as much as possible with language experience stories.
- Encourage extensive reading. Gather basal textbooks from as many different levels as possible. Also acquire easier textbooks in content areas as well as trade books to provide a wide range of reading topics.
- Expose children to the many different types of reading available in the "real" world (magazines, *TV Guide,* newspapers, product labels, signs, etc.).

How Can Teachers Help Parents Better Understand Reading Standards?

Many parents and interested stakeholders are aware of the standards-based movement in education as a result of its politicization and publicity surrounding state testing and the No Child Left Behind (NCLB) legislation. However, most people who are not educators, and probably some who are, find standards-based education to be confusing at best. Fortunately, there are free resources available that you can use to explain reading standards to parents and others. Here are three splendid resources to get you started.

- *Big Dreams: A Family Book About Reading*. Available free online from the National Institute for Literacy at *http://www.nifl.gov/partnershipforreading/publications/pdf/big_dreams.pdf* or order by telephone by calling 1-800-228-8813.
- *Put Reading First: Helping Your Child Learn to Read—A Parent Guide*. Available free online from the National Institute for Literacy at *http://www.nifl.gov/partnershipforreading/publications/Parent_br.pdf* or order by telephone by calling 1-800-228-8813.
- *A Child Becomes a Reader*. Available free online from the National Institute for Literacy at *http://www.nifl.gov/partnershipforreading/publications/reading_pre.pdf* or order by telephone by calling 1-800-228-8813.

Summary

For reading instruction to be effective, teachers must first be aware of the development and sequence of reading skills to the learned. Thus, we began this important chapter with a discussion of the evidence-based skills and related curriculum "standards" for reading instruction. Reading curriculum standards help us understand the progresion of reading development in five essential areas of reading instruction: phonemic awarenes, phonics, vocabulary, comprehension, and fluency.

In the past decade or so, standards-based curriculums and assessments have been prescribed as a cure for the poor performance and accountability of many public schools (Watt, 2005; Zuzovsky & Libman, 2006). Literally billions of dollars have been spent on programs and state tests, in part so that federal and state agencies can rank schools in terms of student achievement. Indeed, the *No Child Left Behind* (NCLB) legislation grew directly out of the standards-based movement. An understanding of the most essential skills adopted by state and other governmental agencies help teachers plan for classroom assessments and subsequent instruction tied to evidence-based research.

Core reading programs, also known as *basal* programs, are a collection of student texts and workbooks, teachers' manuals, and supplemental materials for teaching reading and sometimes writing instruction. Core reading programs are used primarily in the elementary and middle school grades as a foundation for consistent, basic instruction. We learned about a valuable resource in selecting core reading programs known as *A Consumer's Guide to Evaluating a Core Reading Program* which offers evidence as to the effectiveness of different core programs. In the end, core reading programs provide teachers with one of many tools for meeting the reading needs of every child.

When core reading programs are not effective for some learners, there are supplemental reading programs for struggling readers teachers can consider. An online tool to help teachers select programs and other resources is the What Works Clearinghouse *(www.whatworks.ed.gov)*. For example, in 2007 the What Works Clearinghouse identified *Reading Recovery* as an effective supplemental program for meeting the needs of struggling readers in first grade. Other popular supplemental programs we learned about included *Four Blocks* and *Reading Mastery*. However, it is not always necessary to turn to commercial programs for helping struggling readers achieve success. Many teachers use leveled books as one part of guided oral reading instruction, repeated readings to improve reading fluency, and other research-supported practices.

At this point in time, there are few reading programs for English learners (EL) that have been shown effective through rigorous scientific research. However, in this chapter we did learn about some promising practices that may be used to supplement instruction for this growing population. In general, the most logical approach is for teachers to supplement their instruction with strategies proven to be effective with "English-only" students as identified throughout this book in the areas of phonemeic awareness, phonics, reading vocabulary, comprehension, and fluency.

It is important that we help parents understand reading standards and find practical ways to help their children become literate. Parents are the first and often the best teachers. We learned about free, research-supported tools we can use to educate parents about reading standards and home supports. One of these tools we can access is *Put Reading First: Helping Your Child Learn to Read–A Parent Guide*. This booklet is a good place to start and several others were provided to help every child become a successful reader.

Classroom Applications

1. Go to your local school district or university curriculum materials library. Select a leading basal reading series. Locate the following items in the teacher's edition: (a) the scope and sequence chart, (b) the parts of a directed reading lesson, (c) the skill lessons, (d) the workbooks, and (e) the book tests or assessment materials. Use *A Consumer's Guide to Evaluating a Core Reading Program, Grades K–3: A Critical Elements Analysis* by Simmons and Kame'enui (2003) to evaluate the program. Report your results to your class.

2. Plan Block 1 in the Four-Block Reading Program using a basal reader. Determine how you would use the basal for 30 minutes per day for a week of instruction.

3. Select a leveled book. Go through the parts of a Reading Recovery lesson and write a plan about how you would introduce this as a new book to a struggling reader.

4. Interview a teacher in the field about the strengths and weaknesses of the basal. Find out why this teacher uses or does not use the basal. Find out how he or she supplements reading instruction with other materials to meet the needs of all students.

5. Visit a classroom in a local elementary school where Success for All is used. Observe a teacher teaching reading. Which parts of the SFA program did the teacher use? Which parts did the teacher omit? Write an essay about your observations.

6. Prepare a basal reading lesson to be taught in the schools. Secure permission to teach this lesson in a local grade-level appropriate classroom. Write a reflective essay about your experience detailing successes, failures, and necessary changes.

Recommended Readings

Baines, L. A., & Stanley, G. K. (2006). *Clearinghouse: A Journal of Educational Strategies, Issues and Ideas, 79* (3), 119–123.

Dole, J. A., Osborn, J., & Lehr, F. (1990). *A guide to selecting basal reading programs*. Urbana, IL: Center for the Study of Reading.

Duke, N. K. (2000). 3.6 minutes per day: The scarcity of informational texts in first grade. *Reading Research Quarterly, 35*(2), 202–224.

Fountas, I. C., & Pinnell, G. S. (1999). *Matching books to readers: Using leveled books in guided reading, K–3*. Portsmouth, NH: Heinemann.

Hiebert, E. H. (1999). Text matters in learning to read. *The Reading Teacher, 52*(6), 552–566.

Reutzel, D. R., & Larsen, N. S. (1995). Look what they've done to real children's books in the new basal readers. *Language Arts, 72*(7), 495–507.

Simmons, D. C., & Kame'enui, E. J. (2003). *A consumer's guide to evaluating a core reading program, Grades K–3: A critical elements analysis*. Eugene, OR: University of Oregon.

Szymusiak, K., & Sibberson, F. (2001). *Beyond leveled books: Supporting transitional readers in grades 2–5*. Portland, ME: Stenhouse.

REFERENCES

Aardema, V. (1975). *Why mosquitoes buzz in people's ears*. New York: Scholastic.

Aaron, R. L., & Gillespie, C. (1990). Gates-MacGinitie Reading Tests, 3rd Ed. [Test review]. In R. B. Cooter, Jr. (Ed.), *The teacher's guide to reading tests*. Scottsdale, AZ: Gorsuch Scarisbrick.

Abedi, J. (2006). Psychometric issues in the ELL assessment and special education eligibility. *Teachers College Record, 108*(11), 2282–2303.

Adams, M. J. (1990a). *Beginning to read: Thinking and learning about print*. Cambridge, MA: MIT Press.

Adams, M. J. (1990b). *Beginning to read: Thinking and learning about print—a summary*. Urbana, IL: Center for the Study of Reading.

Adams, M. J. (1994). *Beginning to read: Thinking and learning about print*. Cambridge, MA: MIT Press.

Adams, M. J. (2001). Alphabetic anxiety and explicit, systematic phonics instruction: A cognitive science perspective. In S. B. Neuman & D. K. Dickinson (Eds.), *Handbook of early literacy research* (pp. 66–80). New York: Guildford Press.

Adams, M. J. (2002, November). *The promise of speech recognition*. Presentation at A Focus on Fluency Forum, San Francisco, CA. Available at *www.prel.org/programs/rel/fluency/Adams.ppt*

Adams, M. J. (2005). *Insights: Reading fluency*. Watertown, MA: Charlesbridge.

Adams, M. J., Allington, R. L., Chaney, J. H., Goodman, Y. M., Kapinus, B. A., McGee, L. M., et al. (1991). Beginning to read: A critique by literacy professionals and a response by Marilyn Jager Adams. *The Reading Teacher, 44*(6), 370–395.

Adams, M. J., Foorman, B. R., Lundberg, I., & Beeler, T. (1998). *Phonemic awareness in young children: A classroom curriculum*. Baltimore, MD: Paul H. Brookes.

Ahlberg, J., & Ahlberg, A. (1986). *The jolly postman or other people's letters*. Boston: Little, Brown.

Aldridge, J. T., & Rust, D. (1987). A beginning reading strategy. *Academic Therapy, 22*(3), 323–326.

Alexander, J. E. (Ed.). (1983). *Teaching reading,* 2nd Ed. Boston: Little, Brown.

Alexander, J. E., & Filler, R. C. (1976). *Attitudes and reading*. Newark, DE: International Reading Association.

Alexander, J. E., & Heathington, B. S. (1988). *Assessing and correcting classroom reading problems*. Glenview, IL: Scott, Foresman.

Alexander, P. A., & Jetton, T. L. (2000). Learning from text: A multidimensional perspective. In M. L. Kamil, P. B. Mosenthal, P. D. Pearson, and R. Barr (Eds.), *Handbook of reading research* (Vol. 3, pp. 285–310). Mahwah, NJ: Erlbaum.

Aliki. (1985). *Mummies made in Egypt*. New York: Harper Trophy.

Allan, K. K. (1982). The development of young children's metalinguistic understanding of the word. *Journal of Educational Research, 76,* 89–93.

Allington, R. (1997, August/September). Commentary: Overselling phonics. *Reading Today,* 15–16.

Allington, R. L. (1977). If they don't read much, how they ever gonna get good? *Journal of Reading, 21,* 57–61.

Allington, R. L. (1980). Teacher interruption behaviors during primary grade oral reading. *Journal of Educational Psychology, 72,* 371–377.

Allington, R. L. (1983a). Fluency: The neglected goal of reading. *Reading Teacher, 36,* 556–561.

Allington, R. L. (1983b). The reading instruction provided readers of differing reading ability. *Elementary School Journal, 83,* 255–265.

Allington, R. L. (1984). Oral reading. In R. Barr, M. L. Kamil, & P. Mosenthal (Eds.), *Handbook of reading research,* Vol. 1, (pp. 829–864). New York: Longman.

Allington, R. L. (1992). How to get information on several proven programs for accelerating the progress of low-achieving children. *The Reading Teacher, 46*(3), 246–248.

Allington, R. L. (1997, August–September). Overselling phonics. *Reading Today, 14,* 15.

Allington, R. L. (2001). *What really matters for struggling readers: Designing research-based programs*. New York: Addision-Wesley Longman.

Allington, R. L. (2002). *Big brother and the national reading curriculum: How ideology trumped evidence*. Portsmouth, NH: Heinemann Educational Books.

Allington, R. L. (2006). Fluency: Still waiting after all these years. In S. J. Samuels & A. E. Farstrup (Eds.). *What research has to say about fluency instruction* (pp. 94–105). Newark, DE: International Reading Association.

Allington, R. L., & Cunningham, P. (1996). *Schools that work*. New York: HarperCollins College Publishers.

Allington, R. L., & Johnston, P. H. (2002). *Reading to learn: Lessons from exemplary fourth-grade classrooms*. New York: Guilford Press.

Allington, R. L., & Woodside-Jiron, H. (1998). Thirty years of research in reading: When is a research summary not a research summary? In K. S. Goodman (Ed.), *In defense of good teaching: What teachers need to know about the "reading wars"* (pp. 143–158). York: ME: Stenhouse.

Altwerger, B., Edelsky, C., & Flores, B. M. (1987). Whole language: What's new? *The Reading Teacher, 41*(2), 144–154.

Altwerger, B., & Flores, B. (1989). Abandoning the basal: Some aspects of the change process. *Theory Into Practice, 28*(4), 288–294.

Alvermann, D. E. (1991). The discussion web: A graphic aid for learning across the curriculum. *The Reading Teacher, 45*(2), 92–99.

Alvermann, D. E., & Boothby, P. R. (1982). Text differences: Children's perceptions at the transition stage in reading. *The Reading Teacher, 36*(3), 298–302.

Alvermann, D. E., Dillon, D. R., & O'Brien, D. G. (1987). *Using discussion to promote reading comprehension.* Newark; DE: International Reading Association.

Alvermann, D. E., & Phelps, S. F. (1994). *Content reading and literacy.* Boston: Allyn & Bacon.

Alvermann, D. E., & Phelps, P. (2001). *Content reading and literacy: Succeeding in today's diverse classrooms,* 3rd Ed. New York: Allyn & Bacon.

Alvermann, D. E., Smith, L. C., & Readence, J. E. (1985). Prior knowledge activation and the comprehension of compatible and incompatible text. *Reading Research Quarterly, 20* (4), 420–436.

Amarel, M., Bussis, A., & Chittenden, E. A. (1977). *An approach to the study of beginning reading: Longitudinal case studies.* Paper presented at the National Reading Conference, New Orleans, LA.

American Federation of Teachers. (1999). *Teaching reading is rocket science. What expert teachers of reading should know and be able to do.* Washington, DC: Author.

American people, The (Grade 6). (1982). New York: American.

Ancona, G. (1994). *The piñata maker: Piñatero.* San Diego, CA: Harcourt Brace.

Andersen, H. C. (1965). *The ugly duckling* (R. P. Keigwin, Trans., & A. Adams, Illustrator). New York: Scribner.

Anderson, L., Evertson, C., & Brophy, J. (1979). An experimental study of effective teaching in first-grade reading groups. *The Elementary School Journal, 79,* 193–222.

Anderson, R. C. (1970). Control of student mediating processes during verbal learning and instruction. *Review of Educational Research, 40,* 349–369.

Anderson, R. C., & Freebody, P. (1981). Vocabulary knowledge. In J. T. Guthrie (Ed.), *Comprehension and teaching: Research reviews* (pp. 80–82). Newark, DE: International Reading Association.

Anderson, R. C., Hiebert, E. F., Scott, J. A., & Wilkinson, I. A. G. (1985). *Becoming a nation of readers: The report of the commission on reading.* Washington, DC: The National Institute of Education.

Anderson, R. C., Mason, J., & Shirey, L. (1984). The reading group: An experimental investigation of a labyrinth. *Reading Research Quarterly, 20* (1), 6–38.

Anderson, R. C., Osborn, J., & Tierney, R. J. (1984). *Learning to read in American schools.* Hillsdale, NJ: Erlbaum.

Anderson, R. C., & Pearson, P. D. (1984). A schema-theoretic view of basic processes in reading. In P. D. Pearson, (Ed.), *Hand book of reading research* (pp. 255–291). New York: Longman.

Anderson, R. C., Reynolds, R. E., Schallert, D. L., & Goetz, E. T. (1977). Frameworks for comprehending discourse. *American Educational Research Journal, 14,* 367–382.

Anderson, R. C., Wilkinson, I. A. G., & Mason, J. M. (1991). A micro-analysis of the small-group, guided reading lesson: Effects of an emphasis on global story meaning. *Reading Research Quarterly, 26,* 417–441.

Anderson, R. C., Wilson, P. T., & Fielding, L. G. (1988). Growth in reading and how children spend their time outside of school. *Reading Research Quarterly, 23* (3), 285–303.

Anderson, T. H., & Armbruster, B. B. (1980). Studying. In P. D. Pearson (Ed.), *Handbook of reading research* (pp. 657–680). New York: Longman.

Anderson, V. (1991). *A teacher development project in transactional strategy instruction for teacher of severely reading disabled adolescents.* Paper presented at the National Reading Conference annual meeting. Palm Springs, CA.

Anton, W. (1999). *Corn: From farm to table.* New York: Newbridge.

Apple Computer. (1984). *Macwrite* [Computer program]. Cupertino, CA: Author.

Applebee, A. N. (1979). *The child's concept of story: Ages two to seventeen.* Chicago, IL: The University of Chicago Press.

Applebee, A. N., Langer, J. A., & Mullis, I. V. S. (1988). *Who reads best.* Princeton, NJ: Educational Testing Service.

Appleby, E. (2001). *The three billy goats gruff: A Norwegian folktale.* New York: Scholastic, Inc.

Armbruster, B., & Anderson, T. (1981). *Content area textbooks* (Reading Education Report No. 23). Urbana-Champaign: University of Illinois at Urbana-Champaign, Center for the Study of Reading.

Armbruster, B. B. (1984). The problem of "inconsiderate text." In G. G. Duffy, L. R. Roehler, & J. Mason (Eds.), *Comprehension instruction: Perspective and suggestions.* New York: Longman.

Armbruster, B. B., Lehr, F., & Osborn, J. (2001). *Put reading first: The research building blocks for teaching children to read.* Washington, DC: U.S. Department of Education.

Asbjornsen, P. C. (1973). *The three billy goats gruff* (Paul Galdone, Illustrator). New York: Seaburry Press.

Asch, F. (1993). *Moondance.* New York: Scholastic.

Asheim, L., Baker, D. P., & Mathews, V. H. (1983). *Reading and successful living: The family school partnership.* Hamden, CT: Library Professional.

Asher, S. R. (1977). *Sex differences in reading achievement.* (Reading Education Report No. 2). Urbana-Champaign: University of Illinois at Urbana-Champaign, Center for the Study of Reading.

Asher, S. R. (1980). Topic interest and children's reading comprehension. In R. J. Spiro, B. C. Bruce, & W. F. Brewer (Eds.), *Theoretical issues in reading comprehension* (pp. 525–534). Hillsdale, NJ: Erlbaum.

Ashton-Warner, S. (1963). *Teacher.* New York: Touchstone Press.

Atwell, N. (1987). *In the middle: Writing, reading, and learning with adolescents.* Portsmouth, NH: Heinemann.

Au, K. H. (1993). *Literacy instruction in multicultural settings.* Fort Worth, TX: Harcourt Brace.

Au, K. H. (1997). *Literacy instruction in multicultural settings.* Belmont, CA: Wadsworth.

Au, T. K., Depretto, M., & Song, Y. K. (1994). Input vs. constraints: Early word acquisition in Korean and English. *Journal of Memory and Language, 33,* 567–582.

August, D., & Shanahan, T. (2006). *Developing literacy in second-language learners: A report of the national literacy panel on language-minority children and youth.* Mahwah, NJ: Lawrence Erlbaum Associates, Inc.

Aukerman, R. (1981). *The basal reader approach to reading.* New York: Wiley.

Ausubel, D. P. (1959). Viewpoints from related disciplines: Human growth and development. *Teachers College Record, 60,* 245–254.

Avi, W. (1984). *The fighting ground.* Philadelphia: Lippincott.

Bacharach, N., & Alexander, P. (1986). Basal reader manuals: What do teachers think of them? *Reading Psychology, 3,* 163–172.

Bader, L. A. (1984). Instructional adjustments to vision problems. *The Reading Teacher, 37* (7), 566–569.

Baker, L., & Brown, A. L. (1984). Cognitive monitoring in reading. In J. Flood (Ed.), *Understanding reading comprehension* (pp. 21–44). Newark, DE: International Reading Association.

Baker, L., Dreher, M. J., & Guthrie, J. T. (2000). *Engaging young readers: Promoting achievement and motivation.* New York: Guilford Press.

Baldwin, R. S., & Kaufman, R. K. (1979). A concurrent validity study of the Raygor readability estimate. *Journal of Reading, 23,* 148–153.

Baines, L. A., & Stanley, G. K. (2006). *Clearinghouse: A Journal of Educational Strategies, Issues and Ideas, 79*(3), 119–123.

Bank Street Writer [Computer program]. (1990). Jefferson City, MO: Scholastic Software.

Bantam. (1985). *Choose your own adventure.* New York: Bantam.

Barker, R. (1978). Stream of individual behavior. In R. Barker & Associates (Eds.), *Habitats, environments, and human behavior* (pp. 3–16). San Francisco: Jossey-Bass.

Barracca, D., & Barracca, S. (1990). *Taxi dog.* New York: Dial Books.

Barrentine, S. B. (1996). Engaging with reading through interactive read-alouds. *The Reading Teacher, 50*(1), 36–43.

Barrentine, S. J. (1999). *Reading assessment: Principles and practices for elementary teachers.* Newark, DE: International Reading Association.

Barrett, F. L. (1982). *A teacher's guide to shared reading.* Richmond Hill, Ontario, Canada: Scholastic-TAB.

Barrett, J. (1978). *Cloudy with a chance of meatballs* (R. Barrett, Illustrator). Hartford, CT: Atheneum.

Barrett, N. S. (1984). *Trucks* (Tony Bryan, Illustrator). London, NY: F. Watts.

Barrett, N. S. (1989). *Spiders.* London, NY: F. Watts.

Barrett, T. (1972). Taxonomy of reading comprehension. *Reading 360 Monograph.* Boston: Ginn.

Barron, R. F. (1969). The use of vocabulary as an advance organizer. In H. L. Herber & P. L. Sanders (Eds.), *Research in reading in the content areas: First year report.* Syracuse, NY: Reading and Language Arts Center, Syracuse University.

Bartlett, B. J. (1978). *Top-level structure as an organizational strategy for recall of classroom text.* Unpublished doctoral dissertation, Arizona State University.

Barton, D., Miller, R., & Macken, M. A. (1980). Do children treat clusters as one unit or two? *Papers and Reports on Child Language Development, 18,* 137.

Basal reading texts. What's in them to comprehend? (1984). *The Reading Teacher,* 194–195.

Base, G. (1986). *Animalia.* New York: Harry N. Abrams.

Baum, L. F. (1972). *The Wizard of Oz.* World.

Bauman, J. F., & Bergon, B. S. (1993). Story map instruction using children's literature: Effects on first graders' comprehension of central narrative elements. *Journal of Reading Behavior, 25*(4), 407–437.

Baumann, J. F. (1992). Basal reading programs and the deskilling of teachers: A critical examination of the argument. *Reading Research Quarterly, 27*(4), 390–398.

Baumann, J. F. (1993). Letters to the editor: Is it "You just don't understand," or am I simply confused? A response to Shannon. *Reading Research Quarterly, 28*(2), 86–87.

Baumann, J. F. (1996). Do basal readers deskill teachers: A national survey of educators' use and opinions of basals. *Elementary School Journal, 96*(5), 511–526.

Baumann, J. F., & Bergeron, B. S. (1993). Story map instruction using children's literature: Effects on first graders' comprehension of central narrative elements. *Journal of Reading Behavior, 25,* 407–437.

Baumann, J. F., Edwards, E. C., Boland, E. M., Olejnik, S., & Kame'enui, E. (2003). Vocabulary tracks: Effects of instruction in morphology and context on fifth-grade students' ability to derive and infer word meanings. *American Educational Research Journal, 40*(2), 447–494.

Baumann, J. F., Jones, L. A., & Siefert-Kessell, N. (1993). Using think alouds to enhance children's comprehension monitoring abilities. *The Reading Teacher, 47*(3), 184–193.

Baumann, J. F., & Stevenson, J. A. (1986). Teaching students to comprehend anaphoric relations. In J. W. Irwin (Ed.), *Understanding and teaching cohesion comprehension* (pp. 3–8). Newark, DE: International Reading Association.

Baylor, B. (1976). *Hawk, I'm your brother.* New York: Macmillan.

Bear, D. R., Inverizzi, M., Templeton, S., & Johnston, F. (2000). *Words their way: Word study for phonics, vocabulary, and spelling instruction.* Upper Saddle River, NJ: Merrill/Prentice-Hall.

Bear, D. R., Templeton, S., Invernizzi, M., & Johnston, F. (1996). *Words their way: Word study for phonics, vocabulary, and spelling instruction.* Upper Saddle River, NJ: Merrill/Prentice-Hall.

Bear, D. R., Templeton, S., Invernizzi, M., & Johnston, F. (2004). *Words their way: Word study for phonics, vocabulary, and spelling instruction* (3rd ed.). Upper Saddle River, NJ: Merrill/Prentice-Hall.

Beaver, J. (1999). *Development Reading Assessment.* Upper Saddle River, NJ: Pearson Education.

Beaver, J. (2001). *Developmental reading assessment.* Parsippany, NJ: Celebration Press.

Beaver, J. (2006). *Developmental reading assessment—2.* Upper Saddle River, NJ: Pearson Learning Group.

Beck, I. L. (1986). Using research on reading. *Educational Leadership, 43*(7), 13–15.

Beck, I. L. (1997). Response to "Overselling phonics" [Letter to the editor]. *Reading Today,* p. 17.

Beck, I. L., Armbruster, B., Raphael, T., McKeown, M. G., Ringler, L., & Ogle, D. (1989). *Reading today and tomorrow: Treasures. Level 3.* New York: Holt, Rinehart and Winston.

Beck, I. L., & McKeown, M. G. (1981). Developing questions that promote comprehension: The story map. *Language Arts, 58,* 913–918.

Beck, I. L., & McKeown, M. G. (2001). Text talk: Capturing the benefits of read-aloud experiences for young children. *Reading Teacher, 55*(1), 10–20.

Beck, I. L., McKeown, M. G., Omanson, R. C., & Pople, M. T. (1984). Improving the comprehensibility of stories: The effects of revisions that improve coherence. *Reading Research Quarterly, 19,* 263–277.

Beck, I. L., Omanson, R. C., & McKeown, M. G. (1982). An instructional redesign of reading lessons: Effects on comprehension. *Reading Research Quarterly, 17,* 462–481.

Beck, I. L., Perfetti, C. A., & McKeown, M. G. (1982). Effects of long-term vocabulary instruction on lexical access and reading comprehension. *Journal of Educational Psychology, 74,* 506–521.

Bennett, W. J. (2001, April 24). A cure for the illiteracy epidemic. *Wall Street Journal,* p. A24.

Benson & Cummins (2000). *The Power of retelling.* Wright Group/McGraw-Hill, NY.

Berger, M. (1996). *Amazing water.* New York: Newbridge.

Berlak, H. (1992). The need for a new science of assessment. In H. Berlak et al., *Toward a new science of educational testing and assessment.* New York: State University of New York Press.

Betts, E. A. (1946). *Foundation of reading instruction.* New York: American Book.

Biddulph, F., & Biddulph, J. (1992). *How do spiders live?* Bothell, WA: The Wright Group.

Biemiller, A. (2006). Vocabulary development and instruc-tion: A prerequisite for school learning. In D. K. Dickinson & S. B. Neuman (Eds.), *Handbook of early literacy* (Vol. 2) pp. 41–51. New York: Guilford Press.

Bilingual writing center, The. (1992). Fremont, CA: The Learning Company. (Aidenwood Tech Park, 493 Kaiser Drive, Fremont, CA 94555, [800] 852-2255.)

Bintz, W. P. (1991). Staying connected—Exploring new functions for assessment. *Contemporary Education, 62*(4), 307–312.

Birdshaw, D., Burns, S., Carlisle, J. F., Duke, N. K., Garcia, G. E., Hoff-man, J. V. et al. (2001). *Teaching every child to read: Frequently asked questions.* Ann Arbor, MI: Center for the Improvement of Early Reading Achievement.

Bissex, G. L. (1980). *Gnys at wrk: A child learns to write and read.* Cambridge, MA: Harvard University Press.

Blachman, B. A. (1984). Relationship of rapid naming ability and lan-guage analysis skills to kindergarten and first-grade reading achievement. *Journal of Educational Psychology, 76,* 610–622.

Blachowicz, C., & Fisher, P. J. (2006). *Teaching vocabulary in all classrooms* (3rd ed.). Upper Saddle River, NJ: Pearson/Merrill/ Prentice Hall.

Blachowicz, C. L. Z. (1977). Cloze activities for primary readers. *The Reading Teacher, 31*(3), 300–302.

Blachowicz, C. L. Z. (1986). Making connections: Alternatives to the vocabulary notebook. *Journal of Reading, 29*(7), 643–649.

Blackburn, L. (1997). *Whole music: A whole language approach to teaching music.* Westport, CT: Heinemann.

Blair, S. M., and Williams, K. A. (1999). *Balanced reading instruc-tion: Achieving success with every child.* Newark, DE: Interna-tional Reading Association.

Blanchard, J., & Rottenberg, C. J. (1990). Hypertext and hypermedia: Discovering and creating meaningful learning environments. *The Reading Teacher, 43*(9), 656–661.

Blanchard, J. S., Mason, G. E., & Daniel, D. (1987). *Computer applica-tions in reading.* Newark, DE: International Reading Association.

Blanton, W. E., & Moorman, G. B. (1985). *Presentation of reading les-sons. Technical Report No. 1.* Boone, NC: Center for Excellence on Teacher Education, Appalachian State University.

Blanton, W. E., Moorman, G. B., & Wood, K. D. (1986). A model of direct instruction applied to the basal skills lesson. *The Read-ing Teacher, 40,* 299–305.

Blecher, S., & Jaffee, K. (1998). *Weaving in the arts: Widening the learn-ing circle.* Westport, CT: Heinemann.

Bleich, D. (1978). *Subjective criticism.* Baltimore, MD: Johns Hopkins University Press.

Blevins, W. (1997). *Phonemic awareness activities for early reading success.* New York: Scholastic.

Blevins, W. (1998). *Phonics from A to Z: A practical guide.* New York: Scholastic Professional Books.

Block, C. C. (1993). Strategy instruction in a literature-based pro-gram. *Elementary School Journal, 94,* 103–120.

Block, C. C. (2001, December). *Distinctions between the expertise of literacy teachers preschool through grade 5.* Paper presented at the annual meeting of the National Reading Conference, San Antonio, TX.

Block, C. C., Gambrell, L. B., Hamilton, V., Hartman, D. K., Hasselbring, T. S., Klein, A., et al. (2000). *Scholastic literacy place.* New York: Scholastic.

Block, C. C., & Mangieri, J. (1996). *Reasons to read: Thinking strate-gies for life through literature* (Vols. 1–3), Menlo Park, CA: Ad-dison.

Block, C. C., Oakar, M., & Hurt, N. (2002). The expertise of literacy teachers: A continuum from preschool to grade 5. *Reading Re-search Quarterly, 37*(2), 178–206.

Block, J. H. (1989). *Building effective mastery learning schools.* New York: Longman.

Blok, H., Oostdam, R., Otter, M. E., & Overmaat, M. (2002). Com-puter-assisted instruction in support of beginning reading in-struction: A review. *Review of Educational Research, 72*(1), 101–130.

Bloom, A. (1987). *The closing of the American mind: How higher ed-ucation has failed democracy and impoverished the souls of to-day's students.* New York: Simon & Schuster.

Bloom, B. (1956). *Taxonomy of educational objectives.* New York: David McKay.

Blum, I. (1995). Using audiotaped books to extend classroom liter-acy instruction into the homes of second-language learners. *Journal of Reading Behavior, 27*(4), 535–563.

Blume, J. (1972). *Tales of a fourth grade nothing.* New York: Dell.

Bohning, G. (1986). The McGuffey eclectic readers: 1836–1986. *The Reading Teacher, 40,* 263–269.

Bond, G. L., & Dykstra, R. (1967). The cooperative research program in first-grade reading instruction. *Reading Research Quarterly, 2,* 5–142.

Bonne, R. (1985). *I know an old lady.* New York: Scholastic.

Bonners, S. (1989). *Just in passing.* New York: Lothrop, Lee & Shepard.

Booth, J. (1985). *Impressions.* Toronto: Holt, Rinehart and Winston.

Bourgeois, P., & Clark, B. (1986). *Franklin in the dark.* New York: Scholastic.

Boyer, E. L. (1995). *The basic school: A community for learning.* Princeton, NJ: Carnegie Foundation for the Advancement of Teaching.

Boyle, O. F., & Peregoy, S. F. (1990). Literacy scaffolds: Strategies for first- and second-language readers and writers. *The Read-ing Teacher, 44*(3), 194–200.

Brackett, G. (1989). *Super story tree.* Jefferson City, MO: Scholastic.

Branley, F. (1983). *Saturn: The spectacular planet.* New York: HarperCollins.

Bransford, J. C., & Johnson, M. K. (1972). Contextual prerequisites for understanding: Some investiga-tions of comprehension and recall. *Journal of Verbal Learning and Verbal Behavior, 11,* 717–726.

Bransford, J. D., & Franks, J. J. (1971). The abstraction of linguistic ideas. *Cognitive Psychology, 2,* 331–350.

Braun, C. (1969). Interest-loading and modality effects on textual re-sponse acquisition. *Reading Research Quarterly, 4,* 428–444.

Braunger, J., & Lewis, J. P. (2006). *Building a knowledge base in read-ing* (2nd ed.). Newark, DE: International Reading Asssociation.

Brennan, J. (1994, September 3). Been there done that: Three John Grisham stories, one John Grisham plot. *Fort Worth Star Telegram,* p. 1E.

Brent, D. (1994). Writing classes, writing genres, and writing text-books. *Textual Studies in Canada, 4*(1), 5–15.

Bridge, C. (1978). Predictable materials for beginning readers. *Language Arts, 55,* 593–597.

Bridge, C. A., Winograd, P. N., & Haley, D. (1983). Using predictable ma-terials vs. preprimers to teach beginning sight words. *The Reading Teacher, 36,* 84–91.

Brigance, A. H. (1999). *Brigance® comprehensive inventory of basic skills–revised.* North Billerica, MA: Curriculum Associates.

Brimner, L. D. (1992). *A migrant family.* Minneapolis, MN: Lerner.

Bromley, K. D. (1991). *Webbing with literature: Creating story maps with children's books*. Boston: Allyn & Bacon.

Bronfenbrenner, U. (1977). Toward an experimental ecology of human development. *American Psychologist, 32,* 513–531.

Bronfenbrenner, U., McClelland, P., Wethington, E., Moen, P., & Ceci, S. J. (1996). *The state of Americans*. New York: Free Press.

Brooks, G., Cole, P., Davies, P., Davis, B., Frater, G., Harman, J., et al. (2002). *Keeping up with the children*. London: Basic Skills Agency Publishers.

Brown, A., & Smiley, S. S. (1978). The development of strategies for studying texts. *Child Development, 49,* 1076–1088.

Brown, A. (1982). Learning how to learn from reading. In J. A. Langer & M. T. Smith-Burke (Eds.), *Reader meets author: Bridging the gap* (pp. 26–54). Newark, DE: International Reading Association.

Brown, A. L., Day, J. D., & Jones, R. S. (1983). The development of plans for summarizing texts. *Child Development, 54,* 968–979.

Brown, D. J., Engin, A. W., & Wallbrown, F. J. (1979). Developmental changes in reading attitudes during the intermediate grades. *Journal of Experimental Education, 47,* 262–279.

Brown, H., & Cambourne, B. (1987). *Read and retell*. Portsmouth, NH: Heinemann Educational Books.

Brown, K. J. (1999). What kind of text—for whom and when? Textual scaffolding for beginning readers. *The Reading Teacher, 53*(4).

Brown, K. J. (2000). What kind of text—For whom and when? Textual scaffolding for beginning readers. *The Reading Teacher, 53*(4), 292–307.

Brown, M. (1947). *Stone soup*. New York: Scribner.

Brown, R., Pressley, M., Van Meter, P., & Schuder, T. (1996). A quasi-experimental validation of transactional strategies instruction with low-achieving second grade readers. *Journal of Educational Psychology, 88,* 18–37.

Brown, T. (1986). *Hello, amigos*. New York: Holt, Rinehart and Winston.

Brozo, W. G., & Simpson, M. L. (1995). *Readers, teachers, learners: Expanding literacy in secondary schools*. Upper Saddle River, NJ: Merrill/Prentice-Hall.

Bruner, J. (1978). The role of dialog in language acquisition. In A. Sinclair, R. J. Jarvella, & W. M. Levelt (Eds.), *The child's conception of language* (pp. 241–256). New York: Springer-Verlag.

Bruner, J. (1986). *Actual minds, Possible worlds*. Cambridge, MA: Harvard University Press.

Bryan, G., Fawson, P. C., & Reutzel, D. R. (2003). Sustained silent reading: Exploring the value of literature discussion with three non-engaged readers. *Reading Research and Instruction, 43*(1), 47–73.

Burke, C. (1987). Burke reading interview. In Goodman, Y., Watson, D., & Burke, C. (Eds.), *Reading miscue inventory: Alternative procedures*. New York: Owen.

Burkhart, A. L. (2000). Breaking the parental barrier. In T. V. Rasinski, N. D. Padak et al. (Eds.), *Motivating recreational reading and promoting home–school connections* (pp. 110–113). Newark, DE: International Reading Association.

Burnford, S. (1960). *The incredible journey*. Boston: Little, Brown.

Burns, M. (1987). *The I hate mathematics book* (Martha Hairston, Illustrator). Cambridge, MA: Cambridge University Press.

Burns, M. S., Griffin, P., & Snow, C. E. (Eds.). (1999). *Starting out right: A guide to promoting children's reading success*. Committee on the Prevention of Reading Difficulties in Young Children, Commission on Behavioral and Social Sciences and Education, National Research Council. Washington, DC: National Academy Press.

Burns, P. C., Roe, B. D., & Ross, E. P. (1992). *Teaching reading in today's elementary schools,* 5th Ed. Dallas: Houghton Mifflin.

Byars, B. (1970). *The summer of the swans*. New York: Viking.

Byars, B. (1981). *The Cybil war*. New York: Viking.

Byrne, B., & Fielding-Barnsley, R. (1989). Phonemic awareness and letter knowledge in the child's acquisition of the alphabetic principle. *Journal of Educational Psychology, 81,* 313–321.

Byrne, B., & Fielding-Barnsley, R. (1990). Acquiring the alphabetic principle: A case for teaching recognition of phoneme identity. *Journal of Educational Psychology, 82*(4), 805–812.

Byrne, B., Freebody, P., & Gates, A. (1992). Longitudinal data on the relations of word-reading strategies to comprehension, reading time, and phonemic awareness. *Reading Research Quarterly, 27*(2), 140–151.

Cafolla, R., Kauffman, D., & Knee, R. (1997). *World Wide Web for teachers: An interactive guide*. Boston: Allyn & Bacon.

California Department of Education. (1980). *Report on the special studies of selected ECE schools with increasing and decreasing reading scores*. (Available from Publication Sales, California State Department of Education, P.O. Box 271, Sacramento, CA 95802.)

California Reading Task Force. (1995). *Every child a reader: The report of the California Reading Task Force*. Sacramento, CA: California Department of Education.

Calkins, L. (1986). *The art of teaching writing*. Portsmouth, NH: Heinemann.

Calkins, L. (1994). *The art of teaching writing*. Westport, CT: Heinemann.

Calkins, L. (2001). *The art of teaching reading*. New York: Addison Wesley.

Calkins, L. M. (1980). When children want to punctuate: Basic skills belong in context. *Language Arts, 57,* 567–573.

Calkins, L. M., & Harwayne, S. (1987). *The writing workshop: A world of difference* [Video]. Portsmouth, NH: Heinemann.

Cambourne, B. (1988). *The whole story: Natural learning and the acquisition of literacy in the classroom*. New York: Ashton-Scholastic.

Cambourne, B., & Turbill, J. (1990). Assessment in whole-language classrooms: Theory into practice. *Elementary School Journal, 90*(3), 337–349.

Campbell, R. (1992). *Reading real books*. Philadelphia: Open University Press.

Campbell, R. (2001). *Read-alouds with young children*. Newark, DE: International Reading Association.

Canney, G., & Winograd, P. (1979). *Schemata for reading and reading comprehension performance* (Technical Report No. 120). Urbana-Champaign: University of Illinois at Urbana-Champaign, Center for the Study of Reading. (ERIC Document Reproduction Service).

Cantrell, S. C. (1999). Effective teaching and literacy learning: A look inside primary classrooms. *The Reading Teacher, 52*(4), 370–378.

Cantrell, S. C. (1999a). The effects of literacy instruction on primary students' reading and writing achievement. *Reading and Research Instruction, 39*(1), 3–26.

Cantrell, S. C. (1999b). Effective teaching and literacy learning: A look inside primary classrooms. *The Reading Teacher, 52*(4), 370–379.

Carbo, M. (1988). The evidence supporting reading styles: A response to Stahl. *Phi Delta Kappan, 70,* 323–327.

Carle, E. (1986). *The very hungry caterpillar*. New York: Scholastic, Inc.

Carle, E. (1986). *The grouchy ladybug*. New York: HarperCollins.

Carlisle, J. F. (2004). Morphological processes that influence learning to read. In C. A. Stone, E. R. Silliman, B. J. Ehren, & K. Apel (Eds.), *Handbook of language and literacy: Development and disorders* (pp. 318–339). New York: Guilford Press.

Carr, E. (1985). The vocabulary overview guide: A metacognitive strategy to improve vocabulary comprehension and retention. *Journal of Reading, 28*(8), 684–689.

Carr, E., Dewitz, P., & Patberg, J. (1989). Using cloze for inference training with expository text. *The Reading Teacher, 43*(6), 380–385.

Carr, E., & Wixson, K. K. (1986). Guidelines for evaluating vocabulary instruction. *Journal of Reading, 29*(7), 588–589.

Carr, H. K. (1986). *Developing metacognitive skills: The key to success in reading and learning*. For the MERIT, Chapter 2 project, The School District of Philadelphia, H. K. Carr, MERIT supervisor. Philadelphia: School District of Philadelphia.

Carr, S. C., & Thompson, B. (1996). The effects of prior knowledge and schema activation strategies on the inferential reading comprehension of children with and without learning disabilities. *Learning Disability Quarterly, 19*, 48–61.

Carroll, J. B., Davies, P., & Richman, B. (1971). *Word frequency book*. Boston: Houghton Mifflin.

Carroll, L. (1872). *Through the looking glass*. New York: Macmillan.

Cassidy, J. (1981). Grey power in the reading program—a direction for the eighties. *The Reading Teacher, 35*, 287–291.

Cattell, J. M. (1885). Ueber die Zeit der Erkennung und Bennenung von Schriftzeichen, Bildern und Farben. *Philosophische Studien, 2*, 635–650.

Caverly, D. C., & Buswell, J. (1988). Computer assisted instruction that supports whole language instruction. *Colorado Communicator, 11*(3), 6–7.

Center for Research on Education, Diversity and Excellence (CREDE). (2006). *The five standards for effective pedagogy*. Available at the Center for Research on Education, Diversity and Excellence (CREDE) Web site: *http://crede.berkeley.edu/standards/standards.html*.

Chall, J. S. (1967). *Learning to read: The great debate*. New York: McGraw-Hill.

Chall, J. S. (1979). The great debate: Ten years later, with a modest proposal for reading stages. In Resnick, L. B., & Weaver, P. A. (Eds.), *Theory and practice of early reading* (pp. 29–55). Hillsdale, NJ: Erlbaum.

Chall, J. S. (1983). *Stages of reading development*. New York: McGraw-Hill.

Chall, J. S. (1998). My life in reading. In E. Sturtevant, J. Dugan, P. Linder, & W. Linek (Eds.), *Literacy and community, the twentieth yearbook of the College Reading Association, USA*, 12–24.

Chapman, L. J., & Hoffman, M. (1977). *Developing fluent reading*. Milton Keynes, England: Open University Press.

Chard, S. C. (1998). *The project approach: Making curriculum come alive*, Book 1. New York: Scholastic Professional Books.

Chase, R. (1948). *Grandfather tales*. Boston: Houghton Mifflin.

Cheney, L. V. (1990). *Tyrannical machines*. Washington, DC: National Endowment for the Humanities.

Chisom, F. P. (1989). *Jump start: The federal role in adult literacy*. Southport, CT: Southport Institute for Policy Analysis.

Choi, S. N. (1991). *Year of impossible goodbyes*. Boston: Houghton Mifflin.

Chomsky, C. (1971). Write first, read later. *Childhood Education, 47*, 230–237.

Chomsky, N. (1974). *Aspects of the theory of syntax*. (2nd ed.). Cambridge, MA: MIT Press.

Chomsky, N. (1975). *The logical structure of linguistic theory*. Chicago: The University of Chicago Press.

Chomsky, N. (1979). Human language and other semiotic systems. *Semiotica, 25*, 31–44.

Chomsky, N. (1997). *Perspectives on power*. Montreal, Canada: Black Rose Books.

Chomsky, N. A. (1957). *Syntactic structures*. The Hague, The Netherlands: Mouton.

Christopher, J. (1967). *The white mountains*. New York: Macmillan.

Churchland, P. M. (1995). *The engine of reason: The seat of the soul*. Cambridge, MA: MIT Press.

Clark, A. (1997). *Being there: Putting brain, body, and world together again*. Cambridge, MA: MIT Press.

Clark, C. M., Peterson, P. L. (1986). Teachers' thought processes. In M. C. Wittrock (Ed.), *Handbook of reading research on teaching* (pp. 255–296). New York: Macmillan.

Clark, E. (1993). *The lexicon in acquisition*. Cambridge, UK: Cambridge University Press.

Clark, H. H., & Clark, E. V. (1977). *Psychology and language: An introduction to psycholinguistics*. New York: Harcourt Brace Jovanovich.

Clarke, M. A. (1989). Negotiating agendas: Preliminary considerations. *Language Arts, 66*(4), 370–380.

Clay, M. (1966). *Emergent reading behavior*. Unpub-lished doctoral dissertation, University of Auckland.

Clay, M. M. (1967). The reading behaviour of five year old children: A research report. *New Zealand Journal of Educational Studies, 2*(1), 11–31.

Clay, M. M. (1972). *Reading: The patterning of complex behaviour*. Exeter, NH: Heinemann.

Clay, M. M. (1972). *Sand* and *Stones*. Exeter, NH: Heinemann Educational Books, Inc.

Clay, M. M. (1975). *What did I write? Beginning writing behaviour*. Portsmouth, NH: Heinemann.

Clay, M. M. (1979). *Reading: The patterning of complex behaviour*. Exeter, NH: Heinemann Educational Books, Inc.

Clay, M. M. (1985). *The early detection of reading difficulties* (3rd ed.). Portsmouth, NH: Heinemann.

Clay, M. M. (1987). *Writing begins at home: Preparing children for writing before they go to school*. Portsmouth, NH: Heinemann.

Clay, M. M. (1990a). The Reading Recovery Programme, 1984–88: Coverage, outcomes and Education Board district figures. *New Zealand Journal of Educational Studies, 25*, 61–70.

Clay, M. M. (1990b). What is and what might be in evaluation (Research currents). *Language Arts, 67*(3), 288–298.

Clay, M. M. (1991). *Becoming literate: The construction of inner control*. Portsmouth, NH: Heinemann Educational Books.

Clay, M. M. (1993). *An observation survey of early literacy achievement*. Portsmouth, NH: Heinemann.

Clay, M. M. (1993b). *Reading recovery: A guidebook for teachers in training*. Portsmouth, NH: Heinemann.

Clay, M. M. (1997). *Running records for classroom teachers*. Portsmouth, NH: Heinemann.

Clay, M. M. (1998). *By different paths to common outcomes*. York, ME: Stenhouse.

Clay, M. M. (2000a). *New shoes* and *Follow me, moon*. Portsmouth, NH: Heinemann.

Clay, M. M. (2000b). *Concepts about print: What have children learned about the way we print language?* Portsmouth, NH: Heinemann.

Cleary, B. (1952). *Henry and Beezus*. New York: William Morrow.

Clifford, J. (1991). *The experience of reading: Louise Rosenblatt and reader-response theory*. Portsmouth, NH: Heinemann.

Clyne, M., & Griffiths, R. (2005). *Sand*. Parsippany, NJ: Pearson Education.

Cochrane, O., Cochrane, D., Scalena, D., & Buchanan, E. (1984). *Reading, writing and caring*. New York: Owen.

Cohen, M. (1980). *First grade takes a test*. New York: Dell Books.

Cole, B. (1983). *The trouble with mom*. New York: Coward-McCann.

Cole, J. (1986). *This is the place for me*. New York: Scholastic.

Cole, J. (1990). *The magic school bus lost in the solar system*. New York: Scholastic.

Cole, J. E. (2003). What motivates students to read? Four literacy personalities. *The Reading Teacher, 56*(4), 326–336.

Cole, J., & Calmenson, S. (1990). *Miss Mary Mack*. New York: Morrow Junior Books.

Cole, R. (1997). *The world of matter*. New York: Newbridge Educational.

Coleman, E. (1996). *White socks only*. Morton Grove, IL: Albert Whitman & Co.

Coles, G. (2000). *Misreading reading: The bad science that hurts children*. Portsmouth, NH: Heinemann Educational Books.

Collier, J., & Collier, C. (1981). *Jump ship to freedom*. New York: Delacorte.

Collins, A., & Smith, E. (1980). *Teaching the process of reading comprehension* (Tech. Rep. No. 182). Urbana-Champaign: University of Illinois at Urbana-Champaign, Center for the Study of Reading.

Collins, A. M., & Quillian, M. R. (1969). Retrieval time from semantic memory. *Journal of Verbal Learning and Verbal Behavior, 8*, 240–247.

Collins, C. (1988). Research windows. *The Computing Teacher, 15*, 15–16, 61.

Collins C. (1991). Reading instruction that increases thinking abilities. *Journal of Reading, 34*, 510–515.

Collins-Block, C., Gambrell, L. B., & Pressley, M. (2003). *Improving comprehension instruction: Advances in research, theory, and classroom practice*. San Francisco, CA: Jossey-Bass.

Collins-Block, C., & Mangeri, J. (1996). *Reason to read: Thinking strategies for life through literature,* Palo Alto, CA: Addison-Wesley.

Collins-Block, C., Oaker, M., & Hurt, N. (2002). The expertise of literacy teachers: A continuum from preschool to grade 3. *Reading Research Quarterly, 37*(2), 178–206.

Collins-Block, C., & Pressley, M. (2002). *Comprehension instruction: Research-based best practices*. New York: Guilford Press.

Collins-Block, C., Gambrell, L. B., & Pressley, M. (2002). *Improving comprehension instruction: Rethinking research, theory, and classroom practice*. San Francisco, CA: Jossey-Bass.

Commeyras, M., & DeGroff, L. (1998). Literacy professionals' perspectives on professional development and pedagogy: A United States survey. *Reading Research Quarterly, 33*(4), 434–472.

Cone, M. (1964). *A promise is a promise*. Boston: Houghton Mifflin.

Cook, L. K., & Mayer, R. E. (1988). Teaching readers about the nature of science text. *Journal of Educational Psychology, 80*(4), 448–456.

Cooter, K. S. (2003). *Preparing middle school students for the TAKS in writing: A professional development seminar*. Dallas, TX: Seminar series presented for selected middle schools in the Dallas Independent School District. Unpublished manuscript.

Cooter, K. S. (2006a). *Pedagogy to andragogy: CREDE standards in the university classroom*. CREDE Summit, April 7, 2006. University of California at Berkeley, CA.

Cooter, K. S. (2006b). *Tinkertoy writing: A systematic approach for grades K–5*. Memphis, TN: Unpublished manuscript.

Cooter, K. S. (2006c). When mama can't read: Counteracting intergenerational illiteracy. *The Reading Teacher, 59*(7), 698–702.

Cooter, R. B. (Ed.). (2003). *Perspectives on rescuing urban literacy education: Spies, saboteurs & saints*. Mahwah, NJ: Erlbaum.

Cooter, R. B. (2004) The pillars of urban literacy instruction: Prerequisites for change. In R. C. Cooter (Ed.), *Perspectives on rescuing urban literacy education: Spies, saboteurs, and saints*. Mahwah, NJ: Lawrence Erlbaum Associates.

Cooter, R. B., & Cooter, K. S. (2002). *The fluency formula: A comprehensive model of instruction. Creating Comprehensive Reading Programs: Symposium Series for Title I Teachers and Administrators*. Wichita, KS.

Cooter, R. B., Flynt, E. S., & Cooter, K. S. (2007). *The comprehensive reading inventory*. Upper Saddle River, NJ: Pearson Merrill Prentice-Hall.

Cooter, R. B., & Griffith, R. (1989). Thematic units for middle school: An honorable seduction. *Journal of Reading, 32*(8), 676–681.

Cooter, R. B., Jr. (1988). Effects of Ritalin on reading. *Academic Therapy, 23*, 461–468.

Cooter, R. B., Jr. (1993). *Improving oral reading fluency through repeated readings using simultaneous recordings*. Unpublished manuscript, PDS Urban Schools Project, Texas Christian University.

Cooter, R. B., Jr. (1994). Assessing affective and conative factors in reading. *Reading Psychology, 15*(2), 77–90.

Cooter, R. B., Jr. (1998). *Balanced literacy instructional strands*. Reading Research Report #91, Dallas, TX.

Cooter, R. B., Jr. (1999). *Realizing the dream: Meeting the literacy needs of Dallas children*. Dallas, TX: Unpublished manuscript.

Cooter, R. B., Jr. (Ed.). (1990). *The teacher's guide to reading tests*. Scottsdale, AZ: Gorsuch Scarisbrick.

Cooter, R. B., Jr., & Cooter, K. S. (1999). *BLAST!: Balanced Literacy Assessment System and Training*. Ft. Worth, TX: Unpublished manuscript, Ft. Worth TX.

Cooter, R. B., Jr., Diffily, D., Gist-Evans, D., & Sacken, M. A. (1994). *Literacy development milestones research project* (Report No. 94–100). Unpublished manuscript, Texas Christian University, Fort Worth, TX.

Cooter, R. B., Jr., & Flynt, E. S. (1989). Blending basal reader and whole language instruction. *Reading Horizons, 29*(4), 275–282.

Cooter, R. B., Jr., & Flynt, E. S. (1996). *Teaching reading in the content areas: Developing content literacy for all students*. Upper Saddle River, NJ: Merrill/Prentice-Hall.

Cooter, R. B., Jr., & Griffith, R. (1989). Thematic units for middle school: An honorable seduction. *Journal of Reading, 32*(8), 676–681.

Cooter, R. B., Jr., & Reutzel, D. R. (1987). Teaching reading skills for mastery. *Academic Therapy, 23*(2), 127–134.

Cooter, R. B., Jr., & Reutzel, D. R. (1990). *Yakity-yak: A reciprocal response procedure for improving reading comprehension*. Unpublished manuscript, Brigham Young University, Department of Elementary Education, Provo, UT.

Cooter, R. B., Jr., Jacobson, J. J., & Cooter, K. S. (1998). *Technically simple and socially complex: Three school-based attempts to improve literacy achievement*. Paper presented at The National

Reading Conference Annual Convention, Austin, TX, December 5, 1998.

Cooter, R. B., Jr., Joseph, D. G., & Flynt, E. S. (1987). Eliminating the literal pursuit in reading comprehension. *Journal of Clinical Reading, 2*(1), 9–11.

Cooter, R. B., Mathews, B., Thompson, S., & Cooter, K. S. (2004). Searching for lessons of mass instruction? Try reading strategy continuums. *The Reading Teacher, 58*(4), 388–393.

Cooter, R. B., Jr., Mills-House, E., Marrin, P., Mathews, B., & Campbell, S. (1999). Family and community involvement: The bedrock of reading success. *The Reading Teacher, 52*(8), 891–896.

Cooter, R. B., Jr., Reutzel, D. R., & Cooter, K. S. (1998). *Sequence of development and instruction for phonemic awareness.* Unpublished paper.

Cooter, R. B., Mills-House, E., Marrin, P., Mathews, B. A., Campbell, S., and Baker, T. (1999). Family and community involvement: The bedrock of reading. *The Reading Teacher, 52*(8), 891–896.

Cornejo, R. (1972). *Spanish high frequency word list.* Austin, TX: Southwestern Educational Laboratory.

Corno, L., & Randi, J. (1997). Motivation, volition, and collaborative innovation in classroom literacy. In J. T. Guthrie & A. Wigfield (Eds.), *Reading engagement: Motivating readers through integrated instruction.* Newark, DE: International Reading Association.

Cousin, P. T., Weekly, T., & Gerard, J. (1993). The functional uses of language and literacy by students with severe language and learning problems. *Language Arts, 70*(7), 548–556.

Cowley, J. (1980). *Hairy bear.* San Diego, CA: The Wright Group.

Cowley, J. (1982). *What a mess!* San Diego, CA: The Wright Group.

Cox, C. (2002). *Teaching language arts* (4th ed.). Boston: Allyn & Bacon.

Cox, C., & Zarillo, J. (1993). *Teaching reading with children's literature.* Upper Saddle River, NJ: Merrill/Prentice-Hall.

Craft, H., & Krout, J. (1970). *The adventure of the American people.* Chicago, IL: Rand McNally.

CREDE. (2002). *The five standards for effective pedagogy.* Berkeley, CA: Center for Research on Education, Diversity & Excellence, University of California at Berkeley. Retrieved December 21, 2006, from *http://crede.berkeley.edu/standards/standards.html*

Crist, B. I. (1975). One capsule a week—A painless remedy for vocabulary ills. *Journal of Reading, 19*(2), 147–149.

Cronin, V., Farrell, D., & Delaney, M. (1999). Environmental print and word reading. *Journal of Research in Reading, 22*(3), 271–282.

CTB Adams, M. J., & Treadway, J. (2000). *Fox in a box.* Monterey, CA: CTB McGraw-Hill.

CTB McGraw-Hill. (2000). *Fox in a box.* Monterey, CA: CTB McGraw-Hill.

Cudd, E. T., & Roberts, L. L. (1987). Using story frames to develop reading comprehension in a 1st grade classroom. *The Reading Teacher, 41*(1), 74–81.

Cudd, E. T., & Roberts, L. L. (1993). A scaffolding technique to develop sentence sense and vocabulary. *The Reading Teacher, 47*(4), 346–349.

Cunningham, A. E., Perry, K. E., Stanovich, K. E., & Stanovich, P. J. (2004). Disciplinary knowledge of K–3 teachers and their knowledge calibration in the domain of early literacy. *Annals of Dyslexia, 54*(1), 139–167.

Cunningham, A. E., & Stanovich, K. E. (1998). What reading does for the mind. *American Educator, 22,* 8–15.

Cunningham, P. (1980). Teaching were, with, what, and other "four-letter" words. *The Reading Teacher 34,* 160–163.

Cunningham, P. A., Hall, D. P., & Defee, M. (1998). Nonability-grouped, multi-level instruction: Eight years later. *The Reading Teacher, 51*(8), 652–664.

Cunningham, P. M. (1980). Teaching *were, with, what,* and other "four-letter" words. *The Reading Teaching, 34,* 160–163.

Cunningham, P. M. (1995). *Phonics they use: Words for reading and writing* (2nd ed.). New York: HarperCollins.

Cunningham, P. M. (2000). *Phonics they use: Words for reading and writing* (3rd ed.). Boston, MA: Allyn and Bacon.

Cunningham, P. M. (2005). *Phonics they use: Words for reading and writing.* Boston, MA: Allyn and Bacon.

Cunningham, P. M., Hall, D. P., & Sigmon, C. M. (2001). *The teacher's guide to the four-blocks: A multimethod, multilevel framework for grades 1–3.* Greensboro, NC: Carson Dellosa.

Cutting, B., & Cutting, J. (2002). *Is it a fish? –* Sunshine Science Series. Bothell, WA: Wright Group/McGraw-Hill Publishing.

D. E. S. (1975). *A language for life (The Bulloch Report).* London: H.M.S.O.

daCruz-Payne, C. (2005). *Shared reading for today's classroom.* NY: Scholastic, Inc.

Dahl, R. (1961). *James and the giant peach: A children's story* (Nancy Ekholm Burkert, Illustrator). New York: Alfred A. Knopf.

Dahl, R. (1964). *Charlie and the chocolate factory.* New York: Alfred A. Knopf.

Dale, E. (1969), *Audiovisual methods in teaching* (3rd ed.). New York: Holt, Rinehart and Winston.

Dallin, L., & Dallin, L. (1980). *Heritage songster.* Dubuque, IA: William C. Brown.

Dana, C. (1989). Strategy families for disabled readers. *Journal of Reading, 33*(1), 30–35.

Daniels, H. (1994). *Literature circles: Voice and choice in the student-centered classrooms.* York, ME: Stenhouse.

Daniels, H. (2002). *Literature circles: Voice and choice in book clubs and reading groups,* 2nd Ed. York, ME: Stenhouse.

Darling-Hammond, L., Wise, A. E., & Klein, S. P. (1999*). A license to teach.* San Francisco, CA: Jossey-Bass.

Davis, D. (1990). *Listening for the crack of dawn.* Little Rock, AR: August House.

Day, K. C., & Day, H. D. (1979). Development of kindergarten children's understanding of concepts about print and oral language. In M. L. Damil & A. H. Moe (Eds.), *Twenty-eighth yearbook of the National Reading Conference* (pp. 19–22). Clemson, SC: National Reading Conference.

DeBruin-Parecki, A., & Krol-Sinclair, B. (2003). *Family literacy: From theory to practice.* Newark, DE: International Reading Association.

Dechant, E. V. (1970). *Improving the teaching of reading* (2nd ed.). Upper Saddle River, NJ: Prentice-Hall.

DeFord, D., & Harste, J. C. (1982). Child language research and curriculum. *Language Arts, 59*(6), 590–601.

DeFord, D. E. (1985). Validating the construct of theoretical orientation in reading instruction. *Reading Research Quarterly, 20*(3), 351–367.

DeFord, D. E., Lyons, C. A., & Pinnell, G. S. (1991). *Bridges to literacy: Learning from Reading Recovery.* Portsmouth, NH: Heinemann.

DeGroff, L. (1990). Is there a place for computers in whole language classrooms? *The Reading Teacher, 43*(8), 568–572.

DeJong, M. (1953). *Hurry home, Candy.* New York: Harper.

Delacre, L. (1996). *Golden tales: Myths, legends and folktales from Latin America*. New York: Scholastic.

Delpit, L. D. (1988). The silenced dialogue: Power and pedagogy in educating other people's children. *Harvard Educational Review, 58*(3), 280–298.

Denny, T. P., & Weintraub, S. (1966). First graders' responses to three questions about reading. *Elementary School Journal, 66,* 441–448.

Denton, C. A., Ciancio, D. J., & Fletcher, J. M. (2006). Validity, reliability, and utility of the *Observation Survey of Early Literacy Achievement. Reading Research Quarterly, 41*(1), 8–34.

dePaola, T. (1978). *The popcorn book*. New York: Holiday House.

Department of Education. (1985). *Reading in junior classes. Wellington, New Zealand*. New York: Owen.

DeRidder, I. (2002). Visible or invisible links: Does the highlighting of hyperlinks affect incidental vocabulary learning, text comprehension, and the reading process? *Language Learning & Technology, 6*(1), 123–146.

D. E. S. (1975). *A language for life (The Bulloch Report)*. London: H.M.S.O.

Developmental Learning Materials. (1985). *The writing adventure*. Allen, TX: Developmental Learning Materials.

Devillar, R. A., Faltis, C. J., & Cummins, J. P. (1994). *Cultural diversity in schools: From rhetoric to practice*. Albany, NY: SUNY Press.

Dewey, J. (1913). *Interest and effort in education*. New York: Houghton Mifflin.

Dewey, J., & Bentley, A. F. (1949). *Knowing and the known*. Boston: Beacon Press.

Dewitz, P., & Carr, E. M. (1987). Teaching comprehension as a student directed process. In P. Dewitz (Chair), *Teaching reading comprehension, summarizing and writing in content area*. Symposium conducted at the National Reading Conference, Orlando, Florida.

Dewitz, P., Stammer, J., & Jensen, J. (1980). *The development of linguistic awareness in young children from label reading to word recognition*. Paper presented at the annual meeting of the National Reading Conference, San Diego, CA.

Dickinson, D. K., McCabe, A., & Sprague, K. (2003). Teacher Rating of Oral Language and Literacy (TROLL): Individualizing early literacy instruction with a standards-based rating tool. *The Reading Teacher, 56*(6), 554–564.

Dickinson, D. K., & Smith, M. W. (1994). Long-term effects of preschool teachers' book readings on low-income children's vocabulary and story comprehension. *Reading Research Quarterly, 29,* 104–122.

Dickinson, D. K., & Tabors, P. O. (Eds.). (2001). *Young children learning at home and school: Beginning literacy with language*. Baltimore, MD: Paul H. Brookes.

Dickson, S. V., Simmons, D. C., & Kame'enui, E. J. (1998a). Text organization: Instructional and curricular basics and implications. In D. C. Simmons & E. J. Kame'enui (Eds.), *What reading research tells us about children with diverse learning needs*. (pp. 279–302). Mahwah, NJ: Erlbaum;

Dickson, S. V., Simmons, D. C., & Kame'enui, E. J. (1998b). Text organization: Research bases. In D. C. Simmons and E. J. Kame'enui (Eds.), *What reading research tells us about children with diverse learning needs* (pp. 239–278). Mahwah, NJ: Erlbaum.

Dickson, S. V., Simmons, D. C., & Kame'enui, E. J. (1998b). Text organization: Instructional and curricular basics and implications

(279–294). In D. C. Simmons & E. J. Kame'enui (Eds.), *What reading research tells us about children with diverse learning needs: Bases and basics*. Mahwah, NJ: Lawrence Erlbaum Associates.

Diederich, P. B. (1974). *Measuring growth in English*. Urbana, IL: National Council of Teachers of English.

Diffily, D. (1994, April). *Portfolio assessment in early literacy settings*. Paper presented at a professional development schools workshop at Texas Christian University, Fort Worth, TX.

Diffily, D. (2004). *Teachers and families working together*. Boston: Pearson Education/Allyn and Bacon.

Dillner, M. (1993–1994). Using hypermedia to enhance content area instruction. *Journal of Reading, 37* (4), 260–270.

Dixon-Krauss, L. (1996). *Vygotsky in the classroom: Mediated literacy instruction and assessment*. New York: Longman.

Doctorow, M., Wittrock, M. C., & Marks, C. (1978). Generative processes in reading comprehension. *Journal of Educational Psychology, 70* (2), 109–118.

D'Odorico, L. (1984). Nonsegmental features in prelinguistic communications: An analysis of some types of infant cry and noncry vocalizations. *Journal of Child Language, 11,* 17–27.

Dole, J. A., Brown, K. J., & Trathen, W. (1996). The effects of strategy instruction on the comprehension performance of at-risk students. *Reading Research Quarterly, 31,* 62–88.

Dole, J. A., Osborn, J., & Lehr, F. (1990). *A guide to selecting basal reader programs*. Champaign, IL: Center for the Study of Reading.

Dole, J. A., Rogers, T., & Osborn, J. (1987). Improving the selection of basal reading programs: A report of the textbook adoption guidelines project. *Elementary School Journal, 87,* 282–298.

Donelson, K. L., & Nilsen, A. P. (1985). *Literature for today's young adults*. Boston: Scott, Foresman.

Donovan, C. A., & Smolkin, L. B. (2002). Considering genre, context, and visual features in the selection of trade books for science instruction. *The Reading Teacher, 55*(6), 502–520.

Dowd, C. A., & Sinatra, R. (1990). Computer programs and the learning of text structure. *Journal of Reading, 34* (2), 104–112.

Dowhower, S. (1987). Effects of repeated readings on second-grade transitional readers' fluency and comprehension. *Reading Research Quarterly, 22,* 389–406.

Dowhower, S. (1991). Speaking of prosody: Fluency's unattended bedfellow. *Theory Into Practice, 30*(3), 158–164.

Dowhower, S. L. (1989). Repeated reading: Research into practice. *The Reading Teacher, 42* (7), 502–507.

Downing, J. (1970). The development of linguistic concepts in children's thinking. *Research in the Teaching of English, 4,* 5–19.

Downing, J. (1971–72). Children developing concepts of spoken and written language. *Journal of Reading Behavior, 4,* 1–19.

Downing, J. (1977). How society creates reading disability. *The Elementary School Journal, 77,* 274–279.

Downing, J., & Oliver, P. (1973). The child's concept of a word. *Reading Research Quarterly, 9,* 568–582.

Downing, J., & Thomson, D. (1977). Sex role stereotypes in learning to read. *Research in the Teaching of English, 11,* 149–155.

Downing, J. G. (1990). *A study of the relationship between literacy levels and institutional behaviors of incarcerated male felons*. Unpublished doctoral dissertation, Ball State University, Muncie, IN.

Doyle, C. (1988). Creative applications of computer assisted reading and writing instruction. *Journal of Reading, 32* (3), 236–239.

Dreher, M. J., & Gambrell, L. B. (1985). Teaching children to use a self-questioning strategy for studying expository prose. *Reading Improvement, 22,* 2–7.

Drew, D. (1989). *The life of the butterfly*. Crystal Lake, IL: Rigby.

Driscoll, M. P. (1994). *Psychology of learning for instruction*. Boston: Allyn & Bacon.

Drucker, P. F. (1998, August 24). The next information revolution. *Forbes ASAP*. 47–58.

Duffy, G. G. (2003). *Explaining reading: A resource for teaching concepts, skills, and strategies*. New York: Guilford Press.

Duffy, G. G. (2004). *Explaining reading: A resource for teaching concepts, skills, and strategies*. New York: Guilford Press.

Duffy, G. G., Roehler, L. R., & Putnam, J. (1987). Putting the teacher in control: Basal reading textbooks and instructional decision making. *The Elementary School Journal, 87*(3), 357–366.

Duke, N. K. (2000). 3.6 minutes per day: The scarcity of informational texts in first grade. *Reading Research Quarterly, 35*(2), 202–224.

Duke, N. K. (2000a). For the rich it's richer: print experiences and environments offered to children in very low- and very high-socioeconomic status first-grade classrooms. *American Educational Research Journal, 37*, 441–478.

Duke, N. K. (2000b). 3.6 minutes per day: The scarcity of informational texts in first grade. *Reading Research Quarterly, 35*(2), 202–224.

Duke, N. K., & Bennett-Armistead, V. S. (2003). *Reading and writing informational text in the primary grades: Research-based practices*. New York: Scholastic, Inc.

Duke, N. K., Bennett-Armistead, S., Roberts, E. M. (2002). Incorporating informational text in the primary grades 40–54. In C. M. Roller (Ed.), *Comprehensive reading instruction across the grade levels: A collection of papers from the 2001 reading research conference*. Newark, DE: International Reading Association.

Duke, N. K., & Purcell-Gates, V. (In press). Genres at home and at school: Bridging the new to the known. *The Reading Teacher.*

Dunn, L., & Dunn, L. M. (1997). *Peabody picture vocabulary test—third edition* (PPVT-III). Circle Pines, MN: American Guidance Service.

Dunn, L., Lugo, D. E., Padilla, E. R., & Dunn, L. M. (1986). *Test de Vocabulario en Imágenes Peabody* (TVIP). Circle Pines, MN: American Guidance Service.

Dunn, L. M., & Markwardt, F. C. (1970). *Peabody individual achievement test*. Circle Pines, MN: American Guidance Service.

Dunn, R. (1988). Teaching students through their perceptual strengths or preferences. *Journal of Reading, 31*, 304–309.

Dunn, S. (1987). *Butterscotch dreams*. Markham, Ontario: Pembroke.

Durkin, D. (1966). *Children who read early: Two longitudinal studies*. New York: Teachers College Press.

Durkin, D. (1974). A six year study of children who learned to read in school at the age of four. *Reading Research Quarterly, 10*, 9–61.

Durkin, D. (1978). What classroom observations reveal about reading comprehension instruction. *Reading Research Quarterly, 14*(4), 482–533.

Durkin, D. (1981a). Reading comprehension in five basal reader series. *Reading Research Quarterly, 16*(4), 515–543.

Durkin, D. (1981b). What is the value of the new interest in reading comprehension? *Language Arts, 58*, 23–43.

Durkin, D. (1983). *Reading comprehension instruction: What the research says*. Presentation at the first Tarleton State University Reading Conference, Stephenville, TX.

Durkin, D. (1984). Is there a match between what elementary teachers do and what basal reader manuals recommend? *The Reading Teacher, 37*, 734–745.

Durkin, D. (1987). *Teaching young children to read*, (4th ed.) New York: Allyn & Bacon.

Durkin, D. (1989). *Teaching them to read*, 5th Ed. New York: Allyn & Bacon.

Durrell, D. D. (1940). *Improvement of basic reading abilities*. New York: World Book.

Duthie, J. (1986). The web: A powerful tool for the teaching and evaluation of the expository essay. *The History and Social Science Teacher, 21*, 232–236.

Dutro, S., & Moran, C. (2003). Rethinking English language instruction: An architectural approach. In G. G. Garcia (Ed.), *English learning: Reaching the highest level of English literacy* (pp. 227–258). Newark, DE: International Reading Association.

Dyer, P. C. (1992). Reading Recovery: A cost-effectiveness and educational-outcomes analysis. *ERS Spectrum, 10*, 10–19.

Early Childhood-Head Start Taskforce. (2002). *Teaching our youngest: A guide for preschool teachers and child care and family providers*. Washington, DC: U.S. Departments of Education and Health and Human Services.

Eastlund, J. (1980). Working with the language deficient child. *Music Educators Journal, 67*(3), 60–65.

Eckhoff, B. (1983). How reading affects children's writing. *Language Arts, 60*(5), 607–616.

Edelsky, C. (1988). Living in the author's world: Analyzing the author's craft. *The California Reader, 21*, 14–17.

Edelsky, C., Altwerger, B., & Flores, B. (1991). *Whole language: What's the difference?* Portsmouth, NH: Heinemann.

Eder, D. (1983). Ability grouping and student's academic self-concepts: A case study. *The Elementary School Journal, 84*, 149–161.

Educational Testing Service. (1988). *Who reads best?* Princeton, NJ: Educational Testing Service.

Edwards, P. (1999). *A path to follow: Learning to listen to parents*. Portsmouth, NH: Heinemann.

Efta, M. (1984). Reading in silence: A chance to read. In A. J. Harris & E. R. Sipay (Eds.), *Readings on reading instruction* (3rd ed.), (pp. 387–391). New York: Longman.

Ehri, L. C. (1984). How orthography alters spoken language competencies in children. In J. Downing & R. Valtin (Eds.), *Language awareness and learning to read* (pp. 118–147). New York: Springer-Verlag.

Ehri, L. C. & Sweet, J. (1991). Fingerpoint-reading of memorized text: What enables beginners to process the print? *Reading Research Quarterly, 26*, 442–462.

Ehri, L. C., & Wilce, L. C. (1980). The influence of orthography on readers' conceptualization of the phonemic structure of words. *Applied Psycholinguistics, 1*, 371–385.

Ehri, L. C., & Wilce, L. C. (1985). Movement into reading: Is the first stage of printed word learning visual or phonetic? *Reading Research Quarterly, 20*, 163–179.

Ekwall, E. E., & Shanker, J. L. (1989). *Teaching reading in the elementary school* (2nd ed.). Upper Saddle River, NJ: Merrill/Prentice-Hall.

Elbow, P. (1994). Will the virtues of portfolios blind us to their potential dangers? In L. Black, D. Daiker, J. Sommers, & G. Stygall (Eds.), *New directions in portfolio assessment* (pp. 40–55). Portsmouth, NH: Boynton/Cook.

El-Dinary, P. B. (2002). Challenges implementing transactional strategies instruction for reading comprehension. In C. Collins-Block & M. Pressley (Eds.), *Comprehension instruction: Research-based best practices* (pp. 201–218). New York: Guilford Press.

Eldredge, J. L. (1990). Increasing the performance of poor readers in the third grade with a group assisted strategy. *Journal of Educational Research, 84*(2), 69–77.

Eldredge, J. L., & Quinn, D. W. (1988). Increasing reading performance of low-achieving second graders with dyad reading groups. *Journal of Educational Research, 82,* 40–46.

Eldredge, J. L., Reutzel, D. R., & Hollingsworth, P. M. (1996, Summer). Comparing the effectiveness of two oral reading practices: Round-robin reading and the shared book experience. *Journal of Literacy Research, 28*(2), 201–225.

Ellis, A. K., & Fouts, J. T. (1993). *Research on educational innovations.* Princeton Junction, NJ: Eye on Education.

Ellison, C. (1989, January). PCs in the schools: An American tragedy. *PC/Computing,* 96–104.

Engelmann, S., & Bruner, E. C. (1995). *Reading mastery I: Presentation book C,* Rainbow Edition. Columbus, OH: Science Research Associates/ Macmillan/McGraw-Hill.

Engelmann, S., & Bruner, E. C. (2002). *SRA reading mastery plus.* Columbus, OH: SRA-McGraw-Hill.

Englert, C. S., & Tarrant, K. L. (1995). Creating collaborative cultures for educational change. *Remedial and Special Education, 16*(6), 325–336.

Enz, B. J. (2003). The ABCs of family literacy. In A. DeBruin-Parecki & B. Krol-Sinclair (Eds.), *Family literacy: From theory to practice* (pp. 50–67). Newark, DE: International Reading Association.

Epstein, J. L. (2001). *School, family, and community partnerships: Preparing educators and improving schools.* Boulder, CO: Westview Press.

Ericson, L., & Juliebo, M. F. (1998). *The phonological awareness handbook for kindergarten and primary teachers.* Newark, DE: International Reading Association.

Ervin, J. (1982). *How to have a successful parents and reading program: A practical guide.* New York: Allyn & Bacon.

Esch, M. (1991, February 17). Whole language teaches reading. *The Daily Herald* (Provo, UT), p. D1.

Estes, T. H., & Vaughn, J. L. (1978). *Reading and learning in the content classroom.* Boston: Allyn & Bacon.

Fader, D. N. (1976). *The new hooked on books.* New York: Berkley.

Farnan, N., & Dahl, K. (2003). Children's writing: Research and practice. In J. Flood, D. Lapp, J. R. Squire, & J. M. Jensen (Eds.), *Handbook of research on teaching the English language arts* (pp. 993–1007). Mahwah, NJ: Lawrence Erlbaum Associates.

Farr, R. (1991). *Portfolios: Assessment in the language arts.* ED334603.

Farr, R., & Tone, B. (1994). *Portfolio and performance assessment.* Fort Worth, TX: Harcourt Brace.

Farr, R., & Tulley, M. (1989). State level adoption of basal readers: Goals, processes, and recommendations. *Theory Into Practice, 28*(4), 248–253.

Farr, R., Tulley, M. A., & Powell, D. (1987). The evaluation and selection of basal readers. *The Elementary School Journal, 87,* 267–281.

Farr, R., Tulley, M. A., & Pritchard, R. (1989). Assessment instruments and techniques used by the content area teacher. In D. Lapp, J. Flood, & N. Farnan (Eds.), *Content area reading and learning* (pp. 346–356). Englewood Cliffs, NJ: Prentice Hall.

Farrar, E. B. (1985). *Accelerating the oral language of children of low socio-economic status.* Belle Glade, FL: Unpublished Dissertation. (ERIC Document Reproduction Service No. ED 262 913).

Farrar, M. T. (1984). Asking better questions. *The Reading Teacher, 38,* 10–17.

Fawson, P. C., Ludlow, B., Reutzel, D. R., Sudweeks, R., & Smith, J. A. (in press). Examining the reliability of running records: Attaining generalizable results. *Journal of Educational Research.*

Fawson, P. C., & Reutzel, D. R. (2000). But I only have a basal: Implementing guided reading in the early grades. *The Reading Teacher, 54*(1), 84–97.

Fay, L. (1965). Reading study skills: Math and science. In J. A. Figurel (Ed.), *Reading and inquiry.* Newark, DE: International Reading Association.

Felmlee, D., & Eder, D. (1983). Contextual effects in the classroom: The impact of ability groups on student attention. *Sociology of Education, 56,* 77–87.

Ferguson, R. F. (1991). Paying for public education: New evidence on how and why money matters. *Harvard Journal of Legislation, 282,* 465–498.

Ferreiro, E., & Teberosky, A. (1982). *Literacy before schooling.* Portsmouth, NH: Heinemann.

Fielding, L., Kerr, N., & Rosier, P. (1998). *The 90% reading goal.* Kennewick, WA: National Reading Foundation.

Fields, M. V., & Spangler, K. L. (2000). *Let's begin reading right: A developmental approach to emergent literacy.* Upper Saddle River, NJ: Merrill.

Fillmore, D. (1968). The case for case. *Universals of linguistic theory.* New York: Holt, Rinehart and Winston.

Fillmore, L. W., & Snow, C. E. (2000). *What teachers need to know about language.* Special report from ERIC Clearing House on Languages and Linguistics [Online]. Available at *http://www.cal.org/ericcll/ teachers/teachers.pdf*

Finch, J. (2003). *Testing Miss Malarkey.* New York: Walker Books for Young Readers.

Finchler, J. (2001). *Testing Miss Malarkey.* New York: Walker & Company.

Fisher-Nagel, H. (1987). *The life of a butterfly.* Minneapolis: Carolrhoda Books.

Fitzgerald, J. (1993). Literacy and students who are learning English as a second language. *The Reading Teacher, 46*(8), 638–647.

Fitzgerald, J. (1994). Crossing boundaries: What do second-language-learning theories say to reading and writing teachers of English-as-a-second-language learners? *Reading Horizons, 34*(4), 339–355.

Fitzgerald, J. (1995). English-as-a-second-language reading instruction in the United States: A research review. *Journal of Reading Behavior, 27*(2), 115–152.

Fitzgerald, J. (1999). What is this thing called "balance"? *The Reading Teacher, 53*(2), 100–115.

Fleischman, S. (1986). *The whipping boy.* Mahwah, NJ: Troll Associates.

Flesch, R. (1955). *Why Johnny can't read.* New York: HarperCollins.

Flesch, R. (1979, November 1). Why Johnny still can't read. *Family Circle, 26,* 43–46.

Flesch, R. (1981). *Why Johnny still can't read.* New York: HarperCollins.

Flippo, R. F. (2001). *Reading researchers in search of common ground.* Newark, DE: International Reading Association.

Flippo, R. F. (2003). *Assessing readers: Qualitative diagnosis and instruction.* Portsmouth, NH: Heinemann.

Flood, J., & Lapp, D. (1986). Types of texts: The match between what students read in basals and what they encounter in tests. *Reading Research Quarterly, 21,* 284–297.

Flynt, E. S., & Cooter, R. B. (1987). Literal comprehension: The cognitive caboose? *The Kansas Journal of Reading, 3*(1), 8–12.

Flynt, E. S., & Cooter, R. B. (2001). *The Flynt/Cooter Reading Inventory for the Classroom* (4th ed.). Upper Saddle River, NJ: Merrill/Prentice-Hall.

Flynt, E. S., & Cooter, R. B, Jr. (1999). *The Flynt/Cooter English *Español reading inventory.* Upper Saddle River, NJ: Merrill/Prentice-Hall.

Flynt, E. S., & Cooter, R. B., Jr. (2004). *The Flynt/Cooter Reading Inventory for the Classroom* (5th ed.). Upper Saddle River, NJ: Merrill/Prentice-Hall.

Follett, R. (1985). The school textbook adoption process. *Book Research Quarterly, 1,* 19–23.

Foorman, B. R., et al. (1997). Early intervention for children with reading problems: Study designs and preliminary findings. *Learning Disabilities: A Multidisciplinary Journal, 8*(1), 63–71.

Foorman, B. R., Francis, D. J., Fletcher, J. M., Schatschneider, C., & Mehta, P. (1998). The role of instruction in learning to read: Preventing reading failure in at-risk children. *Journal of Educational Psychology, 90,* 37–55.

Forbes, E. (1943). *Johnny Tremain.* Boston: Houghton Mifflin.

Fosnot, C. T. (1996). *Constructivism: Theory, perspectives, and practice.* New York: Teachers College Press.

Fountas, I. C., & Pinnell, G. S. (1996). *Guided reading instruction: Good first teaching for all children.* Portsmouth, NH: Heinemann Educational Books.

Fountas, I. C., & Pinnell, G. S. (1999). *Matching books to readers: Using leveled books in reading, K–3.* Portsmouth, NH: Heinemann Educational Books.

Fountas, I. C., & Pinnell, G. S. (2001). *Guiding readers and writers: Grades 3–6. Teaching comprehension genre, and content literacy.* Portsmouth, NH: Heinemann.

Fowler, G. L. (1982). Developing comprehension skills in primary students through the use of story frames. *The Reading Teacher, 36*(2), 176–179.

Fox, B. J. (1996). *Strategies for word identification: Phonics from a new perspective.* Upper Saddle River, NJ: Merrill/Prentice-Hall.

Fox, B. J. (2004). *Strategies for word identification: Phonics from a new perspective* (3rd ed.). Upper Saddle River, NJ: Merrill/Prentice-Hall.

Fox, B. J., & Hull, M. A. (2002). *Phonics for the teacher of reading* (8th ed.). Upper Saddle River, NJ: Prentice-Hall.

Fox, P. (1973). *The slave dancer.* New York: Bradbury.

Fox, P. (1986). *The moonlight man.* New York: Bradbury.

Fractor, J. S., Woodruff, M. C., Martinez, M. G., & Teale, W. H. (1993). Let's not miss opportunities to promote voluntary reading: Classroom libraries in the elementary school. *The Reading Teacher, 46,* 476–484.

Fredericks, A. D., & Rasinski, T. V. (1990). Working with parents: Involving the uninvolved: How to. *The Reading Teacher, 43*(6), 424–425.

Freeman, D. E., & Freeman, Y. S. (1994). *Between worlds: Access to second language acquisition.* Portsmouth, NH: Heinemann.

Freeman, D. E., & Freeman, Y S. (2000). *Teaching reading in multilingual classrooms.* Portsmouth, NH: Heinemann.

Freeman, Y. S., & Freeman, D. E. (1992). *Whole language for second language learners.* Portsmouth, NH: Heinemann.

Freppon, P. A., & Dahl, K. L. (1998). Balanced instruction: Insights and considerations. *Reading Research Quarterly, 33*(2), 240–251.

Friedman, T. (2005). *The world is flat: A brief history of the twenty-first century.* New York: Farrar, Straus, and Giroux.

Fry, E. (1977). Fry's readability graph: Clarifications, validity, and extension to level 17. *Journal of Reading, 21,* 242–252.

Fry, E. (1980). The new instant word list. *The Reading Teacher, 34,* 284–289.

Fry, E. (2004). Phonics: A large phoneme-grapheme frequency count revisited. *Journal of Literacy Research, 36*(1), 85–98.

Fry, E. B., Kress, J. E., & Fountoukidis, D. L. (2000). *The reading teacher's book of lists* (4th ed.). New York: Jossey-Bass.

Fry, E. B., Polk, J. K., & Fountoukidis, D. (1984). *The reading teacher's book of lists.* Upper Saddle River, NJ: Prentice-Hall.

Gahn, S. M. (1989). A practical guide for teaching writing in the content areas. *Journal of Reading, 33,* 525–531.

Galdone, Paul. *The little red hen.* L. McQueen, Illustrator. New York: Scholastic.

Galindo, R., & Escamilla, K. (1995). A biographical perspective on Chicano educational success. *Urban Review, 27*(1), 1–25.

Gall, M. D., Ward, B. A., Berliner, D. C., Cahen, L. S., Crown, K. A., Elashoff, J. D., et al. (1975). *The effects of teacher use of questioning techniques on student achievement and attitude.* San Francisco: Far West Laboratory for Educational Research and Development.

Gallant, M. G. (1986). *More fun with Dick and Jane.* New York: Penguin Books.

Gallup, G. (1969). *The Gallup poll.* New York: American Institute of Public Opinion.

Gamberg, R., Kwak, W., Hutchings, M., & Altheim, J. (1988). *Learning and loving it: Theme studies in the classroom.* Portsmouth, NH: Heinemann.

Gambrell, L. B. (1978). Getting started with sustained silent reading and keeping it going. *The Reading Teacher, 32,* 328–331.

Gambrell, L. B. (1985). Dialogue journals: Reading-writing instruction. *The Reading Teacher, 38*(6), 512–515.

Gambrell, L. B., & Almasi, J. F. (1996). *Lively discussions: Fostering engaged reading.* Newark, DE: International Reading Association.

Gambrell, L. B., & Bales, R. J. (1986). Mental imagery and the comprehension-monitoring performance of fourth- and fifth-grade poor readers. *Reading Research Quarterly, 21*(4), 454–464.

Gambrell, L. B., & Marnak, B. A. (1997). Incentives and intrinsic motivation to read. In J. T. Guthrie & A. Wigfield (Eds.), *Reading engagement: Motivating readers through integrated instruction* (pp. 205–217). Newark, DE: International Reading Association.

Gambrell, L. B., Morrow, L. M., Neuman, S. B., & Pressley, M. (1999). *Best practices in literacy instruction.* New York: Guilford Press.

Gambrell, L. B., Pfeiffer, W., & Wilson, R. (1985). The effects of retelling upon reading comprehension and recall of text information. *Journal of Educational Research, 78,* 216–220.

Gambrell, L. B., Wilson, R. M., & Gnatt, W. N. (1981). Classroom observations of task-attending behaviors of good and poor readers. *Journal of Educational Research, 74,* 400–404.

Garan, E. M. (2002). *Resisting reading mandates: How to triumph with the truth.* Portsmouth, NH: Heinemann Educational Books.

García, G. E., McKoon, G., & August, D. (2006a). Synthesis: Language and literacy assessment. In D. August & T. Shanahan (Eds.), *Developing literacy in second-language learners: Report of the National Literacy Panel on language-minority children and youth* (pp. 583–596). Mahwah, NJ: Lawrence Erlbaum.

García, G. E., McKoon, G., & August, D. (2006b). Language and literacy assessment of language-minority students. In D. August & T. Shanahan (Eds.), *Developing literacy in second-language learners: Report of the National Literacy Panel on language-minority children and youth* (pp. 597–624). Mahwah, NJ: Lawrence Erlbaum.

Garcia, S. B., & Malkin, D. H. (1993). Toward defining programs and services for culturally and linguistically diverse learners in special education. *Teaching Exceptional Children,* Fall, 52–58.

Gardener, H. (1993). *Frames of mind: The theory of multiple intelligences.* New York: Basic Books.

Gardiner, J. R. (1983). *Stone fox.* New York: HarperTrophy.

Garza, C. L. (1990). *Cuadros de familia: Family pictures.* San Francisco: Children's Book Press.

Gates, A. I. (1921). An experimental and statistical study of reading and reading tests (in three parts). *Journal of Educational Psychology, 12,* 303–314, 378–391, 445–465.

Gates, A. I. (1937). The necessary mental age for beginning reading. *Elementary School Journal, 37,* 497–508.

Gates, A. I. (1961). Sex differences in reading ability. *Elementary School Journal, 61,* 431–434.

Gelman, R. G. (1976). *Why can't I fly?* New York: Scholastic.

Gelman, R. G. (1977). *More spaghetti, I say!* New York: Scholastic.

Gelman, R. G. (1985). *Cats and mice.* New York: Scholastic.

Gentile, L. M. (2003). *The oracy instructional guide: Linking research and theory to assessment and instruction.* Carlsbad, CA: Dominie Press, Inc.

Gentry, R. (1987). *Spel... is a four-letter word.* Portsmouth, NH: Heinemann.

George, J. (1972). *Julie of the wolves.* New York: HarperCollins.

Gersten, R., & Baker, S. (2000). *Effective instruction for English-language learners: What we know about effective instructional practices for English-language learners.* Eugene, OR: University of Oregon, Eugene Research Institute.

Gertson, R., Fuchs, L. S., Williams, J. P., & Baker, S. (2001). Teaching reading comprehension strategies to students with learning disabilities: A review of research. *Review of Educational Research, 71*(2), 279–320.

Gibson, E. J., & Levin, H. (1975). *The psychology of reading.* Cambridge, MA: MIT Press.

Gillet, J. W., & Temple, C. (1986). *Understanding reading problems: Assessment and instruction.* Boston: Little, Brown.

Gingerbread man, The. (1985). (K. Schmidt, Illustrator). New York: Scholastic.

Giordano, G. (2001). *Twentieth-century reading education: Understanding practices of today in terms of patterns of the past.* New York: JAI Press.

Gipe, J. P. (1980). Use of a relevant context helps kids learn new word meanings. *The Reading Teacher, 33,* 398–402.

Gipe, J. P. (1987). *Corrective reading techniques for the classroom teacher.* Scottsdale, AZ: Gorsuch Scarisbrick.

Glatthorn, A. A. (1993). Outcome-based education: Reform and the curriculum process. *Journal of Curriculum and Supervision, 8*(4), 354–363.

Glazer, S. M. (1989). Oral language and literacy development. In D. S. Strickland & L. M. Morrow (Eds.), *Emerging literacy: Young children learn to read and write* (pp. 16–26). Newark, DE: International Reading Association.

Glazer, S. M., & Brown, C. S. (1993). *Portfolios and beyond: Collaborative assessment in reading and writing.* Norwood, MA: Christopher-Gordon.

Gleason, J. B. (1989). *The development of language* (2nd ed.). Upper Saddle River, NJ: Merrill/Prentice-Hall.

Glowacki, D., Lanucha, C., & Pietrus, D. (2001). *Improving vocabulary acquisition through direct and indirect teaching.* Syracuse, NY: Educational Resources Information Center (ERIC) Document Reproduction Service.

Goetz, E. T., Reynolds, R. E., Schallert, D. L., & Radin, D. I. (1983). Reading in perspective: What real cops and pretend burglars look for in a story. *Journal of Educational Psychology, 75*(4), 500–510.

Golden, J. M. (1992). The growth of story meaning. *Language Arts, 69*(1), 22–27.

Good, R. H., & Jefferson, G. (1988). Contemporary perspectives on curriculum-based measurement validity. In M. R. Shinn (Ed.), *Advanced applications of curriculum-based measurement* (pp. 61–88). NY: Guilford Press.

Good, R. H., & Kamiski, R. A. (Eds.). (2002). *Dynamic indicators of basic early literacy skills* (6th ed.). Eugene, OR: Institute for the Development of Educational Achievement. Available: *http://dibelsuoregon.edu/*

Good, R. H., Simmons, D. C., & Kame'enui, E. J. (2001). The importance and decision-making utility of a continuum of fluency-based indicators of foundational reading skills for third-grade high-stakes outcomes. *Scientific Studies of Reading, 5*(3), 257–288.

Good, T. (1979). Teacher effectiveness in the elementary school. *The Journal of Teacher Education, 30,* 52–64.

Goodman, K., Shannon, P., Freeman, Y., & Murphy, S. (1988). *Report card on basal readers.* Katona, NY: Owen.

Goodman, K., Smith, E. B., Meredith, R., & Goodman, Y. M. (1987). *Language and thinking in school: A whole-language curriculum.* Katona, NY: Owen.

Goodman, K. S. (1967). Reading: A psycholinguistic guessing game. *Journal of the Reading Specialist, 6,* 126–135.

Goodman, K. S. (1968). *Study of children's behavior while reading orally* (Final Report, Project No. S 425). Washington, DC: U.S. Department of Health, Education, and Welfare.

Goodman, K. S. (1976). Behind the eye: What happens in reading. In H. Singer & R. B. Ruddell (Eds.), *Theoretical models and processes of reading,* 2nd Ed. (pp. 470–496). Newark, DE: International Reading Association.

Goodman, K. S. (1985). Unity in reading. In H. Singer & R. B. Ruddell (Eds.), *Theoretical models and processes of reading* (3rd ed.). Newark, DE: International Reading Association.

Goodman, K. S. (1986). *What's whole in whole language?* Ontario, Canada: Scholastic.

Goodman, K. S. (1987). Look what they've done to Judy Blume!: The "basalization" of children's literature. *The New Advocate, 1*(1), 29–41.

Goodman, K. S., & Goodman, Y. M. (1983). Reading and writing relationships: Pragmatic functions. *Language Arts, 60*(5), 590–599.

Goodman, Y. M. (1986). Children coming to know literacy. In W. H. Teale & E. Sulzby (Eds.), *Emergent literacy: Writing and reading* (pp. 1–14). Norwood, NJ: Ablex.

Goodman, Y. M., & Altwerger, B. (1981). *Print awareness in preschool children: A study of the development of literacy in preschool children.* Occasional paper, Program in Language and Literacy. Tucson, AZ: University of Arizona.

Gopnik, A., Meltzoff, A. N., & Kuhl, P. K. (1999). *The scientist in the crib: Minds, brains, and how children learn.* New York: William Morrow and Co.

Gordon, C. J., & Braun, C. (1983). Using story schema as an aid to reading and writing. *The Reading Teacher, 37*(2), 116–121.

Gordon, D. (2001). Practical suggestions for supporting speaking and listening in classrooms. In P. G. Smith (Ed.), *Talking classrooms: Shaping children's learning through oral language instruction* (pp. 57–73). Newark, DE: International Reading Association.

Gordon, N. (Ed.). (1984). *Classroom experiences: The writing process in action*. Exeter, NH: Heinemann.

Goswami, U. (2000). Phonological and lexical processes. In M. L. Kamil, P. B. Mosenthal, P. D. Pearson, & R. Barr (Eds.), *Handbook of reading research* (Vol. 3) (pp. 251–268). Mahwah, NJ: Lawrence Erlbaum Associates.

Goswami, U. (2001). Early phonological development and the acquisition of literacy. In S. B. Neuman & D. K. Dickinson (Eds.), *Handbook of early literacy research* (pp. 111–125). New York: Guildford Press.

Goswami, U., & Bryant, P. (1990). *Phonological skills and learning to read*. East Sussex, UK: Erlbaum.

Goswami, U., & Mead, F. (1992). Onset and rime awareness and analogies in reading. *Reading Research Quarterly, 27*(2), 152–163.

Gough, P. B. (1972). One second of reading. In J. F. Kavanagh & I. G. Mattingly (Eds.), *Language by ear and by eye*. Cambridge, MA: MIT Press.

Gove, M. K. (1983). Clarifying teacher's beliefs about reading. *The Reading Teacher, 37*(3), 261–268.

Graesser, A., Golding, J. M., & Long, D. L. (1991). Narrative representation and comprehension. In R. Barr, M. L. Kamil, P. Mosenthal, & P. D. Pearson (Eds.), *Handbook of reading research:* Vol. 2. (pp. 171–205). New York: Longman.

Graves, D. H. (1983). *Writing: Teachers and children at work*. Portsmouth, NH: Heinemann.

Graves, M. F., & Slater, W. H. (1987). Development of reading vocabularies in rural disadvantaged students, intercity disadvantaged students and middle class suburban students. Paper presented at AERA conference, Washington, DC.

Greaney, V. (1994). World illiteracy. In F. Lehr & J. Osborn (Eds.), *Reading, language, and literacy: Instruction for the twenty-first century*. Hillsdale, NJ: Erlbaum.

Greene, F. P. (1970). *Paired reading*. Unpublished manuscript, Syracuse University, New York.

Greene, F. P. (1973). *OPIN*. Unpublished paper, McGill University, Montreal, Quebec, Canada.

Greenhalgh, K. S., & Strong, C. J. (2001). Literate language features in spoken narratives of children with typical language and children with language impairments. *Language, Speech, & Hearing Services in Schools, 32*(2), 114–126.

Greenwald, R., Hedges, L., & Laine, R. (1996). The effect of school resources on student achievement. *Review of Educational Research, 66*, 361–396.

Gregg, M., & Sekeres, D. C. (2006). Supporting children's reading of expository text in the geography classroom. *The Reading Teacher, 60*(2), 102–110.

Gregory, G. H., & Chapman, C. (2002). *Differentiated instructional strategies: One size doesn't fit all*. Thousand Oaks, CA: Corwin Press.

Griffith, L. W., & Rasinski, T. V. (2004). A focus on fluency: How one teacher incorporated fluency with her reading curriculum. *The Reading Teacher 58*(2), 126–137.

Griffith, P. L., & Olson, M. W. (1992). Phonemic awareness helps beginning readers break the code. *The Reading Teacher, 45*, 516–523.

Grigg, W. S., Daaine, M. C., Jin, Y., & Campbell, J. R. (2003). *The nation's report card: Reading 2002* (NCES Report No. 2003-521). Washinton, DC: U.S. Department of Education, National Center for Educational Statistics.

Groff, P. J. (1984). Resolving the letter name controversy. *The Reading Teacher, 37*(4), 384–389.

Groom, W. (1986). *Forrest Gump*. New York: Pocket Books.

Gross, A. D. (1978). The relationship between sex differences and reading ability in an Israeli kibbutz system. In D. Feitelson (Ed.), *Cross-cultural perspectives on reading and reading research* (pp. 72–88). Newark, DE: International Reading Association.

Grossen, B. (1997). *30 years of research: What we know about how children learn to read*. Santa Cruz, CA: The Center for the Future of Teaching and Learning.

Guilfoile, E. (1957). *Nobody listens to Andrew*. Cleveland, OH: Modern Curriculum Press.

Gunderson, L. (1991). *ESL literacy instruction: A guidebook to theory and practice*. Upper Saddle River, NJ: Prentice-Hall.

Gunn, B., Biglan, A., Smolkowski, K., & Ary, D. (2000). The efficacy of supplemental instruction in decoding skills for Hispanic and non-Hispanic students in early elementary school. *The Journal of Special Education, 34*, 90–103.

Gunn, B. Smolkowski, K., Biglan, A., & Black, C. (2002). Supplemental instruction in decoding skills for Hispanic and non-Hispanic students in early elementary school: A follow-up. *The Journal of Special Education, 36*, 69–79.

Guskey, T. R., Smith, J. K., Smith, L. F., Crooks, T., & Flockton, L. (2006). Literacy assessment, New Zealand style. *Educational Leadership, 64*(2), 74–79.

Guszak, F. J. (1967). Teacher questioning and reading. *The Reading Teacher, 21*(1), 227–234.

Guthrie, J. T. (1982). Effective teaching practices. *The Reading Teacher, 35*(7), 766–768.

Guthrie, J. T., & McCann, A. D. (1997). Characteristics of classrooms that promote motivations and strategies for learning. In J. T. Guthrie & A. Wigfield (Eds.), *Reading engagement: Motivating readers through integrated instruction*. Newark, DE: International Reading Association.

Guthrie, J. T., Seifert, M., Burnham, N. A., & Caplan, R. J. (1974). The maze technique to assess and monitor reading comprehension. *The Reading Teacher, 28*(2), 161–168.

Guthrie, J. Y., Hoa, L. W., Wigfield, A., Tonks, S. M., & Perencevich, K. C. (2006). From spark to fire: Can situational reading interest lead to long-term reading motivation? *Reading Research and Instruction, 45*(2), 91–117.

Gwynne, F. (1970). *A chocolate moose for dinner*. New York: Windmill Books.

Gwynne, F. (1976). *The king who rained*. New York: Windmill Books.

Gwynne, F. (1999). *A chocolate moose for dinner*. New York: Bt Bound.

Hagerty, P. (1992). *Reader's workshop: Real reading*. New York: Scholastic.

Haggard, M. R. (1986). The vocabulary self-collection strategy: Using student interest and world knowledge to enhance vocabulary growth. *Journal of Reading, 29*(7), 634–642.

Hagood, B. F. (1997). Reading and writing with help from story grammar. *Teaching Exceptional Children, 29*(4), 10–14.

Hall, L. (2004). Comprehending expository text: Promising strategies for struggling readers and students with reading disabilities? *Reading Research and Instruction, 44*(2), 75–95.

Hall, M. A. (1978). *The language experience approach for teaching reading: A research perspective.* Newark, DE: International Reading Association.

Hall, M. A. (1981). *Teaching reading as a language experience,* 3rd Ed. Upper Saddle River, NJ: Merrill/Prentice-Hall.

Hall, N. (1987). *The emergence of literacy.* Portsmouth, NH: Heinemann.

Hall, R. (1984). *Sniglets.* New York: Collier Books.

Haller, E. J., & Waterman, M. (1985). The criteria of reading group assignments. *The Reading Teacher, 38,* 772–781.

Halliday, M. A. K. (1975). *Learning how to mean: Explorations in the development of language.* London: Edward Arnold.

Hallinan, M. T., & Sorensen, A. B. (1985). Ability grouping and student friendships. *American Educational Research Journal, 22,* 485–499.

Halpern, H. (1981). An attitude survey of uninterrupted sustained silent reading. *Reading Horizons, 21,* 272–279.

Hammill, D., & Larsen, S. C. (1974). The relationship of selected auditory perceptual skills and reading ability. *Journal of Learning Disabilities, 7,* 429–435.

Handel, R. D. (1999). The multiple meanings of family literacy. *Education of Urban Society, 32*(1), 127–144.

Hansen, J. (1981). The effects of inference training and practice on young children's reading comprehension. *Reading Research Quarterly, 16*(3), 391–417.

Hansen, J. (1987). *When writers read.* Portsmouth, NH: Heinemann.

Hare, V. C, & Borchordt, K. M. (1984). Direct instruction of summarization skills. *Reading Research Quarterly, 20*(1), pp. 62–78.

Harkrader, M. A., & Moore, R. (1997). Literature preferences of fourth graders. *Reading Research and Instruction, 36*(4), 325–339.

Harp, B. (1988). When the principal asks: "Why are your kids singing during reading time?" *The Reading Teacher, 41*(4), 454–457.

Harp, B. (1989a). What do we do in the place of ability grouping? *The Reading Teacher, 42,* 534–535.

Harp, B. (1989b). When the principal asks: "Why don't you ask comprehension questions?" *The Reading Teacher, 42*(8), 638–639.

Harris, A. J., & Hodges, R. E. (Eds.). (1981). *A dictionary of reading and related terms.* Newark, DE: International Reading Association.

Harris, A. J., & Sipay, E. R. (1990). *How to increase reading ability: A guide to developmental and remedial methods* (9th ed.). New York: Longman.

Harris, T., Matteoni, L., Anderson, L., & Creekmore, M. (1975). *Keys to reading.* Oklahoma City: Economy.

Harris, T. L., & Hodges, R. E. (Eds.). (1981). *A dictionary of reading and related terms.* Newark, DE: International Reading Association.

Harris, T. L., & Hodges, R. E. (Eds.). (1995). *The literacy dictionary: The vocabulary of reading and writing.* Newark, DE: International Reading Association.

Harste, J. C., & Burke, C. L. (1977). A new hypothesis for reading teacher research: Both the teaching and learning of reading are theoretically based. In Pearson, D. P. (Ed.). *Reading: Theory, research, and practice* (pp. 32–40). Clemson, SC: National Reading Conference.

Harste, J. C., Short, K. G., & Burke, C. (1988). *Creating classrooms for authors: The reading writing connection.* Portsmouth, NH: Heinemann.

Harste, J. C., Woodward, V. A., & Burke, C. L. (1984). *Language stories and literacy lessons.* Portsmouth, NH: Heinemann.

Hart, B., & Risley, T. R. (1995). *Meaningful differences in the everyday experience of young American children.* Baltimore, MD: Paul H. Brookes.

Hart, B., & Risley, T. R. (2002). *The social world of children: Learning to talk.* Baltimore, MD: Paul H. Brookes.

Harwayne, S. (1992). *Lasting impressions.* Portsmouth, NH: Heinemann.

Hasbrouck, J., & Tindal, G. (2006). Oral reading fluency norms: A valuable assessment tool for reading teachers. *The Reading Teacher, 59*(7), 636–645.

Hasbrouck, J. E., & Tindal, G. (1992). Curriculum-based oral reading fluency for students in grades 2 through 5. *Teaching Exceptional Children, 24*(3), 41–44.

Haselkorn, D., & Harris, L. (2001). *The essential profession: American education at the crossroads.* Belmont, MA: Recruiting New Teachers.

Hawking, S. W. (1988). *A brief history of time: From the big bang to black holes.* Toronto: Bantam.

Heald-Taylor, G. (1989). *The administrator's guide to whole language.* Katona, NY: Owen.

Heald-Taylor, G. (1991). *Whole language strategies for ESL students.* San Diego, CA: Dominie Press.

Heald-Taylor, G. (2001). *The beginning reading handbook: Strategies for success.* Portsmouth, NH: Heinemann.

Healy, J. M. (1990). *Endangered minds: Why children don't think and what can be done about it.* New York: Touchstone.

Heath. (no date). *Quill* [computer program]. Lexington, MA: Heath.

Heathington, B. S. (1990). Test review: Concepts about print test. In R. B. Cooter, Jr. (Ed.). *The teacher's guide to reading tests* (pp. 110–114). Scottsdale, AZ: Gorsuch Scarisbrick.

Heckleman, R. G. (1966). Using the neurological impress remedial reading technique. *Academic Therapy, 1,* 235–239, 250.

Heckleman, R. G. (1969). A neurological impress method of remedial reading instruction. *Academic Therapy, 4,* 277–282.

Heide, F. P., & Gilliland, J. H. (1990). *Day of Ahmed's secret.* New York: Lothrop, Lee & Shepard Books.

Heilman, A. W., Blair, T. R., & Rupley, W. H. (2001). *Principles and practices of teaching reading,* 10th Ed. Upper Saddle River, NJ: Merrill/Prentice-Hall.

Henderson, J. (2001). *Incidental vocabulary acquisition: Learning new vocabulary from reading silently and listening to stories read aloud.* Syracuse, NY: Educational Resources Information Center (ERIC) Document Reproduction Service.

Henk, W. A. (1983). Adapting the NIM to improve comprehension. *Academic Therapy, 19,* 97–101.

Henk, W. A., & Holmes, B. C. (1988). Effects of content-related attitude on the comprehension and retention of expository text. *Reading Psychology, 9*(3), 203–225.

Hennings, K. (1974). Drama reading: An on-going classroom activity at the elementary school level. *Elementary English, 51,* 48–51.

Henwood, C. (1988). *Frogs* (Barrie Watts, Photographer). London, NY: Franklin Watts.

Herber, H. L. (1978). *Teaching reading in the content areas,* 2nd Ed. Upper Saddle River, NJ: Prentice-Hall.

Heymsfeld, C. R. (1989, March). Filling the hole in whole language. *Educational Leadership,* pp. 65–68.

Hiebert, E. (1978). Preschool children's understanding of written language. *Child Development, 49,* 1231–1241.

Hiebert, E. (1981). Developmental patterns and interrelationships of preschool children's print awareness. *Reading Research Quarterly, 16,* 236–260.

Hiebert E., & Ham, D. (1981). *Young children and environmental print.* Paper presented at the annual meeting of the National Reading Conference, Dallas, TX.

Hiebert, E. H. (1983). An examination of ability grouping for reading instruction. *Reading Research Quarterly, 18,* 231–255.

Hiebert, E. H. (1999). Text matters in learning to read. *The Reading Teacher, 52*(6), 552–566.

Hiebert, E. H. (2006). Becoming fluent: Repeated reading with scaffolded texts. In S. J. Samuels & A. E. Farstrup (Eds.), *What research has to say about fluency instruction* (pp. 204–226). Newark, DE: International Reading Association.

Hiebert, E. H., & Colt, J. (1989). Patterns of literature-based reading. *The Reading Teacher, 43*(1), 14–20.

Hiebert, E. H., & Fisher, P. (2006). Fluency from the first: What works with first graders. In T. V. Rasinski, C. Blachowicz, & K. Lems (Eds.). *Fluency instruction: Research-based best practices* (pp. 279–294). New York: Guilford Press.

Hiebert, E. H., & Martin, L. A. (2001). The texts of beginning reading instruction. In S. B. Neuman & D. K. Dickinson (Eds.), *Handbook of Early Literacy.* New York: Guilford Press.

Hiebert, E. H., Pearson, P. D., Taylor, B. M. Richardson, V., & Paris, S. G. (1998). *Every child a reader: Applying reading research in the classroom.* Ann Arbor, MI: Center for the Improvement of Early Reading Achievement.

Hill, B., & Ruptic, C. (1994). *Practical aspects of authentic assessment: Putting the pieces together.* Norwood, MA: Christopher-Gordon.

Hill, S. (1990a). *Raps and rhymes.* Armadale, Victoria, Australia: Eleanor Curtain.

Hill, S. (1990b). *Readers theatre: Performing the text.* Armadale, Victoria, Australia: Eleanor Curtain.

Hintze, J. M., & Christ, T. J. (2004). An examination of variability as a function of passage variance in CBM progress monitoring. *School Psychology Review, 33*(2), 204–217.

Hirsch, E. D. (1987). *Cultural literacy: What every American needs to know.* Boston: Houghton Mifflin.

Hirschfelder, A. B., & Singer, B. R. (1992). *Rising voices: Writing of young Native Americans.* New York: Scribner's.

Hobbs, R. (2005). Literacy for the information age. In J. Flood, S. B. Heath, & D. Lapp (Eds.), *Handbook of research on teaching literacy through the communicative and visual arts* (pp. 7–14). Mahwah, NJ: Lawrence Erlbaum Associates.

Hoffman, J. V. (1987). Rethinking the role of oral reading in basal instruction. *The Elementary School Journal, 87*(3), 367–374.

Hoffman, J. V. (2001). *WORDS (on Words in Leveled Texts for Beginning Readers).* Paper presented at 2001 National Reading Conference, San Antonio, Texas.

Hoffman, J. V. (2003). Foreword. In T. V. Rasinski's *The Fluent Reader: Oral reading strategies for building word recognition, fluency, and comprehension* (pp. 5–6). New York: Scholastic.

Hoffman, J. V., McCarthey, S. J., Abbott, J., Christian, C., Corman, L., Curry, et al. (1994). So what's new in the new basals? A focus on first grade. *Journal of Reading Behavior, 26*(1), 47–73.

Hoffman, J. V., Roser, N., & Battle, J. (1993). Reading aloud in classrooms: From the modal to a "model." *The Reading Teacher, 46*(6), 496–503.

Hoffman, J. V., Sailors, M., Duffy, G., & Beretvas, S. N. (2004). The effective classroom literacy environment: Examining the validity of the TEX-IN3 Observation System. *Journal of Literacy Research, 36*(3), 303–334.

Hoffman, J. V., & Segel, K. W. (1982). *Oral reading instruction: A century of controversy.* (ERIC Document Reproduction Service).

Hoffman, M. (1991). *Amazing grace.* New York: Dial Books.

Holdaway, D. (1979). *The foundations of literacy.* Exeter, NH: Heinemann.

Holdaway, D. (1981). Shared book experience: Teaching reading using favorite books. *Theory Into Practice, 21,* 293–300.

Holdaway, D. (1984). *Stability and change in literacy learning.* Portsmouth, NH: Heinemann.

Hollingsworth, P. M. (1970). An experiment with the impress method of teaching reading. *The Reading Teacher, 24,* 112–114.

Hollingsworth, P. M. (1978). An experimental approach to the impress method of teaching reading. *The reading Teacher, 31,* 624–626.

Hollingsworth, P. M., & Reutzel, D. R. (1988). Get a grip on comprehension. *Reading Horizons, 29*(1), 71–78.

Hollingsworth, P. M., & Reutzel, D. R. (1990). Prior knowledge, content-related attitude, reading comprehension: Testing Mathewson's affective model of reading. *The Journal of Educational Research, 83*(4), 194–200.

Holmes, J. A. (1953). *The substrata-factor theory of reading.* Berkeley, CA: California Books.

Homan, S. P., Klesius, J. P., & Hite, C. (1993). Effects of repeated readings and non-repetitive strategies on students' fluency and comprehension. *Journal of Educational Research, 87*(2), 94–99.

Honig, B., Diamond, L., & Gutlohn, L. (2000). *Teaching reading: Sourcebook for kindergarten through eighth grade.* Novato, CA: Arena Press.

Hook, P. E., & Jones, S. (2002). The importance of automaticity and fluency for efficient reading comprehension. *Perspectives, 28*(1), 9–14.

Hopkins, C. (1979). Using every-pupil response techniques in reading instruction. *The Reading Teacher, 33,* 173–175.

Hoskisson, K., & Tompkins, G. E. (1987). *Language arts: Content and teaching strategies.* Upper Saddle River, NJ: Merrill/Prentice-Hall.

Houston, J. (1977). *Frozen fire.* New York: Atheneum.

Hoyt, L. (1999). *Revisit, reflect, retell: Strategies for improving reading comprehension.* Portsmouth, NH: Heinemann.

Huber, J. A. (2004). A closer look at SQ3R. *Reading Improvement, 41*(2), 108–112.

Huck, C. S., Helper, S., & Hickman, J. (1987). *Children's literature in the elementary school.* New York: Holt, Rinehart and Winston.

Huck, C. S., & Kuhn, D. Y. (1968). *Children's literature in the elementary school.* New York: Holt, Rinehart and Winston.

Hudson, R. F., Lane, H. B., & Pullen, P. C. (2005). Reading fluency assessment and instruction: What, why, and how? *The Reading Teacher, 58*(8), 702–714.

Huebner, C. E. (2000). Promoting toddlers language development: A randomized trial of a community-based intervention. *Journal of Applied Developmental Psychology, 21,* 513–535.

Huebner, C. E. (2001). *Hear-and-say reading with toddlers.* Bainbridge Island, WA: Bainbridge Island Rotary (instructional video). To order, contact: Hear and Say Reading Program, Rotary Club of Bainbridge Island, PO Box 11286, Bainbridge Island, WA 98110.

Huebner, C. E., & Meltzoff, A. N. (2005). Intervention to change parent-child reading syle: A comparison of instructional methods. *Applied Developmental Psychology, 26,* 296–313.

Huey, E. B. (1908). *The psychology and pedagogy of reading.* New York: Macmillan.

Hughes, T. O. (1975). *Sentence-combining: A means of increasing reading comprehension.* Kalamazoo: Western Michigan University, Department of English.

Hull, M. A. (1989). *Phonics for the teacher of reading.* Upper Saddle River, NJ: Merrill/Prentice-Hall.

Hunt, J. (2004). *Volcano!* Northborough, MA: Sundance.

Hunt, L. C. (1970). Effect of self-selection, interest, and motivation upon independent, instructional, and frustrational levels. *Reading Teacher, 24,* 146–151.

Hunter, M. (1984). Knowing, teaching and supervising. In P. L. Hosford (Ed.), *Using what we know about teaching.* Alexandria, VA: Association for Supervision and Curriculum Development.

Hunter, P. (2003). "A tale of two schools" takes an intimate look at the national reading crisis. Available at *http://www.readingrockets. org/pressrelease/632*

Huot, B., & Neal, M. (2006). Writing assessment. In C. A. MacArthur, S. Graham, & J. Fitzgerald (Eds.), *Handbook of writing research.* New York: Guilford.

Hymes, D. (Ed.). (1964). *Language in culture and society.* New York: HarperCollins.

Ihnot, C., & Ihnot, T. (1996). *Read Naturally: The Fluency Co.* Saint Paul, MN: Read Naturally.

International Dyslexia Society. (n.d.). Frequently asked questions about dyslexia. Retrieved October 14, 2007, from the World Wide Web: http://www.interdys.org/FAQ.htm.

Invernizzi, M., Juel, C., & Rosemary, C. (1997). A community volunteer tutorial that works. *Reading Teacher, 50*(4), 304–311.

Irvin, J. L. (2001). Assisting struggling readers in building vocabulary and background knowledge. *Voices from the Middle, 8*(4), 37–43.

Irwin, J. W. (1996). *Teaching reading comprehension processes* (2nd ed.). Englewood Cliffs, NJ: Prentice-Hall.

Jachym, N. K., Allington, R. L., & Broikou, K. A. (1989). Estimating the cost of seatwork. *The Reading Teacher, 43,* 30–37.

Jacobs, H. H., & Borland, J. H. (1986). The interdisciplinary concept model: Theory and practice. *Gifted Child Quarterly, 30*(4), 159–163.

Jaffe, N. (1993). *The uninvited guest and other Jewish holiday tales.* New York: Scholastic.

Jancoloa, L. (n.d.). *Six-trait writing.* Retrieved November 3, 2006, from *http://www.kent.k12.wa.us/staff/LindaJancola/6Trait/6-trait.html*

Jenkins, J. R., Fuchs, L. S., Van den Broek, P., Espin, C., & Deno, S. L. (2003). Accuracy and fluency in list and context reading of skilled and RD groups: Absolute and relative performance levels. *Learning Disabilities Research and Practice, 18*(4), 237–245.

Jenkins, R. (1990). *Whole language in Australia.* Scholastic Co. workshop at Brigham Young University, Provo, UT.

Jennings, J. H., Caldwell, J., & Lerner, J. W. (2006). *Reading problems: Assessment and teaching strategies* (5th ed.). Boston: Pearson Allyn and Bacon.

Jobe, F. W. (1976). *Screening vision in schools.* Newark, DE: International Reading Association.

Johns, J. L. (1980). First graders' concepts about print. *Reading Research Quarterly, 15,* 529–549.

Johns, J. L. (1986). Students: Perceptions of reading: Thirty years of inquiry. In D. B. Yaden, Jr. & S. Templeton (Eds.), *Awareness and beginning literacy: Conceptualizing what it means to read and write* (pp. 31–40). Portsmouth, NH: Heinemann.

Johns, J. L., & Ellis, D. W. (1976). Reading: Children tell it like it is. *Reading World, 16,* 115–128.

Johns, J. L., & Johns, A. L. (1971). How do children in the elementary school view the reading process? *The Michigan Reading Journal, 5,* 44–53.

Johns, J. L., & Lunn, M. K. (1983). The informal reading inventory: 1910–1980. *Reading World, 23*(1), 8–18.

Johnson, D. (1989). *Pressing problems in world literacy: The plight of the homeless.* Paper presented at the 23rd annual meeting of the Utah Council of the International Reading Association, Salt Lake City, UT.

Johnson, D., & Pearson, P. D. (1984). *Teaching reading vocabulary.* New York: Holt, Rinehart and Winston.

Johnson, D. D. (1973). Sex differences in reading across cultures. *Reading Research Quarterly, 9*(1), 67–86.

Johnson, D. D. (2001). *Vocabulary in the elementary and middle school.* Needham Heights, MA: Allyn & Bacon.

Johnson, D. D., & Baumann, J. F. (1984). Word identification. In P. D. Pearson (Ed.), *Handbook of reading research* (pp. 583–608). New York: Longman.

Johnson, D. D., & Pearson. P. D. (1975). Skills management systems: A critique. *The Reading Teacher, 28,* 757–764.

Johnson, D. D., & Pearson. P. D. (1984). *Teaching reading vocabulary.* New York: Holt, Rinehart and Winston.

Johnson, D. W. (1976). *Jack and the beanstalk* (D. William Johnson, Illustrator). Boston: Little, Brown.

Johnson, D. W., & Johnson, R. T. (1999). *Learning together and alone: Cooperative, competitive, and individualistic learning* (5th ed.). Boston: Allyn & Bacon.

Johnson, D. W., Maruyama, G., Johnson, R. T., Nelson, D., & Skon, L. (1981). Effects of cooperative, competitive, and individualistic goal structures on achievement: A meta-analysis. *Psychological Bulletin, 89,* 47–62.

Johnson, T. D., & Louis, D. R. (1987). *Literacy through literature.* Portsmouth, NH: Heinemann.

Johnston, F. R. (1998). The reader, the text, and the task: Learning words in first grade. *The Reading Teacher, 51,* 666–676.

Johnston, P. H. (1992). *Constructive evaluation of literate activity.* New York, NY: Longman Publishers.

Jones, M. B., & Nessel, D. D. (1985). Enhancing the curriculum with experience stories. *The Reading Teacher, 39,* 18–23.

Jongsma, K. S. (1989). Questions & answers: Portfolio assessment. *The Reading Teacher, 43*(3), 264–265.

Jongsma, K. S. (1990). Questions & Answers: Collaborative Learning, *The Reading Teacher, 43*(4), 346–347.

Jordan, G. E., Snow, C. E., & Porche, M. V. (2000). Project EASE: The effect of a family literacy project on kindergarten students' early literacy skills. *Reading Research Quarterly, 35,* 524–546.

Joseph, D. G., Flynt, E. S., & Cooter, R. B., Jr. (1987, March). *Diagnosis and correction of reading difficulties: A new model.* Paper presented at the National Association of School Psychologists annual convention, New Orleans, LA.

Juel, C. (1988). Learning to read and write: A longitudinal study of the fifty-four children from first through fourth grade. *Journal of Educational Psychology, 80*(4), 437–447.

Juel, C. (1991). Cross-age tutoring between student athletes and at-risk children. *Reading Teacher, 45*(3), 178–186.

Juel, C., & Minden-Cupp, C. (2004). Learning to read words: Linguistic units and instructional strategies. In R. B. Ruddell, & N. J. Unrau (Eds.), *Theoretical models and processes of reading* (5th ed.) (pp. 313–364). Newark DE: International Reading Association.

Juster, N. (1961). *The phantom tollbooth*. New York: Random House.

Justice, L. M., Pence, K., Bowles, R. B., & Wiggins, A. (2006). An investigation of four hypotheses concerning the order by which 4-year-old children learn the alphabet letters. *Early Childhood Research Quarterly, 21*(3), 374–389.

Kaderavek, J. N., & Justice, L. M. (2005). The effect of book genre in repeated readings of mothers and their children with language impairment: A pilot investigation. *Child Language Teaching and Therapy, 21*(1), 75–92.

Kagan, J. (1966). Reflection-impulsivity: The generality and dynamics of conceptual tempo. *Journal of Abnormal Psychology, 71,* 17–24.

Kame'enui, E. J., & Simmons, D. C. (2001). The DNA of reading fluency. *Scientific Studies of Reading, 5*(3), 203–210.

Kang, H. W. (1994). Helping second language readers learn from content area text through collaboration and support. *The Journal of Reading, 37*(8), 646–652.

Karlsen, B., & Gardner, E. F. (1984). *Stanford diagnostic reading test* (3rd ed.). New York: Harcourt Brace.

Kaufman, A. S., & Kaufman, N. L. (1997). *Kaufman Test of Educational Achievement-Normative Update (K-TEA/NU)*. Circle Pines, MN: AGS.

Kearsley, R. (1973). The newborn's response to auditory stimulation: A demonstration of orienting and defensive behavior. *Child Development, 44,* 582–590.

Keegan, M. (1991). *Pueblo boy: Growing up in two worlds*. New York: Cobblehill Books.

Keene, E. O., & Zimmerman, S. (1997). *Mosaic of thought: Teaching comprehension in a reader's workshop*. Portsmouth, NH: Heinemann.

Keillor, G., Pankake, J., & Pankake, M. (1988). *A prairie home companion folk song book*. New York: Viking.

Keith, S. (1981). *Politics of textbook selection* (Research report No. 81-AT). Stanford, CA: Stanford University School of Education, Institute for Research on School Finance and Governance.

Kemp, M. (1987). *Watching children read and write*. Portsmouth, NH: Heinemann.

Kessen, W., Levine, J., & Wendrich, K. (1979). The imitation of pitch in infants. *Infant Behavior and Development, 2,* 93–100.

Kiefer, Z., Levstik, L. S., & Pappas, C. C. (1998). *An integrated language perspective in the elementary school: An action approach* (3rd ed.). Boston: Addison-Wesley.

Killilea, M. (1954). *Karen*. New York: Dodd, Mead.

Kintsch, W. (1974). *The representation of meaning in memory*. Hillsdale, NJ: Erlbaum.

Kintsch, W. (1998). *Comprehension: A paradigm for cognition*. Cambridge: Cambridge University Press.

Kintsch, W. (2004). The construction-integration model of text comprehension and its implications for instruction. In R. B. Ruddell & N. J. Unrau (Eds.), *Theoretical models and processes of reading* (5th ed.) (pp. 94–120). Newark, DE: International Reading Association.

Kintsch, W., & Kintsch, E. (2005). Comprehension. In S. G. Paris & S. A. Stahl (Eds.), *Children's reading comprehension and assessment* (pp. 71–92). Mahwah, NJ: Lawrence Erlbaum Associates.

Kirsch, I. S., Jungeblut, A., Jenkins, L., & Kolstad, A. (1993). *Adult literacy in America: A first look at the results of the national adult literacy survey*. Washington, DC: National Center for Educational Statistics.

Kirshner, D., & Whitson, J. A. (1997). *Situated cognition: Social, semiotic, and psychological perspectives*. Mahwah, NJ: Lawrence Erlbaum Associates.

Klare, G. R. (1963). Assessing readability. *Reading Research Quarterly, 10,* 62–102.

Klenk, L., & Kibby, M. W. (2000). Remediating reading difficulties: Appraising the past, reconciling the present, constructing the future. In M. L. Kamil, P. B. Mosenthal, P. D. Pearson, and R. Barr (Eds.), *Handbook of reading research,* Vol. 3. (pp. 667–690). Mahwah, NJ: Lawrence Erlbaum Associates.

Klobukowski, P. (2000). Parents, buddy journals, and teacher response. In T. V. Rasinski, N. D. Padak, et al. (Eds.), *Motivating recreational reading and promoting home-school connections* (pp. 51–52). Newark, DE: International Reading Association.

Knapp, M. S. (1991). *What is taught, and how, to the children of poverty: Interim report from a two-year investigation*. Menlo Park, CA: SRI.

Kornblith, G. J., & Lasser, C. (2005). "The truth, the whole truth, and nothing but the truth": Writing, producing, and using college-level American history textbooks. *Journal of American History, 91*(4), 1380–1382.

Koskinen, P., Wilson, R., & Jensema, C. (1985). Closed-captioned television: A new tool for reading instruction. *Reading World, 24,* 1–7.

Koskinen, P. S., Blum, I. H., Bisson, S. A., Phillips, S. M., Creamer, T. S., & Baker, T. K. (1999). Shared reading, books, and audiotapes: Supporting diverse students in school and at home. *The Reading Teacher, 52*(5), 430–444.

Kownslar, A. O. (1977). *People and our world: A study of world history*. New York: Holt, Rinehart and Winston.

Kozol, J. (1985). *Illiterate America*. New York: New American Library.

Kozol, J. (1991). *Savage inequalities*. New York: Harper Perennial.

Krashen, S. (1982). *Principles and practices in second language acquisition*. New York: Pergamon Press.

Krashen, S. (1992). *The power of reading*. Englewood, CO: Libraries Unlimited.

Krashen, S. (1993). *The power of reading: Insights from the research*. Englewood. CO: Libraries Unlimited.

Krashen, S., & Biber, D. (1988). *On course*. Sacramento, CA: CABE.

Krashen, S. D. (1985). *The input hypothesis: Issues and implication*. New York: Longman.

Krauss, R. (1945). *The carrot seed*. New York: Scholastic, Inc.

Krech, B. (2000). *Fresh & fun: Teaching with kids' names* (Grades K–2). New York: Scholastic, Inc.

Krulik, N. E. (1991). *My picture book of the planets*. New York: Scholastic.

Kuby, P., & Aldridge, J. (1994). Direct vs. indirect environmental print instruction and early reading ability in kindergarten children. *Reading Psychology 18*(2), 91–104.

Kuby, P., & Aldridge, J. (1997). Direct vs. indirect environmental print instruction and early reading ability in kindergarten children. *Reading Psychology 15*(1), 1–9.

Kuby, P., Aldridge, J., & Snyder, S. (1994). Developmental progression of environmental print recognition in kindergarten children. *Reading Psychology 18*(2), 91–104.

Kuby, P., Kirkland, L., & Aldridge, J. (1996). Learning about environmental print through picture books. *Early Childhood Education Journal, 24*(1), 33–36.

Kuchinskas, G., & Radencich, M. C. (1986). *The semantic mapper*. Gainesville, FL: Teacher Support Software.

Kuhn, M. (2005a). Helping students become accurate, expressive readers: Fluency instruction for small groups. *The Reading Teacher, 58*(4), 338–345.

Kuhn, M. (2005b). A comparative study of small group fluency instruction. *Reading Psychology, 26,* 127–146.

Kuhn, M. R., & Schwanenflugel, P. J. (2006). Fluency-oriented reading instruction: A merging of theory and practice. In K. A. Stahl & M. C. McKenna (Eds.), *Reading research at work: Foundations of effective practice* (pp. 205–216). New York: Guilford Press.

Kuhn, M. R., & Stahl, S. A. (2000). *Fluency: A review of developmental and remedial practices.* Center for the Improvement of Early Reading Achievement—Report #2-008, University of Michigan, Ann Arbor, Michigan.

Kulik, C. C., & Kulik, J. A. (1982). Effects of ability grouping on secondary students: A meta-analysis of evaluation findings. *American Educational Research Journal, 19,* 415–428.

L'Engle, M. (1962). *A wrinkle in time.* New York: Dell.

Labbo, L. D. (2001). Supporting children's comprehension of informational text through interactive read alouds. *Literacy and Nonfiction Series, 1*(2), 1–4.

Labbo, L. D., & Teale, W. H. (1990). Cross age reading: A strategy for helping poor readers. *The Reading Teacher, 43,* 363–369.

LaBerge, D., & Samuels, S. J. (1974). Toward a theory of automatic information processing in reading. *Cognitive Psychology, 6,* 293–323.

LaBerge, D., & Samuels, S. J. (1985). Toward a theory of automatic information processing in reading. In H. Singer & R. B. Ruddell (Eds.), *Theoretical models and processes of reading* (pp. 689–718). Newark, DE: International Reading Association.

Lamme, L. L., & Hysmith, C. (1991). One school's adventure into portfolio assessment. *Language Arts, 68,* 629–640.

Lamoreaux, L., & Lee, D. M. (1943). *Learning to read through experience.* New York: Appleton-Century-Crofts.

Langer, J. (1981). From theory to practice: A prereading plan. *Journal of Reading, 25,* 152–156.

Langer, J. A. (1984). Examining background knowledge and text comprehension. *Reading Research Quarterly, 19,* 468–481.

Langer, J. A. (1985). Levels of questioning: An alternative view. *Reading Research Quarterly, 20*(5), 586–602.

Langer, P., Kalk, J. M., & Searls, D. T. (1984). Age of admission and trends in achievement: A comparison of blacks and Caucasians. *American Educational Research Journal, 21,* 61–78.

Larsen, N. (1994). *The publisher's chopping block: What happens to children's trade books when they are published in a basal reading series?* Unpublished master's projects, Brigham Young University.

Lass, B., & Davis, B. (1985). *The remedial reading handbook.* Upper Saddle River, NJ: Prentice-Hall.

Lathlaen, P. (1993). A meeting of minds: Teaching using biographies. *The Reading Teacher, 46*(6), 529–531.

Law, B., & Eckes, M. (1990). *The more than just surviving handbook: ESL for every classroom teacher.* Winnipeg, Canada: Peguis.

Lee-Daniels, S. L., & Murray, B. A. (2000). DEAR me: What does it take to get my children reading? *The Reading Teacher, 54,* 154–155.

Leinhardt, G., Zigmond, N., & Cooley, W. (1981). Reading instruction and its effects. *American Educational Research Journal, 18,* 343–361.

Lemann, N. (1997, November). The reading wars. *The Atlantic Monthly, 280*(5), 128–134.

Lenneberg, E. H. (1964). *New directions in the study of language.* Cambridge, MA: MIT Press.

Leslie, L., & Caldwell, J. (2001). *Qualitative reading inventory–3.* New York: Longman.

Leu, D. J. (2006). *Preparing all students for the new literacies of online reading comprehension: Ten easy steps.* Presentation at the Texas State Reading Association Annual Conference, November 10, 2006.

Levin, J.-R., Johnson, D. D., Pittelman, S. D., Levin, K., Shriberg, L. K., Toms-Bronowski, S., & Hayes, B. (1984). A comparison of semantic- and mnemonic-based vocabulary-learning strategies. *Reading Psychology, 5,* 1–15.

Levin, J. R., Levin, M. E., Glasman, L. D., & Nordwall, M. B. (1992). Mnemonic vocabulary instruction: Additional effectiveness evidence. *Contemporary Educational Psychology, 17,* 156–174.

Levine, S. S. (1976). *The effect of transformational sentence-combining exercises on the reading comprehension and written composition of third-grade children.* Unpublished doctoral dissertation, Hofstra University, NY.

Lewis, C. S. (1961). *The lion, the witch, and the wardrobe.* New York: Macmillan.

Liberman, I. Y., Shankweiler, D., Liberman, A., Fowler, C., & Fischer, F. (1977). Phonetic segmentation and decoding in the beginning reader. In A. S. Reber & D. L. Scarborough (Eds.), *Toward a psychology of reading* (pp. 207–225). Hillsdale, NJ: Erlbaum.

Lightbrown, P. M., & Spada, N. (1999). *How languages are learned* (Rev. ed.). New York: Oxford University Press.

Lima, C., & Lima, J. (1993). *A to zoo: A subject access to children's picture books.* New York: Bowker.

Lindsay, P. H., & Norman, D. A. (1977). *Human information processing: An introduction to psychology.* New York: Academic Press.

Lipson, M. Y. (1983). The influence of religious affiliation on children's memory for text information. *Reading Research Quarterly, 18*(4), 448–457.

Lipson, M. Y. (1984). Some unexpected issues in prior knowledge and comprehension. *The Reading Teacher, 37*(8), 760–764.

Lisle, J. T. (1989). *Afternoon of the elves.* New York: Franklin Watts.

Littlejohn, C. (1988). *The lion and the mouse.* New York: Dial Books for Young Readers.

Livingston, N., & Birrell, J. R. (1994). Learning about cultural diversity through literature. *BYU Children's Book Review, 54*(5), 1–6.

Loban, W. (1976). *Teaching language and literature: Grades seven–twelve* (NCTE Research Report No. 18). Urbana, IL: National Council of Teachers of English.

Loban, W. D. (1963). *The language of elementary school children* (Research Report No. 1). Urbana, IL: National Council of Teachers of English.

Loban, W. D. (1964). *Language ability: Grades seven, eight, and nine.* Berkeley, CA: University of California. ERIC Ed 001275.

Lobel, A. (1981). *On market street.* New York: Scholastic.

Lobel, A. (1983). *Fables.* New York: Harper & Row.

Lock, S. (1980). *Hubert hunts his hum* (J. Newnham, Illustrator). Sydney, Australia: Ashton Scholastic.

Lomax, R. G., & McGee, L. M. (1987). Young children's concepts about print and reading: Toward a model of word reading acquisition. *Reading Research Quarterly, 22*(2), 237–256.

Long, M. H. (1991). Focus on form: Design features in language teaching methodology. In K. de Bot, D. Coste, R. Ginsberg, & C. Kramsch (Eds.), *Foreign language research in cross-cultural perspective* (pp. 39–52). Amsterdam: John Benjamins.

Loranger, A. L. (1997). Comprehension strategies instruction: Does it make a difference? *Reading Psychology, 18*(1), 31–68.

Loughlin, C. E., & Martin, M. D. (1987). *Supporting literacy: Developing effective learning environments.* New York: Columbia Teachers College Press.

Lowery, L. F., & Grafft, W. (1967). Paperback books and reading attitudes. *The Reading Teacher, 21*(7), 618–623.

Luria, A. R., & Yudovich, F. I. (1971). *Speech and the development of mental processes in the child.* London: Staples Press.

Lyman, F. (1988). Think-Pair-Share, Wait time two, and on . . . *Mid-Atlantic Association for Cooperation in Education Cooperative News, 2,* 1.

Lyon, G. R. (1997). Statement of G. Reid Lyon to The Committee on Education and the Workforce, U.S. House of Representatives (July 19, 1997). Washington, DC.

Lyon, G. R. (1998). Why reading is not a natural process. *Educational Leadership, 55*(6), 14–18.

Lyon, G. R. (1999). Reading development, reading disorders, and reading instruction: Research-based findings. ASHA Special Interest Division I Newsletter. *Language Learning and Education, 6*(1), 8–16.

Lyon, R. (1977). Auditory-perceptual training: The state of the art. *Journal of Learning Disabilities, 10,* 564–572.

Lyons, C. A., & Beaver, J. (1995). Reducing retention and learning disability placement through reading recovery: An educationally sound, cost-effective choice. In R. L. Allington & S. A. Walmsley (Eds.), *No quick fix: Rethinking literacy programs in America's elementary schools.* New York: Teachers College Press.

MacGinitie, W. H. (1969). Evaluating readiness for learning to read: A critical review and evaluation of research. *Reading Research Quarterly, 4,* 396–410.

MacGinitie, W. H., & MacGinitie, R. K. (1989). *Gates-MacGinitie reading tests* (3rd ed.). Chicago: Riverside.

Macmillan/McGraw-Hill. (1993). *Macmillan/McGraw-Hill reading/language: A new view.* New York: Author.

Manarino-Leggett, P., & Salomon, P. A. (1989, April–May). *Cooperation vs. competition: Techniques for keeping your classroom alive but not endangered.* Paper presented at the Thirty-Fourth Annual Convention of the International Reading Association, New Orleans, LA.

Mandler, J. M., & Johnson, N. S. (1977). Remembrance of things parsed: Story structure and recall. *Cognitive Psychology, 9,* 111–151.

Manning, G. L., & Manning, M. (1984). What models of recreational reading make a difference? *Reading World, 23,* 375–380.

Manzo, A. V. (1969). The request procedure. *The Journal of Reading, 13,* 123–126.

Manzo, A. V., & Manzo, U. C. (1990). *Content area reading: A heuristic approach.* Upper Saddle River, NJ: Merrill/Prentice-Hall.

Manzo, A. V., Manzo, U. C., & Estes, T. (2000). *Content area literacy: Interactive teaching for active learn ing* (3rd ed.). San Francisco, CA: John Wiley & Sons.

Marchionini, G. (1988). Hypermedia and learning: Freedom and chaos. *Educational Technology, 28,* 8–12.

Martin, B. (1990). *Brown bear, brown bear, what do you see?* New York: Henry Holt.

Martin, B. (1991). *Polar bear, polar bear, what do you hear?* New York: Henry Holt.

Martin, B., & Archambault, J. (1987). *Knots on a counting rope.* New York: Holt, Rinehart and Winston.

Martin, J. H. (1987). *Writing to read* [Computer program]. Boca Raton, FL: IBM.

Martinez, M. (1993). Motivating dramatic story reenactments. *The Reading Teacher, 46*(8), 682–688.

Martinez, M., & Nash, M. F. (1990). Bookalogues: Talking about children's literature. *Language Arts, 67,* 576–580.

Martorella, P. H. (1985). *Elementary social studies.* Boston: Little, Brown.

Martorella, P. H. (2000). *Teaching social studies in middle and secondary schools.* Upper Saddle River, NJ: Prentice-Hall.

Maryland Evaluation Committee. (2006). *Final report of the Maryland Evaluation Committee for selecting supplemental and intervention programs and materials.* Baltimore, MD: Maryland State Department of Education.

Marzano, R. J. (1993–1994). When two world views collide. *Educational Leadership, 51*(4), 6–11.

Marzano, R. J. (1998). *A theory-based meta-analysis of research on instruction* (Contract No. RJ96006101). Aurora, CO: Office of Educational Research and Improvement, Department of Education, Mid-continent Regional Educational Laboratory.

Marzano, R. J. (2004). *Building background knowledge for academic achievement: Research on what works in schools.* Alexandria, Virginia: Association for Supervision and Curriculum Development.

Marzollo, J., & Marzollo, C. (1982). *Jed's junior space patrol: A science fiction easy to read.* New York: Dial.

Mason, J. (1983). An examination of reading instruction in third and fourth grades. *The Reading Teacher, 36*(9), 906–913.

Mason, J., Herman, P. A., & Au, K. H. (1991). Reading: Children's developing knowledge of words. In J. Flood, J. M. Jensen, D. Lapp, & J. R. Squire (Eds.), *Handbook of research on teaching the language arts.* New York: Macmillan.

Mason, J. M. (1980). When do children begin to read: An exploration of four-year-old children's letter and word reading competencies. *Reading Research Quarterly, 15,* 203–227.

Masonheimer, P. E., Drum, P. A., & Ehri, L. C. (1984). Does environmental print identification lead children into word reading? *Journal of Reading Behavior, 16,* 257–271.

Math, I. (1981). *Wires and watts: Understanding and using electricity.* New York: Scribner's.

Mathes, P. G. (1997). Cooperative story mapping. *Remedial and Special Education, 18*(1), 20–27.

Mathes, P. G., Denton, C. A., Fletcher, J. M., Anthony, J. L., Francis, D. J., & Schatschneider, C. (2005). The effects of theoretically different instruction and student characteristics on the skills of struggling readers. *Reading Research Quarterly, 40*(2), 148–183.

Mathes, P. G., Simmons, D. C., & Davis, B. I. (1992). Assisted reading techniques for developing reading fluency. *Reading Research and Instruction, 31*(4), 70–77.

Mathewson, G. C. (1985). Toward a comprehensive model of affect in the reading process. In H. Singer & R. B. Ruddell (Eds.), *Theoretical models and processes of reading* (3rd ed.). (pp. 841–856). Newark, DE: International Reading Association.

Mathewson, G. C. (1994). Model of attitude influence upon reading and learning to read. In H. Singer & R. B. Ruddell (Eds.), *Theoretical models and processes of reading* (4th Ed.) (pp. 1131–1161). Newark, DE: International Reading Association.

Maxim, G. (1989). *The very young: Guiding children from infancy through the early years* (3rd ed.). Upper Saddle River, NJ: Merrill/Prentice-Hall.

May, F. B., & Elliot, S. B. (1978). *To help children read: Mastery performance modules for teachers in training* (2nd ed.). Upper Saddle River, NJ: Merrill/Prentice-Hall.

May, F. B., & Rizzardi, L. (2002). *Reading as communication* (6th ed.). Upper Saddle River, NJ: Merrill/Prentice-Hall.

Mayer, M. (1976a). *Ah-choo.* New York: Dial Books.

Mayer, M. (1976b). *Hiccup.* New York: Dial Books.

McCallum, R. D. (1988). Don't throw the basals out with the bath water. *The Reading Teacher, 42,* 204–209.

McCardle, P., & Chhabra, V. (2004). *The voice of evidence in reading research.* Baltimore, MD: Paul H. Brookes.

McCarrier, A., Pinnell, G. S., & Fountas, I. C. (1999). *Interactive writing: How language and literacy come together, K–2.* Portsmouth, NH: Heinemann.

McCarthey, S. J., Hoffman, J. V., Christian, C., Corman, L., Elliott, B., Matherne, D., & Stahle, D. (1994). Engaging the new basal readers. *Reading Research and Instruction, 33*(3), 233–256.

McCormick, C. E., & Mason, J. (1986). Intervention procedures for increasing preschool children's interest in and knowledge about reading. In W. H. Teale & E. Sulzby (Eds.), *Emergent literacy: Writing and reading* (pp. 90–115). Norwood, NJ: Ablex Publishing.

McCormick, S. (1995). *Instructing students who have literacy problems.* Upper Saddle River, NJ: Merrill/Prentice-Hall.

McCracken, R. A., & McCracken, M. J. (1978). Modeling is the key to sustained reading. *The Reading Teacher, 31,* 406–408.

McDermott, G. (1993). *Raven: Trickster tale from the Pacific Northwest.* San Diego, CA: Harcourt Brace.

McGee, L. M. (1982). Awareness of text structure: Effects on children's recall of expository text. *Reading Research Quarterly, 17*(4), 581–590.

McGee, L. M., Lomax, R. G., & Head, M. H. (1988). Young children's written language knowledge: What environmental and functional print reading reveals. *Journal of Reading Behavior, 20*(2), 99–118.

McGee, L. M., Ratliff, J. L., Sinex, A., Head, M., & LaCroix, K. (1984). Influence of story schema and concept of story on children's story compositions. In J. A. Niles & L. A. Harris (Eds.), *Thirty-third yearbook of the National Reading Conference* (pp. 270–277). Rochester, NY: National Reading Conference.

McGee, L. M., & Richgels, D. J. (2000). *Literacy's beginnings: Supporting young readers and writers* (3rd ed.). Needham, MA: Allyn & Bacon.

McGee, L. M., & Richgels, D. J. (2003). *Designing early literacy programs: Strategies for at-risk preschool and kindergarten children.* New York: Guilford.

McGuire, F. N. (1984). How arts instruction affects reading and language: Theory and research. *The Reading Teacher, 37*(9), 835–839.

McInnes, J. (1983). *Networks.* Toronto: Nelson of Canada.

McKee, D. (1990). *Elmer.* London: Red Fox.

McKenna, M. C., & Stahl, S. A. (2003). *Assessment for reading instruction.* New York: Guilford Press.

McKeown, M. G., & Beck, I. L. (1988). Learning vocabulary: Different ways for different goals. *Remedial and Special Education, 9*(1), 42–52.

McKeown, M. G., Beck, I. L., Omanson, R. C., & Pople, M. T. (1985). Some effects of the nature and frequency of vocabulary instruction on the knowleldge and use of words. *Reading Research Quarterly, 20,* 522–535.

McKeown, M. G., Beck, I. L., & Worthy, M. J. (1993). Grappling with text ideas: Questioning the author. *The Reading Teacher, 46*(7), 560–565.

McKissack, P. C. (1986). *Flossie & the fox.* New York: Dial Books for Young Readers.

McKuen, R. (1990). Ten books on CD ROM. *MacWorld, 7*(12), 217–218.

McMahon, S. I., & Raphael, T. E. (1997). *The book club connection: Literacy learning and classroom talk.* New York: Teachers College Press.

McNabb, M. (2006). *Evaluation study of Language, Literacy, & Vocabulary!* St. Charles, IL: Learning Gauge.

McNeil, J. D. (1987). *Reading comprehension* (2nd ed.). Glenview, IL: Scott, Foresman.

McQueen, L. (1985). *The little red hen.* New York, NY: Scholastic Books, Inc.

McQuillan, J. (1998). *The literacy crisis: False claims, real solutions.* Portsmouth, NH: Heinemann Educational Books.

McTighe, J., & Lyman, F. T. (1988). Cueing thinking in the classroom: The promise of theory-embedded tools. *Educational Leadership, 45*(7), 18–24.

Meade, E. L. (1973). The first R-A point of view. *Reading World, 12,* 169–180.

MECC. (1984). *Writing a narrative* (computer program). St. Paul, MN: Minnesota Educational Computing Consortium.

Medina, M., & Escamilla, K. (1994). Language acquisition and gender for limited-language-proficient Mexican Americans in a maintenance bilingual program. *Hispanic Journal of Behavioral Sciences, 16*(4), 422–437.

Meisinger H., Schwanenflugel, P. J., Bradley, E., Kuhn, M. R., & Stahl, S. A. (2002). *Interaction quality during partner reading.* Paper presented at the Annual Meeting of the National Reading Conference, Miami, FL.

Meltzer, N. S., & Himse, R. (1969). The boundaries of written words as seen by first graders. *Journal of Reading Behavior, 1,* 3–13.

Menke, D. J., & Pressley, M. (1994). Elaborative interrogation: Using "why" questions to enhance learning from text. *Journal of Reading, 37*(8), 642–645.

Menon, S., & Hiebert, E. H. (2005). A comparison of first graders' reading with little books or literature-based basal anthologies. *Reading Research Quarterly, 40*(1), 12–36.

Menyuk, P. (1988). *Language development knowledge and use.* Glenview, IL: Scott, Foresman/Little, Brown College Division.

Merrill Mathematics (Grade 5). (1985). Upper Saddle River, NJ: Merrill/Prentice-Hall.

Merrill Science (Grade 3). (1989). Upper Saddle River, NJ: Merrill/Prentice-Hall.

Messaris, P. (2005). Introduction. In J. Flood, S. B. Heath, & D. Lapp (Eds.), *Handbook of research on teaching literacy through the communicative and visual arts* (pp. 3–6). Mahwah, NJ: Lawrence Erlbaum Associates.

Metsala, J. L., & Wharton-McDonald, R. (1997). Effective primary-grades literacy instruction equals balanced literacy instruction. *The Reading Teacher, 50*(6), 518–521.

Meyer, B., Brandt, D., & Bluth, G. (1980). Use of top-level structure in text for reading comprehension of ninth-grade students. *Reading Research Quarterly, 16,* 72–103.

Meyer, B. J. (1979). Organizational patterns in prose and their use in reading. In M. L. Kamil & A. J. Moe (Eds.), *Reading research: Studies and applications* (pp. 109–117). Twenty-eighth Yearbook of the National Reading Conference.

Meyer, B. J. F., & Freedle, R. O. (1984). Effects of discourse type on recall. *American Educational Research Journal, 21*(1), 121–143.

Meyers, P. A. (2006). The princess storyteller, Clara clarifier, Quincy questioner, and the wizard: Reciprocal teaching adapted for kindergarten students. *The Reading Teacher, 59*(4), 314–325.

Mezynski, K. (1983). Issues concerning the acquisition of knowledge: Effects of vocabulary training on reading comprehension. *Review of Educational Research, 53*(2), 253–279.

Michaels, J. R. (2001). *Dancing with words: Helping students love language through authentic vocabulary instruction.* Urbana, IL: National Council of Teachers of English.

Miesels, S. J., & Piker, R. A. (2001). *An analysis of early literacy assessments used for instruction, CIERA Report #2-013.* Ann Arbor, MI: Center for the Improvement of Early Reading Achievement.

Miller, B. F., Rosenberg, E. B., & Stackowski, B. L. (1971). *Investigating your health.* Boston: Houghton Mifflin.

Mindplay. (1990). *Author! Author!* Danvers, MA: Methods and Solutions.

Missal, K. N., & McConnell, S. R. (2004). *Technical report: Psychometric characteristics of individual growth and development indicators: Picture naming, rhyming, and alliteration.* Minneapolis, MN: University of Minnesota.

Moats, L. (1999) *Teaching Reading IS Rocket Science.* Washington, DC: American Federation of Teachers.

Moats, L. C. (1994). The missing foundation in teacher education: Knowledge of the structure of spoken and written language. *Annuals of Dyslexia, 44,* 81–102.

Moats, L. C. (1999). *Teaching reading is rocket science: What expert teachers of reading should know and be able to do.* Washington, DC: American Federation of Teachers.

Moats, L. C. (2000). *Speech to print: Language essentials for teachers.* Baltimore, MD: Paul H. Brookes.

Moe, A. J., & Irwin, J. W. (1986). Cohesion, coherence, and comprehension. In J. W. Irwin (Ed.), *Understanding and teaching cohesion comprehension* (pp. 3–8). Newark, DE: International Reading Association.

Moffett, J. (1983). *Teaching the universe of discourse.* Boston: Houghton Mifflin.

Moffett, J., & Wagner, B. J. (1976). *Student-centered language arts and reading K–13. A handbook for teachers,* 2nd Ed. Boston: Houghton Mifflin.

Mohr, K. A. J. (2003). Children's choices: A comparison of book preferences between Hispanic and non-Hispanic first-graders. *Reading Psychology: An International Quarterly, 24*(2), 163–176.

Mohr, K. A. J. (2006). Children's choices for recreational reading: A three-part investigation of selection preferences, rationales, and processes. *Journal of Literacy Research, 38*(1), 81–104.

Monjo, F. N. (1970). *The drinking gourd.* New York: HarperCollins.

Montelongo, J., Jiménez, L. B., Hernández, A. C., & Hosking, D. (2006). Teaching expository text structures. *The Science Teacher, 73*(2), 28–31.

Mooney, M. E. (1990). *Reading to, with, and by children.* Katonah, NY: Owen.

Moore, G. (1986). Effects of the spatial definition of behavior settings on children's behavior: A quasi-experimental field study. *Journal of Personality and Social Psychology, 6,* 205–231.

Moore, J. C., Jones, C. J., & Miller, D. C. (1980). What we know after a decade of sustained silent reading. *The Reading Teacher, 33,* 445–450.

Moore, M. A. (1991). Electronic dialoguing: An avenue to literacy. *The Reading Teacher, 45*(4), 280–286.

Moran, C. (1996). *Content area instruction for students acquiring English: Power of two languages.* New York: MacMillan/McGraw-Hill.

Morphett, M. V., & Washburne, C. (1931). When should children begin to read? *Elementary School Journal, 31,* 496–503.

Morris, D., Bloodgood, J. M., Lomax, R. G., & Perney, J. (2003). Developmental steps in learning to read: A longitudinal study in kindergarten and first grade. *Reading Research Quarterly, 38*(3), 302–328.

Morris, D., Shaw, B., & Perney, J. (1990). Helping low readers in grades 2 & 3: An after-school volunteer tutoring program. *Elementary School Journal, 91,* 133–150.

Morrow, L. M. (1984). Reading stories to young children: Effects of story structure, and traditional questioning strategies on comprehension. *Journal of Reading Behavior, 16,* 273–288.

Morrow, L. M. (1985). Retelling stories: A strategy for improving children's comprehension, concept of story structure, and oral language complexity. *Elementary School Journal, 85,* 647–661.

Morrow, L. M. (1988a). Retelling as a diagnostic tool. In S. M. Glazer, L. W. Searfoss, & L. Gentile (Eds.), *Re-examining reading diagnosis: New trends and procedures in classrooms and clinics* (pp. 128–149). Newark, DE: International Reading Association.

Morrow, L. M. (1988b). Young children's responses to one-to-one story reading in school settings. *The Reading Teacher, 23*(1), 89–107.

Morrow, L. M. (1990). Preparing the classroom environment to promote literacy during play. *Early Childhood Education Research Quarterly, 5,* 537–554.

Morrow, L. M. (1993). *Literacy development in the early years: Helping children read and write* (2nd ed.). Boston: Allyn & Bacon.

Morrow, L. M. (1995). *Family literacy: Connections in schools and communities.* Newark, DE: International Reading Association.

Morrow, L. M. (2001). *Literacy development in the early years: Helping children read and write* (4th ed.). Needham Heights, MA: Allyn & Bacon.

Morrow, L. M. (2002). *The literacy center: Contexts for reading and writing* (2nd ed.). Portland, ME: Stenhouse.

Morrow, L. M. (2005). *Literacy development in the early years: Helping children read and write* (5th ed.). Boston, MA: Allyn & Bacon.

Morrow, L. M., & Casey, H. K. (2003). A comparison of exemplary characteristics in 1st and 4th grade teachers. *The California Reader, 36*(3), 5–17.

Morrow, L. M., & Gambrell, L. B. (2001). Literature-based instruction in the early years. In S. B. Neuman & D. K. Dickinson (Eds.), *Handbook of early literacy research* (pp. 348–360). New York: Guilford Press.

Morrow, L. M., & Rand, M. K. (1991). Promoting literacy during play by designing early childhood classroom environments. *The Reading Teacher, 44*(6), 396–402.

Morrow, L. M., Gambrell, L. B., Kapinus, B., Koskinen, P. S., Marshall, N., & Mitchell, J. N. (1986). Retelling: A strategy for reading instruction and assessment. In J. A. Niles and R. V. Lalik (Eds.), *Solving problems in literacy: Learners, teachers and researchers: Thirty-fifth yearbook of the National Reading Conference* (pp. 73–80). Rochester, NY: National Reading Conference.

Morrow, L. M., Reutzel, D. R., & Casey, H. (2006). Organization and management of language arts teaching: Classroom environments, grouping practices, and exemplary instruction. In C. Evertson (Ed.), *Handbook of classroom management* (pp. 559–582). Mahwah, NJ: Lawrence Erlbaum Associates.

Morrow, L. M., Tracey, D. H., Woo, D. G., & Pressley, M. (1999). Characteristics of exemplary first-grade literacy instruction. *The Reading Teacher, 52*(5), 462–476.

Mosenthal, J., Lipson, M., Torncello, S., Russ, B., & Mekkelsen, J. (2004). Contexts and practices of six schools successful in obtaining reading achievement. *Elementary School Journal, 104*(5),343–367.

Mosenthal, P. B. (1989a). From random events to predictive reading models. *The Reading Teacher, 42*(7), 524–525.

Mosenthal, P. B. (1989b). The whole language approach: Teachers between a rock and a hard place. *The Reading Teacher, 42*(8), 628–629.

Moskal, B. M. (2003). Developing classroom performance assessments and scoring rubrics: Part II. College Park, MD: ERIC Clearinghouse on Assessment and Evaluation. ED 481715.

Moss, B. (1997). A qualitative assessment of first graders' retelling of expository text. *Reading Research and Instruction, 37*(1), 1–13.

Moss, B. (2004). Teaching expository text structures through information trade book retellings. *The Reading Teacher, 57*(8), 710–718.

Moss, B., & Newton, E. (2001). An examination of the information text genre in basal readers. *Reading Psychology, 23*(1), 1–13.

Moustafa, M. (1997). *Beyond traditional phonics: Research discoveries and reading instruction.* Portsmouth, NH: Heinemann.

Moustafa, M., & Maldonado-Colon, E. (1999). Whole-to-parts phonics instruction: Building on what children know to help them know more. *The Reading Teacher, 52*(5), 448–458.

Mullis, I. V. S., Campbell, J. R., & Farstrup, A. E. (Eds.). (1993). *NAEP 1992 reading report card for the nation and the states* (Report No. 23-ST06). Washington, DC: National Center for Education Statistics, USDOE.

Munsch, R. (1980). *The paper bag princess.* Toronto: Annick Press.

Murray, A. D. (1990). Fine-tuning of utterance length to preverbal infants: Effects on later language development. *Journal of Child Language, 17*(3), 511–525.

Mustafa, M. (1997). *Beyond traditional phonics: Research discoveries and reading instruction.* Portsmouth, NH: Heinemann.

Muth, K. D. (1989). *Children's comprehension of text: Research into practice.* Newark, DE: International Reading Association.

Myers, W. D. (1975). *Fast Sam, Cool Clyde, and Stuff.* New York: Puffin Books.

Nagy, W. (1988). *Teaching vocabulary to improve reading comprehension.* Unpublished manuscript, Champaign, IL: Center for the Study of Reading.

Nagy, W. E., Anderson, R., & Herman, P. (1987). Learning word meanings from context during normal reading. *American Educational Research Journal, 24,* 237–270.

Nagy, W. E., & Anderson, R. C. (1984). How many words are there in printed school English? *Reading Research Quarterly, 19*(3), 304–330.

Nagy, W. E., Herman, P. A., & Anderson, R. C. (1985). Learning words from context. *Reading Research Quarterly, 20,* 233–253.

Naiden, N. (1976). Ratio of boys to girls among disabled readers. *The Reading Teacher, 29*(6), 439–442.

Namioka, L. (1992). *Yang the youngest and his terrible ear.* Boston: Little, Brown.

Nash, B., & Nash, G. (1980). *Pundles.* New York: Stone Song Press.

Nash, B., & Nash, G. (1983). *Pundles.* New York: GD/Perigee Book.

Naslund, J. C., & Samuel, J. S. (1992). Automatic access to word sounds and meaning in decoding written text. *Reading and Writing Quarterly, 8*(2), 135–156.

National assessment of educational progress report, 1994: Reading. Washington, DC: National Center for Educational Statistics and the U.S. Department of Education.

National Assessment of Educational Progress, Reading Report Card. (2002). Washington, DC: U.S. Department of Education.

National Assessment of Educational Progress. (1990). *Learning to read in our nation's schools: Instruction and achievement in 1988 at grades 4, 8, and 12.* Princeton, NJ: Author.

National Assessment of Educational Progress. (2000). Washington, DC: Department of Education.

National Assessment of Educational Progress NAEP. (1996). *Results from the NAEP 1994 reading assessment—at a glance.* Washington, DC: National Center for Educational Statistics.

National Association for the Education of Young Children. (1986). Position statement on developmentally appropriate practice in programs for 4- and 5-year-olds. *Young Children, 41*(6), 20–29.

National Center for Education Statistics. (1999). *NAEP 1998 Reading Report Card: National & state highlights.* Washington, DC: National Center for Education Statistics.

National Commission on Teaching and America's Future. (1996). *What matters most: Teachers for America's future.* Woodbridge, VA: Author.

National Commission on Teaching and America's Future (NCTAF). (2006). *NCTAF emphasizes need for 21st century teaching and learning: Meeting summary.* St. Paul, MN: NCTAF.

National Education Association (NEA). (2000). *Report of the National Education Association's Task Force on Reading 2000.* Washington, DC: Author.

National Education Association. *Report of the NEA Task Force on Reading 2000.* Washington, DC. Retrieved from *https://www.nea. org/reading/images/ readingtaskforce2000.pdf*

National Institute of Child Health and Human Development. (2000). *Report of the National Reading Panel: Teaching children to read.* Washington, DC.

National Institute of Child Health and Human Development. (2000). *Why children succeed or fail at reading. Research from NICHD's program in learning disabilities.* Retrieved from *http:// wwwnichd.nih.gov/publications/pubs/readbro.htm*

National Institutes of Health. (Ed.). (2006). Retrieved from *http://www.nih.gov/.*

National Reading Panel (NRP). (2000). *Report of the National Reading Panel: Teaching children to read.* Washington, DC: National Institute of Child Health and Human Development.

National Research Council. (1998). Preventing Reading Difficulties in Young Children. Washington, DC: National Academy Press.

National Research Council. (2001). *Scientific research in education.* (Report of the Committee on Scientific Principles for Education Research). Washington, DC: National Academy Press.

Nelson, T. (1988, January). Managing immense storage. *Byte,* 225–238.

Neuman, S. B. (1981). Effect of teaching auditory perceptual skill on reading achievement in first grade. *The Reading Teacher, 34,* 422–426.

Neuman, S. B. (1999a). Books make a difference: A study of access to literacy. *Reading Research Quarterly, 34,* 286–311.

Neuman, S. B. (1999b). *The importance of classroom libraries: Research monograph.* New York: Scholastic, Inc.

Neuman, S. B. (2001). The role of knowledge in early literacy. *Reading Research Quarterly, 36*(4), 468–475.

Neuman, S. B., & Celano, D. (2001). Access to print in low-income and middle-income communities: An ecological study of four neighborhoods. *Reading Research Quarterly, 36*(1), 8–26.

Neuman, S. B., & Celano, D. (2006). The knowledge gap: Implications of leveling the playing field for low-income and middle-income children. *Reading Research Quarterly, 42*(2), 176–201.

Neuman, S. B., & Koskinen, P. (1992). Captioned television as comprehensible input: Effects of incidental word learning from context for language minority students. *Reading Research Quarterly, 27*(1), 94–106.

Neuman, S. B., & Roskos, K. (1990). Play, print, and purpose: Enriching play environments for literacy development. *The Reading Teacher, 44*(3), 214–221.

Neuman, S. B., & Roskos, K. (1990). The influence of literacy-enriched play settings on preschooler's engagement with written language. In J. Zutell & S. McCormick (Eds.), *Literacy theory and research: Analysis from multiple paradigms* (pp. 179–187). Chicago, IL: National Reading Conference.

Neuman, S. B., & Roskos, K. (1992). Literacy objects as cultural tools: Effects on children's literacy behaviors in play. *Reading Research Quarterly, 27*, 202–225.

Neuman, S. B., & Roskos, K. (1993). Access to print for children of poverty: Differential effects of adult mediation and literacy-enriched play settings on environmental and functional print tasks. *American Educational Research Journal, 30*(1), 95–122.

Neuman, S. B., & Roskos, K. (1993). *Language and literacy learning in the early years: An integrated approach.* New York: Harcourt Brace.

Neuman, S. B., & Roskos, K. (1997). Literacy knowledge in practice: Contexts of participation for young writers and readers. *Reading Research Quarterly, 32*(1), 10–33.

Neuman, S., & Roskos, K. (1992). Literacy objects as cultural tools: Effects on children's literacy behaviors in play. *Reading Research Quarterly, 27*(3), 203–225.

Neuman, S., & Roskos, K. (1997). Literacy knowledge in practice: Contexts of participation for young writers and readers. *Reading Research Quarterly, 32*(1), 10–33.

Newman, J. M. (1985a). Yes, that's an interesting idea, but. . . . In J. M. Newman (Ed.), *Whole language: Theory in use* (pp. 181–186). Portsmouth, NH: Heinemann.

Newman, J. M. (Ed.). (1985b). *Whole language: Theory in use.* Portsmouth, NH: Heinemann.

Newman, M. L. (1996). *The association of academic achievement, types of offenses, family, and other characteristics of males who have been adjudicated as juvenile delinquents.* Unpublished masters thesis, California State University, Long Beach, CA.

Nichols, J. N. (1980 assignments). Using paragraph frames to help remedial high school students with writing. *Journal of Reading, 24*(3), 228–231.

Nilsen, A. P., & Nilsen, D. L. F. (2002). Lessons in the teaching of vocabulary from September 11 and Harry Potter. *Journal of Adolescent & Adult Literacy, 46*(3), 254–260.

Nist, S. L., & Simpson, M. L. (1993). *Developing vocabulary concepts for college thinking.* Lexington, MA: Heath.

Nolan, E. A., & Berry, M. (1993). Learning to listen. *The Reading Teacher, 46*(7), 606–608.

Nordquist, V. M., & Twardosz, S. (1990). Preventing behavior problems in early childhood special education classrooms through environmental organization. *Education and Treatment of Children, 13*(4), 274–287.

Norton, D. (2007). *Through the eyes of a child: An introduction to children's literature* (7th ed.). Upper Saddle River, NJ: Pearson/Merrill/Prentice-Hall.

Norton, D. E. (1998). *Through the eyes of a child: An introduction to children's literature* (5th ed.). Upper Saddle River, NJ: Merrill/Prentice-Hall.

Norton, D. E., & Norton, S. (2003). *Through the eyes of a child: An introduction to children's literature* (6th ed.). Upper Saddle River, NJ: Merrill/Prentice-Hall.

Norton, D. E., & Norton, S. E. (2003). *Language arts activities for children* (4th ed.). Upper Saddle River, NJ: Merrill Prentice-Hall.

Novick, R. (2002). Learning to read the heart: Nurturing emotional literacy. *Young Children, 57*(3), 84–89.

Noyce, R. M., & Christie, J. F. (1989). *Integrating reading and writing instruction.* Boston: Allyn & Bacon.

Numeroff, L. J. (1985). *If you give a mouse a cookie.* New York: Scholastic.

Nurss, J. R., Hough, R. A., & Goodson, M. S. (1981). Prereading/language development in two day care centers. *Journal of Reading Behavior, 13,* 23–31.

O'Bruba, W. S. (1987). Reading through the creative arts. *Reading Horizons, 27*(3), 170–177.

O'Huigin, S. (1988). *Scary poems for rotten kids.* New York: Firefly Books.

Oakes, J. (1992). Can tracking research inform practice? *Educational Researcher, 21*(4), 12–21.

Oczkus, L. (2003). *Reciprocal teaching at work: Strategies for improving reading comprehension.* Newark, DE: International Reading Association.

Ogle, D. M. (1986). K-W-L: A teaching model that develops active reading of expository text. *The Reading Teacher, 39*(6), 564–570.

Ohanian, S. (1984). Hot new item or same old stew? *Classroom Computer Learning, 5,* 30–31.

O'Haigin, S. (1988). Scary poems for rotten kids. New York: Firefly Books.

Olson, M. W., & Gee, T. C. (1988). Understanding narratives: A review of story grammar research. *Childhood Education, 64*(4), 302–306.

Olson, M. W., & Longnion, B. (1982). Pattern guides: A workable alternative for content teachers. *Journal of Reading, 25,* 736–741.

Opitz, M. F. (1992). The cooperative reading activity: An alternative to ability grouping. *The Reading Teacher, 45*(9), 736–738.

Opitz, M. F. (1998). *Flexible grouping in reading: Practical ways to help all students become better readers.* New York: Scholastic.

Opitz, M. F., & Ford, M. P. (2001). *Reaching readers: Flexible and innovative strategies for guided reading.* Portsmouth, NH: Heinemann.

Opitz, M. F., & Rasinski, T. V. (1998). *Good-bye round robin: 25 effective oral reading strategies.* Portsmouth, NH: Heinemann.

Orellana, M. F., & Hernandez, A. (1999). Talking the walk: Children reading urban environmental print. *The Reading Teacher, 52*(6), 612–619.

ORFC Curriculum Review Panel. (2004). *Oregon Reading First Center (ORFC): Review of comprehensive programs.* Eugene, OR: University of Oregon.

Osborn, J. (1984). The purposes, uses, and contents of workbooks and some guidelines for publishers. In R. C. Anderson, J. Osborn, & R. J. Tierney (Eds.), *Learning to read in American schools* (pp. 45–112). Hillsdale, NJ: Erlbaum.

Osborn, J. (1985). Workbooks: Counting, matching, and judging. In J. Osborn, P. T. Wilson, & R. C. Anderson (Eds.), *Reading education: Foundations for a literate America* (pp. 11–28). Lexington, MA: Lexington Books.

Osborn, J., Lehr, M. A., & Hiebert, E. H. (2003). *Focus on fluency: Research-based practices in early reading series.* Honolulu, HI: Pacific Resources for Education and Learning (PREL).

Otto, J. (1982). The new debate in reading. *The Reading Teacher, 36*(1), 14–18.

Palincsar, A. M. (2003). Collaborative approaches to comprehension instruction. In C. E. Snow & A. P. Sweet (Eds.), *Rethinking reading comprehension* (pp. 99–114). New York: Guilford Press.

Palincsar, A. M., & Brown, A. L. (1984). Reciprocal teaching of comprehension-fostering and monitoring activities. *Cognition and Instruction, 1,* 117–175.

Palincsar, A. S., & Brown, A. L. (1985). Reciprocal teaching: A means to a meaningful end. In J. Osborn, P. T. Wilson, & R. C. Anderson (Eds.), *Reading education: Foundations for a Literate America* (pp. 299–310). Lexington, MA: Heath.

Pankake, M., & Pankake, J. (1988). *A Prairie Home Companion folk song book.* New York: Viking.

Pappas, C. C., Kiefer, B. Z., & Levstik, L. S. (1990). *An integrated language perspective in the elementary school.* New York: Longman.

Paradis, E., & Peterson, J. (1975). Readiness training implications from research. *The Reading Teacher, 28*(5), 445–448.

Paradis, E. E. (1974). The appropriateness of visual discrimination exercises in reading readiness materials. *Journal of Educational Research, 67,* 276–278.

Paradis, E. E. (1984). *Comprehension: Thematic units* (videotape). Laramie: University of Wyoming.

Paratore, J. R. (2003). Building on family literacies: Examining the past and planning the future. In A. DeBruin-Parecki & B. Krol-Sinclair (Eds.), *Family literacy: From theory to practice* (pp. 8–27). Newark, DE: International Reading Association.

Paris, S. G., Carpenter, R. D., Paris, A. H., & Hamilton, E. E. (2005). Spurious and genuine correlates of children's reading comprehension. In S. G. Paris & S. A. Stahl (Eds.), *Children's reading comprehension and assessment* (pp. 131–160). Mahwah, NJ: Lawrence Erlbaum Associates.

Paris, S. G., Lipson, M. Y., & Wixson, K. K. (1983). Issues concerning the acquisition of knowledge: Effects of vocabulary training on reading comprehension. *Review of Educational Research, 53,* 293–316.

Paris, S. G., & Stahl, S. A. (2005). *Children's reading comprehension and assessment.* Mahwah, NJ: Lawrence Erlbaum Associates.

Parish, P. (1963). *Amelia Bedelia.* New York: HarperCollins.

Park, L. S. (2001). *A single shard.* New York: Clarion.

Parker, A., & Paradis, E. (1986). Attitude development toward reading in grades one through six. *Journal of Educational Research, 79*(5), 313–315.

Parkes, B. (1986a). *The enormous watermelon.* Crystal Lake, IL: Rigby.

Parkes, B. (1986b). *Who's in the shed?* Crystal Lake, IL: Rigby.

Parsons, L. (1990). *Response journals.* Portsmouth, NH: Heinemann.

Partnership for Reading (2001). Put reading first: The research building blocks for teaching children to read. Washington. DC: The Partnership for Reading. Report available online at *www.nifl.gov/partnershipforreading*

Pashler, H. (2006). *Optimizing resistance to forgetting.* Paper presented at the 2006 Institute of Education Sciences 2006 Research Conference, Washington, DC.

Paterson, K. (1977). *Bridge to Terabithia.* New York: Thomas Y. Crowell.

Paterson, W. A., Henry, J. J., O'Quin, K., Ceprano, M. A., & Blue, E. V. (2003). Investigating the effectiveness of an integrated learning system on early emergent readers. *Reading Research Quarterly, 38*(2), 172–207.

Paul, R. (2001). *Language disorders from infancy through adolescence* (2nd ed.). St. Louis, MO: Mosby.

Paulsen, G. (1987). *Hatchet.* New York: Simon & Schuster.

Payne, C. (2005). *Shared reading for today's classroom.* NY: Scholastic, Inc.

Payne, C. D., & Schulman, M. B. (1998). *Getting the most out of morning message and other shared writing lessons.* New York: Scholastic. Inc.

Payne, R. (1998). *A framework for understanding poverty.* Highlands, TX: RFT.

Payne, R. K. (1998). *A framework for understanding poverty.* Highlands, TX: RFT Publishing Co.

Pearson, P. D. (1974). The effects of grammatical complexity on children's comprehension, recall, and conception of certain semantic relations. *Reading Research Quarterly, 10*(2), 155–192.

Pearson, P. D. (1985). Changing the face of reading comprehension instruction. *The Reading Teacher, 38*(8), 724–738.

Pearson, P. D. (1989a). *Improving national reading assessment: The key to improved reading instruction.* Paper presented at the 1989 annual reading conference of the Utah Council of the International Reading Association, Salt Lake City, UT.

Pearson, P. D. (1989b). Reading the whole language movement. *Elementary School Journal, 90*(2), 231–242.

Pearson, P. D. (2000). *What sorts of programs and practices are supported by research? A reading from the radical middle.* Ann Arbor, MI: Center for the Improvement of Early Reading Instruction.

Pearson, P. D. (2006). Forward. In K. S. Goodman (Ed.), *The truth about DIBELS: What it is–What it does.* (pp. v–xx) Portsmouth, NH: Heinemann.

Pearson, P. D., & Duke, N. (2002). Comprehension instruction in the primary grades. In C. Collins-Block & M. Pressley (Eds.), *Comprehension instruction: Research-based best practices* (pp. 247–258). New York: Guilford Press.

Pearson, P. D., & Fielding, L. (1982). Listening comprehension. *Language Arts, 59*(6), 617–629.

Pearson, P. D., & Gallagher, M. C. (1983). The instruction of reading comprehension. *Contemporary Educational Psychology, 8*(3), 317–344.

Pearson, P. D., & Johnson, D. D. (1978). *Teaching reading comprehension.* New York: Holt, Rinehart and Winston.

Pearson, P. D., Hansen, J., & Gordon, C. (1979). The effect of background knowledge on children's comprehension of implicit and explicit information. *Journal of Reading Behavior, 11*(3), 201–209.

Peregoy, S. F., & Boyle, O. F. (1993). *Reading, writing, and learning in ESL.* New York: Longman.

Perez, S. A. (1983). Teaching writing from the inside: Teachers as writers. *Language Arts, 60*(7), 847–850.

Perfetti, C. A., & Lesgold, A. M. (1977). Discourse comprehension and sources of individual differences. In M. A. Just & P. A. Carpenter (Eds.), *Cognitive processes in comprehension* (pp. 141–184). Hillsdale, NJ: Erlbaum.

Perkins, J. H. (2001). Listen to their teachers' voices: Effective reading instruction for fourth grade African American students. *Reading Horizons, 41*(4), 239–255.

Perspectives on basal readers (Special issue). (1989). *Theory Into Practice, 28*(4).

Peterson, B. (1991). Selecting books for beginning readers. In D. E. DeFord, C. A. Lyons, & G. S. Pinnell (Eds.), *Bridges to literacy: Learning from reading recovery* (pp. 119–147). Portsmouth, NH: Heinemann.

Peterson, P., Carta, J., & Greenwood, C. (2005). Teaching milieu language skills to parents in multiple-risk families. *Journal of Early Intervention, 27*, 94–109.

Peterson, R., & Eeds, M. (1990). *Grand conversations: Literature groups in action*. New York: Scholastic.

Pfeffer, S. B. (1989). *Future forward*. New York: Holt.

Piaget, J. (1955). *The language and thought of the child*. New York: World.

Piaget, J. (1959). *The language and thought of the child* (3rd ed.). London: Routledge & Kegan.

Pikulski, J. J. (1985). Questions and answers. *The Reading Teacher, 39*(1), 127–128.

Pikulski, J. J. (2006). Fluency: A developmental and language perspective. In S. J. Samuels & A. E. Farstrup (Eds.), *What research has to say about fluency instruction* (pp. 70–93). Newark, DE: International Reading Association.

Pikulski, J. J., & Chard, D. J. (2005). Fluency: Bridge between decoding and reading comprehension. *The Reading Teacher, 58*(6), 510–519.

Pikulski, J. J., & Templeton, S. (1997). The role of phonemic awareness in learning to read. *Invitations to Literacy*. Boston: Houghton Mifflin.

Pinkney, A. D. (1993). *Alvin Ailey*. New York: Hyperion Books for Children.

Pinnell, G. S. (1998). *The language foundation of reading recovery*. Keynote address to the Third International Reading Recovery Institute: Cairns, Australia.

Pinnell, G. S., Deford, D. E., & Lyons, C. A. (1994). Comparing instructional models for the literacy education of high-risk first graders. *Reading Research Quarterly, 29*(1), 8–39.

Pinnell, G. S., & Fountas, I. C. (1997a). *A handbook for volunteers: Help America read*. Portsmouth, NH: Heinemann.

Pinnell, G. S., & Fountas, I. C. (1997b). *Help America read: Coordinator's guide*. Portsmouth, NH: Heinemann.

Pinnell, G. S., & Fountas, I. C. (1998). *Word matters*. Portsmouth, NH: Heinemann.

Pinnell, G. S., & Fountas, I. C. (2002). *Leveled books for readers grades 3–6: A companion volume to guiding readers and writers*. Portsmouth, NH: Heineman.

Pinnell, G. S., Fried, M. D., & Estice, R. M. (1990). Reading recovery: Learning how to make a difference. *The Reading Teacher, 43*, 282–295.

Pinnell, G. S., & Jaggar, A. M. (2003). Oral language: Speaking and listening in elementary classrooms. In J. Flood, D. Lapp, J. R. Squire, & J. M. Jensen (Eds.), *Handbook of research on teaching the English language arts* (2nd ed.) (pp. 881–913). New York: MacMillan.

Pinnell, G. S., Lyons, C. A., DeFord, D. E., Bryk, A. S., & Seltzer, M. (1994). Comparing instructional models for the literacy education of high-risk first graders. *Reading Research Quarterly, 29*(1), 8–39.

Pino, E. (1978). *Schools are out of proportion to man*. Seminar on discipline, Utah State University, Logan, UT.

Pintrich, P. R., & DeGroot, E. V. (1990). Motivational and self-regulated learning components of classroom academic performance. *Journal of Educational Psychology, 82*, 33–40.

Piper, T. (1993). *Language for all our children*. New York: Merrill/Macmillan.

Piper, T. (1998). *Language and learning: The home and school years* (2nd ed.). Upper Saddle River, NJ: Merrill/Prentice-Hall.

Point/counterpoint. The value of basal readers. (1989, August–September). *Reading Today, 7*, 18.

Polacco, P. (2002). *When lightning comes in a jar*. New York: Philomel.

Pollack, P. (1982). *Keeping it secret*. New York: Putnam.

Potter, B. (1903). *The tale of Peter Rabbit*. New York: F. Warne.

Potter, B. (1986). *The tale of Peter Rabbit*. New York: Scholastic, Inc.

Powell, D. A. (1986). *Retrospective case studies of individual and group decision making in district-level elementary reading textbook selection*. Unpublished doctoral dissertation, Indiana University, Bloomington, IN.

Pray, R. T. (1983). *A comparison of good and poor readers in an adult, incarcerated population*. Unpublished doctoral dissertation, Harvard University, Cambridge, MA.

Prelutsky, J. (1976). *Nightmares: Poems to trouble your sleep*. New York: Greenwillow Books.

Prelutsky, J. (1984). *A new kid on the block*. New York: Greenwillow Books.

Prelutsky, J. (1990). *Something big has been here*. New York: Greenwillow Books.

Prelutsky, J. (1991). *Poems for laughing out loud*. New York: Alfred A. Knopf.

Prelutsky, J. (1996). *A pizza the size of the sun*. New York: Greenwillow Books.

Pressley, M. (2000). What should comprehension instruction be the instruction of? In M. L. Kamil, P. B. Mosenthal, P. D. Pearson, & R. Barr (Eds.), *Handbook of reading research,* Vol. 3 (pp. 545–561). Mahwah, NJ: Erlbaum.

Pressley, M. (2002a). *Beginning reading instruc-tion: The rest of the story from research*. Washington, DC: National Education Association. *http://www.nea.org/reading/images/beginningreading.pdf*

Pressley, M. (2002b). Comprehension strategies instruction: A turn-of-the-century status report. In C. Collins-Block & M. Pressley (Eds.), *Comprehension instruction: Research-based best practices,* (pp. 11–27). New York: Guilford Press.

Pressley, M. (2002c). *Reading instruction that works: The case for balanced teaching* (2nd ed.). New York: Guilford Press.

Pressley, M. (2002d). Comprehension strategies instruction: A turn-of-the-century status report. In C. Collins-Block, & M. Pressley (Eds.) *Improving comprehension instruction: Advances in research, theory, and classroom practice* (pp. 11–27). New York: Guilford Press.

Pressley, M. (2006). *Reading instruction that works: The case for balanced teaching* (3rd ed.). New York: Guilford Press.

Pressley, M., Allington, R. L., Wharton-McDonald, R., Collins-Block, C., and Morrow, L. M. (2001). *Learning to read: Lessons from exemplary first-grade classrooms*. New York: Guildford Press.

Pressley, M., Gaskin, I. W., Wile, D., Cunicelli, E. A., & Sheridan, J. (1991). Teaching literacy strategies across the curriculum: A case study at Benchmark School. In J. Zutell & S. McCormick (Eds.), *Learner factors/teacher factors: Issues in literacy research and instruction: Fortieth yearbook of the National Reading Conference* (pp. 219–228). Chicago: National Reading Conference.

Pressley, M., Rankin, J., & Yokoi, L. (1996). A survey of instructional practices of primary teachers nominated as effective in promoting literacy. *Elementary School Journal, 96*(4), 363–383.

Prince, A. T., & Mancus, D. S. (1987). Enriching comprehension: A schema altered basal reading lesson. *Reading Research and Instruction, 27*, 45–53.

Proudfoot, G. (1992). Pssst! There is literacy at the laundromat. *English Quarterly, 24*(1), 10–11.

Provensen, A., & Provensen, M. (1983). *The glorious flight: Across the channel with Louis Bleriot.* New York: Viking Penguin.

Puckett, M. B., & Black, J. K. (1994). *Authentic assessment of the young child.* Upper Saddle River, NJ: Merrill/Prentice-Hall.

Pulver, C. J. (1986). Teaching students to understand explicit and implicit connectives. In J. W. Irwin (Ed.), *Understanding and teaching cohesion comprehension* (pp. 3–8). Newark, DE: International Reading Association.

Put reading first: The research building blocks for teaching children to read. Washington, DC: The Partnership for Reading. Report available online at *www.nifl.gov/partnershipforreading.*

Radencich, M., Beers, P., & Schumm, J. S. (1995). *Handbook for the K–12 reading specialist.* Boston, MA: Allyn and Bacon.

Radencich, M. C. (1995). *Administration and supervision of the reading/writing program.* Boston: Allyn & Bacon.

Ramey, S. L., & Ramey, C. T. (2006). Early educational interventions: Principles of effective and sustained benefits from targeted early educational programs. In D. K. Dickenson & S. B. Neuman (Eds.), *Handbook of early literacy research* (Vol. 2) (pp. 445–459). New York: Guilford Press.

Ramirez, G., & Ramirez, J. L. (1994). *Multiethnic literature.* Albany, NY: Delmar.

RAND Reading Study Group. (2001). *Reading for understanding: Towards an R & D program in reading comprehension.* Washington, DC: Author/OERI/Department of Education.

RAND Reading Study Group. (2002). *Reading for understanding: Toward an R & D program in reading comprehension.* Santa Monica, CA: Science and Technology Policy Institute, RAND Education.

Raphael, T. E. (1982). Question-answering strategies for children. *The Reading Teacher, 36,* 186–191.

Raphael, T. E. (1986). Teaching question answer relationships, revisited. *The Reading Teacher, 39*(6), 516–523.

Raphael, T. E., & Au, K. H. (2005). QAR: Enhancing comprehension and test-taking across grade and content areas. *The Reading Teacher, 59*(3), 206–221.

Raphael, T. E., Florio-Ruane, S., Kehus, M. J., George, M., Hasty, N. L., & Highfield, K. (2003). Constructing curriculum for differentiated instruction: Inquiry in the teachers' learning collaborative. In R. L. McCormick & J. R. Paratore (Eds.), *After early intervention, then what? Teaching struggling readers in grades 3 and beyond* (pp. 94–116). Newark, DE: International Reading Association.

Raphael, T. E., Pardo, L., Highfield, K., & McMahon, S. I. (1997). *Book club: A literature-based curriculum.* Littleton, MA: Small Planet Communications.

Raphael, T. E., & Pearson, P. D. (1982). *The effect of metacognitive awareness training on children's question answering behavior* (Tech. Rep. No. 238). Urbana-Champaign: University of Illinois at Urbana-Champaign, Center for the Study of Reading.

Raphael, T. E., & Pearson, P. D. (1985). Increasing students' awareness of sources of information for answering questions. *American Educational Research Journal, 22*(2), 217–235.

Rasinski, T. (1989). Fluency for everyone: Incorporating fluency instruction in the classroom. *The Reading Teacher, 42*(9), 690–693.

Rasinski, T. (1990). Investigating measure of reading fluency. *Educational Research Quarterly, 14*(3), 37–44.

Rasinski, T. (1998, September). *Reading to learn: Vocabulary development strategies.* Paper presented at the Fall Session of the Dallas Reading Plan Grades 4–6 Professional Development Series, Dallas, TX.

Rasinski, T. (2000). Speed does matter. *The Reading Teacher, 54*(2), 146–151.

Rasinski, T. V. (1984). *Developing Models of Reading Fluency.* ERIC Document Reproduction Service No. ED269721.

Rasinski, T. V. (1990). Effects of repeated reading and listening-while-reading on reading fluency. *Journal of Educational Research, 83*(2), 147–150.

Rasinski, T. V. (1995). *Parents and teachers: Helping children learn to read and write.* New York: Harcourt Brace.

Rasinski, T. V. (2000). Speed does matter. *The Reading Teacher, 54*(2), 146–151.

Rasinski, T. V. (2003). *The fluent reader: Oral reading strategies for building word recognition, fluency, and comprehension.* NY: Scholastic, Inc.

Rasinski, T. V. (2006a). A brief history of reading fluency. In S. J. Samuels & A. E. Farstrup (Eds.), *What research has to say about fluency instruction* (pp. 4–23). Newark, DE: International Reading Association.

Rasinski, T. V. (2006b). Reading fluency instruction: Moving beyond accuracy, automaticity, and prosody. *The Reading Teacher, 59*(7), 704–707.

Rasinski, T. V., & Fredericks, A. D. (1988). Sharing literacy: Guiding principles and practices for parent involvement. *The Reading Teacher, 41,* 508–512.

Rasinski, T. V., & Fredericks, A. D. (1989). Working with parents: What do parents think about reading in the schools? *The Reading Teacher, 43*(3), 262–263.

Rasinski, T. V., & Hoffman, J. V. (2006). Seeking understanding about reading fluency: The contributions of Steven A. Stahl. In K. A. Stahl & M. C. McKenna (Eds.), *Reading research at work: Foundations of effective practice,* (pp.169–176). New York: Guilford Press.

Rasinski, T. V., & Padak, N. (1996). Five lessons to increase reading fluency. In L. R. Putnam (Ed.), *How to become a better reading teacher: Strategies for assessment and intervention* (pp. 255–266). Englewood Cliffs, NJ: Merrill/Prentice-Hall.

Rasinski, T. V., Blachowicz, C., & Lems, K. (2006). *Fluency instruction: Research-based best practices.* New York: Guilford Press.

Rasinski, T., & Opitz, M. F. (1998). *Good-bye round robin: 25 effective oral reading strategies.* Portsmouth, NH: Heinemann.

Rasinski, T., & Padak, N. D. (1990). Multicultural learning through children's literature. *Language Arts, 69,* 14–20.

Rathvon, N. (2004). *Early reading assessment: A practitioner's handbook.* New York: Guilford Press.

Raven, J. (1992). A model of competence, motivation, and behavior, and a paradigm for assessment. In H. Berlak, *Toward a new science of educational testing and assessment.* New York: State University of New York Press.

Ravitch, D., & Finn, C. E., Jr. (1987). *What do our 17-year-olds know?* New York: HarperCollins.

Rawls, W. (1961). *Where the red fern grows.* New York: Doubleday.

Raygor, A. L. (1977). The Raygor readability estimate: A quick and easy way to determine difficulty. In P. D. Pearson (Ed.), *Reading: Theory, research and practice* (pp. 259–263). Clemson, SC: National Reading Conference.

Rayner, K., Foorman, B. R., Perfetti, C. A., Pesetsky, D., and Seidenberg, M. S. (2001). How psychological science informs the teaching of reading. *Psychological Science in the Public Interest 2*(2), 31–74.

Rayner, K., Foorman, B. R., Perfetti, C. A., Pesetsky, D., and Seidenberg, M. S. (2002, March). How should reading be taught? *Scientific American,* 85–91.

Read, C. (1971). Preschool children's knowledge of English phonology. *Harvard Educational Review, 41,* 1–34.

Read, S. J., & Rosson, M. B. (1982). Rewriting history: The biasing effects of attitudes on memory. *Social Cognition, 1,* 240–255.

Readence, J. E., Bean, T. W., & Baldwin, R. S. (1992). *Content area reading: An integrated approach* (4th ed.). Dubuque, IA: Kendall/Hunt.

Reid, J. F. (1966). Learning to think about reading. *Educational Research, 9,* 56–62.

Reimer, B. L. (1983). Recipes for language experience stories. *The Reading Teacher, 36*(4), 396–401.

Reinking, D. (Ed.) (1987). *Computers and reading: Issues for theory and practice.* New York: Teachers College Press.

Reinking, D., & Rickman, S. S. (1990). The effects of computer-mediated texts on the vocabulary learning and comprehension of intermediate-grade readers. *Journal of Reading Behavior, 22*(4), 395–409.

Remaly, B. K. (1990). *Strategies for increasing the expressive vocabulary of kindergarten children.* Fort Lauderdale, FL: Nova University. (ERIC Document Reproduction Service No. ED 332 234).

Reutzel, D. R. (1985a). Reconciling schema theory and the basal reading lesson. *The Reading Teacher, 39,* 194–197.

Reutzel, D. R. (1985b). Story maps improve comprehension. *The Reading Teacher, 38*(4), 400–405.

Reutzel, D. R. (1991). Understanding and using basal readers effectively. In Bernard L. Hayes (Ed.), *Reading instruction and the effective teacher* (pp. 254–280). New York: Allyn & Bacon.

Reutzel, D. R. (1992). Breaking the letter a week tradition: Conveying the alphabetic principle to young children. *Childhood Education, 69*(1), 20–23.

Reutzel, D. R. (1995). Fingerpoint-reading and beyond: Learning about print strategies (LAPS). *Reading Horizons, 35*(4), 310–328.

Reutzel, D. R. (1996a). A balanced reading approach. In J. Baltas & S. Shafer (Eds.), *Scholastic guide to balanced reading: Grade 3–6,* 7–11. New York: Scholastic.

Reutzel, D. R. (1996b). A balanced reading approach. In J. Baltas & S. Shafer (Eds.), *Scholastic guide to balanced reading: K–2.* New York: Scholastic.

Reutzel, D. R. (1999a). On balanced reading. *The Reading Teacher, 52*(4), 2–4.

Reutzel, D. R. (1999b). Organizing literacy instruction: Effective grouping strategies and organizational plans. In L. M Morrow, L. B. Gambrell, S. Neuman, & M. Pressley (Eds.), *Best practices for literacy instruction.* New York: Guilford Press.

Reutzel, D. R. (2006). Hey teacher, when you say fluency, what do you mean?: Developing fluency and meta-fluency in elementary classrooms. In T.V. Rasinski, C. Blachowicz, & K. Lems (Eds.), *Fluency instruction: Research-based best practices* (pp. 62–85). New York: Guilford Press.

Reutzel, D. R., Camperell, K., & Smith, J. A. (2002). Helping struggling readers make sense of reading. In C. Collins-Block, L. B. Gambrell, & M. Pressley (Eds.), *Improving comprehension instruction: Advances in research, theory, and classroom practice.* San Francisco, CA: Jossey-Bass.

Reutzel, D. R., & Cooter, R. B. (2000). *Teaching children to read: Putting the pieces together* (3rd ed.). Upper Saddle River, NJ: Merrill/Prentice-Hall.

Reutzel, D. R., & Cooter, R. B. (2003). *Strategies for reading assessment and instruction: Helping every child succeed* (2nd ed.). Upper Saddle River, NJ: Merrill/Prentice-Hall.

Reutzel, D. R., & Cooter, R. B. (2004). *Teaching children to read: Putting the pieces together* (4th ed.). Upper Saddle River, NJ: Merrill/Prentice-Hall.

Reutzel, D. R., & Cooter, R. B. (2005). *Essentials of teaching children to read.* Upper Saddle River, NJ: Merrill/Prentice-Hall.

Reutzel, D. R., & Cooter, R. B. (2007). *Strategies for reading assessment and instruction: Helping every child succeed* (3rd ed.). Upper Saddle River, NJ: Merrill/Prentice-Hall.

Reutzel, D. R., & Cooter, R. B., Jr. (1990). Whole language: Comparative effects on first-grade reading achievement. *Journal of Educational Research, 83,* 252–257.

Reutzel, D. R., & Cooter, R. B., Jr. (1991). Organizing for effective instruction: The reading workshop. *The Reading Teacher, 44*(8), 548–555.

Reutzel, D. R., & Cooter, R. B., Jr. (1999). *Balanced reading strategies and practices: Assessing and assisting readers with special needs.* Upper Saddle River, NJ: Merrill/Prentice-Hall.

Reutzel, D. R., & Daines, D. (1987a). The instructional cohesion of reading lessons in seven basal reading series. *Reading Psychology, 8,* 33–44.

Reutzel, D. R., & Daines, D. (1987b). The text-relatedness of seven basal reading series. *Reading Research and Instruction, 27,* 26–35.

Reutzel, D. R., & Fawson, P. C. (1989). Using a literature webbing strategy lesson with predictable books. *The Reading Teacher, 43*(3), 208–215.

Reutzel, D. R., & Fawson, P. C. (1990). Traveling tales: Connecting parents and children in writing. *The Reading Teacher, 44,* 222–227.

Reutzel, D. R., & Fawson, P. C. (1991). Literature webbing predictable books: A prediction strategy that helps below-average, first-grade readers. *Reading Research and Instruction, 30*(4), 20–30.

Reutzel, D. R., & Fawson, P. C. (1998). Global literacy connections: Stepping into the future. *Think, 8*(2), 32–34.

Reutzel, D. R., & Fawson, P. C. (2002). *Your classroom library—giving it more teaching power: Research-based strategies for developing better readers and writers.* New York: Scholastic Professional Books.

Reutzel, D. R., Fawson, P. C., & Smith, J. A. (2006). *Words to Go!:* Evaluating a firstgrade parent involvement program for "making" words at home. *Reading Research and Instruction 2,* 119–159.

Reutzel, D. R., Fawson, P., Young, J., & Morrison, T. (2003). Reading environmental print: What is the role of concepts about print in discriminating young readers' responses? *Reading Psychology, 24*(2), 123–162.

Reutzel, D. R., & Gali, K. (1998). The art of children's book selection: A labyrinth unexplored. *Reading Psychology, 19*(1), 3–50.

Reutzel, D. R., & Hollingsworth, P. M. (1988a). Highlighting key vocabulary: A generative-reciprocal procedure for teaching selected inference types. *Reading Research Quarterly, 23*(3), 358–378.

Reutzel, D. R., & Hollingsworth, P. M. (1988b). Whole language and the practitioner. *Academic Therapy, 23*(4), 405–416.

Reutzel, D. R., & Hollingsworth, P. M. (1991a). Investigating the development of topic-related attitude: Effect on children's reading and remembering text. *Journal of Educational Research, 84*(5), 334–344.

Reutzel, D. R., & Hollingsworth, P. M. (1991b). Reading comprehension skills: Testing the skills distinctiveness hypothesis. *Reading Research and Instruction, 30*(2), 32–46.

Reutzel, D. R., & Hollingsworth, P. M. (1991c). Reading time in school: Effect on fourth graders' performance on a criterion-referenced comprehension test. *Journal of Educational Research, 84*(3), 170–176.

Reutzel, D. R., & Hollingsworth, P. M. (1991d). Using literature webbing for books with predictable narrative: Improving young readers' predictions, comprehension, & story structure knowledge. *Reading Psychology, 12*(4), 319–333.

Reutzel, D. R., & Hollingsworth, P. M. (1993). Effects of fluency training on second graders' reading comprehension. *Journal of Educational Research, 86*(6), 325–331.

Reutzel, D. R., Hollingsworth, P. M., & Eldredge, J. L. (1994). Oral reading instruction: The impact on student reading development. *Reading Research Quarterly, 23*(1), 40–62.

Reutzel, D. R., & Larsen, N. S. (1995). Look what they've done to real children's books in the new basal readers. *Language Arts, 72*(7), 495–507.

Reutzel, D. R., & Mitchell, J. P. (2005). High-stakes accountability themed issue: How did we get here from there? *The Reading Teacher, 58*(4), 2–4.

Reutzel, D. R., & Morgan, B. C. (1990). Effects of prior knowledge, explicitness, and clause order on children's comprehension of causal relationships. *Reading Psychology: An International Quarterly, 11,* 93–114.

Reutzel, D. R., & Morrow, L. M. (in press). Promoting and assessing effective literacy learning classroom environments. In J. Paratore & C. McCormick (Eds.), *Classroom literacy assessment: Making sense of what students know and do.* New York: Guilford Press.

Reutzel, D. R., Oda, L. K., & Moore, B. H. (1989). Developing print awareness: The effect of three instructional approaches on kindergartners: Print awareness, reading readiness, and word reading. *Journal of Reading Behavior, 21*(3), 197–217.

Reutzel, D. R., & Sabey, B. (1995). Teacher beliefs about reading and children's conceptions: Are there connections? *Reading Research and Instruction, 35*(4), 323–342.

Reutzel, D. R., Smith, J. A., & Fawson, P. C. (2005). An evaluation of two approaches for teaching reading comprehension strategies in the primary years using science information texts. *Early Childhood Research Quarterly, 20,* 276–305.

Reutzel, D. R., Smith, J. A., & Fawson, P. C. (in preparation). *Reconsidering silent sustained reading (SSR): A comparative study of modified SSR with oral repeated reading practice.* Logan, UT: Utah State University.

Reutzel, D. R., & Wolfersberger, M. (1996). An environmental impact statement: Designing supportive literacy classrooms for young children. *Reading Horizons, 36*(3), 266–282.

Reznitskaya, A., & Anderson, R. C. (2002). The argument schema and learning to reason. In C. Collins-Block, L. B. Gambrell, & M. Pressley (Eds.) *Improving comprehension instruction: Advances in research, theory, and classroom practice* (pp. 319–334). San Francisco, CA: Jossey-Bass.

Rhodes, L. K., & Dudley-Marling, C. (1988). *Readers and writers with a difference.* Portsmouth, NH: Heinemann.

Rhodes, L. K., & Shanklin, N. (1993). *Windows into literacy: Assessing learners K–8.* Portsmouth, NH: Heinemann.

Ribowsky, H. (1985). *The effects of a code emphasis approach and a whole language approach upon emergent literacy of kindergarten children* (Report No. CS-008-397). (ERIC Document Reproduction Service)

Rice, P. E. (1991). Novels in the news. *The Reading Teacher, 45*(2), 159–160.

Rich, E. S. (1964). *Hannah Elizabeth.* New York: HarperCollins.

Richards, M. (2000). Be a good detective: Solve the case of oral reading fluency. *The Reading Teacher, 53*(7), 534–539.

Richek, M. A. (1978). Readiness skills that predict initial word learning using 2 different methods of instruction. *Reading Research Quarterly, 13,* 200–222.

Richgels, D. J. (2001). Invented spelling, phonemic awareness, and reading and writing instruction. In Neuman, S. B., & Dickinson, D. K. (Eds.), *Handbook of early literacy research* (pp. 142–155). New York: Guilford Press.

Richgels, D. J., & Wold, L. S. (1998). Literacy on the road: Backpacking partnerships between school and home. *The Reading Teacher, 52*(1), 18–29.

Rijlaarsdam, G., & van den Bergh, H. (2006). Writing process theory. In C. A. MacArthur, S. Graham, & J. Fitzgerald (Eds.), *Handbook of writing research.* New York: Guilford.

Riley, R. E. (1993). *Adult literacy in America.* Washington, DC: United States Department of Education.

Rinehart, S. D., Stahl, S. A., & Erickson, L. G. (1986). Some effects of summarization training on reading and studying. *Reading Research Quarterly, 21*(4), 422–438.

Ring, S. (2003). *Bridges.* Boston, MA: Newbridge.

Roberts, B. (1992). The evolution of the young child's concept of word as a unit of spoken and written language. *Reading Research Quarterly, 27*(2), 124–139.

Roberts, T. (1975). Skills of analysis and synthesis in the early stages of reading. *British Journal of Educational Psychology, 45,* 3–9.

Robertson, C., Keating, I., Shenton, L., & Roberts, I. (1996). Uninterrupted, sustained, silent reading: The rhetoric and the practice. *Journal of Research in Reading, 19,* 25–35.

Robinson, A. (In press). *American Reading Instruction.* Newark, DE: International Reading Association.

Robinson, B. (1972). *The best Christmas pageant ever.* New York: HarperCollins.

Robinson, F. (1946). *Effective study.* New York: Harper Brothers.

Robinson, H. M. (1972). Perceptual training—does it result in reading improvement? In R. C. Aukerman (Ed.), *Some persistent questions on beginning reading* (pp. 135–150). Newark, DE: International Reading Association.

Rodriqeuz-Brown, F., Fen Li, R., & Alborn, J. A. (1999). Hispanic parents' awareness and use of literacy-rich environments at home and in the community. *Education and Urban Society, 32,* 41–57.

Rodriquez-Brown, F., & Meehan, M. A. (1998). Family literacy and adult education: Project FLAME. In M. C. Smith (Ed.), *Literacy for the 21st century: Research, policy, practices and the National Adult Literacy Survey* (pp. 175–193). Westport, CT: Greenwood.

Rogg, L. J. (2001). *Early literacy instruction in kindergarten.* Newark, DE: International Reading Association.

Roller, C. M. (2002). *Comprehensive reading instruction across the grade levels: A collection of papers from the Reading Research 2001 Conference.* Newark, DE: International Reading Association.

Romero, G. G. (1983). *Print awareness of the preschool bilingual Spanish English speaking child.* Unpublished doctoral dissertation, University of Arizona Tucson.

Rosenbaum, J. (1980). *Making inequality: The hidden curriculum of high school tracking.* New York: Wiley.

Rosenblatt, L. M. (1978). *The reader, the text, and the poem.* Carbondale, IL: Southern Illinois University Press.

Rosenblatt, L. M. (1989). Writing and reading: The transactional theory. In J. M. Mason (Ed.), *Reading and writing connections* (pp. 153–175). Boston: Allyn & Bacon.

Rosenblatt, L. M. (2004). The transactional theory of reading and writing. In R. B. Ruddell & N. J. Unrau (Eds.), *Theoretical models and processes of reading* (5th ed.) (pp. 1363–1398). NWP Publications.

Rosenhouse, J., Feitelson, D., & Kita, B. (1997). Interactive reading aloud to Israeli first graders: its contribution to literacy development. *Reading Research Quarterly, 32,* 168–183.

Rosenshine, B., & Meister, C. (1994). Reciprocal teaching: A review of nineteen experimental studies. *Review of Educational Research, 64,* 479–530.

Rosenshine, B. V. (1980). Skill hierarchies in reading comprehension. In R. J. Spiro, B. C. Bruce, & W. F. Brewer (Eds.), *Theoretical issues in reading comprehension* (pp. 535–554). Hillsdale, NJ: Erlbaum.

Roser, N. L., Hoffman, J. V., & Farest, C. (1990). Language, literature, and at-risk children. *The Reading Teacher, 43*(8), 554–561.

Roskos, K., & Neuman, S. B. (2001). Environment and its influences for early literacy teaching and learning. In S. B. Neuman & D. K. Dickinson (Eds.), *Handbook of Early Literacy Research* (pp. 281–294). New York: Guildford Press.

Roswell, F. G., & Chall, J. S. (1963). *Auditory Blending Test.* New York: Essay Press.

Rouse, H. L., & Fantuzzo, J. W. (2006). Validity of the *Dynamic Indicators for Basic Early Literacy Skills* as an indicator of early literacy for urban kindergarten children. *The School Psychology Review, 35*(3) 341–355.

Routman, R. (1988). *Transitions: From literature to literacy.* Portsmouth, NH: Heinemann.

Routman, R. (1996). *Literacy at the crossroads: Crucial talk about reading, writing, and other teaching dilemmas.* Portsmouth, NH: Heinemann.

Routman, R. (2003). *Reading Essentials: The specifics you need to know to teach reading well.* Portsmouth, NH: Heinemann.

Rowe, M. B. (1974). Wait-time and rewards as instructional variables, their influence on language, logic, and fate control: Part one—wait time. *Journal of Research in Science Teaching, 11,* 81–94.

Rowling, J. K. (1998). *Harry Potter and the Sorcerer's Stone.* New York: Scholastic.

Ruddell, R. (1974). *Reading-language instruction: Innovative practices.* Upper Saddle River, NJ: Prentice-Hall.

Ruddell, R. B., & Harris, P. (1989). A study of the relationship between influential teachers' prior knowledge and beliefs and teaching effectiveness: Developing higher order thing in content areas. In S. McCormick & J. Zutell (Eds.), *Cognitive and social perspective for literacy research and instruction, 38th Yearbook of the National Reading Conference* (pp. 461–472). Chicago, IL: National Reading Conference.

Ruddell, R. B., & Kern, R. B. (1986). The development of belief systems and teaching effectiveness of influential teachers. In M. P. Douglas (Ed.), *Reading: The quest for meaning* (pp. 133–150). Claremont, CA: Claremont Graduate School Yearbook.

Ruddell, R. B., & Ruddell, M. R. (1995). *Teaching children to read and write: Becoming an influential teacher.* Boston: Allyn & Bacon.

Ruddell, R. B., & Unrau, N. J. (1997). The role of responsive teaching in focusing reader intention and developing reader motivation. In J. T. Guthrie & A. Wigfield (Eds.), *Reading engagement: Motivating readers through integrated instruction.* Newark, DE: International Reading Association.

Ruddell, R. B., & Unrau, N. J. (2004). *Theoretical models and processes of reading* (5th ed.). Newark, DE: International Reading Association.

Rule, A. C. (2001). Alphabetizing with environmental print. *The Reading Teacher, 54*(6), 558–562.

Rumelhart, D. E. (1975). Notes on a schema for stories. In D. G. Bobrow & A. Collins (Eds.), *Representation and understanding: Studies in cognitive science* (pp. 211–236). New York: Academic Press.

Rumelhart, D. E. (1980). Schemata: The building blocks of cognition. In R. J. Spiro (Ed.), *Theoretical issues in reading comprehension* (pp. 33–58). Hillsdale, NJ: Erlbaum.

Rumelhart, D. E. (1981). Schemata: The building blocks of cognition. In Guthrie, J. T. (Ed.), *Comprehension and teaching: Research reviews* (pp. 3–26). Newark, DE: International Reading Association.

Rumelhart, D. E. (1984). Understanding understanding. In J. Flood (Ed.), *Understanding reading comprehension* (pp. 1–20). Newark, DE: International Reading Association.

Rupley, W., & Blair, T. (1987). Assignment and supervision of reading seatwork: Looking in on 12 primary teachers. *The Reading Teacher, 40*(4), 391–393.

Rupley, W. H., & Blair, T. R. (1978). Teacher effectiveness in reading instruction. *The Reading Teacher, 31,* 970–973.

Ryder, R. J., & Graves, M. F. (1994). Vocabulary instruction presented prior to reading in two basal readers. *Elementary School Journal, 95,* 139–153.

Rye, J. (1982). *Cloze procedure and the teaching of reading.* Portsmouth, NH: Heinemann.

Sadoski, M., & Pavio, A. (2004). A dual coding theoretical model of reading. In R. B. Ruddell & N. J. Unrau (Eds.), *Theoretical models and processes of reading* (5th ed.) (pp. 1329–1362). Newark, DE: International Reading Association.

Sadoski, M., & Quast, Z. (1990). Reader response and long-term recall for journalistic text: The roles of imagery, affect, and importance. *Reading Research Quarterly, 24*(4), 256–272.

Sadow, M. W. (1982). The use of story grammar in the design of questions. *The Reading Teacher, 35,* 518–523.

Salvia, J., & Ysseldyke, J. E. (2004). *Assessment in special and inclusive education* (9th ed.). Boston: Houghton Mifflin.

Samuels, S. J. (1967). Attentional process in reading: The effect of pictures on the acquisition of reading responses. *Journal of Educational Psychology, 58,* 337–342.

Samuels, S. J. (1970). Effects of pictures on learning to read, comprehension, and attitudes. *Review of Educational Research, 40,* 397–408.

Samuels, S. J. (1979). The method of repeated reading. *The Reading Teacher, 32,* 403–408.

Samuels, S. J. (2006). Toward a model of reading fluency. In S. J. Samuels & A. E. Farstrup (Eds.), *What research has to say about fluency instruction* (pp. 24–46). Newark, DE: International Reading Association.

Samuels, S. J., & Farstrup, A. E. (2006). *What research has to say about fluency instruction.* Newark, DE: International Reading Association.

Sanders, W. A., & Rivers, J. C. (1996). *Cumulative and residual effects of teachers on future student academic achievement.* Knoxville: University of Tennessee Value-Added Research and Assessment Center.

Sandora, C., Beck, I. L, & McKeown, M. G. (1999). A comparison of two discussion strategies on students' comprehension and interpretation of complex literature. *Reading Psychology, 20*(3), 177–212.

Sanford, A. J., & Garrod, S. C. (1981). *Understanding written language.* New York: Wiley.

Santa, C. (1990). *Reporting on the Montana Teacher Change Project: Kallispell reading/language initiative.* Utah Council of the International Reading Association, Salt Lake City, UT.

Santa, C. M. (1997). School change and literacy engagement: Preparing teaching and learning environments. In J. T. Guthrie & A. Wigfield (Eds.), *Reading engagement: Motivating readers through integrated instruction.* Newark, DE: International Reading Association.

Santa, C. M., & Hoien, T. (1998). An assessment of Early Steps: A program for early interventions of reading problems. *Reading Research Quarterly, 34*(1), 54–79.

Savage, J. F. (1994). *Teaching reading using literature.* Madison, WI: Brown & Benchmark.

Scarborough, H. S. (2001). Connecting early language and literacy to later reading (dis) abilities: Evidence, theory, and practice. In S. B. Neuman & D. K. Dickinson (Eds.), *Handbook of early literacy research* (Vol. 1) (pp. 97–110). New York: Guilford.

Scarborough, H. S., & Dobrich, W. (1994). On the efficacy of reading to preschoolers. *Developmental Review, 14,* 245–302.

Schmidt, K. (1985). *The gingerbread man.* New York, NY: Scholastic Books.

Schneider, W., & Shiffrin, R. M. (1977). Controlled and automatic human information processing: 1. Detection, search, and attention, *Psychological Review, 84*(1), 1–66.

Scholastic. (1986). *Talking text* (computer program). Jefferson City, MO: Scholastic.

Scholastic. (1990). *Bank Street writer III* (computer program). Jefferson City, MO: Scholastic Software.

Scholastic. (1995). *Literary place program.* New York: Author.

Schreiber, A., & Tuchman, G. (1997). *Scholastic Phonics Readers The Big Hit: Book 14.* New York: Scholastic.

Schunk, D. H., & Zimmerman, B. J. (1997). Developing self-efficacious readers and writers: The role of social and self-regulatory processes. In J. T. Guthrie and A. Wigfield (Eds.), *Reading engagement: Motivating readers through integrated instruction* (pp. 34–50). Newark, DE: International Reading Association.

Schwartz, D. M. (1985). *How much is a million?* Richard Hill, Ontario: Scholastic-TAB.

Schwartz, R. M., & Raphael, T. E. (1985). Concept of definition: A key to improving students' vocabulary. *The Reading Teacher, 39*(2), 198–205.

Scieszka, J. (1989). *The true story of the 3 little pigs: By A. Wolf.* New York: Viking Kestrel.

Searfoss, L. W. (1975). Radio reading. *The Reading Teacher, 29,* 295–296.

Searfoss, L. W., & Readence, J. E. (1989). *Helping children learn to read* (2nd ed.). Upper Saddle River, NJ: Prentice-Hall.

Seefeldt, C., & Barbour, N. (1986). *Early childhood education: An introduction.* Upper Saddle River, NJ: Merrill/Prentice-Hall.

Seidenberg, P. L. (1989). Relating text-processing research to reading and writing instruction for learning disabled students. *Learning Disabilities Focus, 5*(1), 4–12.

Sendak, M. (1962). *Chicken soup with rice.* New York: Scholastic.

Sendak, M. (1963). *Where the wild things are.* New York: HarperCollins.

Senechal, M., & Cornell, E. H. (1993). Vocabulary acquisition through shared reading experiences. *Reading Research Quarterly, 28*(4), 361–373.

Seuss, D. (1954). *Horton hears a Who!* New York: Random House.

Shake, M. (1986). Teacher interruptions during oral reading instruction: Self-monitoring as an impetus for change in corrective feedback. *Remedial and Special Education, 7*(5), 18–24.

Shake, M. C., & Allington, R. L. (1985). Where do teacher's questions come from? *The Reading Teacher, 38,* 432–439.

Shanahan, T. (1984). Nature of the reading-writing relation: An exploratory multi-variate analysis. *Journal of Educational Psychology, 76,* 466–477.

Shanahan, T. (2003a). Research-based reading instruction: Myths about the National Reading Panel report. *The Reading Teacher, 56*(7), 646–655.

Shanahan, T. (2003b). *A framework for improving reading achievement.* Paper presented at the National Conference on Family Literacy and the California Family Literacy Conference. Long Beach, California, March 16, 2003.

Shanahan, T. (2004). Critiques of the National Reading Panel report: Their implications for research, policy, and practice. In P. McCardle & V. Chhabra (Eds.), *The voice of evidence in reading research* (pp. 235–266). Baltimore: MD: Paul H. Brookes.

Shanahan, T. (2004, November). *How do you raise reading achievement?* Paper presented at the Utah Council of the International Reading Association Meeting, Salt Lake City, UT.

Shanahan, T. (2006). Relations among oral language, reading, and writing. In C. A. MacArthur, S. Graham, & J. Fitzgerald (Eds.), *Handbook of writing research* (pp. 171–186). New York: Guilford Press.

Shanahan, T. (2006). Relations among oral language, reading, and writing development. In C. A. MacArthur, S. Graham, & J. Fitzgerald (Eds.), *Handbook of writing research* (pp. 171–186). New York: Guilford Press.

Shanahan, T., & Barr, R. (1995). Reading Recovery: An independent evaluation of the effects of an early intervention for at-risk learners. *Reading Research Quarterly, 30*(40), 958–996.

Shanahan, T., & Lomax, R. G. (1986). An analysis and comparison of theoretical models of the reading-writing relationship. *Journal of Educational Psychology, 78,* 116–123.

Shanahan, T., Mulhern, M., & Rodriquez-Brown, F. (1995). Project FLAME: Lessons learned from a family literacy program for minority families. *The Reading Teacher, 48,* 40–47.

Shanklin, N. L., & Rhodes, L. K. (1989). Comprehension instruction as sharing and extending. *The Reading Teacher, 43*(7), 496–500.

Shannon, P. (1983). The use of commercial reading materials in American elementary schools. *Reading Research Quarterly, 19,* 68–85.

Shannon, P. (1989a). Basal readers: Three perspectives. *Theory Into Practice, 28*(4), 235–239.

Shannon, P. (1989b). *Broken promises.* Granby, MA: Bergin & Garvey.

Shannon, P. (1992). *Becoming political: Readings and writings in the politics of literacy education.* Portsmouth, NH: Heinemann.

Shannon, P. (1993). Letters to the editor: Comments on Baumann. *Reading Research Quarterly, 28*(2), 86.

Shannon, P., & Goodman, K. (1994). *Basal readers: A second look.* New York: Owen.

Sharmat, M. W. (1980). *Gila monsters meet you at the airport.* New York: Aladdin.

Shaywitz, S. E., & Shaywitz, B. A. (2004). Neurobiologic basis for reading and reading disability. In P. McCardle & V. Chhabra (Eds.), *The voice of evidence in reading research* (pp. 417–444). Baltimore: MD: Paul H. Brookes.

Shermis, M. D., Burstein, J., & Leacock, C. (2006). Applications of computers in assessment and analysis of writing. In

C. A. MacArthur, S. Graham, & J. Fitzgerald (Eds.), *Handbook of writing research*. New York: Guilford.

Shinn, M. R. (Ed.). (1989). *Curriculum-based measurement: Assessing special children*. NY: Guilford.

Shockley, B., Michalove, B., & Allen, J. (1995). *Engaging Families*. Portsmouth, NH: Heinemann.

Short, K. G., Harste, J. C., & Burke, C. (1996). *Creating classrooms for authors and inquirers*. Portsmouth, NH:Heinemann.

Shulman, L. (2001). *Ways of measuring: Then and now*. Northborough, MA: Sundance Publishers.

Siegel, M. (1983). *Reading as signification*. Unpublished doctoral dissertation, Indiana University.

Silvaroli, N. J. (1986). *Classroom reading inventory* (5th ed.). Dubuque, IA: William C. Brown.

Silverstein, S. (1974). *Where the sidewalk ends*. New York: HarperCollins.

Silverstein, S. (1996). *Falling Up*. New York: HarperCollins.

Simmons, D. C., & Kame'enui, E. J. (1998). *What reading research tells us about children with diverse learning needs: Bases and basics*. Mahwah, NJ: Erlbaum.

Simmons, D. C., & Kame'enui, E. J. (2003). *A consumer's guide to evaluating a core reading program, Grades K–3: A critical elements analysis*. Eugene, OR: University of Oregon.

Sinatra, R. C., Stahl-Gemake, J., & Berg, W. (1984). Improving reading comprehension of disabled readers through semantic mapping. *Reading Teacher, 38*(1), 22–29.

Singer, H. (1960). *Conceptual ability in the substrata-factor theory of reading*. Unpublished doctoral dissertation, University of California at Berkeley.

Singer, H. (1978a). Active comprehension: From answering to asking questions. *The Reading Teacher, 31*, 901–908.

Singer, H. (1978b). Research in reading that should make a difference in classroom instruction. In *What research has to say about reading instruction* (pp. 57–71). Newark, DE: International Reading Association.

Singer, H., & Donlan, D. (1989). *Reading and learning from text* (2nd ed.). Hillsdale, NJ: Erlbaum.

Sippola, A. E. (1994). Holistic analysis of basal readers: An assessment tool. *Reading Horizons, 34*(3), 234–246.

Skaar, G. (1972). *What do the animals say?* New York: Scholastic.

Slaughter, H. B. (1988). Indirect and direct teaching in a whole language program. *The Reading Teacher, 42*(1), 30–35.

Slaughter, J. J. (1993). *Beyond storybooks: Young children and the shared book experience*. Newark, DE: International Reading Association.

Slavin, R. E. (1987). Ability grouping and student achievement in elementary schools: A best-evidence synthesis. *Review of Educational Research, 57*(3), 293–336.

Slavin, R. E. (1988). Cooperative learning and student achievement. *Educational Leadership, 45*, 31–33.

Slavin, R. E. (1991). Are cooperative learning and "untracking" harmful to the gifted? *Education Leadership, 48*(6), 68–71.

Slavin, R. E. (1995). *Cooperative learning: Theory, research, and practice*. Needham Heights, MA: Allyn & Bacon.

Slavin, R. E., & Madden, N. (1995). Effects of success for all on the achievement of English language learners. Paper presented at the annual meeting of the American Educational Research Association, San Francisco, CA, April, 1995.

Slavin, R. E., Madden, N. A., Karweit, N. L., Livermon, B. J., & Dolan, L. (1990). Success for all: First-year outcomes of a comprehensive

plan for reforming urban education. *American Educational Research Journal, 27,* 255–278.

Slavin, R. E., Madden, N. L., Dolan, L., & Wasik, B. A. (1996). *Every child, every school: Success for all*. Thousand Oaks, CA: Corwin.

Slavin, R. E., Madden, N. L., Karweit, N. L., Dolan, L., & Wasik, B. A. (1992). *Success for all: A relentless approach to prevention and early intervention in elementary schools*. Arlington, VA: Educational Research Services.

Slosson, R. L. (1971). *Slosson intelligence test*. East Aurora, NY: Slosson Educational Publications.

Sloyer, S. (1982). *Reader's theater: Story dramatization in the classroom*. Urbana, IL: National Council of Teachers of English.

Smith, D. E. P. (1967). *Learning to learn*. New York: Harcourt Brace.

Smith, E. B., Goodman, K. S., & Meredith, R. (1976). *Language and thinking in school* (2nd ed.). New York: Holt, Rinehart and Winston.

Smith, F. (1977). The uses of language. *Language Arts, 54*(6), 638–644.

Smith, F. (1983). *Essays into literacy*. Exeter, NH: Heinemann.

Smith, F. (1985). *Reading without nonsense* (2nd ed.). New York: Teachers College Press.

Smith, F. (1987). *Insult to intelligence*. New York: Arbor House.

Smith, F. (1988). *Understanding reading* (4th ed.). Hillsdale, NJ: Erlbaum.

Smith, K. A. (1989). *A checkup with the doctor*. New York: McDougal, Littell.

Smith, M. W. & Dickinson, D. K. (2002). *Early language and literacy classroom observation (ELLCO)*. Baltimore, MD: Paul H. Brookes.

Smith, M. W., Dickinson, D. K., Sangeorge, A., & Anastasopoulos, L. (2002). *Early language and literacy classroom observation (ELLCO) toolkit*. Baltimore, MD: Paul H. Brookes.

Smith, N. B. (1965). *American reading instruction*. Newark, DE: International Reading Association.

Smith, N. B. (1986). *American reading instruction*. Newark, DE: International Reading Association.

Smith, N. B. (2002). *American reading instruction—special edition*. Newark, DE: International Reading Association.

Smith, P. G. (2001). *Talking classrooms: Shaping children's learning through oral language instruction*. Newark, DE: International Reading Association.

Smith, R. B. (1981). *Jelly belly*. New York: Dell.

Smolkin, L. B., & Donovan, C. A. (2000). *The contexts of comprehension: Information book read alouds and comprehension acquisition*. (CIERA Report #2-009). Ann Arbor, MI: Center for the Improvement of Early Reading Achievement.

Smoot, R. C., & Price, J. (1975). *Chemistry, a modern course*. Upper Saddle River, NJ: Merrill/Prentice-Hall.

Snow, C. (1999). *Preventing reading difficulties*. Keynote address at the Second Annual Commissioner's Reading Day, Austin, TX.

Snow, C. E., Burns, M. N., & Griffin, P. (1998). *Preventing reading difficulties in young children*. Washington: National Academy Press.

Snow, C. E., Griffin, P., & Burns, M. S. (2005). *Knowledge to support the teaching of reading: Preparing teachers for a changing world*. San Francisco, CA: Jossey-Bass.

Snow, C. E., Scarborough, H. S., & Burns, M. S. (1999). What speech-language pathologists need to know about early reading. *Topics in Language Disorders, 20*(1), 48–58.

Snowball, D., & Bolton, F. (1999). *Spelling K–8: Planning and teaching*. York, ME: Stenhouse.

Soto, G. (1993). *Local news*. San Diego, CA: Harcourt Brace.

Spache, G., & Spache, E. (1977). *Reading in the elementary school* (4th ed.). Boston: Allyn & Bacon.

Spady, W., & Marshall, K. J. (1991). Beyond traditional outcome-based education. *Educational Leadership, 48,* 67–72.

Spangler, K. L. (1983). Reading interests vs. reading preferences: Using the research. *The Reading Teacher, 36*(9), 876–878.

Speare, E. G. (1958). *The witch of Blackbird Pond.* New York: Dell.

Sperry, A. (1940). *Call it courage.* New York: Macmillan.

Spiegel, D. L. (1981). Six alternatives to the directed reading activity. *The Reading Teacher, 34,* 914–922.

Spiegel, D. L. (1999). The perspective of the balanced approach. In S. M. Blair-Larsen & K. A. Williams (Eds.), *The balanced reading program: Helping all students achieve success* (pp. 8–23). Newark, DE: International Reading Association.

Spier, P. (1977). *Noah's ark.* Garden City, NY: Doubleday.

Spinelli, J. (1991). Catching Maniac Magee. *The Reading Teacher, 45*(3), 174–176.

Spivak, M. (1973). Archetypal place. *Architectural Forum, 140,* 44–49.

Squire, J. R. (1983). Composing and comprehending: Two sides of the same basic process. *Language Arts, 60*(5), 581–589.

Squire, J. R. (1989). A reading program for all seasons. *Theory into Practice, 28*(4), 254–257.

St. John, E. P., & Loescher, S. A. (2001). *Improving early reading: A resource guide for elementary schools.* Bloomington, IN: Indiana Education Policy Center.

St. Pierre, R. G., Gamse, B., Alamprese, J., Rimdzius, T., & Tao, F. (1998). *National evaluation of the Even Start family literacy program: Evidence from the past and a look to the future.* Washington, DC: U.S. Department of Education Planning and Evaluation Service.

Stage, S., Sheppard, J., Davidson, M. M., & Browning, M. M. (2001). Prediction of first-graders' growth in oral reading fluency using kindergarten letter fluency. *Journal of School Psychology, 39*(3), 225–237.

Stahl, K. (2004). Proof, practice, and promise: Comprehension strategy instruction in the primary grades. *The Reading Teacher, 57*(7), 598–609.

Stahl, K. A., & McKenna, M. C. (2006). *Reading research at work: Foundations of effective practice.* New York: Guilford Press.

Stahl, S. (2004). What do we do about fluency? In P. McCardle & V. Chhabra (Eds.), *The voice of evidence in reading research* (pp. 187–211). Baltimore: MD: Paul H. Brookes.

Stahl, S. A. (1986). Three principles of effective vocabulary instruction. *Journal of Reading, 29*(7), 662–668.

Stahl, S. A., Bradley, B., Smith, C. H., Kuhn, M. R., Schwanenglugel, P., Meisinger, E., et al. (2003). *Teaching children to become fluent and automatic readers.* Paper presented at the annual meeting of the American Educational Research Association, Chicago.

Stahl, S. A., & Fairbanks, M. M. (1986). The effects of vocabulary instruction: A model-based meta-analysis. *Review of Educational Research, 56*(1), 72–110.

Stahl, S. A., Hare, V. C., Sinatra, R., & Gregory, J. F. (1991). Defining the role of prior knowledge and vocabulary in reading comprehension: The retiring of number 41. *Journal of Reading Behavior, 23*(4), 487–507.

Stahl, S. A., Heuback, K., & Cramond, B. (1997). *Fluency-oriented reading instruction.* Athens, GA and Washington, D.C.: National Reading Research Center and U.S. Department of Education, Office of Educational Research and Improvement, Educational Resources Information Center.

Stahl, S. A., Heubach, K., & Cramond, B. (1997). *Fluency-oriented reading instruction* (Reading Research Report No. 79) Athens, GA: National Reading Research Center.

Stahl, S. A., & Jacobson, M. G. (1986). Vocabulary difficulty, prior knowledge, and text comprehension. *Journal of Reading Behavior, 18*(4), 309–319.

Stahl, S. A., & Kapinus, B. (2001). *Word power: What every educator needs to know about teaching vocabulary.* Washington, DC: National Education Association.

Stahl, S. A., & Miller, P. D. (1989). Whole language and language experience approaches for beginning reading: A quantitative research synthesis. *Review of Educational Research, 59,* 87–116.

Stahl, S. A., & Murray, B. A. (1993). Environmental print, phonemic awareness, letter recognition, and word recognition. In D. J. Leu & C. I. Kinzer (Eds.), *Examining central issues in literacy research, theory, and practice* (pp. 227–233). Chicago: National Reading Conference.

Stahl, S. A., & Nagy, W. E. (2006). *Teaching word meaning.* Mahwah, NJ: Lawrence Erlbaum Associates.

Standard for the English Language Arts. (1996). A project of The International Reading Association and National Council of Teachers of English. Newark, DE: International Reading Association.

Stanovich, E., & West, R. F. (1989). Exposure to print and orthographic processing. *Reading Research Quarterly, 24,* 402–433.

Stanovich, K. (1980). Toward an interactive-compensatory model of individual differences in the development of reading fluency. *Reading Research Quarterly, 16*(1), 37–71.

Stanovich, P. J., & Stanovich, K. E. (2003). *Using research and reason in education: How teachers can use scientifically-based research to make curricular and instructional decisions.* Washington, DC: National Institute for Literacy.

Stauffer, R. G. (1969). *Directing reading maturity as a cognitive process.* New York: HarperCollins.

Stauffer, R. G. (1975). *Directing the reading-thinking process.* New York: HarperCollins.

Stayter, F., & Allington, R. (1991). Fluency and the understanding of texts. *Theory Into Practice, 30*(3), 143–148.

Stead, T. (2001). *Is that a fact? Teaching nonfiction writing K–3.* Portland, ME: Stenhouse.

Stead, T. (2006). *The use of non-fiction informational text in developing comprehension.* Presentation at the Texas State Reading Association Annual Conference, November 11, 2006.

Stedman, L. C., & Kaestle, C. E. (1987). Literacy and reading performance in the United States from 1880 to the present. *Reading Research Quarterly, 22,* 8–46.

Steele, W. O. (1958). *The perilous road.* Orlando, FL: Harcourt Brace.

Stein, M. (1993). *The beginning reading instruction study.* Syracuse, NY: Educational Resources Information Center (ERIC) Document Reproduction Service.

Stein, N. L., & Glenn, C. G. (1979). An analysis of story comprehension in elementary school children. In R. O. Freedle (Ed.), *New directions in discourse processing* (pp. 53–120). Hillsdale, NJ: Erlbaum.

Steinbeck, J. (1937). *The red pony.* New York: Bantam Books.

Stenner, A. J. (1996). *Measuring reading comprehension with the Lexile framework.* Washington, DC: Paper presented at the 4th North American Conference on Adolescent/Adult Literacy.

Stenner, A. J., & Burdick, D. S. (1997). *The objective measurement of reading comprehension.* Durham, NC: MetaMetrics.

Steptoe, J. (1987). *Mufaro's beautiful daughters: An African tale.* New York: Lothrop, Lee, & Shepard Books.

Stern, D. N., & Wasserman, G. A. (1979). *Maternal language to infants*. Paper presented at a meeting of the Society for Research in Child Development. Ann Arbor, MI.

Stevens, R., & Rosenshine, B. (1981). Advances in research on teaching. *Exceptional Education Quarterly, 2,* 1–9.

Stevens, R. J., Madden, N. A., Slavin, R. E., & Farnish, A. (1987a). *Cooperative integrated reading and composition: A brief overview of the CIRC program*. Baltimore, MD: Johns Hopkins University, Center for Research on Elementary and Middle Schools.

Stevens, R. J., Madden, N. A., Slavin, R. E., & Farnish, A. M. (1987b). Cooperative integrated reading and composition: Two field experiments. *Reading Research Quarterly, 22*(4), 433–454.

Stevens, R. J., & Slavin, R. E. (1995). Effects of a cooperative learning approach in reading and writing on academically handicapped and nonhandicapped students. *Elementary School Journal, 95*(3), 241–262.

Stolz, M. (1963). *Bully on Barkham Street*. New York: HarperCollins.

Stoodt, B. D. (1989). *Reading instruction*. New York: HarperCollins.

Straub, S. B. (2003). Read to me: A family literacy program for young mothers and their babies. In A. DeBruin-Parecki & B. Krol-Sinclair (Eds.), *Family literacy: From theory to practice* (pp. 184–201). Newark, DE: International Reading Association.

Straub, S. B., & DeBruin-Parecki, A. (2002, May). *Read to me: A unique high school program linking teenage mothers, their babies, and books*. Paper presented at the 47th Annual Convention of the International Reading Association, San Francisco, CA.

Strickland, D. S. (1998). *Teaching phonics today: A primer for educators*. Newark, DE: International Reading Association.

Strickland, D. S., Feeley, J. T., & Wepner, S. B. (1987). *Using computers in the teaching of reading*. New York: Teachers College Press.

Strickland, D. S., Snow, C., Griffin, P., Burns, M. S., & McNamara, P. (2002). *Preparing our teachers: Opportunities for better reading instruction*. Washington, DC: John Henry Press.

Sucher, F., & Allred, R. A. (1986). *Sucher-Allred group reading placement test*. Oklahoma City: Economy.

Sukhomlinsky, V. (1981). *To children I give my heart*. Moscow, USSR: Progress.

Sulzby, E. (1985). Children's emergent reading of favorite storybooks: A developmental study. *Reading Research Quarterly, 20*(4), 458–481.

Sulzby, E. (1991). Assessment of emergent literacy: Storybook reading. *The Reading Teacher, 44*(7), 498–500.

Sulzby, E., Hoffman, J., Niles, J., Shanahan, T., & Teale, W. (1989). *McGraw-Hill reading*. New York: McGraw-Hill.

Sunburst. (1987). *The puzzler*. Pleasantville, NY: Sunburst Communications.

Swafford, J. (1995). I wish all my groups were like this one: Facilitating peer interaction during group work. *Journal of Reading, 38*(8), 626–631.

Sweet, A. (1997). Teacher perceptions of student motivation and their relation to literacy learning. In J. T. Guthrie & A. Wigfield (Eds.), *Reading engagement: Motivating readers through integrated instruction*. Newark, DE: International Reading Association.

Sweet, A. P., & Snow, C. E. (2003). *Rethinking reading comprehension*. New York: Guilford Press.

Szymusiak, K., & Sibberson, F. (2001). *Beyond leveled books: Supporting transitional readers in grades 2–5*. Portland, ME: Stenhouse.

Taba, H. (1975). *Teacher's handbook for elementary social studies*. Reading, MA: Addison-Wesley.

Tarver, S. G., & Dawson, M. M. (1978). Modality preference and the teaching of reading: A review. *Journal of Learning Disabilities, 11*(1), 5–17.

Taxel, J. (1993). The politics of children's literature: Reflections on multiculturalism and Christopher Columbus. In V. J. Harris (Ed.), *Teaching multicultural literature in grades K–8* (pp. 1–36). Norwood, MA: Christopher Gordon.

Taylor, B., Harris, L. A., & Pearson, P. D. (1988). *Reading difficulties: Instruction and assessment*. New York: Random House.

Taylor, B. M., & Pearson, P. D. (2002). *Teaching reading: Effective schools, accomplished teachers*. Mahwah, NJ: Lawrence Erlbaum Associates.

Taylor, B. M., Frye, B. J., & Gaetz, T. M. (1990). Reducing the number of reading skill activities in the elementary classroom. *Journal of Reading Behavior, 22*(2), 167–180.

Taylor, B. M., Graves, M. F., & Van den Broek, P. (2000). *Reading for meaning: Fostering comprehension in the middle grades*. New York: Teachers College Press.

Taylor, B. M., Pearson, P. D., & Clark, K. (2000). Effective schools and accomplished teachers: Lessons about primary-grade reading instruction in low-income schools. *Elementary School Journal, 101*(2), 121–165.

Taylor, B. M., Pearson, P. D., Clark, K. E., & Walpole, S. (1999). *Beating the odds in teaching all children to read* (Ciera Report No.2–006). Ann Arbor, MI: Center for the Improvement of Early Reading Achievement.

Taylor, B. M., Pearson, P. D., Clark, K. F., & Walpole, S. (2000). Effective schools and accomplished teachers: Lessons about primary grade reading instruction in low-income schools. *Elementary School Journal, 101,* 121–165.

Taylor, B. M. Pearson, P. D., Peterson, D. S., & Rodriguez, M. C. (2005). The CIERA School Change Framework: An evidence-based approach to professional development and school reading improvement. *Reading Research Quarterly, 40*(1), 40–69.

Taylor, D. (1983). *Family literacy: Young children learning to read and write*. Portsmouth, NH: Heinemann.

Taylor, D., & Strickland, D. S. (1986). *Family storybook reading*. Portsmouth, NH: Heinemann.

Taylor, G. C. (1981). ERIC/RCS report: Music in language arts instruction. *Language Arts, 58,* 363–368.

Taylor, M. D. (1990). *Road to Memphis*. New York: Dial Books.

Taylor, N. E. (1986). Developing beginning literacy concepts: Content and context. In D. B. Yaden, Jr., & S. Templeton (Eds.), *Metalinguistic awareness and beginning literacy* (pp. 173–184). Portsmouth, NH: Heinemann.

Taylor, N. E., Blum, I. H., & Logsdon, M. (1986). The development of written language awareness: Environmental aspects and program characteristics. *Reading Research Quarterly, 21*(2), 132–149.

Taylor, W. L. (1953). Cloze procedure: A new tool for measuring readability. *Journalism Quarterly, 30,* 415–433.

Teale, W. H. (1987). Emergent literacy: Reading and writing development in early childhood. In J. E. Readence, R. S. Baldwin, J. P. Konopak, & H. Newton (Eds.), *Research in literacy: Merging perspectives* (pp. 45–74). Rochester, NY: National Reading Conference.

Teale, W. H., & Martinez, M. (1986a). Reading in a kindergarten classroom library. *The Reading Teacher, 41*(6), 568–573.

Teale, W. H., & Martinez, M. (1986b). *Teachers reading to their students: Differing styles, different effects?* ERIC Document Reproduction Service.

Teale, W. H., & Sulzby, E. (1986). *Emergent literacy: Writing and reading*. Norwood, NJ: Ablex.

Temple, C., & Gillet, J. (1996). *Language and literacy: A lively approach*. New York: HarperCollins.

Temple, C., Nathan, R., Burris, N., & Temple, F. (1993). *The beginnings of writing* (3rd ed.). Newton, MA: Allyn & Bacon.

Templeton, S. (1995). *Children's literacy: Contexts for meaningful learning*. Princeton, NJ: Houghton Mifflin.

Texas Education Agency. (2003–2004). *Texas primary reading inventory* (TPRI). Austin, TX: Author. Available online, in both English and Spanish, at Reading Initiative at *http://www.tea.state.tx.us/reading/*

Thaler, M. (1989). *The teacher from the Black Lagoon*. New York: Scholastic.

Tharp, R. (1982). The effective instruction of comprehension: Results and description of the Kamehameha Early Education Program. *Reading Research Quarterly, 17*(4), 503–527.

Tharpe, R. G., & Gallimore, R. (1988). *Rousing minds to life*. Cambridge, MA: Cambridge University Press.

Thelen, J. N. (1984). *Improving reading in science*. Newark, DE: International Reading Association.

Thomas, D. G., & Readence, J. E. (1988). Effects of differential vocabulary instruction and lesson frameworks on the reading comprehension of primary children. *Reading Research and Instruction, 28*, 1–13.

Thompson, R. (1997). The philosophy of balanced reading instruction. *The Journal of Balanced Reading Instruction, 4*(D1), 28–29.

Thorndike, E. L., & Lorge, I. (1944). *Thorndike-Lorge magazine count: Entries from* The teacher's word book of 30,000. New York: Columbia University.

Thorndike, R. L. (1973). *Reading comprehension education in fifteen countries: An empirical study*. New York: Wiley.

Thorndyke, P. N. (1977). Cognitive structure in comprehension and memory of narrative discourse. *Cognitive Psychology, 9*(1), 77–110.

Tierney, R. J. (1992). Setting a new agenda for assessment. *Learning, 21*(2), 61–64.

Tierney, R. J., Carter, M. A., & Desai, L. E. (1991). *Portfolio assessment in the reading-writing classroom*. Norwood, MA: Christopher-Gordon.

Tierney, R. J., & Cunningham, J. W. (1984). Research on teaching reading comprehension. In P. D. Pear-son (Ed.), *Reading research handbook* (pp. 609–656). New York: Longman.

Tierney, R. J., & Pearson, P. D. (1983). Toward a composing model of reading. *Language Arts, 60*(5), 568–580.

Tierney, R. J., Readence, J. E., & Dishner, E. K. (1985). *Reading strategies and practices: A compendium* (2nd ed.). Boston: Allyn & Bacon.

Tierney, R. J., & Shanahan, T. (1991). Research on the reading-writing relationship: Interactions, transactions, and outcomes. In R. Barr, M. L. Kamil, P. Mosenthal, & P. D. Pearson (Eds.), *Handbook of reading research* (Vol. II). New York: Longman, Inc.

Tierney, R. J., & Shanahan, T. (1996). Research on the reading-writing relationship: Interactions, transactions, and outcomes. In R. Barr, M. L. Kamil, P. Mosenthal, & P. D. Pearson (Eds.), *Handbook of reading research* (Vol. 2, pp. 246–280). Mahwah, NJ: Erlbaum.

Tindal, G., Martson, D., & Deno, S. L. (1983). *The reliability of direct and repeated measurement*. (Research Rep. No. 109).

Minneapolis: University of Minnesota Institute for Research on Learning Disabilities.

Tomasello, M. (1996). Piagetian and Vygotskian approaches to language acquisition. *Human Development, 39*, 269–276.

Tomlinson, C. A. (1999). *The differentiated classroom: Responding to the needs of all learners*. Alexandria, VA: Association for Supervision and Curriculum Development.

Tomlinson, C. A. (2001). *How to differentiate instruction in mixed-ability classrooms* (2nd ed.). Alexandria, VA: Association for Supervision and Curriculum Development.

Tompkins, G. (2006). *Literacy for the 21st century: A balanced approach*. Upper Saddle River, NJ: Merrill Prentice-Hall.

Tompkins, G. E. (1998). *Language arts: Content and teaching strategies* (4th ed.). Upper Saddle River, NJ: Merrill Prentice-Hall.

Tompkins, G. E. (2000). *Teaching writing: Balancing process and product* (3rd ed.). Upper Saddle River, NJ: Merrill/Prentice-Hall.

Tompkins, G. E. (2003). *Literacy for the 21st Century*, 3rd Ed. Upper Saddle River, NJ: Merrill/Prentice-Hall.

Tompkins, G. E. (2004). *Teaching writing: Balancing process and product* (4th ed.). Upper Saddle River, NJ: Merrill Prentice-Hall Pearson.

Tompkins, G. E. (2005). *Language arts essentials*. Upper Saddle River, NJ: Merrill Prentice-Hall.

Tompkins, G. E. (2006). *Literacy for the 21st century: A balanced approach*. Upper Saddle River, NJ: Merrill Prentice-Hall.

Tompkins, G. E., & Hoskisson, K. (1995). *Language arts: Content and teaching strategies* (3rd ed.). Upper Saddle River, NJ: Merrill/Prentice-Hall.

Topping, K. (1989). Peer tutoring and paired reading: Combining two powerful techniques. *The Reading Teacher, 42*, 488–494.

Torgesen, Wagner, Rashotte, Alexander, & Conroy, 1997. Prevention and remediation of severe reading disabilities: Keeping the end in mind. *Scientific Studies of Reading, 1*(3), 217–234.

Torrey, J. W. (1979). Reading that comes naturally. In G. Waller & G. E. MacKinnon (Eds.), *Reading research: Advance in theory and practice*, Vol. 1, (pp. 115–144). New York: Academic Press.

Tovey, D. R., & Kerber, J. E. (Eds.) (1986). *Roles in literacy learning*. Newark, DE: International Reading Association.

Towers, J. M. (1992). Outcome-based education: Another educational bandwagon. *Educational Forum, 56*(3), 291–305.

Towle, (1993). *The real McCoy: The life of an African American inventor*. New York: Scholastic.

Town, S., & Holbrook, N. M. (1857). *Progressive Primer*. Boston: Carter, Bazin & Company.

Trabasso, T. (1980). *On the making of inferences during reading and their assessment*. (Tech. Rep. No. 157). Urbana-Champaign: University of Illinois, Center for the Study of Reading.

Tracey, D. H., & Morrow, L. M. (2006). *Lenses on reading: An introduction to theories and models*. New York: Guilford Press.

Treiman, R. (1985). Onsets and rimes as units of spoken syllables: Evidence from children. *Journal of Experimental Child Psychology, 39*, 161–181.

Trelease, J. (1995). *The new read-aloud handbook* (4th ed.). New York: Penguin.

Tunnell, M. O., & Jacobs, J. S. (1989). Using "real" books: Research findings on literature based reading instruction. *The Reading Teacher, 42*, 470–477.

Turner, J., & Paris, S. (1995). How literacy tasks influence children's motivation for literacy. *The Reading Teacher, 48*(8), 662–673.

Tutolo, D. (1977). The study guide: Types, purpose and value. *Journal of Reading, 20,* 503–507.

Tyner, B. (2004). *Small-group reading instruction: A differentiated teaching model for beginning and struggling readers.* Newark, DE: International Reading Association.

U.S. Bureau of Labor. (1995). *Final report: Governor's Council on School-to-Work Transition.* Washington, DC: U.S. Department of Education.

U.S. Department of Education. (1997). *President Clinton's America's Reading Challenge.* Washington, DC: U.S. Department of Education.

U.S. Department of Education. *National Assessment of Educational Progress: The Nation's Report Card Reading 2000.* Washington, DC: U.S. Department of Education, Office of Educational Research and Improvement.

United States and the other Americas, The (Grade 5). (1980). Upper Saddle River, NJ: Merrill/Prentice-Hall.

United States: Its history and neighbors, The (Grade 5). (1985). San Diego. CA: Harcourt Brace.

Unsworth, L. (1984). Meeting individual needs through flexible within-class grouping of pupils. *The Reading Teacher, 38*(3), 298–304.

Vacca, J. L., Vacca, R. T., & Gove, M. K. (1995). *Reading and learning to read* (3rd ed.). Boston: Little, Brown.

Vacca, R. T., & Vacca, J. L. (2001). *Content area reading: Literacy and learning across the curriculum* (7th ed.). New York: Allyn & Bacon.

Vacca, R. T., Vacca, J. L., Gove, M. K., Burkey, L. C., Lenhart, L. A., & McKeon, C. A. (2003). *Reading and learning to read* (5th ed.). Needham Heights, MA: Allyn & Bacon.

Valencia, S. (1990). A portfolio approach to classroom reading assessment: The whys, whats, and hows. *The Reading Teacher, 43*(4), 338–340.

Valencia, S. (1998). *Portfolios in action.* New York: HarperCollins.

Valencia, S., McGinley, W., & Pearson, P. D. (1990). *Assessing reading and writing: Building a more complete picture for middle school assessment* (Tech. Rep. No. 500). Urbana, IL: Center for the Study of Reading. (ERIC Document Reproduction Service).

Valencia, S., & Pearson, P. D. (1987). Reading assessment: Time for a change. *The Reading Teacher, 40*(8), 726–733.

Vallecorsa, A. L., & deBettencourt, L. U. (1997). Using a mapping procedure to teach reading and writing skills to middle grade students with learning disabilities. *Education and the Treatment of Children, 20*(2), 173–188.

Van Allsburg, C. (1985). *The polar express.* Boston: Houghton Mifflin.

Van Allsburg, C. (1987). *The Z was zapped.* Boston: Houghton Mifflin.

Van Dijk, T. A. (1999). *Context models in discourse processing.* Mahwah, NJ: Lawrence Erlbaum Associates.

Van Manen, M. (1986). *The tone of teaching.* Ontario: Scholastic.

Van Meter, P., Aleksic, M., & Schwartz, A. (2006). Learner-generated drawing as a strategy for learning from content area text. *Contemporary Educational Psychology, 31*(2), 142–166.

Varble, M. E. (1990). Analysis of writing samples of students taught by teachers using whole language and traditional approaches. *Journal of Educational Research, 83*(5), 245–251.

Veatch, J. (1968). *How to teach reading with children's books.* New York: Owen.

Veatch, J. (1978). *Reading in the elementary school,* 2nd Ed. New York: Owen.

Veatch, J., & Cooter, R. B., Jr. (1986). The effect of teacher selection on reading achievement. *Language Arts, 63*(4), 364–368.

Vellutino, F. R., & Scanlon D. M. (2002). The Interactive Strategies approach to reading intervention. *Contemporary Educational Psychology, 27*(4), 573–635.

Viorst, J. (1972). *Alexander and the terrible, horrible, no good, very bad day* (R. Cruz, Illustrator). New York: Atheneum.

Viorst, J. (1972). *Alexander and the terrible, horrible, no good, very bad day.* New York: Atheneum.

Viorst, J. (1987). *Alexander and the terrible, horrible, no good, very bad day.* New York: Aladdin.

Voltz, D. L., & Demiano-Lantz, M. (1993, Summer). Developing ownership in learning. *Teaching Exceptional Children,* pp. 18–22.

Vopat, J. (1994). *The parent project: A workshop approach to parent involvement.* York, ME: Stenhouse.

Vopat, J. (1998). *More than bake sales: The resource guide for family involvement in education.* York: ME: Stenhouse.

Vukelich, C. (1994). Effects of play interventions on young children's reading of environmental print. *Early Childhood Research Quarterly, 9*(2), 153–170.

Vygotsky, L. S. (1939). Thought and speech. *Psychiatry, 2,* 29–54.

Vygotsky, L. S. (1962). *Thought and language.* Cambridge, MA: MIT Press.

Vygotsky, L. S. (1978). *Mind in society.* Cambridge, MA: Harvard University Press.

Vygotsky, L. S. (1986). *Thought and language.* Boston: MIT Press.

Vygotsky, L. S. (1990). *Mind in society.* Boston: Harvard University Press.

Wade, S. E., & Moje, E. B. (2000). The role of text in classroom learning. In M. L. Kamil, P. B. Mosenthal, P. D. Pearson, & R. Barr (Eds.), *Handbook of Reading Research,* Vol. 3. Mahwah, NJ: Erlbaum.

Wagner, R., Torgesen, J., & Rashotte, C. (1999). *Comprehensive Test of Phonological Processing (CTOPP).* Circle Pines, MN: AGS.

Walker, B. J. (2004). *Diagnostic teaching of reading: Techniques for instruction and assessment.* Upper Saddle River, NJ: Merrill/Prentice-Hall.

Walker, J. E. (1991, May). *Affect in naturalistic assessment: Implementation and implications.* Paper presented at the 36th annual convention of the International Reading Association, Las Vegas, NV.

Wallach, L., Wallach, M. A., Dozier, M. G., & Kaplan, N. E. (1977). Poor children learning to read do not have trouble with auditory discrimination but do have trouble with phoneme recognition. *Journal of Educational Psychology, 69,* 36–39.

Walley, C. (1993). An invitation to reading fluency. *The Reading Teacher, 46*(6), 526–527.

Walpole, S., & McKenna, M. C. (2004). *The literacy coach's handbook: A guide to research-based practice.* New York: Guilford Press.

Walters, K., & Gunderson, L. (1985). Effects of parent volunteers reading first language (L1) books to ESL students. *The Reading Teacher, 39*(1), 66–69.

Wang, C. X., & Dwyer, F. M. (2006). Instructional effects of three concept mapping strategies in facilitating student achievement. *International Journal of Instructional Media, 33*(2), 135–151.

Wang, M., Haertel, G., & Walberg, H. (1994, December). What helps students learn? *Educational Leadership,* 74–79.

Warren, S. F. (2001). The future of early communication and language intervention. *Topics in Early Childhood Special Education, 20*(1), 33–38.

Warren, S. F., & Yoder, P. J. (1997). Emerging model of communication and language intervention. *Mental Retardation and Developmental Disabilities Research Reviews, 3,* 358–362.

Washington, DC: National Institute of Child Health and Human Development.

Wasik, B. A. (1998). Using volunteers as reading tutors: Guidelines for successful practices. *The Reading Teacher, 51*(7), 562–573.

Watson, D., & Crowley, P. (1988). How can we implement a whole-language approach? In C. Weaver (Ed.), *Reading process and practice* (pp. 232–279). Portsmouth, NH: Heinemann.

Watson, R. (2001). Literacy and oral language: Implications for early literacy acquisition. In S. B. Neuman & D. K. Dickinson (Eds), *Handbook of Early Literacy Research* (pp. 43–53). New York: Guilford Press.

Watson, S. (1976). *No man's land*. New York: Greenwillow.

Watt, M. G. (2005). *Standards-based reforms in the United States of America: An overview*. Online Submission. (ERIC Document Reproduction Service No. ED490562)

Weaver, C. (1994). *Reading process and practice: From socio-psycholinguistics to whole language* (2nd ed.). Portsmouth, NH: Heinemann.

Weaver, C. (1998). *Reconsidering a balanced approach to reading*. Urbana, IL: National Council of Teachers of English.

Weaver, C. A., & Kintsch, W. (1996). Expository text. In R. Barr, M. L. Kamil, P. Mosenthal, & P. D. Pearson (Eds.), *Handbook of reading research, volume II* (pp. 230–245). Mahwah, NJ: Lawrence Erlbaum.

Weaver, C., Chaston, J., & Peterson, S. (1993). *Theme exploration: A voyage of discovery*. Portsmouth, NH: Heinemann.

Webb, K., & Willoughby, N. (1993). An analytic rubric for scoring graphs. *The Texas School Teacher, 22*(3), 14–15.

Webb, M., & Schwartz, W. (1988, October). Children teaching children: A good way to learn. *PTA Today*, 16–17.

Weimans, E. (1981). *Which way courage?* New York: Atheneum.

Weinstein, R. S. (1976). Reading group membership in first grade: Teacher behaviors and pupil experience over time. *Journal of Educational Psychology, 68*, 103–116.

Weintraub, S., & Denny, T. P. (1965). What do beginning first graders say about reading? *Childhood Education, 41*, 326–327.

Wells, R. (1973). *Noisy Nora*. New York: Scholastic.

Wepner, S. B. (1985). Linking logos with print for beginning reading success. *The Reading Teacher, 38*(7), 633–39.

Wepner, S. B. (1990). Holistic computer applications in literature-based classrooms. *The Reading Teacher, 44*(1), 12–19.

Wepner, S. B. (1992). Technology and text sets. *The Reading Teacher, 46*(1), 68–71.

Wepner, S. B. (1993). Technology and thematic units: An elementary example on Japan. *The Reading Teacher, 46*(5), 442–445.

Wepner, S. B., & Feeley, J. T. (1993). *Moving forward with literature: Basals, books, and beyond*. Upper Saddle River, NJ: Merrill/Prentice-Hall.

Wepner, S. B., Feeley, J. T., & Strickland, D. S. (1995). *The administration and supervision of reading programs* (2nd ed.). New York: Teacher's College Columbia Press.

Wepner, S. B., Valmont, W. J., & Thurlow, R. (2000). *Linking literacy and technology: A guide for K–8 classrooms*. Newark, DE: International Reading Association.

Wessells, M. G. (1990). *Computer, self, and society*. Upper Saddle River, NJ: Prentice-Hall.

West, L. S., & Egley, E. H. (1998). Children get more than a hamburger: Using labels and logos to enhance literacy. *Dimensions of Early Childhood, 26*(3–4), 43–46.

Whaley, J. F. (1981). Readers' expectations for story structures. *Reading Research Quarterly, 17*, 90–114.

Wharton-McDonald, R., Pressley, M., Rankin, J., & Mistretta, J. (1997). Effective primary-grades literacy instruction equals balanced literacy instruction. *The Reading Teacher, 6*(50), 518–521.

Wharton-McDonald, R., Pressley, M., Rankin, J., Mistretta, J., Yokoi, L., & Ettenberger, S. (1997). Effective primary-grades literacy instruction = balanced literacy instruction. *The Reading Teacher, 50*(6), 518–521.

Wheatley, E. A., Muller, D. H., & Miller, R. B. (1993). Computer-assisted vocabulary instruction. *Journal of Reading, 37*(2), 92–102.

Whitaker, B. T., Schwartz, E., & Vockell, E. (1989). *The computer in the reading curriculum*. New York: McGraw-Hill.

White, C. S. (1983). Learning style and reading instruction. *The Reading Teacher, 36*, 842–845.

White, E. B. (1952). *Charlotte's web*. New York: HarperCollins.

White, E. B. (1970). *The trumpet of the swan*. New York: Harper-Collins.

Whitehurst, G. J., Arnold, D. S., & Epstein, J. N. (1994). A picture book reading intervention in day care and home for children from low income families. *Developmental Psychology, 30*, 679–689.

Whitehurst, G. J., Falco, F. L., & Lonigan, C. J. (1988). Accelerating language development through picture book reading. *Developmental Psychology, 24*, 552–559.

Wiener, R. B., & Cohen, J. H. (1997). *Literacy portfolios: Using assessment to guide instruction*. Upper Saddle River, NJ: Merrill/Prentice-Hall.

Wiesendanger, W. D. (1986). Durkin revisited. *Reading Horizons, 26*, 89–97.

Wigfield, A. (1997). Motivations, beliefs, and self-efficacy in literacy development. In J. T. Guthrie & A. Wigfield (Eds.), *Reading engagement: Motivating readers through integrated instruction*. Newark, DE: International Reading Association.

Wigfield, A. (1997b). Children's motivations for reading and reading engagement. In J. T. Guthrie and A. Wigfield (Eds.), *Reading engagement: Motivating reading through integrated instruction* (pp. 14–33). Newark, DE: International Reading Association.

Wigfield, A. (2000). Facilitating children's reading motivation. In L. Baker, M. J. Dreher, and J. T. Guthrie (Eds.), *Engaging young readers: Promoting achievement and motivation* (pp. 140–158). New York: Guilford Press.

Wigfield, A., & Guthrie, J. T. (1997). Relations of children's motivation for reading to the amount and breadth of their reading. *Journal of Educational Psychology, 89*, 420–432.

Wiggins, R. A. (1994). Large group lesson/small group follow-up: Flexible grouping in a basal reading program. *The Reading Teacher, 47*(6), 450–460.

Wiig, E. H., Becker-Redding, U., & Semel, E. M. (1983). A cross-cultural comparison of language abilities of 7-to 8- and 12-to-13-year-old children with learning disabilities. *Journal of Learning Disabilities, 16*(10) 576–585.

Wilde, S. (1997). *What's a schwa sound anyway?* Portsmouth, NH: Heinemann Educational Books.

Williams, J. P. (2005). Instruction in reading comprehension for primary-grade students: A focus on text structure. *Journal of Special Education, 39*(1), 6–18.

Williams, J. P., Brown, L. G., Silverstein, A. K., & deCari, J. S. (1994). An instructional program in comprehension of narrative themes for adolescents with learning disabilities. *Learning Disability Quarterly, 17*, 205–221.

Willman, A. T. (2000). "Hello, Mrs. Willman, it's me!: Keep kids reading over the summer by using voice mail." In T. V. Rasinski,

N. D. Padak, et al. (Eds.), *Motivating recreational reading and promoting home-school connections* (pp. 51–52). Newark, DE: International Reading Association.

Wilson, R. M., & Gambrell, L. B. (1988). *Reading comprehension in the elementary school.* Boston: Allyn & Bacon.

Wilson, R. M., Hall, M. A., Leu, D. J., & Kinzer, C. K. (2001). *Phonics, phonemic awareness, and word analysis for teachers: An interactive tutorial* (7th ed.). Upper Saddle River, NJ: Prentice-Hall.

Winograd, P. (1989). Improving basal reading instruction: Beyond the carrot and the stick. *Theory Into Practice, 28*(4), 240–247.

Winograd, P. N. (1989). Introduction: Understanding reading instruction. In P. N. Winograd, K. K. Wixson, & M. Y. Lipson (Eds.). *Improving basal reader instruction* (pp. 1–20). New York: Teachers College Press.

Winograd, P. N., Paris, S., & Bridge, C. (1991). Improving the assessment of literacy. *The Reading Teacher, 45*(2), 108–116.

Winograd, P. N., Wixson, K. K., & Lipson, M. Y. (Eds.). (1989). *Improving basal reader instruction.* New York: Teachers College Press.

Wiseman, D. L. (1992). *Learning to read with literature.* Boston: Allyn & Bacon.

Wittrock, M. C. (1974). Learning as a generative process. *Educational Psychologist, 11,* 87–95.

Wixson, K. K., Peters, C. W., Weber, E. M., & Roeber, E. D. (1987). New directions in statewide reading assessment. *The Reading Teacher, 40*(8), 749–755.

Wolf, M., & Katzir-Cohen, T. (2001). Reading fluency and its intervention. *Scientific Studies of Reading, 5*(3), 211–229.

Wolfersberger, M., Reutzel, D. R., Sudweeks, R., & Fawson, P. F. (2004). Developing and validating the Classroom Literacy Environmental Profile (CLEP): A tool for examining the "print richness" of elementary classrooms. *Journal of Literacy Research, 36*(2), 211–272.

Wong, H., & Wong, R. (1998). *The first days of school: How to be an effective teacher.* Mountain View, CA: Harry K. Wong.

Wong, H. K., & Wong, R. (1998). *The first days of school: How to be an effective teacher.* Mountain View, CA: Harry K. Wong.

Wong, J. W., & Au, K. H. (1985). The concept-text-application approach: Helping elementary students comprehend expository text. *The Reading Teacher, 38*(7), 612–618.

Wood, A. (1984). *The napping house* (Don Wood, Illustrator). San Diego, CA: Harcourt Brace.

Wood, A. (1990). *Weird parents.* New York: Dial Books for Young Readers.

Wood, A., & Wood, D. (1988). *Elbert's bad word.* New York: Harcourt, Brace, & Jovanovich.

Wood, E., Pressley, M., & Winne, P. H. (1990). Elaborative interrogation effects on children's learning of factual content. *Journal of Educational Psychology, 82,* 741–48.

Wood, K. D. (1983). A variation on an old theme: 4-way oral reading. *The Reading Teacher, 37*(1), 38–41.

Wood, K. D. (1987). Fostering cooperative learning in middle and secondary level classrooms. *Journal of Reading, 31,* 10–18.

Woodcock, R., Mather, N., & Barnes, E. K. (1987). *Woodcock reading mastery tests–revised.* Circle Pines, MN: American Guidance Service.

Woodcock, R. W. (1997). *Woodcock Reading Mastery Tests–Revised (WRMT–R).* Circle Pines, MN: AGS.

Woodcock, R. W., & Muñoz-Sandoval, A. F. (1993). *Woodcock-Muñoz language survey* (WMLS), English and Spanish forms. Chicago: Riverside.

Worby, D. Z. (1980). *An honorable seduction: Thematic studies in literature.* Arlington, VA: ERIC Document Reproduction Service. (ERIC Document Reproduction Service).

Worthy, J., & Broaddus, K. (2002). Fluency beyond the primary grades: From group performance to silent, independent reading. *The Reading Teacher, 55*(4), 334–343.

Worthy, J., Moorman, M., & Turner, M. (1999). What Johnny likes to read is hard to find in school. *Reading Research Quarterly, 34*(1), 12–27.

Yaden, D. B., Jr. (1982). A multivariate analysis of first graders' print awareness as related to reading achievement, intelligence, and gender. *Dissertation Abstracts International, 43,* 1912A. (University Microfilms No. 82–25, 520)

Yaden, D. B., Jr., & S. Templeton (Eds.). (1986). *Reading research in metalinguistic awareness: A classification of findings according to focus and methodology.* Portsmouth, NH: Heinemann Educational Books.

Yashima, T. (1983). *Crow boy.* New York: Viking.

Yeh, S. (2003). An evaluation of two approaches for teaching phonemic awareness to children in Head Start. *Early Childhood Research Quarterly, 18*(1), 511–529.

Yellin, D., & Blake, M. E. (1994). *Integrating language arts: A holistic approach.* New York: HarperCollins.

Yep, L. (1989). *The rainbow people.* New York: HarperCollins.

Ylisto, I. P. (1967). An empirical investigation of early reading responses of young children (doctoral dissertation, The University of Michigan, 1967). *Dissertation Abstracts International, 28,* 2153A. (University Microfilms No. 67–15, 728).

Yolen, J. (1976). *An invitation to a butterfly ball: A counting rhyme.* New York: Philomel.

Yolen, J. (1988). *The devil's arithmetic.* New York: Viking Kestrel.

Yopp, H. K. (1988). The validity and reliability of phonemic awareness tests. *Reading Research Quarterly, 23,* 159–177.

Yopp, H. K. (1992). Developing phonemic awareness in young children. *The Reading Teacher, 45*(9), 696–703.

Yopp, H. K., & Troyer, S. (1992). *Training phonemic awareness in young children.* Unpublished manuscript.

Yopp, R. H., & Yopp, H. K. (2000). *Literature-based reading activities* (3rd Ed.). New York: Allyn & Bacon.

Young, E. (1989). *Lon Po Po.* New York: Philomel Books.

Young, T. A., & Vardell, S. (1993). Weaving readers theatre and nonfiction into the curriculum. *The Reading Teacher, 46,* 396–406.

Zahar, R., Cobb, T., & Sapda, N. (2001). Acquiring vocabulary through reading: Effects of frequency and contextual richness. *Canadian Modern Language Review, 57*(4), 541–572.

Zarillo, J. (1989). Teachers' interpretations of literature-based reading. *The Reading Teacher, 43*(1), 22–29.

Zemelman, S., Daniels, H., & Hyde, A. (1993). *Best practice: New standards for teaching and learning in America's schools.* Portsmouth, NH: Heinemann.

Zeno, S. M., Ivens, S. H., Millard, R. T., & Duvvuri, R. (1995). *The educator's word guide.* New York: Touchstone Applied Science Associates, Inc.

Zentall, S. S. (1993). Research on the educational implications of attention deficit hyperactivity disorder. *Exceptional Children, 60*(2), 143–153.

Zintz, M. V., & Maggart, Z. R. (1989). *The reading process: The teacher and the learner.* Dubuque, IA: William C. Brown.

Zlatos, B. (1993). Outcomes-based outrage. *Executive Educator, 15*(9), 12–16.

Zutell, J., & Rasinski, T. (1991). Training teachers to attend to their students' oral reading fluency. *Theory Into Practice, 30*(3), 211–217.

Zuzovsky, R., & Libman, Z. (2006). Standards of teaching and teaching tests: Is this the right way to go? *Studies in Educational Evaluation, 32*(1), 37–52.

Zwann, R. A. (1999). Embodied cognition, perceptual symbols, and situated cognition. *Discourse Processes, 28*(1), 81–88.

NAME INDEX

SUBJECT INDEX

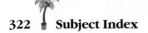

D. Ray Reutzel

D. Ray Reutzel is the Emma Eccles Jones Distinguished Professor and Endowed Chair of Early Childhood Education at Utah State University. Ray is a former Provost and Vice President for Academic Affairs at Southern Utah University; Associate Dean of Teacher Education in the David O. McKay School of Education; and former Chair of the Department of Elementary Education at Brigham Young University. While at BYU, he was the recipient of the 1992 Karl G. Maeser Distinguished Research and Creative Arts Professor Award and was an integral part of developing BYU's nationally celebrated Public School Partnership, the field-based Elementary Education program, the Center for Improvement of Teacher Education and Schooling (CITES) and the Utah/CITES Balanced Literacy initiative as a part of the U.S. and Utah's Goals 2000 funding. He has served as technical assistant to the Reading Excellence Act and the Reading First federal reading reform projects in the state of Utah. Several years ago, he took a leave from his university faculty position to return to full-time, first-grade classroom teaching in Sage Creek Elementary School. Ray has taught in Kindergarten, 1st grade, 3rd grade, and 6th grade.

Dr. Reutzel is the author of more than 165 refereed research reports, articles, books, book chapters, and monographs published in *Early Childhood Research Quarterly, Reading Research Quarterly, Journal of Literacy Research, Journal of Educational Research, Reading Psychology, Reading Research and Instruction, Language Arts, Journal of Adolescent and Adult Literacy,* and *The Reading Teacher,* among others. He has received more than $5.5 million in research/professional development funding from private, state, and federal funding agencies. He was recently awarded a $1 million research grant as principal investigator under the Teacher Quality Research Program of the Institute of Education Sciences, U.S. Department of Education.

He is the past editor of *Reading Research and Instruction,* the journal of the College Reading Association. He is co-author, with Robert B. Cooter, Jr., of *The Essentials for Teaching Children to Read,* First Edition, *Teaching Children to Read: The Teacher Makes the Difference,* Fifth Edition and *Strategies for Reading Assessment and Instruction: Helping Every Child Succeed,* Third Edition published by Merrill/Prentice-Hall. He has written a professional book titled, *Your Classroom Library: How to Give It More Teaching Power,* with Parker C. Fawson, published by Scholastic, Inc. He is or has been a reviewer for *The Reading Teacher, Reading Research Quarterly, Reading Psychology, Journal of Educational Research, Early Childhood Research Quarterly, Reading Research and Instruction, Journal of Reading Behavior, Journal of Literacy Research* and *the Elementary School Journal.* He was an author of Scholastic Incorporated's Literacy Place, 1996, 2000® school reading program.

Dr. Reutzel received the A.B. Herr Award from the College Reading Association in 1999 for Outstanding Research and Published Contributions to Reading Education. He was the editor of the International Reading Association's professional elementary section journal *The Reading Teacher* from 2002–2007. He was awarded the Researcher/Scholar of the Year Award by the College of Education and Human Services at Utah State University in May, 2004. And he was elected Vice-President of the College Reading Association in April of 2005 and will serve as that organization's President in 2007. Dr. Reutzel was recognized as a recipient of the College of Education's 2006 Distinguished Alumni Award at the University of Wyoming in Laramie, Wyoming and is the D. Wynne Thorne Outstanding University Researcher Award recipient from Utah State University in April 2007. Dr. Reutzel was given the John C. Manning Public School Service Award from the International Reading Association in May 2007. Ray will also serve as a member of the Board of Directors of the International Reading Association from 2007–2010.

Dr. Robert B. Cooter, Jr.
Bellarmine University

Dr. Robert B. Cooter, Jr. is the Ursuline Endowed Chair of Teacher Education at Bellarmine University in Louisville, Kentucky. Prior to moving to Bellarmine University, Dr. Cooter was Distinguished Professor of Urban Literacy Research at The University of Memphis. Professor Cooter teaches courses at the undergraduate and graduate levels in reading/literacy education, and his research focuses on the improvement of reading instruction for children living at the poverty level. In November 2007, Robert Cooter and colleagues J. Helen Perkins and Kathleen Spencer Cooter received the 2007 Urban Impact Award from the Council of Great City Schools for their work creating and implementing the Memphis Literacy Academy for teacher capacity-building in high poverty schools.

In March of 2006, Robert Cooter and J. Helen Perkins (University of Memphis) were selected by the International Reading Association to serve as editors through 2011 of *The Reading Teacher,* the largest literacy education journal in the world.

Professor Cooter founded the award-winning Memphis Literacy Academy, an outreach program in Memphis City Schools dedicated to raising the expertise and of hundreds of inner-city teachers of reading, and is also co-principal investigator for the Memphis Striving Readers Program (grades 6-9 content areas), a $16 million middle school literacy research project in Memphis City Schools funded under a major grant by the U.S. Department of Education for 2006-2011. Dr. Cooter formerly served as the first "Reading Czar" (associate superintendent) for the Dallas Independent School District (TX) and engineered the district's highly acclaimed Dallas Reading Plan involving the training of approximately 3,000 teachers in comprehensive literacy instruction. In 1998 then-Texas governor George W. Bush and First Lady Laura Bush named him a Texas Champion for Reading for his development of the Dallas Reading Plan.

Cooter has authored or co-authored more than 60 journal articles and some 19 books in reading education. His books include the best-selling *Teaching Children to Read: The Teacher Makes the Difference*, 5th ed. (Merrill/Prentice Hall), an evidence-based reading (SBRR) text currently used at over 200 universities; *Strategies for Reading Assessment and Instruction: Helping Every Child Succeed* (Merrill/Prentice Hall) which is at present the top text in reading assessment in the U.S., *Perspectives on Rescuing Urban Literacy Education: Spies, Saboteurs, & Saints* (Lawrence Erlbaum Associates), *The Flynt/Cooter Reading Inventory for the Classroom* (Merrill/Prentice-Hall), and the new *Comprehensive Reading Inventory* (Merrill/Prentice Hall), a norm-referenced reading assessment for classroom use.

Robert Cooter lives in Louisville, Kentucky, with his wife and colleague, Kathleen Spencer Cooter. Kathleen is Professor of Special Education at Bellarmine University and directs a new national center focused on promoting "literacy as the path to social justice." They love to vacation on their houseboat, *Our Last Child*, with their twelve grandchildren and two Golden Retrievers of dubious utility.